W9-CDT-729

ECONOMICS AND THE PUBLIC INTEREST

ECONOMICS AND THE PUBLIC INTEREST

FIFTH EDITION

RICHARD T. GILL

Bristlecone Books

Mayfield Publishing Company
Mountain View, California
London • Toronto

Copyright 1991 by Bristlecone Books, Mayfield Publishing Company

All rights reserved. No portion of this book may be reproduced in any form or by any means without written permission of the publisher.

Library of Congress Cataloging-in-Publication Data

Gill, Richard T.
   Economics and the public interest / Richard T. Gill.—5th ed.
     p.   cm.
   "Bristlecone books."
   Includes index.
   ISBN 1-55934-008-8 (pbk.)
   1. Economics.   2. United States—Economic conditions.   I. Title.
HB171.5.G47   1991
330—dc20   90-23049
                                                    CIP

Manufactured in the United States of America
10 9 8 7 6 5 4 3 2 1

Bristlecone Books
Mayfield Publishing Company
1240 Villa Street
Mountain View, California

Managing editor, Linda Toy; production editor, April Wells; copy editor, Andrea McCarrick; text and cover designer, Jeanne M. Schreiber; cover art, Richard Diebenkorn, purchased with funds from the Coffin Fine Arts Trust, Nathan Emory Coffin Collection of Des Moines Art Center; illustrator, Judith Ogus. The text was set in 10/12 Times Roman and printed on 50# Finch Opaque by Arcata Graphics.

3 2280 00477 1481

PREFACE

This book is intended to serve three possible purposes. It can be used for the *macroeconomics* half of a two-semester course in economics, or, standing alone, as a text for a one-semester course in economics. It can also be used by interested citizens who wish a general introduction to modern economic analysis.

Structurally, *Economics and the Public Interest* attempts to fill the gap between the comprehensive textbook that treats every conceivable aspect of the field and the occasional popular article that describes (without analyzing) what modern economics is about. Its focus is on the great macroeconomic topics: national income, inflation, unemployment, and growth. However, these topics are developed in relation to basic economic principles and placed in a context that recognizes differing economic systems and approaches.

In this fifth edition, I have tried to keep in mind the stated objective of earlier editions: to locate those issues of public concern on which economic analysis has the most direct and immediate bearing. These issues are, of course, constantly changing. An obvious example is given by the revolutionary developments in the Soviet Union and the Eastern bloc nations which have required a major rewriting of Chapter 3 on central planning and alternative systems.

More significant for the textbook writer have been changes in economics itself. Reluctant to relinquish the simplicity of what has been called the "Keynesian cross" analysis—simplicity which is of great importance to the beginning student—I have finally had to introduce the entire apparatus of aggregate supply and demand curves. Since this cannot be done piecemeal, it has required a thorough reorganization of the macroeconomic theory on which the book is centrally based. The problem for the author here was to introduce what in effect is a new layer of complexity to the text while at the same time a) keeping the material understandable, and b) keeping the book short. To have expanded it substantially would in fact have defeated its particular purpose.

In the end the book did expand slightly though it still remains far shorter and, I trust, more concise than the truly encyclopedic texts that now dominate much of the field. As to its comprehensibility, all that can be said is that the author has tried, as before, to present the subject as clearly and straightforwardly as possible.

For those who use *Economics and the Public Interest* as the text for the macroeconomics half of a two-semester course, there is now a new edition of the complementary text available: *Economics and the Private Interest: An Introduction to Microeconomics*. In this complementary text, I have tried to observe the same principles of brevity and relevance discussed above.

In preparing the present book, I have drawn heavily on some twenty years of teaching at Harvard College, including nine years as director of Harvard's Principles of Economics course. From the beginning, this book has also benefitted from my television teaching. This teaching involved giving a fifteen-week television course on economics (called "Economics and the Public Interest") on the New England public television channel and, more recently, serving as Economic Analyst for a 28-program nationally-televised series, "Economics U$A." In these television courses, I was obliged to observe a principle of selectivity similar to that which has guided the writing of this book. The experience made me aware of some of the difficulties of conveying the principles of economics in a brief compass, but it also made me aware of the desirability of doing so.

One's indebtedness to other people in writing a book of this nature is always large. I wish to thank my invariably helpful publisher, Gary Burke, my editor, Andrea McCarrick, and the extremely efficient staff of Mayfield Publishing Company. Professor Carol Adams, who did the excellent Study Guide, offered numerous helpful comments on my manuscript as did Professor Paul Barkley of Washington State University, Professor Walter J. Wessels of North Carolina State University, and Professor Norman J. Simler of the University of Minnesota. I also thank Professor Gunther Mattersdorff of Lewis and Clark College for sending me his comments, and also the comments of his entire class, on the previous edition of the text.

More generally, I am indebted to all my colleagues and former students for what I have learned from them and to my wife, who has always tried to keep my writing clear and uncomplicated.

CONTENTS

CHAPTER 7   National Income Determination with Constant Prices

CHAPTER 8   The Multiplier, Business Cycles, and Elementary Fiscal Policy

PART 3

THE ECONOMY IN THE AGGREGATE: MONEY, PRICES, AND INFLATION

CHAPTER 9   Inflation and Aggregate Supply and Demand

ECONOMICS
AND THE
PUBLIC
INTEREST

For Betty

PART 1

THE MODERN ECONOMY: PROBLEMS, INSTITUTIONS, AND SYSTEMS

CHAPTER 1.

THE ECONOMIC PROBLEM

We all know something about economics because we are everyday participants in the economic life of our society. "Getting and spending, we lay waste our powers," complained Wordsworth, and the complaint has decided relevance for a modern industrial economy. We do pass a great many of our waking hours "getting and spending." If we are clever, we even try to economize during the process. We try to economize on the things we buy, and we try to economize on the time and effort we put into producing the products or services we are offering for sale.

In these respects, we are taking part in the economic system of the country, and we daily gain certain insights into how that system functions.

At other times, however, economics seems to be dealing with matters that are far removed from our personal knowledge and experience and, indeed, that seem far outside our personal control. The stock market rises or falls. Millions of people in Asia or Africa are suffering from malnutrition. The cost of living is going up. At such moments, we feel we are being managed by external forces, and we are inclined to say, as Mark Twain did about the weather, "Everybody talks about it, but nobody does anything about it." At such moments, the study of economics seems interesting, but also obscure and difficult.

ECONOMIC BREAKDOWNS—PAST AND PRESENT

The remarkable thing about a modern industrial economy is that it functions so smoothly. We become *aware* of this remarkable fact, however, mainly

3

when the system breaks down. And let no one mistake the fact: economic systems do break down, and, when they do, the costs and consequences are incalculable.

Hyperinflation after World War I

Take the problem of inflation after World War I. Prices rose in all European countries in the aftermath of the war, and at what rates! In Britain and France, prices rose by three or four times their prewar levels. In Austria, the rise was 14,000 times the prewar level. In Hungary, it was 23,000 times; in Poland, 2,500,000 times; and in Russia, 4 *billion* times the prewar level. But even their extraordinary increases pale beside those of Germany, where the forces of inflation went so wild that they virtually destroyed the fabric of the society. Figure 1-1 shows what happened to the wholesale price level in Germany in the 1920s, but only up to a point. By 1922, the numbers would push the curve off the top of the page of this book and, indeed, up through the ceiling of any ordinary-sized room. By 1923, the curve would be out of sight in the clouds. In September 1923, German wholesale prices, in terms of marks, had risen 24 million times above the level of a decade earlier; two months later, the figure was close to a *trillion!* No wonder that people used

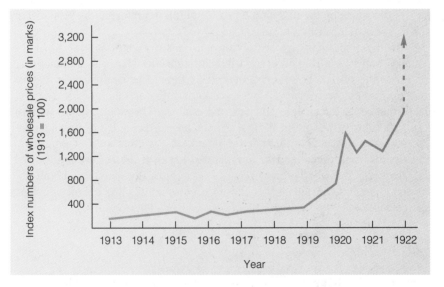

Figure 1-1   The German Hyperinflation of the 1920s   This is an example of an inflation that got completely out of hand. By November 1923 in Germany, the index of wholesale prices that had stood at 100 in 1913 reached the level of 73 trillion!

wheelbarrows to bring home their weekly pay or found marks cheaper than wallpaper for the walls of their homes!

The Great Depression

Or take the United States in the year 1933. This was the worst year of the Great Depression, when 12 to 14 million Americans were out of work—25 percent or more of our entire labor force. The personal suffering involved in this social catastrophe is hard to imagine. The mayor of Youngstown, Ohio, recorded this not untypical newspaper item of the period:

FATHER OF TEN DROWNS SELF

**Jumps from Bridge, Starts to Swim
Gives Up, Out of Work Two Years**

> Out of work two years, Charles Wayne, aged 57, father of ten children, stood on the Spring Common bridge this morning, watching hundreds of other persons moving by on their way to work. Then he took off his coat, folded it carefully, and jumped into the swirling Mahoning River. Wayne was born in Youngstown and was employed by the Republic Iron and Steel Company for twenty-seven years as a hot mill worker.
> "We were about to lose our home," sobbed Mrs. Wayne. "And the gas and electric companies had threatened to shut off the service." [1]

The Great Depression in the United States lasted from 1929 until our entry into the Second World War in 1941; it is estimated that during this period unemployment cost us the waste of 104 million man-years of labor. [2]

Current Economic Problems

These are historic episodes, but they could easily be duplicated in various parts of the world today. We have already mentioned malnutrition in the less developed countries. Rapid population growth combined with bad weather in particular years can lead to widespread famine even in the late twentieth century. Political upheavals can cause severe economic problems, as they have in recent years in Central America, Ethiopia, the Sudan, and, very dramatically, in the Soviet Union and Eastern Europe.

Nor do we have to go abroad to find evidence of breakdowns in modern economic life. Curiously, the very affluence of American society has raised

---

[1] Joseph L. Heffernan, "The Hungry City: A Mayor's Experience with Unemployment," *The Atlantic Monthly* (May 1932).
[2] Lester V. Chandler, *America's Greatest Depression, 1929–41* (New York: Harper & Row, Publishers, 1970), 6.

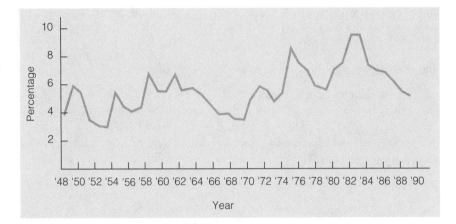

Figure 1-2   U.S. Unemployment as a Percentage of the Labor Force (Seasonally adjusted)   Although the post–World War II years have been prosperous compared to the Depression of the 1930s, unemployment (with inflation) remains a serious problem in the American economy. Source: U.S. Department of Labor.

serious questions about our future. For one thing, it underlines the paradox of continuing poverty among certain groups in our society, including increasing numbers of our children. It also makes some critics wonder about the sustainability of modern economic growth. Are we overheating our planet, destroying our ozone layer, acidifying our lakes and forests?

Meanwhile, the traditional problems of inflation and unemployment are still with us. Figure 1-2 shows that we experienced our worst unemployment of the post–World War II era in the early 1980s. Indeed, during the whole preceding decade, both unemployment and inflation were getting worse. In the late 1980s, things began to improve, with unemployment and inflation both falling somewhat. But then we were faced with the largest budget deficits and international trade deficits in our country's history. Were we borrowing trouble for the future?

Problems of this sort do not represent a breakdown of our economic system comparable to the Great Depression. But they do indicate that the economic mechanisms of even highly successful national economies have deep flaws. And this causes us to wonder why such flaws should occur. Or— what comes to the same thing—it causes us to wonder how the modern economic system functions in the first place.

CHARACTERISTICS OF ECONOMIC PROBLEMS

If we were to try to link together the various problems we have been discussing, we should find that they have certain common characteristics.

Economics and Numbers

One such characteristic is that they usually have a *quantitative* side to them. If we look deeply enough at almost any economic problem, we will sooner or later find some quantities—numbers—involved. We spoke of "getting and spending," and what we get and spend is, among other things, money; and money is measured numerically: so many dollars, so many marks, so many pesos. Furthermore, we typically get money by working at the production of certain goods and services that we sell for certain prices. How much money we get depends on what quantities of goods and services we produce and how many dollars per unit the goods and services will sell for—both numbers.

Indeed, whenever we consider what we loosely think of as "economic" problems, we invariably seem to meet with these numbers. We may be concerned about the price level (a number) or the percentage of the labor force unemployed (a number) or the rate of growth (a number) of per capita income (a number) in India or China or the size of the U.S. federal debt ($2.9 trillion in 1989). And so on. Mind you, some of these numbers are hard to come by. Some are even philosophically complicated. But there is hardly any major economic problem into which a number does not enter somewhere.

This fact is important because it helps explain certain aspects of the approach of modern economists to their subject. This approach is slightly different from that of the historian or of many other students of society. It is more statistical, more mathematical, more like the approach one might find in the natural sciences. Economists actually like to think of their subject as a science. Take a look at a typical professional economics journal of today, its pages covered with differential equations and matrix algebra, and you might think that you had wandered into physics or biochemistry by mistake!

Economics and Institutions

But if this quantitative side is the first common characteristic of economic problems, the second—their *institutional* side—is almost the reverse. Economic problems are not generally reducible to simple scientific formulae. They deal with society, they deal with people, they deal with institutions, history, culture, ideology. The field may be a science, but it is a social (not a natural) science. Behind the numbers, behind the hard facts of resources and technological capabilities, we ultimately come face to face with human beings and the psychology of their behavior, whether individual or collective. Because this behavior is, in turn, conditioned by the past history of their society and its relationships to other societies, there is really no aspect of history, political science, or sociology that does not have some relevance to most major economic problems. Without knowing the history of twentieth-century wars, who could follow the movements of price levels in our century? Without knowing the differences of history and culture that separate the continents, who could explain why people eat well in Western Europe and North America and starve in certain countries in Africa and Asia?

Economics and Controversy

Furthermore, and largely as a consequence of the above, there is a third and final characteristic of most economic problems: they are usually *controversial*. This, by the way, is not unfortunate. Indeed, most economists have been drawn to the field at one time or another because of its controversial side. Economic problems are full of zest and spice, and economic discussions are quite capable of turning friends into distant acquaintances and vice versa. The controversial side does, however, demand a special kind of self-awareness when we pursue the analysis of an economic problem. We have to know whether what we are saying is true because we have carefully and objectively verified it or whether we are mainly expressing our own opinions—our own value judgments—that may conflict sharply with someone else's. Is my friend (or former friend) John wrong about the national debt because of logical error, empirical misinformation (he simply does not know the facts), or flaws in his moral character? Because John may also be asking the same questions about me, it is worthwhile to try to get the matter straight. Because economic problems characteristically weave these different threads together, it takes a particular effort of mental discipline to disentangle them.

SCARCITY AND CHOICE

So much for general characteristics. Now, let us probe a bit more deeply. Can we define the nature of economic problems in a more fundamental way?

The answer will vary somewhat from economist to economist, but a fairly central definition would go something like this:

> Economic problems in general arise because of the fact that the means society has for satisfying the material wants of its citizens are limited relative to those wants. Human desires for material goods—for survival, for luxury, for ostentation, whatever—generally exceed the volume of goods that can be made available for satisfying these desires.

Another way of putting this is to say that there is, in most economic matters, a fundamental problem of *scarcity* involved. Our desires are relatively unlimited. Our resources are relatively limited. The tension between desire and means of satisfying that desire is a reflection of the degree of scarcity involved.

This way of looking at the matter brings out immediately some important points about most economic problems. For one thing, it helps explain why many people when they talk about economics sometimes say, "It's all a matter of supply and demand!" Actually, this is one of those interesting statements that are true in some interpretations and quite false in others. In the technical sense in which economists sometimes use the terms *supply* and *demand*,[3] the statement is not true at all. In this technical sense, supply and demand analysis only applies to certain market structures. In the general sense of our present discussion, however, the statement does have some validity. What it says is that there is this fundamentally two-sided nature of economic problems—human desires and scarce resources—and that economics is deeply concerned with the relationship of these two different sides.

Another point that this way of looking at the economic problem brings out very clearly is that economic problems are frequently concerned with *choice*. We want all these various goods. But we cannot produce them all at once. We must therefore choose. Either this or that. But not both. Scarcity forces choice on us, and a great many economic problems are concerned with the choices a society must make: what particular goods shall we produce? What scarce resources should we use in producing this or that good? And so on. Scarcity forces choice upon society, and the mechanisms a society employs to make its economic choices are quite as significant facts about that society as are its political system or the way it organizes its family life. Indeed, these economic, political, and social matters are, as we have said, usually very much interrelated.

ECONOMIC POSSIBILITIES—A DIAGRAM

It is desirable now for us to illustrate this choice problem with the aid of a diagram. Economists often find simple diagrams useful both in explaining their subject to others and in understanding it themselves. The diagram we turn to now is a good example of the help such drawings can give, for it enables us to show quite straightforwardly some of the fundamental economic problems with which all societies must cope.

The Production-Possibility Curve

The diagram is called a production-possibility curve or, sometimes, a transformation curve.[4] In order to draw it, let us imagine a very simple, hypothetical society that is capable of producing only two products: food and

---

[3] See chapter 2, pp. 22–35, where the applicability of the technical terms *supply* and *demand* is discussed.
[4] The word *transformation* is sometimes used because the diagram is designed to show how a society, using all its resources, can produce different combinations of goods; that is, how it can transform (by different resource use) one good into another. For the use of this same diagram in a microeconomic setting, see my *Economics and the Private Interest,* 3d ed., especially chapters 1 and 7.

TABLE 1-1

When Food Production Is (Million Bushels)	Then the Maximum Possible Steel Production Is (Thousand Tons)
0	1,050
20	1,035
40	990
60	930
80	840
100	720
120	595
140	410
160	190
175	0

steel. The technologists in the society have given us the information contained in Table 1-1. They have told us what is the maximum amount of steel we can produce for each possible amount of food that we are producing. We begin by producing zero units of food; that is, all our resources are going into steel production. We then begin diverting our resources from steel to food production until, finally, when we are producing 175 million bushels of food, there are no resources left over, and steel production is zero. The table, in theory, describes all the possible combinations of food and steel that the society can produce—its *production possibilities*—when all its resources of land, labor, and machines are fully employed.

The figures from Table 1-1 are displayed graphically in Figure 1-3. If we had a piece of graph paper, we could plot on it all the points shown in Table 1-1. Then if we joined them together in a smooth curve, we would have the diagram shown in Figure 1-3.

The Shape of the Curve

Now, this diagram is nothing but a representation of the material presented in Table 1-1—basically, it gives us no new information—but it does show us something that is not obviously read off the table: the *shape* of the production-possibility curve. We notice, in particular, that the curve is bowed out, or, technically, "concave to the origin"; it is not simply a straight line from the y-axis (vertical) to the x-axis (horizontal).

What does this bowed-out shape mean? And why is it a fairly characteristic shape for the production-possibility curve?

The *meaning* of the shape of the curve is fairly easy to see. It states that

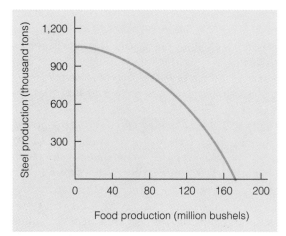

Figure 1-3 Production-Possibility, or Transformation, Curve This curve graphically presents the hypothetical data from Table 1-1. It shows the characteristic bowed-out shape of the production-possibility curve.

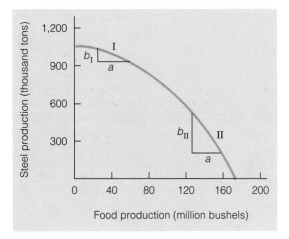

Figure 1-4 The shape of the production-possibility curve illustrates this important generalization: as we produce more of one good, we must usually give up more of other commodities to increase production of that good still further.

as we increase our production of one commodity, it will be harder and harder to get still further units of that commodity. Harder in what sense? Harder in the sense that we will have to give up more units of the other commodity to add another unit of the first commodity. In other words, as we increase food production, we shall have to give up more and more units of steel to increase our food production by one unit.

The meaning of this last statement is illustrated in Figure 1-4. In the portion of the curve indicated by the roman numeral I, we are producing relatively little food and a great deal of steel. To increase food production by a given amount (a) is relatively easy—we have to give up only b_1 steel to do so. Now, contrast this with the situation in area II. Food production is much higher here. To increase food production by the same amount as before (a), we must now give up much more steel; that is, b_{II} is much greater than b_I. And the same of course would be true if we were speaking of increasing steel production as opposed to increasing food production.

This, then, is what the shape of the curve *means,* but now we ask, Why does it have this particular shape? The fundamental answer to this question derives from the fact that not all productive agents and resources—*factors of production* as economists usually call them—are equally well suited to the production of different commodities. If *all* commodities were the product of *one* factor of production—say, homogeneous labor—then there would be no need for the curve to bow out as it does. But this is obviously not so. In our particular case, steel production requires iron ore, while food production requires fertile, cultivable soils. There is no reason to expect that the best farming land will also be the land containing the richest iron deposits; quite the contrary in fact. What happens then as we keep increasing our food production?

> In the beginning, when we are producing a great deal of steel and almost no food, we are using excellent cultivable soil in our search for whatever bit of iron ore it may yield. By giving up just a bit of steel production, we release this rich land to the farmer and, consequently, gain a great deal of food production for a relatively small loss (b_I) of steel. As we keep increasing our food production, however, the situation changes. Now all the really good farming land has been used. If we wish to increase food production any more, we must take over the land rich in iron ore but relatively poor for crops. This means that to get the same increase in food production we must make major sacrifices (to the amount of b_{II}) in our steel production.

Thus, it is empirically (though not universally or necessarily) true that it usually costs us more to produce more of a particular good, the more of it we have. The *opportunity cost*—the steel we have to give up to get more food—generally goes up as we proceed further and further in any one line of production.

APPLICATION TO MAJOR ECONOMIC PROBLEMS

We can now use this diagram to illustrate specifically and meaningfully some of the fundamental economic problems all societies have.

The Choice Problem

Figure 1-5 illustrates the choice problem that we have emphasized so much in our earlier discussion. Should the society locate itself at point A (lots of steel, little food) or at point B (little steel, lots of food) on its production-possibility

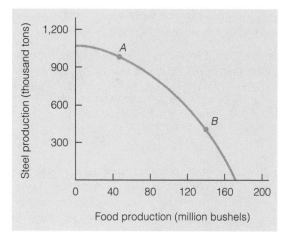

Figure 1-5   The Choice Problem   Among the fundamental choices a society must make is the choice of the composition of its output (*A* or *B* or some other point). This choice will reflect not only the stage of development of the economy, but also its economic system. Is choice decentralized, centralized, mixed, or what?

curve? This is not the only kind of choice a society must make, but because economic problems tend to be interrelated, this choice is reflective of the solutions to many other choice problems as well.

How can or should this choice be made between *A* and *B?* Clearly, the choice the society will want to make will depend on a whole host of different factors. For example, if it has a very large population, then presumably it will need a fairly large production of food. If it is a very rich country, then it will presumably consume a higher proportion of industrial products (steel) as opposed to agricultural products (food). Even if it is a poor country, it may decide to sacrifice food production today to make machines (steel) so that it can produce *both* more food and more steel in the future.

These are simply a few of the many considerations that will influence a society's choice between *A* and *B* on its production-possibility curve. *How* these factors influence that choice, moreover, is dependent upon a still further variable: the kind of economic *system* operating in that particular society. Does it have a traditional economy? A market economy? A planned or command economy? A mixed economy? The way in which these different possible economic systems work to influence economic choices will be a major concern for us in our remaining chapters of part 1.

Before carrying these matters further, however, let us use our diagram to illustrate two additional major economic problems. These two additional problems have received great attention among economists since the 1930s, and we shall devote much of the remaining parts of this book to their study.

It is useful in this connection to note an important distinction that economists make between *macroeconomics* and *microeconomics:*

> *Macroeconomics* is the branch of economics that studies the behavior of broad aggregates, such as national income, total employment and unemployment, or the overall price level.

Microeconomics is the branch of economics that studies the behavior of individual decision-making units, such as consumers, laborers, or business firms.

The following two problems are central concerns in the field of macroeconomics, the main subject of this book. Microeconomic problems are discussed in detail in a companion volume, *Economics and the Private Interest*.[5]

The Unemployment Problem

The first problem deals with *short-run* macroeconomics. It asks, What factors determine the state of health of the economy as a whole in the short run? One of the most important aspects of this question has to do with the employment problem. Are we utilizing all our available labor and other resources in production, or do we have men and factories standing idle and, consequently, a national income that is less than it might be? In terms of Figure 1-6, the two situations are contrasted at points *FE* (full-employment production) and *UE* (unemployment or undercapacity production). The production-possibility curve does not tell us where the society *will* be, but where, technologically, it *can* be. It will take us a good bit of analysis to show the forces that determine where the economy in the aggregate will, in fact, be located at any given moment of time.[6]

The Growth Problem

The other problem that can be illustrated by our diagram is that of *long-run economic growth*. Here, as Figure 1-7 indicates, we are concerned with the shifting outward of the production-possibility curve over time. What these curves tell us is that in 1975 we were able to produce *both* more food and more steel than in 1950 and that, by 2000, we had, hypothetically, advanced still further.

Now this growth process—this shifting out of the production-possibility curve—does not happen automatically with the passage of time. Indeed, it is not too much of an exaggeration to say that economic growth, in its modern sense, was really unknown to the world until the British industrial revolution of the late eighteenth and early nineteenth centuries. Even today, there are vast areas of the world, especially in Asia and Africa, where this process has not yet fully taken root. In the advanced industrial countries, however, growth is now a characteristic feature of economic life. Through a

---

[5] Richard T. Gill, *Economics and the Private Interest*. Mountain View, CA: Mayfield Publishing Co., Bristlecone Books, 1991.

[6] "Full employment" is not quite as precise a concept as it may seem from this discussion. Thus, it is possible to have *over*-full employment for certain periods of time; also, there is always *some* unemployment even when the economy is "fully" employed (see below, p. 22 and p. 35).

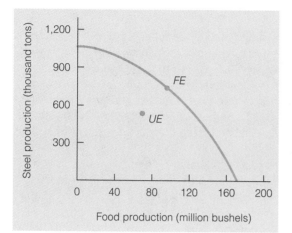

Figure 1-6   The Unemployment Problem   Will total output be at its full-employment potential level (on the production-possibility curve), or will it be at a point *inside* the curve, signifying unemployment? Note that at *UE* we can have more of both food and steel if we can only get our laborers and machinery back into full operation.

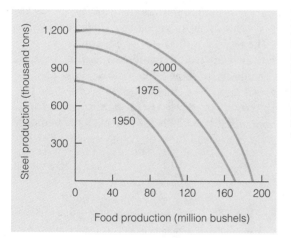

Figure 1-7   The Growth Problem   Most modern economies do not remain static but grow, as suggested by these outward shifts of the production-possibility curve. How to stimulate long-run growth is a special concern for many of today's less developed countries.

continuing process that involves population growth, the accumulation of machines and other capital goods, and, above all, a constant attention to invention and innovation—new products, new discoveries, new technologies of production—these modern economies are able to shift out their production-possibility curves.

Economic growth is not the cure-all for the social and moral ills of humanity; indeed, people are increasingly concerned with the sustainability of modern technology, and its *costs*. These matters we shall discuss later on. Still, growth is an economic fact of the first magnitude; and like the other economic problems we have mentioned, it, too, will require our serious attention.

SUMMARY

We become aware of the workings of our economic system when there is some dramatic malfunction in one of its parts. Such malfunctions have occurred historically, as in the German hyperinflation of the 1920s or the worldwide Great Depression of the 1930s. But they also occur today, most obviously in the less developed countries of Asia, Africa, and Latin America, but even in the affluent United States, where poverty, pollution, unemployment, inflation, and large fiscal and trade deficits are matters of serious concern.

The character of these various economic problems is similar in that (1) they usually involve a *quantitative* element—numbers appear in most economic problems; (2) they also involve an *institutional* element—they require a knowledge of the institutions, culture, and ideology of a particular society; and (3) they are often *controversial* problems—one must be careful to isolate value judgments from questions of fact or logic.

More deeply, these various economic problems ultimately arise from the problem of scarcity: the fact that human desires for material goods and services generally exceed the volume of those goods and services the economy is capable of providing. The problems of scarcity and, consequently, of choice among alternatives are illustrated in a production-possibility, or transformation, curve. This curve enables us to show hypothetically how a society might choose between this or that different combination of goods.

The production-possibility diagram is also useful in allowing us to illustrate important macroeconomic problems such as (1) short-run unemployment and undercapacity production and (2) long-run economic growth.

Key Concepts for Review

Hyperinflation after World War I
The Great Depression
Less developed countries
U.S. economic problems
    Poverty
    Pollution
    Unemployment
    Inflation
    Federal deficit
    Trade deficit
Character of economic problems
    Quantitative
    Institutional
    Controversial

Scarcity and choice
Production-possibility (transformation)
    curve
Factors of production
Opportunity cost
Supply and demand
Macroeconomics
Microeconomics
Full employment
Economic growth

Questions for Discussion

1. List a few of the major economic problems facing the United States at the present time. What features of these problems lead you to characterize them as *economic* problems?

2. Economists a century or two ago worried about the so-called "paradox of value": water is very useful but cheap, while diamonds are much less useful but expensive. How does the fundamental role of scarcity in economic problems help you to understand this paradox?

3. Under what special circumstances might the production-possibility curve have a shape such as the following?

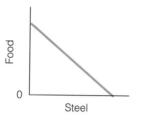

Could you imagine any circumstances in which it might have a shape such as this?

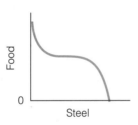

4. At the height of World War II, the United States was devoting some 50 percent of its total production to the war effort; yet private consumption, except for a few commodities, remained high. Use the production-possibility analysis to illustrate how these facts might be reconciled.

CHAPTER 2

THE MARKET ECONOMY

The hard fact of scarcity can force many choices upon a society; and these choices, as we have indicated, will be deeply influenced by the kind of economic *system* operating in that society. In the next three chapters, we shall be examining some of the different systems by which fundamental economic choices can be made. In this chapter, we shall focus on what economists sometimes call a *market economy*. We shall try to show how, through the operation of prices and markets, without any central planning or guidance, a society can solve its economic problems in a coherent way.

CHOICE THROUGH THE MARKET

Because everyone brought up in the United States is familiar with the workings of prices and markets of various kinds, the subject of a market economy may seem one of the easier topics in economics.

But this view is misleading for two reasons. The first is that the successful functioning of a market economy is intrinsically complicated. Indeed, it is something of a social miracle. For the essence of such an economy is that nobody guides or even thinks about the economy as a whole. Everything is decentralized into the thousands and, indeed, millions of private, individual decisions being made by consumers, producers, and laborers, here, there, and everywhere. That such apparently haphazard means should produce anything like an orderly result is not something to be taken for granted—in fact, it should be regarded as rather astonishing.

The second reason for caution is that a pure market economy does not really exist in the modern world. Although we have all seen various markets—from the supermarket to the stock market—operating in the United States, it would be quite wrong to believe that this country makes all its crucial choices through the market mechanism. The government plays a considerable role in the present-day American economy, as, indeed, it does in all economies in the modern world. Furthermore, even in the private sector, the roles of business and labor in real life are often quite different from those described by standard economic theory. We shall return to these matters in chapter 4. For the moment, the important point to keep in mind is that the pure market economy is something of an abstraction. Its great importance for the student of economics is not as a description of reality, but as a tremendously useful point of departure from which the complexities of modern industrial organization can be approached.

The tasks that our market economy must perform are numerous. For one thing, it must determine in one way or another how the income of a society is distributed. One person earns $20,000 a year; another, $5,000; another, $100,000. Whether one applauds or objects to any particular arrangement, it is clear that every economic system must have *some* determinate way of distributing its goods and services among its members. Anything less would bring social chaos.

Similarly, every economic system must provide some determinate way of deciding how the goods and services of the society are to be produced. One might think that this question of how to produce potatoes or automobiles or tablelamps is a purely technological—not an economic—question. But this is not so. For there are many different ways of producing any given product. All these ways are feasible in a physical or engineering sense, but some may be better than others in an *economic* sense. Automation may be excellent for a society with a great deal of machinery and a shortage of labor, but it would hardly make sense for a society that is overflowing with unskilled labor and can barely afford the most rudimentary tools and machines. The question of how to produce different goods is vitally affected by the relative scarcities of the different factors of production. Thus, it falls squarely in the province of the economist; and, like the question of the distribution of income, it is another problem for the market economy to solve.

Finally, there is the problem we have already spent some time on: what goods to produce? In terms of our earlier diagram (repeated here in Figure 2-1), shall we produce at point *A* (lots of steel, little food) or at point *B* (little steel, lots of food)? In this chapter, we shall put particular emphasis on this aspect of the choice problem, for it will allow us to bring out quite clearly the essential features of the market economy in its overall operations.

Figure 2-1 The Familiar Choice Problem In this chapter, we shall try to show how a decentralized market economy can make the choice between points *A* and *B* through the supply-and-demand mechanism.

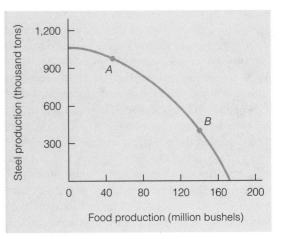

THE SOLUTION OF THE CLASSICAL ECONOMISTS

Now the notion that a good way to handle these choice problems—in fact, the notion that the best way to handle them—is through a price-and-market mechanism was really born sometime during the eighteenth century. Around the 1750s and 1760s, a number of French economists (sometimes called physiocrats) began to stress the view that there was a natural harmony between the decisions individuals made privately and the general social welfare. *Physiocracy* means "rule of nature." Private self-interest and the social welfare were seen not as in conflict but as in a fundamental union more or less as a matter of "natural law."

The British Classical School

The most important development of this concept, however, came in Great Britain. Early British economists were interested in analyzing the implications of a market economy and in trying to demonstrate that if the government stayed in the background, the price-and-market mechanism could handle things quite satisfactorily. Because these early British economists did much to establish the field of economics as we know it today, it is worthwhile to say a word about them.

The key date is probably the year 1776. This year saw not only the beginning of the American Revolution; it saw also the publication of one of the most important economic treatises of all times: *The Wealth of Nations* by Adam Smith. Smith was a quite remarkable man, although his life was notably without incident. He never married. Except for a grand tour of the Continent—when, incidentally, he met some of the leading French physiocrats—he never traveled extensively. But he was a philosopher, a historian of science, and, above all, the greatest economist of his day. *The Wealth of Nations* is a spacious book that can be read for pleasure even now. It is filled with rolling eighteenth-century sentences but also with sharp phrases that catch whole pages of argumentation in a word or two. When Smith speaks of an "invisible hand" that brings private and social interest into harmony, he is not simply writing vividly; he is pinpointing an entire philosophy of economic life.

Smith is important not only because of his work, but because of the influence of that work on others. *The Wealth of Nations* became the rock on which a whole school of economists was founded. This school is usually called the *classical economists,* and it included, in the decades following Adam Smith, some of the most important writers in the history of the subject. There was Thomas Robert Malthus, the English parson whose ideas on population cast a pessimistic pall over nineteenth-century thought and greatly influenced the evolutionist Charles Darwin. There was David Ricardo, who published his *Principles of Political Economy and Taxation* in 1817 after a highly successful career in business. Ricardo was one of a small number of economists who really have done well on the stock market. His work in economic theory was rigorous and systematic. Although not well known to the general public, he had an enormous impact on the development of technical economics. Even in the middle of the nineteenth century, Smith's influence was still strong, and John Stuart Mill, who once had Ricardo for a tutor, is often regarded as a classical economist. Mill, of course, was a many-sided genius whose works in philosophy and political science easily match his very substantial contributions to economics.

Adam Smith and Laissez-faire

Smith's message, however, carried beyond his fellow economists to the world at large. And this message was, in essence, that except for certain unavoidable responsibilities,[1] the State ought to stay fairly well out of the economic sphere. Laissez-faire was the motto: leave the economy alone; have the state keep a hands-off policy. Or, in terms of our discussion in this chapter, let the society solve its economic problems largely through the functioning of a market economy.

Smith's general reasons for advancing this view are fairly clear. He

---

[1] Smith acknowledged that the state had certain duties that would bring it actively into the economy: (1) national defense, (2) the administration of justice, and (3) the provision of certain socially necessary institutions—for example, educational institutions—that private interests might neglect. Thus, neither he nor any of the classical economists advocated a truly *pure* market economy. The question was how much (or little) intervention was needed.

combined a belief in the frugality and industry of private individuals with an insight into the ways in which competition among individuals could keep their actions in line with the interests of society. Smith said something like this: If you have everyone operating according to his own self-interest and if, at the same time, you have a great deal of competition among different individuals and businesses, then these private parties will be more or less forced to produce the goods that the consumers want and to make those goods available at reasonable prices.

Or we can state the same thing beginning at the other end: Consumers have certain preferences with respect to, say, food and steel products. How are these preferences translated into economic reality in an economy in which everything is decentralized and works through the market? Smith's answer was that it will be in the self-interest of the producers to make the goods the consumers want (this will bring them greater profits); furthermore, the competition among these producers will be sufficient to keep profits moderate and to ensure that no consumer is overcharged. The consumer will have to pay only what, in Smith's phrase, "the good is worth."

The corollary was: If the private sector can handle things so well, then the state need not intervene except for rather special and limited functions.

THE DEMAND CURVE

Today, we are aware of many qualifications to the "classical" view of the world, but we can also state their own arguments more precisely than they could because we have developed certain analytic tools that were not at their disposal. One of the most important of these tools is the *demand curve*. Together with the *supply curve*, which we shall take up momentarily, this tool will enable us to explain some of the essential features of a market economy.

A Definition of the Demand Curve

A *demand curve* may be defined as follows:

> A demand curve is a hypothetical construction that tells us how many units of a particular commodity consumers would be willing to buy over a period of time at all possible prices, assuming that consumer tastes, the prices of other commodities, and the money incomes of the consumers are unchanged.

The last phrase in this definition is of some importance. It is usually called a *ceteris paribus,* or "all-other-things-equal," phrase. It brings out the fact that we are isolating a particular part of economic life for close inspection and holding other areas in abeyance. This is clearly necessary here. How can we tell how many units of steak a consumer will buy at $5 a pound if we

TABLE 2-1

At Price (Per Pound of Apples)	Consumers Wish to Buy Per Month (Thousand Pounds)
$2.00	20
1.80	90
1.60	150
1.40	212
1.20	278
1.00	340
.92	365
.80	402
.60	465
.40	530
.20	590
.02	650

do not know what the consumer's income is or what the price of lamb or chicken is? Hence, the need to proceed in this one-step-at-a-time fashion.

In Table 2-1, we have set out the raw data for a demand curve for a commodity: apples. (We have chosen a food because, ultimately, we want to come back to the food-steel choice problem raised earlier in this chapter.) We have asked consumers to tell us how many pounds of apples they would be willing to buy in a given month at prices ranging from $2.00 to 2 cents per pound. Notice that we must specify the period of time involved: presumably the number of apples purchased at a given price will be twelve times as much in a year as in a month, and so on.

The Shape of the Demand Curve

Figure 2-2 represents the material in Table 2-1 in a smooth curve. The procedure here is the same as in the case of our production-possibility curve of chapter 1. The points from Table 2-1 are charted on graph paper and then joined together in a continuous line (as if, in fact, we actually had information on how many apples consumers would purchase at 97 cents, 98 cents, 99 cents, and so on per pound). This curve is the consumer demand curve for apples.

Now you notice that the curve slopes downward from left to right. Why this particular shape? Actually, this is not too difficult to understand. At high prices for apples, the consumers will find that buying too many apples makes

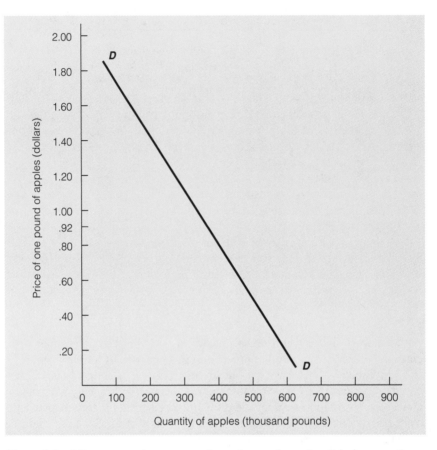

Figure 2-2   *DD* represents the consumer demand curve for apples. It is drawn on the assumption that money incomes of consumers are constant and that prices of other commodities (for example, oranges) are constant.

too big a dent in their budgets; they will have to cut down their purchases. Furthermore, when apple prices are high, even the dedicated apple lover will be tempted to substitute pears or peaches or oranges for apples. This, too, will mean fewer purchases. Thus, although we could imagine a few very curious exceptions if we wished to,[2] the customary shape of a consumer

---

[2] A famous (among economists) exception to the rule of a downward-sloping demand curve is the so-called "Giffen paradox," named after a nineteenth-century British economist, Sir Robert Giffen. He noticed that when the price of potatoes goes up, very poor families may buy *more* potatoes. Why? Because the rise in the price of potatoes makes them poorer, and when they are poorer, they substitute potatoes for meat. This, however, is a very exceptional case and implies, among other things, that the commodity looms very large in the budgets of the consumers involved.

demand curve will be as we have drawn it: sloping downward toward the southeast.

Shifts of the Demand Curve

Two further points will help the reader in understanding the concept of the demand curve. For one thing, you might ask yourself what will happen to our demand curve if some of the "other-things-equal" items happen to change. Suppose all consumers have a 50-percent rise in their money incomes. Suppose the price of bananas goes up. Suppose the price of oranges goes down. Suppose consumer tastes change. In each case, the answer is that the whole demand curve will *shift* its position. You should determine the direction of the shift and the reason why it shifts in each case.

Also, you should carefully distinguish in your mind between a *shift* in the curve as just described and a movement *along* the curve. Figure 2-3 indicates what could be two quite different meanings for the phrase "an increase in demand." It could mean a shift in the total demand curve from *DD* to *D'D'*, *or* it could mean an increase in the quantity demanded as the price of apples falls; that is, as we moved *along* the demand curve *DD* from *a* to *b*. The economic significance of these two phenomena is quite different. A *shift* in the curve means a change either in the "other-things-equal" (*ceteris paribus*) assumptions or a basic change in consumer tastes: people may have suddenly developed a new taste for apples. A movement *along* the curve from *a* to *b* involves no such basic changes; indeed, it simply tells us that, other things equal, consumers will demand more apples at lower prices. By convention, economists usually reserve the phrase "increase (or decrease) in demand" for a shift in the curve as a whole. Movements along the curve are described in detail for what they are: an increase (or decrease) in the quantity of the commodity demanded as the price falls (or rises). This terminology is purely conventional; the distinction between the two different phenomena, however, is clear and important.

ELASTICITY OF DEMAND—AN APPLICATION

The demand curve seems a simple enough concept, yet it took economists many years after Adam Smith to pin this concept down; and, indeed, once understood, the demand curve can help us explain one of the great "mysteries" that puzzles many beginning students of economics. Why was it, during the Great Depression—a time of general economic need—that farmers actually destroyed crops and livestock? Why is it, to this day, that when

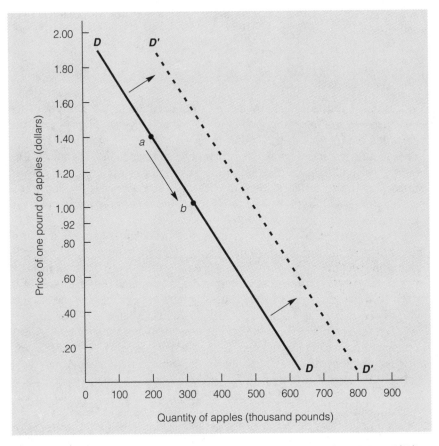

Figure 2-3   It is important to distinguish *shifts* in a demand curve (from *DD* to *D'D'*) from movements *along* a demand curve (from *a* to *b* on *DD*).

farmers are in economic trouble, the first thing they or the government think of is acreage or crop restrictions?

To answer these questions, we need to introduce the term *elasticity of demand,* or, more specifically, *price elasticity of demand.* We define this term as follows:

> Price elasticity of demand is measured by the percentage change in the quantity of a commodity demanded divided by the percentage change in its price.

If the quantity of a commodity demanded goes up by 10 percent, when the price falls by 10 percent we say that the price elasticity of demand is 1.0. If the quantity demanded goes up by 20 percent, when the price falls by 10 percent we say that the price elasticity is 2.0 and that the demand curve is relatively *elastic* at that point. If the quantity goes up by only 5 percent under

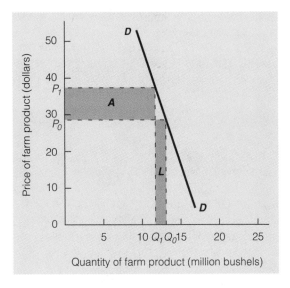

Figure 2-4 Inelastic Agricultural Demand If farmers can find some way (for example, through a government production control program) of reducing their output from Q_0 to Q_1, they will actually raise their total revenues and incomes. Area A will exceed area L when demand is inelastic.

these circumstances, we say that price elasticity is 0.5 and that the demand curve is relatively *inelastic* at this point.[3]

The relevance of these comments for American agriculture is that it is generally the case that the demand for farm products is relatively *price inelastic*. People do not greatly alter the quantity of farm products they purchase in response to a given change in price. Or, to put it the other way around, consumers will pay considerably higher farm prices rather than substantially cut their consumption of farm products.

Thus, in Figure 2-4, because of the price inelasticity of demand, a reduction of crop sales from Q_0 to Q_1 raises the price (from P_0 to P_1) by a much higher percentage. This means that total farm revenues increase. You can see this by comparing area A ($=$ added revenue) to area L ($=$ lost revenue). The loss

---

[3] In the accompanying figure I have drawn three demand curves: the center one has a price elasticity of 1; the steeper one is less price elastic (more inelastic); the flatter one is more elastic. You should determine why this is so, given our definition of price elasticity of demand.

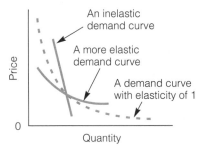

from lower sales is more than compensated by the higher price on the remaining sales, and, hence, farm income will go up.

Thus, the "mystery" is solved. Crop restrictions in hard times may hurt the consumer (because of higher prices), but they will generally improve the economic condition of the farmers. An interesting application of the principle that "less is more"!

THE SUPPLY CURVE

The second tool we need for our analysis of the market economy is the *supply curve*.

This curve tells us not about the consumers of apples but about the *producers* of apples. Instead of going around to consumers and asking, "How many apples would you buy this month at such-and-such a price?" we now ask producers, "How many apples would you produce and sell this month at such-and-such a price?"

The supply curve is derived by graphing Table 2-2, which is similar to Table 2-1, except that this time we are questioning producers rather than consumers. "If the market establishes a price of $1.40 a pound, how many thousand pounds of apples will you bring to market?" we ask the apple producers. Their answer, according to Table 2-2, is 631 thousand pounds. If this and the other points are plotted on a graph, we get a curve like *SS* in Figure 2-5: a supply curve for apples.

Now, in some respects, the supply curve is a bit more complicated to grasp than the demand curve, or at least it seems so at first glance. Two problems arise: Under what assumptions can a determinate supply curve be drawn? What explains the upward (northeasterly) slope of the supply curve?

TABLE 2-2

At Price (Per Pound of Apples)	Producers Are Willing to Supply Per Month (Thousand Pounds)
$ .40	76
.60	187
.80	298
.92	365
1.00	410
1.20	521
1.40	631
1.60	743
1.80	854

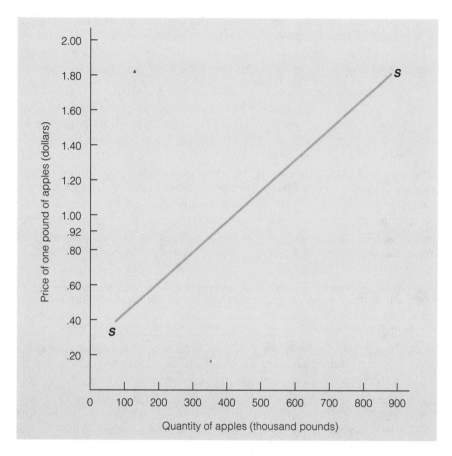

Figure 2-5   Supply Curve   *SS* represents the producers' supply curve for apples. It tells us that producers are willing to supply more apples only if the price of apples goes up. A lower price, conversely, will lead to a smaller quantity supplied.

ASSUMPTIONS BEHIND THE SUPPLY CURVE

The supply curve, like the demand curve, is constructed on a number of *ceteris paribus* assumptions, but it also assumes a certain particular market structure.

The Assumption of Perfect Competition

More specifically, the supply curve is drawn on the assumption that apple producers take the prices of apples as given *by the market* and not as subject in any significant way to their personal control. They are price takers, not price setters. In technical economics terminology, they are *perfect competitors*.

By the term *perfect competition* in economics we mean: A market structure is perfectly competitive when the business firms comprising the industry in question are selling a homogeneous product and are so small in relation to the industry as a whole that they take the price of their product as a "given."

Perfect competition exists when we have large numbers of very small business units each selling what is, for practical purposes, an identical product. When we come to chapter 4, we shall see that other market structures are quite pervasive in a modern "mixed economy." *Pure monopoly*—a single large seller of a given commodity—is fairly rare, but there are many intermediate cases. There may be *monopolistic competition,* a seeming contradiction in terms, where there are large numbers of firms but each has a "monopoly" of its own particular brand of a product. Or there may be a few large firms that effectively dominate a particular industry. This market structure is usually called *oligopoly,* meaning "few sellers." Often oligopolistic firms also use brands and other devices to separate off—to *differentiate,* as economists say—their products from those of their rivals. The American automobile industry, for example, consists of a small number of large firms, and each of these firms produces similar, but not identical, products.

The point is that where firms are either large in relation to the market or where they have a "monopoly" of their particular product (say, Ford Escorts or Kellogg's Corn Flakes), the producers are likely to have some influence over the price of their product. They have at least some freedom to *set* the price of their product. But in our supply curve, as we have said, the business firms are assumed to be price *takers*. This can be seen very clearly by reflecting a moment on the question we asked each apple producer: "How many apples would you offer for sale at such-and-such a price per pound?" The producer is being asked to respond to a *given price*. If this were not the case, the only relevant question we could ask would be, "What price do you plan to *set* for apples this month?" But that is not the question we asked. Our question—the question underlying the supply curve—does build in the assumption of price taking, or perfect competition.

Ceteris Paribus Assumptions

The supply curve is based on other assumptions as well, and after our discussion of the demand curve, we should not be surprised to find that each supply curve has its *ceteris paribus* clause attached. In the case of the supply curve, the meaning of this clause seems a bit more complicated, however, for it is so obviously affected by considerations of time. It was the late-nineteenth-century British economist Alfred Marshall who pointed out the great importance of time in speaking of producer behavior and the supply curve. In the *very* short run, when we hold virtually everything constant except the price of apples, the apple producer really has nothing to offer but his given stock of apples. The supply curve in this case might be a straight, vertical line—that is, producers would offer their given supplies of apples at any price.

In the more ordinary short run of a few weeks or months, producers will have time to adjust their production somewhat to different market conditions. They may make more trips to the market, hire more labor to help during the picking season. Production of apples can be expanded or contracted to a limited degree.

In the long run, producers can go still further if conditions look favorable. They can buy more land, plant more orchards, construct more storage bins, buy more tools and farm machinery. Indeed, if conditions look favorable enough, other potential producers who were not in the industry before may now decide to enter apple production themselves. In this case, the expansions or contractions of apple production may be very large indeed.

The basic point we are making is that the number of things held constant under a *ceteris paribus* clause attached to a supply curve depends very much on the time period under consideration. One common definition of the *short run* in economics is that period in which there is insufficient time for business firms to alter their basic productive capacity (the amount of land, buildings, and machinery at their disposal) or for firms to leave or enter any particular industry. In other words, in the short run so defined, the firm can expand its production by hiring more laborers and buying more raw materials, but its fixed capital, its machines, its buildings, its land, and so on will not change. Also, in the same short run, it is assumed that the number of firms in the industry will remain constant. There is not enough time for exit or entry into the industry.

By contrast, in the *long run*, there will be much greater flexibility. Firms can go in and out of apple production. New acreage can be planted; tractors and other farm machinery can be acquired. Even then, the supply curve will have a *ceteris paribus* clause attached; for example, it will be assumed that the basic technology of apple production is given.[4] But many other of the items held fixed in the short run will be allowed to vary.

THE SHAPE OF THE SUPPLY CURVE

These same "time" considerations also have an important bearing on our second problem—explaining the upward (northeasterly) slope of the supply

---

[4] Not that the basic technology cannot change as well. Clearly, modern industrial society is characterized by a constant flow of new inventions and new methods of production of all kinds. If the basic technology of apple production did change, we would indicate this by a *shift* in the supply curve. It would be very much like the shift in the demand curve when there was, say, a change in consumer tastes.

curve—for the shape of the supply curve will ordinarily be affected by what factors are being held constant and what time period is envisaged.

Now the main *general* reason that the supply curve goes in this north-easterly direction is that costs tend to rise as the production of any particular commodity is increased. This is most easy to see in the short run. In the short run, as we have defined it, we are dealing with a given number of firms in the industry, each of which will be operating with roughly fixed quantities of land, buildings, and machinery. Each firm can expand production to some degree by adding more laborers and raw materials, but because of the limited capacity of the available plant, it will become increasingly difficult to expand production further; eventually costs will start to go up.

The Law of Diminishing Returns

Actually, what we are elucidating here is a version of one of the most famous of all economic "laws": *the law of diminishing returns*. We will be coming back to this law later on (chapter 15), but let us present it now:

> The *law of diminishing returns* states that in the production of any commodity, as we add more units of one factor of production (the "variable" factor) to a given quantity of other factors of production (the "fixed" factors), the addition to total product with each subsequent unit of the variable factor will eventually begin to diminish.

To put it in terms of short-run apple production, we might say: As we hire more labor to increase apple production from a fixed amount of orchard land, we will find eventually that the added number of apples we get from each extra laborer begins to diminish. If the laborers come at a fixed wage, this means, in turn, that the *added cost* of getting apples will rise higher and higher, the more apples we try to produce.[5]

This law of diminishing returns is not an a priori law of nature, true in each and every circumstance. But it is a useful generalization about the production process, depending finally on the fact that as we keep adding labor (or any other "variable" factor) to a fixed quantity of other factors, each laborer will have increasingly less of the fixed factor (fewer acres of land, fewer tools, and so on) to work with. The result in most instances will be diminishing returns and increasing costs.

---

[5] Economists have a term to cover the *added cost* of producing one more unit of a commodity: *marginal cost*. The word *marginal*, indeed, is a very common word in economics, meaning "an addition to a total of something." We could rephrase our statement in the text to say that, *given* the law of diminishing returns and *given* a fixed wage per laborer, the marginal cost of apples will rise as more apples are produced in the short run.

Rising Costs and Supply

What we have said should help to explain why costs generally rise as a firm expands production in the short run. But how is this fact connected with the shape of the supply curve? The answer, essentially, is that if costs rise with output, business firms will be willing to expand output only if they can receive higher prices for their products. If they did not get higher prices and still went ahead to expand output, they would find that the additional output cost them more than the revenues it brought in. It will only be at the higher price that the expansion of output will prove to be *profitable*.[6]

This analysis, of course, applies only to the short run. In the long run, the shape of the supply curve is somewhat more difficult to explain, though even in the long run the normal shape will still be upward sloping in a northeasterly direction. The main difference will be that the rise in costs will be less steep. This, in turn, reflects the fact that, in the long run, there are many different ways of expanding output, both by varying plant and capacity and by the entry and exit of new firms into the industry. Thus, the long-run supply curve for a firm and for an industry will generally rise less steeply than the short-run supply curve for such a firm or industry.[7]

We have here an example of the workings of Adam Smith's principle of private self-interest. Individual, private producers will expand production at higher prices because it is in *their* interest to do so. A higher price will give producers in the industry greater profits. This will encourage them to expand production. In the long run, higher profits in this industry will also encourage other business firms to enter this industry to share the spoils. It is ultimately the operation of the profit motive that is involved in the upward-sloping supply curve, such as we have shown in Figure 2-5.

THE LAW OF SUPPLY AND DEMAND

We have explained the general meaning and shape of both the demand and the supply curves. Now we are in a position to combine them. In Figure 2-6, we have put the demand curve for apples and the supply curve for apples in one diagram. With the aid of this diagram, we shall now be able to determine

---

[6] Indeed, we can state this more exactly, using the term *marginal cost* (see footnote 5). A firm under perfect competition will maximize its profits when it produces to the point where the price of the product equals the marginal cost of producing a unit of the product ($P = MC$). Why? If it produced *more* than this, the extra cost of the additional output would exceed its price because of increasing costs. If it produced *less* than this, it would be missing an opportunity to make additional profits.
[7] The ultimate reason that costs rise in the long run, even when all factors of production are variable, is that different commodities are produced by different kinds and combinations of the various factors of production. It was this reason, we recall, that explained the shape of our production-possibility curve in chapter 1 (pp. 10–12).

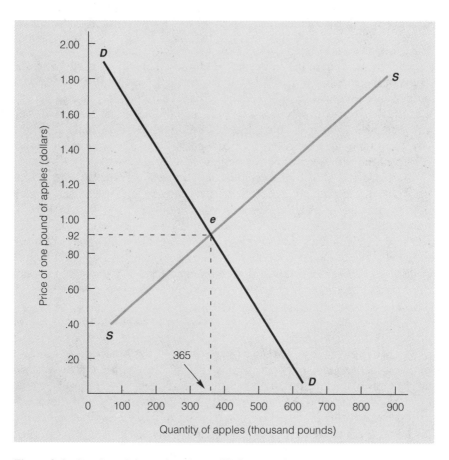

Figure 2-6   Supply and demand are in equilibrium at point *e*, where the price of a pound of apples is 92 cents and the quantity bought and sold is 365 thousand pounds.

the equilibrium market price of apples and the quantity of apples that will be bought and sold. This determination of the price and quantity of a particular product is what the law of supply and demand is all about.

Needless to say, it seems likely that the key point will be where the two curves intersect. And, indeed, it is at this point that the equilibrium price and quantity are determined. In our diagram, the market price will be 92 cents a pound, and the equilibrium quantity produced will be 365 thousand pounds.

The deeper question is: Why is this intersection point significant? Why couldn't the price be somewhere else? The answer to this, in essence, is that it is only at this particular price (92 cents) that the quantity of apples consumers are demanding and the quantity of apples producers are willing to supply are exactly equal; that is, supply = demand. At any other price, either the quantity supplied will be greater than the quantity demanded—in which case producers will be accumulating large quantities of unwanted and unsold apples—*or* the quantity demanded will be greater than the quantity supplied—in which case buyers will be clamoring for apples that producers simply do not have for sale. It is clear that neither of these alternatives could last long. If producers were accumulating unwanted apples, sooner or later they would decide to cut back on the production of apples. If, conversely, buyers kept asking for nonexistent apples, producers would sooner or later get the idea that it was time to raise prices and expand apple production.

It is only at this intersection point that these problems cannot arise. There is no accumulation of unsold apples; there are no lines of buyers trying to get apples that do not exist. We have, then, an equilibrium price—a price that will stay put unless some new fundamental change occurs—and this is the price at which supply and demand are equated.

CONSUMER SOVEREIGNTY—A SIMPLIFIED EXAMPLE

Our analysis so far has shown how the price and quantity of a particular commodity are determined in a market economy, all other things equal. This is an important step in understanding how such a decentralized, private economy can function.

Now, however, let us use these tools to go a step further. We want to show how a market economy makes some of those fundamental economic choices that all societies must face. It will not be possible to do this rigorously in two or three pages, but we can illustrate the general process satisfactorily, and this is a matter of great importance to all students of economics.

One of these central choice problems, we recall, was whether to locate at point A (lots of steel, little food) or at point B (little steel, lots of food) on our production-possibility curve. Now, in a market economy, as Adam Smith understood, the essence of the process is that producers will adjust their production of different commodities so that they are in accord with consumer desires. This is what is meant by the concept of *consumer sovereignty*. If the economy is at point A and consumers prefer to be at B, the market will operate to shift production in the desired direction.

With our newly acquired supply and demand curves, we can give a bit more definition to this process. Let us imagine that we are dealing with two commodities. Apples will be our food commodity; our steel commodity will be, say, washing machines.

Now, let us imagine that, for whatever reason, there is a shift in consumer desires from washing machines to apples. The example is a bit far-fetched, but the principle is clear enough: consumer preferences have changed. How is this reflected through the market in changed production of these two commodities?

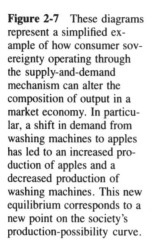

Figure 2-7 These diagrams represent a simplified example of how consumer sovereignty operating through the supply-and-demand mechanism can alter the composition of output in a market economy. In particular, a shift in demand from washing machines to apples has led to an increased production of apples and a decreased production of washing machines. This new equilibrium corresponds to a new point on the society's production-possibility curve.

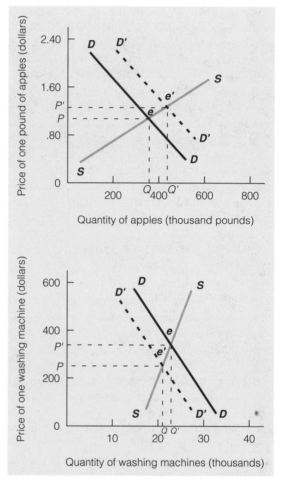

The general nature of the answer is given in Figure 2-7. The increased demand for apples has resulted in an upward shift of the demand curve for apples. The decreased demand for washing machines has resulted in a downward shift in the demand curve for washing machines. The consequences of these shifts according to our diagrams are:

1. A greater production of apples at a higher price
2. A lesser production of washing machines at a lower price

Consumer preferences have shifted from washing machines to apples, and the result has been an increased production of apples and a decreased production of washing machines, and this without any planning or governmental intervention, but solely through the laws of supply and demand working in the marketplace.

Now, this example is simplified, and it should be taken as suggestive rather than definitive.[8] Actually, it wasn't until the late nineteenth century, 100 years after Adam Smith wrote *The Wealth of Nations,* that economists began to pin down the full theoretical implications of a competitive market economy. Beginning around 1870, however, a number of important economists developed a very comprehensive view of such an economy. Alfred Marshall, whom we have already mentioned, was one of these. Another, less known to the general public but very highly regarded by professional economists, was a French-Swiss economist by the name of Léon Walras. Walras was one of the early breed of mathematical economists. He developed the kind of supply and demand analysis that we have been discussing in such an elaborate way that it could cover not only the supply and demand for products, like apples and washing machines, but also the supply and demand for the factors of production (land, labor, capital goods). What emerged from Walras's writings was a view of the interdependent structure of a market economy in a grand design known as *general equilibrium* analysis. And this whole structure—very theoretical, of course—could be expressed in mathematical terms as, indeed, an elaborate set of simultaneous equations.

The point of these remarks about general equilibrium analysis is to make us realize that to follow through any significant change in an economy—even a shift of tastes involving apples and washing machines—we ultimately have to inspect the whole system at once. Even though we cannot achieve this large objective here, our progress with the supply and demand apparatus has shown us the general nature of the process. We can see at least some of the links that join the consumer on the one hand with the productive apparatus of the society on the other. And in so doing, we understand how the social miracle of the market economy is possible.

THE MARKET AND THE PUBLIC INTEREST

The market economy, then, is a possible system. Is it also, as Adam Smith was inclined to believe, the *best* possible system? It is with this second

---

[8] In a more detailed treatment, we should want to take into account some further consequences of a shift in consumer tastes. Such a shift would affect not only the quantities of different goods (apples and washing machines) produced, but also the methods of producing different goods and the distribution of income in the society. The reason is that when consumers shift their preferences, they are indirectly affecting the demand for the different productive agents (land, labor, and capital) that produced the different goods. In our example, we might imagine that apple production used a great deal of land (relative to labor), whereas washing machine production used a great deal of labor (relative to land). When consumers demand more apples and fewer washing machines, they are, in effect, creating an increased demand for land relative to labor. This will tend to raise the price of land relative to labor. And this, in turn, will affect (1) methods of production in the economy—businesses will try to economize on the more expensive land by using labor whenever possible—and (2) the distribution of income—landowners will receive increased income relative to laborers.

question that "economics" and the "public interest" come into critical confrontation.

The answer, as one might expect, is very complicated and subject to much disagreement among the experts. In a preliminary way, however, we can indicate at least two lines of argument that must affect all serious thinking about the subject.

The first line of argument really stems from the kind of analysis we have been presenting in this chapter. It emphasizes the essential viability of the market system. It says in effect: Consider how beautifully the supply and demand apparatus works, how remarkable it is that, without governmental intervention or planning or forethought, all these thousands of individual decisions nevertheless do lead to such desirable social results. This is in the full tradition of classical economic thought.

A second line of argument leads in quite a different direction. It stresses that there are important areas of economic life where competition and markets do not produce the results we want. Take, for example, the problem of unemployment. In our washing machines and apples example we have essentially been assuming a full-employment economy. But we know that unemployment can exist. Can a market economy solve that problem? Or take pollution. Half the air pollution in the United States comes from automobiles. How can the "market" possibly handle this problem when the immediate self-interest of car producers and car owners does not lead them to take corrective steps? In this area and, indeed, in many other areas, the critics can point to significant divergences between private and social interest in a market economy.

History is partly on each side. The great industrial revolution of the late eighteenth and early nineteenth centuries was born at a time when the market system was triumphing over earlier forms of economic organization. Furthermore, history strongly suggests that most centralized, planned economies in the long run lead to economic stagnation. The near collapse of the economies of the Soviet Union and Eastern Europe during the late 1980s was strong testimony to the costs of paying too little attention to the market mechanism (see below, pp. 50–54). On the other hand, it has been true in the past and it is certainly true in the present that a *pure* market economy was never an actual reality. In one way or another, citizens of every country in the world have asked that governments step in to change this or that aspect of the functionings of the price and market mechanism. The need for regulation is especially evident in the modern period, when all thoughtful people have become aware of the potential "costs" of indiscriminate industrial and technological advance.

Thus, the crucial question, as far as the public interest is concerned, is not whether there should be *any* intervention—that question has really been settled by history—but what *degree* of intervention should be permitted.

This question has been debated for over two centuries now. And, as we shall see in the remaining pages of this book, the debate rages on with undiminished intensity to this very day.

SUMMARY

A market economy is one in which the crucial economic decisions and choices are made in a decentralized fashion by private individuals operating through a price and market mechanism. In a *pure* form, such an economy does not exist in the modern world, but the study of its workings is fundamental to the understanding of modern economics.

The British classical economists of the late eighteenth and early nineteenth centuries, and especially Adam Smith, stressed the virtues of limiting government intervention in economic life so that private self-interest and competition could bring consumers the goods they wanted at reasonable prices. With modern analysis, we can give much sharper expression to Smith's views through the interaction of *supply* and *demand* curves.

A demand curve for a product shows the quantities of the product that consumers are willing to buy over a given period of time at different prices. A supply curve shows the amounts of the commodity that producers are willing to sell over a given period of time at different prices. Both curves are drawn under certain important *ceteris paribus,* or "other-things-equal," assumptions. In the case of the supply curve, it is particularly important to notice the element of time, whether short run or long run, because, generally, costs will rise more steeply (and, hence, the supply curve will rise more steeply) in the short run than in the long run.

Equilibrium price and quantity are determined in a market economy where supply and demand curves intersect. This is the so-called law of supply and demand, a law valid only under the special conditions of *perfect competition* where business firms are small and respond to prices as given by the market.

Using supply and demand curves, we can illustrate in a general way how consumer preferences are carried through the price system to affect the kinds of goods produced in the economy. If consumers want more apples and fewer washing machines in a market economy, supply and demand will work to produce this general result.

To prove that the market economy is a "possible" economy is one thing; to prove that it is the "best possible" economy is another. Economic analysis indicates points on both sides, as does historical experience. History does strongly suggest, however, that the issue is (and was) never one of a *pure* market economy, but rather one of what *degree* of government intervention should be allowed or encouraged.

Key Concepts for Review

Market economy
Fundamental choices
    What goods to produce
    How to produce them
    How income is distributed
Classical economists
    Adam Smith
    David Ricardo
    Thomas Robert Malthus
    John Stuart Mill
Laissez-faire
Demand curve
Elasticity of demand
Supply curve

Market structures
    Perfect competition
    Monopoly
    Monopolistic competition
    Oligopoly
Ceteris paribus
Law of diminishing returns
Law of supply and demand
Equilibrium price and quantity
Consumer sovereignty
Degrees of government intervention

Questions for Discussion

1. Adam Smith was aware that certain business firms, if given the opportunity, might overcharge consumers, but he felt that the forces of competition would ordinarily keep prices at a reasonable level. How might competition produce this result? Can you imagine circumstances in which the process would not work satisfactorily?

2. The choice of methods of producing different commodities is not only a technological but also an economic question. Discuss.

3. What does the phrase "other things equal" mean when applied to the ordinary consumer demand curve?

4. Suppose that there is an invention that substantially lowers the costs of producing a certain commodity. What general effect would this invention have on the supply curve of that commodity? What would be the resulting effect on the equilibrium price and quantity produced of the commodity in question?

5. Discuss the role of the time period of adjustment in analyzing producers' responses to changes in market prices. Might consumer responses to different prices (as shown by the demand curve) also be affected by the length of the time period under consideration?

6. "When some people are very rich and others are very poor, the whole notion of 'consumer sovereignty' in a market economy is misleading and prejudicial." Discuss some of the issues raised by this statement.

7. Suppose that we have a farm product with a relatively inelastic demand curve and a perfectly inelastic (vertical) supply curve as follows:

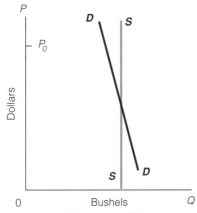

The government has two (politically feasible) alternatives:
(a) Support the price at P_0 by buying up all the product that consumers will not buy at that price; or
(b) Guarantee the farmers the same total revenue as under the price support program, but do this by direct subsidy after the farmers have sold their entire crop to the public at the supply-and-demand-determined price.

Which program will cost the government more money? Can you see any possible advantages to the more expensive program?

CHAPTER 3

CENTRAL PLANNING AND
ALTERNATIVE SYSTEMS

In the last chapter, we said that a *pure* market economy was something of an abstraction, not to be encountered in its pristine form in the real world. Much the same can be said of any of the major *alternatives* to the market system, which we will be discussing in this chapter. In general, these alternatives involve a decisive role for the *state* in planning, regulating, owning, or directing the expenditure of the resources of an economy. In no case, however, has any viable economy been able to survive without some intrusion of market forces such as we have just described. Indeed, at the beginning of the decade of the 1990s, the virtues of the market mechanism were being appreciated, though sometimes resisted, in virtually every planned economy in the world.

THE MARXIAN CRITIQUE OF CAPITALISM

One major alternative to the market economy is the *centrally planned economy,* such as has existed in one form or another in the Soviet Union since 1917, in much of Eastern Europe since World War II, in China, and in a number of other less developed countries since the late 1940s. This particular approach, though not the only path leading away from the world of Adam Smith, owes its spiritual allegiance to Karl Marx (1818–1883). In all the countries mentioned, Marx was regarded—at least until very recently—as the founder of scientific economic thought.

Actually, if we go to Marx in the hope of finding a detailed blueprint of how a planned economy should work, we shall be largely disappointed. Marx gave comparatively little attention to this important problem. What he did was two rather different things. First, he provided a massive critique of the workings of the capitalistic market economy. Second, he provided a revolutionary ideology that proved to be very effective in causing the overthrow of established economic systems and the installation of highly centralized economies.

Class Conflict

His critique begins with the notion of *class conflict*. By definition, *capitalism* is a system under which there is private ownership of the means of production.[1] Looking at our description of a market economy in the last chapter, Marx would have scoffed at its failure to consider what he felt to be a fundamental feature of capitalism: the conflict between the capitalistic class and the laboring class, between the owners of factories and machines and the dispossessed proletariat. To write about the beauties of supply and demand and how they reflect consumer preferences, but to ignore the struggle between the wealthy capitalists and the downtrodden laborers—this, in Marx's eyes, would be to shut out the fundamental facts of the real world.

Monopoly Capitalism

He would have objected, also, that we failed to recognize the importance of *monopoly* elements in the price system. Our supply curve, we recall, was drawn on the assumption that producers are perfect competitors, or price takers; that is, each firm is too small to have any appreciable direct effect on the price of its product. As far as Marx was concerned, however, the result of free markets in the modern industrial world almost certainly would be that big, monopolizing firms would swallow up the small, individual producers. In his view, it was not the small firm but the giant industrial corporation that was characteristic of capitalism, particularly in its advanced stages. Indeed, he believed that these large firms would come to control not only the economies, but, to a great degree, the governments of capitalistic countries. In such a world, the notion of producers responding meekly to the will and wishes of consumers would be a mockery.

Crises and Depressions

Finally, he would have objected, as we ourselves have recognized, that our description of a market economy takes insufficient notice of the *unemploy-*

---

[1] By contrast, *socialism* is usually defined as a system under which there is government ownership of the means of production: capital (factories, buildings, and so on) and land. (See below, p. 55.)

ment problem. For Marx, this would have meant living in a fairy-tale world. In his theoretical structure, unemployment was not an accidental but an intrinsic feature of a capitalistic economy. One reason for this was quite simply that capitalists had to find some way to keep wages down. The way they chose, according to Marx, was to introduce machinery in place of labor whenever wages started to rise. This machinery displaced the laborers; consequently, there was serious general unemployment. If any laborer asked for a raise, his employer simply took him to the factory window and showed him the line of workers who had no jobs at all, a crude but effective means of settling wage disputes! In terms of our production-possibility curve, Marx would have said that a market economy characteristically operates at some point, *UE,* inside the production frontier (see Figure 1-6, p. 15). Indeed, Marx argued that this problem would get worse and worse as time went on. Capitalism would be increasingly subject to great crises and depressions. These crises would, in fact, do much to make the Communist revolution inevitable.

The Revolution—Theory and Practice

As is evident from what we just said, Marx argued that the weaknesses in capitalism would cause the eventual collapse of the system after capitalistic evolution had run its full course. In point of fact, the real-world revolutions have come not in the advanced capitalistic countries, but rather in poor, relatively backward countries that have scarcely had time to go through the capitalistic stage. Russia, in 1917, although it had made some economic progress by that time, was still economically far behind the advanced capitalistic countries of Western Europe and North America. The Chinese claimed to be true Marxists, yet they had their revolution in the 1940s, before they could truly be said to have had any experience at all with modern industrial capitalism.

Thus, it is accurate to say not only that Marx left no blueprint for the functioning of a Communist-run economy but that his theories failed to predict why, when, and how Communist revolutions would actually take place. That they did take place is, however, a major fact of the twentieth century. It is this fact, moreover, that explains the emergence of the most serious attempts to replace the market mechanism we described in chapter 2 with the quite different mechanism of central planning.

THE FUNCTIONING OF A COMMAND ECONOMY

In their purest form, centrally planned economies are sometimes referred to as *command economies.* By using this term, we emphasize that the decision process generally goes not from individual consumers to individual producers, but from central planning boards or ministries to enterprises that are either state owned or highly regulated by the state. Consumer sovereignty largely gives way to the collective preferences of the central planners.

Basically, a centralized command economy must face the same fundamental economic problems as a decentralized market economy. It must somehow determine the incomes of different kinds of labor and the salaries of production managers, artists, doctors, and bureaucrats. It must determine the planned outputs of all the different productive enterprises in the economy and the allocation of resources to each. In terms of our earlier examples, it would set, and attempt to secure the fulfillment of, targets for food production and steel production, for the output of apples and washing machines.

Now, such a task, if carried through into every single corner of a modern economy, would be hopelessly complex and really beyond the capabilities of any group of planners, however sophisticated. Consequently, in most real-life command economies, at least some of these decisions are decentralized either to lower levels of authority or, in some cases, to what is a rough facsimile of a price-and-market mechanism. It is frequently the case that a command economy will direct its main planning energies to certain broad areas of the economy or to certain particular targets that, for some reason, have special priority in the minds of the central planners.

Even when the task is limited in this fashion, it still involves a number of difficult and, in the long run, possibly insuperable problems. These include problems of organization, coordination, efficiency, incentives, and basic goals.

Organization

The first and most obvious requirement of a command economy is a bureaucratic *organization* that makes it possible for anything like effective planning to proceed. It is one thing to make decisions about what the pattern of economic activity in the society should be and another to see that these are carried out.

> There must be, first, an organizational chain of command that makes it possible to transmit the decisions, targets, and directives of the central body *down* through the system to the level of the actual production units in the economy. There must also be an organizational structure that permits information and data from the production units to *rise up* through the system to furnish the ultimate decision makers with the knowledge required for any kind of intelligent planning. It should be clear that many countries do not possess, or could build up only very slowly, the massive administrative mechanism necessary to carry out these vital functions. Even under the best of circumstances, there is a tremendous burden of bureaucracy to carry in the command economy, which is at least partially avoided in a more decentralized system.

Coordination

It is not enough that targets and directives be quickly communicated through the system; they must also be economically consistent. There is a serious problem of *coordination* in any command economy, arising from the interdependent nature of the modern industrial economy.

> The problem may be put in terms of what economists refer to as *input-output analysis*.[2] The outputs of one industry in the economy can be thought of as inputs into some other industry in the economy. Machines are necessary to produce steel, but steel is necessary to produce machines. Actually, steel output will be used as inputs into literally hundreds of other industries in the economy: machines, tractors, automobiles, airplanes, building construction, and so on. And, indeed, a modern economy is an infinitely complex network of interdependence in which the production of one sector depends on the inputs it can receive from a host of other sectors, while its own output simultaneously feeds back inputs into these and still other sectors. The point is that one cannot simply set a target for industry *A* and then, *independently*, set targets for industries *B*, *C*, and *D*. One must be sure that there is sufficient production of *A* so that the input requirements of *B*, *C*, and *D* are met, and vice versa. With the large number of industries involved and their intricate interconnections, the coordination problem facing a command economy is necessarily extremely complex.

Efficiency

Even consistency is not sufficient, however; for it is necessary or at least desirable that a command economy be *efficient*—that is, that it employ its scarce resources in such a way that it gets as much output as possible from them.

> The subject of economic efficiency is a very large and difficult one.[3] Suffice it to say here that a market economy is provided with some rough guidelines for the efficient use of its resources, because the prices of the factors of production—land, labor, capital goods—will reflect their relative scarcities; hence, it will be profitable for firms to economize on the use of particularly scarce (therefore expensive) productive factors. In a command economy, difficulties may arise in this area, particularly if there is an aversion to using anything that may look like "capitalistic" market pricing. Historically, indeed, this has been a fairly serious problem for many actual command or near-command economies.

Incentives

In the command economy—as, indeed, in any economy—the workers, managers, and executives, not the central planners, produce the goods. Hence,

---

[2] The father of input-output analysis is the Nobel Prize-winning economist Wassily Leontief. This analysis can be described as an attempt to apply general equilibrium theory (mentioned in the last chapter) to real-life economies under certain special assumptions.

[3] Technically, we have an *efficient* economic system when it is impossible to improve anyone's economic situation without hurting someone else's.

there must be sufficient *incentives* established, monetary or otherwise, to ensure a vigorous labor force and intelligent managerial direction.

> Many critics of the command economy in the past felt that since the avowed objective of most socialists was to achieve a more equal distribution of income in society, they would be denying any special rewards to those producers who contributed most to the social product—thus diminishing the incentives for productive work. However, there is nothing intrinsic in the nature of a command economy that requires an equal distribution of income, and, in fact, most command economies have set up fairly elaborate bonuses, awards, and other incentives to spur managers and workers to the fulfillment or, if possible, overfulfillment of their production targets. Problems do arise, however, when the incentives are skewed—for example, emphasizing sheer quantity and ignoring quality.

Basic Goals

We have left for last in this brief description what in some sense should have come first: the question of *basic goals*. If the central planners do not rely on the wishes and preferences of consumers to set society's basic economic targets, what then do they rely on?

> This is a complex question, for, ultimately, its answer depends on the particular political organization of the command economy and the psychology of its effective leaders. There is no question that, as a matter of historical fact, all command economies have had what, in the West, would be considered authoritarian, nondemocratic political regimes. These regimes have also tended historically to put primary stress on (1) military priorities and (2) promoting economic growth through an emphasis on capital investment, industry above agriculture, and, within industry, heavy industry as opposed to light industry. In these economies, the interests of consumers have been sacrificed—at least until quite recently—to these higher priority objectives.

These last comments raise an important question: Is this choice of goals—with substantial neglect of consumer interests—intrinsic to the command economy model, or is it more of an historical happenstance? More generally, we have to wonder about the basic relationship between individual choice economically and individual choice politically. Can command economies really function in a political democracy? Conversely, can a market economy survive and prosper in a politically repressive system? As everyone who reads a newspaper knows, these questions are no longer academic.

THE SOVIET UNION—A COMMAND ECONOMY IN CRISIS

The Soviet economy has never been a pure command economy. In 1980, perhaps a quarter of Soviet agricultural output was produced on "private plots"; half the Soviet population lived in privately owned housing; private services could be offered for sale in certain professions such as medicine, tutoring, and the like. In addition to these legal activities, there was evidence of widespread *illegal* activity outside the command mechanism. Still, in 1980 and even as late as 1990, the Russian economy was probably the closest approximation to, and certainly the most important example of, the command model that existed anywhere in the world.

Whether this model could possibly persist through the 1990s was, however, another question. For the USSR and the entire Soviet bloc in Eastern Europe began this new decade in a state of crisis and turmoil.

Achievement of Modern Growth in the USSR

Because of the obvious existence of major difficulties facing the system recently, it is perhaps all the more necessary to acknowledge the fact that, historically speaking, the USSR did manage to achieve a very respectable rate of economic growth over the 70-year period following the revolution in 1917. She achieved this growth despite the turmoil of the revolution itself, the enormous dislocations produced by changes in the economic system and especially the collectivization of agriculture, and, of course, the devastation caused by World War II. During this whole period, she also faced the problems of organization, coordination, efficiency, incentives, and so on that we have just discussed.

Still, significant growth was achieved, and under a highly centralized system based on a series of five-year plans. Over the period from 1928 to 1985, Western scholars estimate that total production in the Soviet Union grew at an annual rate of 4.2 percent per year. If the World War II years are excluded, the annual rate was 4.7 percent. This is not an unparalleled rate of growth for a country trying to "catch up" with the West—Japan, for example, has shown a higher growth rate—but it is a substantial achievement. At these rates, total output doubles in around 15 or 16 years, growing more than eightfold in a half-century. Russia transformed herself over these decades from an economically backward nation to a superpower fully capable of posing a serious military threat to the West.

Given what seem to be a number of intrinsic problems with a command economy, how could this transformation have been accomplished? Part of the answer lies in the fact that there are certain advantages to "backwardness," particularly the fact that there is a vast storehouse of new technology already developed by the more economically advanced nations that can simply be borrowed and installed by the "late developer." But there are also certain advantages inherent in the command model that help to offset its disadvantages. In particular, if the central planners focus—as the Russians did—on forcing a rapid rate of industrialization and growth, they are likely to devote a larger proportion of their total output to growth-fostering production (investment) as opposed to raising living standards (consumption).

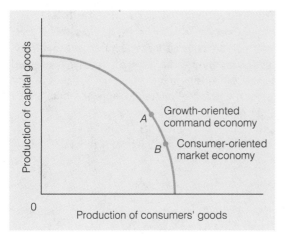

Production of capital goods

A Growth-oriented
   command economy

B Consumer-oriented
   market economy

0   Production of consumers' goods

Figure 3-1 In the determination of basic goals, most near-command economies in real life have put a heavy emphasis on investment and economic growth. They have moved in the direction of *A* (as opposed to *B*) on their production-possibility curve.

This issue can be seen fairly clearly through the use of our production-possibility curve. In Figure 3-1, we have drawn another such diagram, but this time we have placed "consumers' goods" on the *x*-axis and "capital goods" on the *y*-axis. One of the choices all societies face is how much of their output to devote to immediate consumption and how much to *invest* in machines, tools, equipment, and plant—what we call *capital goods*—which will make possible a larger productive capacity in the future.

Now, the Soviet leaders, with their urgency about raising the rate of growth, have historically "commanded" that a very high proportion of their national product be devoted to such investment. In 1980, for example, while most Western European countries were devoting something over 20 percent and the United States well under 20 percent of national product to investment, the Soviet Union was devoting anywhere from 28 to 33 percent to investment, depending on the measure used.[4] Since the USSR also spends more in percentage terms on defense than any of these other countries, these figures represent a substantial direction of the economy toward the desired targets of the central planners. In Figure 3-1, this is represented by the fact that the growth-oriented command economy may locate itself at point *A*, whereas the ordinary market economy, being more responsive to consumer preferences, may locate itself at point *B*.

A final reason for the relatively successful Soviet growth record may have been due to the fact that the command mechanism was well suited to the demands of the growth process in Russia's particular circumstances and over

---

[4] As we shall see in chapter 6, the measurement of aggregate terms like national income or total investment is quite complicated. The different Soviet percentages quoted here depend on the particular prices used. For a discussion of these figures, see Gur Ofer, "Soviet Economic Growth, 1928–55," *Journal of Economic Literature*, vol. 25, no. 4 (December 1987): 1789.

that particular historical era. Russia had an abundance of underutilized labor; her capital stock was meager; the great industries of the period—steel, machinery, heavy industrial products—required large, centralized factories. During this period of what has been called *extensive* growth, the command mechanism, with its forceful (and often inhumane) methods for mobilizing resources could make up for inefficiencies that could appear under other circumstances.

So the Soviet economy grew, and, by the late 1950s, Nikita Khrushchev even began to brag that the USSR would soon overtake and, indeed, "bury" the United States.

Problems Become More and More Serious

Not only did this burial not take place, but during the decade of the 1980s, severe cracks began to appear in the structure of Russia's command economy. Actually, the problems had started earlier, and careful observers of the Soviet scene had noted during the 1970s that Russian growth was definitely slowing down. In Table 3-1, we present Western estimates of the annual rate of

TABLE 3-1 Average Annual Rates of Growth of Soviet Total Production (GNP),* 1951–1989

Period	Average Percentage of Annual Growth
1951–1955	5.5%
1956–1960	5.9
1961–1965	4.8
1966–1970	5.0
1971–1975	3.1
1976–1983	2.3
1984	1.4
1985	.9
1986	4.1
1987	1.2
1988	2.1
1989**	1.9

SOURCES: U.S. Congress, Joint Economic Committee, *USSR: Measures of Economic Growth, 1950–1980;* figures from 1961 on are from the *Economic Report of the President* (February 1990), Table C-110.

*The term "GNP" stands for "gross national product." It is defined in chapter 6, pp. 103–113.

**The figure for 1989 is estimated.

growth of total Soviet production over the period from 1951 to 1989. It is abundantly clear that Soviet growth has been decelerating in recent years. From the mid-1970s on, the USSR, though operating from a much lower base, has been growing less rapidly than the United States and the countries of Western Europe, and far less rapidly than Japan.

The strains that this has put on the Soviet consumer have been intensified by a number of factors:

1. Investment is not only high in the Soviet Union, but has been increasing in percentage terms during the post–World War II period. Depending on the measure used, the percentage of total Soviet production going to gross investment increased either from 17 to 28 percent or 14 to 33 percent between 1950 and 1980. In a certain sense, the command approach, with its heavy emphasis on capital goods, seems to have required the Soviets to run ever faster, even to keep moving forward at a crawl.

2. Defense expenditures have also grown as a percentage of total Soviet production. During the period from 1950 to 1980, the percentage of total production going to defense has been estimated to have increased from 9 to 16 percent (as compared to around 5 percent for the United States in 1980). Of course, Soviet defense expenditures are to some extent shrouded in secrecy, which means that no one can be sure exactly where they are headed. However, it seems certain that during the 1980s, increasing defense expenditures placed very severe strains on the Soviet economy. The U.S. defense buildup under President Reagan was undoubtedly partly responsible for this pressure, though a large part was also due to the more expensive nature of modern defense technologies.

3. As a corollary to the above, consumption was declining as a percentage of Soviet production. Although living standards for the Soviet consumer have clearly risen since the beginning of the five-year plans in 1928, consumption has been declining as a percentage of total production, from nearly three-quarters of total output in 1928 to something above one-half of total output in the 1980s. At the present time, it is probable that average consumption standards in the USSR on a per capita basis are no more than a third of what they are in the United States.

4. Agriculture has been a particular disaster area for the Soviet command economy. Giving agriculture a low priority in the aggressive industrialization drives of Stalin and subjecting it to enforced collectivization, the central planners have effectively turned the Soviet Union from a major agricultural exporter to a major agricultural importer. Table 3-2 shows that, even as late as 1960, Russia was still a major grain exporter. By the mid-1970s and through the 1980s, she has become a persistent importer of large quantities of grain from abroad. Her total grain harvest in 1986 (210 million metric tons), though higher than that of any earlier year in the 1980s, was actually below those achieved in 1973, 1976, and 1978. In this case, it seems clear that the command mechanism, operating through collectives and state farms, has

TABLE 3-2 Soviet Grain Exports and Imports, 1950–1986
(Millions of Metric Tons)

Year	Exports (+)	Imports (−)	Net Exports (+) or Imports (−)
1950	2.9	0.2	+2.7
1955	3.7	0.3	+3.4
1960	6.8	0.3	+6.6
1965	4.3	6.4	−2.1
1970	5.7	2.2	+3.5
1975	3.6	15.9	−12.3
1980	0.5	34.8	−34.3
1982	0.5	32.5	−32.0
1984	1.0	55.5	−54.5
1986	1.0	30.0	−29.0

SOURCE: Marshall I. Goldman, *Gorbachev's Challenge* (New York: W. W. Norton, 1987), 32–34.

provided insufficient incentives for efficient agricultural production. It is notable that on the *3 percent* of arable land allotted to private plots, Soviet peasants are able to produce 60 percent of the USSR's potatoes and honey, 40 percent of her fruits, berries, and eggs, 30 percent of her milk, meat, and vegetables, and around a quarter of her total crop output.

5. *The new high technology era seems particularly ill suited to the mechanisms of the command economy.* In the new era of computers, artificial intelligence, and information technology, the command economy, at least of the traditional Soviet variety, seems hopelessly inadequate. Instead of quantity, the new emphasis is on quality. Instead of well-defined, heavy industrial targets, we have constant technological change, requiring quick, nimble responses. Instead of economic development that requires huge, centralized effort and control, we have a need for numerous, relatively small-scale "start-up" units. Indeed, it can be argued that, in the particular case of the Soviet economy, the demands of the information revolution run counter to her entire history. A society built heavily on the principles of secrecy and political control, where even the mimeograph machine (let alone the modern copier, fax, and computer network) was looked upon with suspicion, could be expected to have severe problems adjusting to a world in which the free and rapid flow of information is not only a desirable but an intrinsic feature of technological advance.

In this new world, where many shifting centers of initiative and creative effort are required, it is likely that the centrally planned command economy is at a fatal disadvantage. In the Soviet Union, what was being "buried" at the end of the 1980s was a seven-decade-long politico-economic organization. New goals were needed, and with them, a far greater attention to efficiency, and especially individual incentives, than in the past.

Enter *Glasnost* and *Perestroika*

Officials in the Soviet Union could not help being aware of these mounting problems, and, as far back as 1965, under the stimulus of the writings of Soviet economist E. G. Liberman, the USSR began various experiments in the greater use of prices, markets, and the criterion of profitability in the management of Soviet industry. All these experiments were piecemeal and short lived, however, and it was only with the ascendancy of Mikhail Gorbachev in March 1985 that a wholesale assault on the command system was even contemplated. Gorbachev pulled no punches in his assessment of the sad state to which the Soviet economy had fallen:

> In the last fifteen years the national income growth rates had declined by more than a half and by the beginning of the eighties had fallen to a level close to economic stagnation. A country that was once quickly closing on the world's advanced nations began to lose one position after another. Moreover, the gap in the efficiency of production, quality of products, scientific and technological development, the production of advanced technology and the use of advanced techniques began to widen. . . .[5]

The terms that were widely introduced to herald a new era in Soviet life were *glasnost* (openness) and *perestroika* (restructuring). Both political and economic mechanisms in the USSR were to be made over apparently into something quite different.

But how? And how serious were the reforms to be? And how long would they last?

The answers to these questions cannot be given at this writing in the early 1990s since the Soviet system is still in a tremendous state of flux. One thing that seems apparent already is that the changes going on are very much more momentous than anything that has occurred since the revolution of 1917. The proof of this is in the relinquishing of Soviet control over the satellite nations of Eastern Europe. The coming down of the Berlin Wall in itself was an unthinkable development just a few months before it happened. Since each of the liberated Warsaw Pact nations is now scurrying to abandon the command economy model as rapidly as it can manage, it can safely be said that, at least in terms of foreign affairs, Gorbachev's regime has shown a willingness to accept wholesale departures from the previous Marxist-Leninist orthodoxy.

But what of the Soviet Union itself? Here, answers must be much more tentative. There is no question that revolutionary changes were being *consid-*

---

[5] Mikhail Gorbachev, *Perestroika* (New York: Harper & Row, 1987), 19.

ered. In the spring of 1990, American newspapers were filled with reports of drastic reforms being discussed by Gorbachev and his advisers. These would involve a much more widespread market-oriented economy, a new pricing mechanism, and laws to allow economic activity without government control in perhaps as much as 70 percent of the economy.

However, consideration is one thing, *implementation* is quite another. The economic reforms actually undertaken by the end of 1990 were relatively minor, and some may have been counterproductive. In general, the Soviet Union faces the following very serious problems in undertaking reforms on the scale most Western observers feel may be necessary to reverse her stagnation:

1. The gradual introduction of economic reforms, however beneficial in the long run, may easily worsen the current situation while adjustments are being made. There is every evidence that GNP growth under *perestroika* has been declining, and by 1990 (and perhaps even earlier), it may have turned *negative*. This poses obvious threats to reform.

2. Not only in the short run, but even in the long run, certain groups stand to lose from economic reform. One cannot build up a huge, powerful national bureaucracy over seven decades without creating numerous vested interests who find reform a serious threat. Even ordinary people—for example, laborers who have had a reasonable degree of job security without having to press themselves very hard—may find reform uncongenial and unsettling.

3. A very important vested interest is the military establishment. Some Western scholars believe that we have been regularly overestimating Soviet GNP and underestimating the proportion of that GNP going to defense.[6] Under any circumstances, the attempt to lift the very heavy military burden from the back of the civilian economy may very well produce a serious backlash on the part of the defense establishment.

4. This backlash may be all the more serious given the centrifugal forces that political liberalization has set into motion throughout the Soviet empire. For it is obviously not only the Eastern European nations, but also various regions, ethnic groups, and previously absorbed nations (like the Baltic states) *within* the Soviet Union who are threatening to break free from Russian domination.

And if the military reasserts itself and any serious hopes of democracy are abandoned in order to stem the collapse of the nation, is it really possible that market reforms will persist? Or will they, too, perish (as have most previous attempts at reform) as the hardliners, temporarily pushed aside, return to power?

---

[6] See, for example, Henry S. Rowen and Charles Wolf, Jr., eds., *The Impoverished Superpower: Perestroika and the Soviet Military Burden* (Institute for Contemporary Studies: San Francisco, 1990).

IS MARKET SOCIALISM REALLY POSSIBLE?

Quite apart from the specific problems of the Soviet Union is the general question: Is it really possible to introduce market elements into a largely centrally controlled economic system? Can we, in effect, *use* the market mechanism to give effect to the objectives of the state and/or society in general.

What we are inquiring about is the viability of what is called *market socialism.* Let us imagine a system in which we have what is usually considered the defining characteristic of socialism—state ownership of the basic means of production—in all or very large parts of the economy. Let us assume also that the state has certain objectives it wishes to secure: say, the way income is distributed, the rate at which capital accumulation takes place, and the balancing of certain social costs and benefits.

Having selected these objectives, however, market socialism then turns to the forces of supply and demand to determine the prices and quantities produced of most consumers' goods. Since society itself would own the basic factors of production, there would be no overt market for land, resources, machinery, factories, and the like, but the producing units in the economy could be instructed to behave *as if* these factors did have markets. They would be told to obey certain rules—rules essentially derived from the competitive market economy we described in the last chapter. By adhering to these rules, production managers would be guaranteeing an "efficient" economic outcome and solving, in a decentralized way, many of the coordination and consistency problems that central planning would otherwise create.

The general analysis demonstrating that market socialism is theoretically possible was developed many, many years ago by economist Oscar Lange.[7] The practical question, however, is whether this route represents a viable evolutionary path for any of today's real-life command economies. In point of fact, there have been at least three serious attempts to move from a command economy toward market socialism in the post–World War II world. Each has its special features, and also its serious problems. The three examples are Yugoslavia, Hungary, and China.

Yugoslavia

Yugoslavia was the first of the European command economies to attempt a drastic reorganization of her economic system and, until the late 1970s, was widely regarded as an example of successful market socialism. After World War II, Yugoslavia had embarked on a Stalinist-style planned economy with a detailed five-year plan aimed at fostering rapid industrial development,

---

[7] Oscar Lange, "On the Economic Theory of Socialism," *Review of Economic Studies,* 4th ser., no. 1 (October 1936).

with priority being given to heavy industries (electrical power, steel, coal) and with arbitrarily fixed prices and an elaborate bureaucracy at both the federal and regional levels.

This highly centralized approach was modified and then abandoned at the end of the First Five-Year Plan in 1951. A political break with Stalin had already occurred (1948); plans for industrial enterprises had proved to be unrealistic or inconsistent; consumers' goods output had fallen far short of expectations; and agriculture was facing one disaster after another. Yugoslavia turned then to a system that, while retaining a one-party communist state, nevertheless did abandon central planning and compulsory collectivization and introduced substantial elements of a market economy, including a rather special feature called worker "self-management."

For 25 years or so, this amalgam of ingredients seemed to work very well. Between 1950 and 1979, the Yugoslav economy grew at an estimated 6.3 percent per year, with per capita output growing at 5.3 percent. And then decline set in. Over the next decade, output *fell* at a rate of 0.9 percent per year, and worker productivity and earnings declined even more. Meanwhile, inflation soared, and Yugoslavia's foreign debt, often wasted on consumption or on investment projects of dubious value, has become a serious burden. Although hardly attributable to her experiment in "market socialism," tensions between different ethnic groups were beginning by 1990 to threaten the viability of the nation itself.

From success story to apparent disaster—Did the attempt to combine markets with socialism have anything to do with this result? Some observers think so. Says Ivan Ribnikar, an economist at Yugoslavia's University of Ljubljana:

> The lesson of Yugoslavia is that there is no compromise between a market economy and a centrally planned economy. One must have a true market economy. It can be harder, like America, or softer, like Sweden or Austria. But it surely shouldn't be like Yugoslavia.[8]

Clearly, one example is not enough to prove this large contention. Still, the Yugoslav case does make it clear that the joining together of markets and socialism is far from easy and, if handled improperly, may prove a total failure. This lesson is also apparent from the two following examples.

Hungary

After the crushing of her 1956 revolution by the Soviets, Hungary proceeded cautiously and with a certain readiness to compromise, where necessary, to

---

[8] Ivan Ribnikar, quoted in Craig Forman, "Yugoslavia's Problems Show Risks in Reform of Socialist Systems," *Wall Street Journal*, 20 February 1990. For a detailed discussion of Yugoslavia's problems, see Harold Lydall, *Yugoslavia in Crisis* (Oxford: Clarendon Press, 1989).

modify her socialism in the direction of a greater market orientation. Agricultural reforms were followed in 1968 by the so-called New Economic Mechanism, which was designed to give market-determined prices an important role in at least certain areas of the economy. For a time, the economy flourished, but then there was a conservative reaction in 1972, and the subsequent OPEC-engineered oil price increases set Hungary back even further.

Still, reforms continued forward in the late 1970s, and, by the late 1980s, Hungary was in the forefront of Eastern European economies in allowing citizens to own private property, including stocks on her embryonic stock exchange. She had become the most attractive East European market for foreign investors, her regulations permitting Westerners to acquire 50 percent ownership in Hungarian enterprises, and, in some cases, up to 100 percent. She was also, however, a nation (like Yugoslavia) where inflation was high and where the foreign debt (at around $20 billion in 1989) was heavy for a nation of only 11 million people.

Does the Hungarian experience give substance to the Lange model of market socialism we described above? Again, specific factors make it difficult to generalize, although it is significant that one of the most eminent observers of the Hungarian scene feels that this judgment is unwarranted. On the contrary, Janos Kornai, professor of Economics at the Hungarian Academy of Sciences and at Harvard University, concludes that Hungary's experience has departed massively from the Lange model. The view that we can combine central regulation and the market, with the latter simply becoming a useful "instrument" in the hands of central policy makers, he regards as "naive." He also notes the deep problem of making a transition from a command economy to a more market-oriented economy: "There is, therefore, a stubborn inner contradiction in the whole reform process: how to get the active participation of the very people who will lose a part of their power if the process is successful." [9]

As to the future of the Hungarian experiment, Kornai is hesitant to judge. Whether a truly competitive, hard-nosed, market-oriented mechanism can be introduced while retaining state ownership over large portions of the resources of the economy, he is unsure. "Up to now," he writes, "Hungary does not provide a conclusive answer." [10]

China

What, then, can we say of our third example—China? With over a billion people and almost a third of the total population of the world's less developed

---

[9] Janos Kornai, "The Hungarian Reform Process," in *Remaking the Economic Institutions of Socialism: China and Eastern Europe*, ed. V. Nee and D. Stark (Stanford, CA: Stanford University Press, 1989), 88.
[10] Ibid., 94.

countries, China commands a special interest for any student of the international scene.

In line of succession, China is the third country (after Yugoslavia and Hungary) to attempt serious market-oriented reforms. It should be understood that ever since the 1949 revolution, while China has consistently been a one-party Communist state with a basic command economy approach, her policies—political, economic, and social—have often fluctuated sharply. This has been true, for example, of her population policies (see chapter 17, p. 346). But it has also been true of her broad ideological outlook as suggested by the periods of the Great Leap Forward and the Cultural Revolution, and the subsequent abandonment of both experiments.

Beginning in 1978, however, China entered a decade of economic reforms that were designed to move the Chinese economy away from Soviet-style central planning and toward a greater reliance on prices, competition, profits, and markets. The reforms began in agriculture, with an approval of the concept that payments could be "based on output with bonuses for overproduction" and a movement from collectivized agriculture to an agricultural policy based on "family responsibility." After a family met certain obligations to the state, it was permitted to sell the remainder of its crop on the market at whatever price it could get.

The results of the agricultural reforms were immediate and strongly positive, with, for example, agricultural output increasing at a strikingly high 11 percent per year in the early 1980s. Industrial reforms soon followed, a basic innovation being that, within limits, business enterprises and their workers could retain a portion of their sales revenues after meeting their obligations to the state. Private businesses were permitted outside the central plan, and by the late 1980s, over 20 million Chinese were engaged in such private ventures. A more open international economy was encouraged, and joint Sino-foreign investment activity began to appear. Although the industrial sector reforms did not show anything like the immediately favorable results produced in agriculture and although serious criticisms were sometimes leveled at the weakening of central planning, the reform process seemed so deeply rooted as to be unstoppable.

And then, abruptly, it was stopped. The popular demonstrations for democracy in 1989 produced a massacre in Tiananmen Square, and also justification for the reversal of the reforms by conservatives who were already unhappy with the drift away from the command economy (and one-party rule) that was occurring. In a vitriolic speech in March 1990, conservative Premier Li Peng announced a variety of counterreform measures under which the government would "tighten control" over prices, business enterprises, investment funds, foreign trade, and any "unduly high" earnings of private firms.

Whether the counterreform movement will soon be replaced by another proreform movement, no one can confidently predict. The Chinese experience does, however, add further evidence to the lessons already observed in Yugoslavia and Hungary: namely, that piecemeal reforms are very difficult to sustain effectively and that there are often powerful vested interests who are ready to clamp down at the first sign of trouble with the reform process. As of the beginning of the 1990s, it has to be said that there is as yet no clear-cut example of (1) a conclusively successful economy based on market socialism or (2) a conclusively successful transition of a Soviet-style command economy to a more market-oriented system of any kind. The relevance of these rather grim observations to the present Soviet reform efforts is all too obvious.

THE WELFARE STATE

In the bulk of this chapter, we have considered economies that have been evolving out of the command economy mode established originally by the Soviet Union in the early decades of this century. But market economies also evolve. In the next chapter, we shall see the particular form that this evolution has taken in the case of the United States.

Suffice it to say here that the evolution of a market economy, carried far enough, creates what is in effect *another* alternative system, what is often called the *welfare state*. A welfare state is like market socialism in that the state is very heavily involved in the operations of the economy, usually, though not exclusively, to promote what is considered to be a more "equitable" distribution of the society's income and resources. Unlike market socialism, however, the welfare state need not involve total or even very substantial government ownership of the means of production. Also, since the welfare state has evolved in the context of Western-style democracies (as opposed to the one-party rule common among command economies), the state that is intervening in the economy is a popularly elected one. In principle (although not always in practice), the state is simply giving voice to the wishes of the general electorate.

In the early post–World War II decades, the drift of the industrial democracies of the West toward welfare statism was quite notable. For example, a study of 13 European countries revealed that, between 1953 and 1973, government expenditures rose on the average from 34 percent of national income to 49 percent.[11] In many of these countries, there were a number of nationalized industries, including everything from telecommunications, electricity, gas, and railroads, to coal, steel, airlines, and even (for example, in France) major ownership in the automotive industry. More generally, there was a trend to increased governmental intervention to promote certain "wel-

---

[11] Warren G. Nutter, *Growth of Government in the West,* American Enterprise Institute for Public Policy Research Studies, no. 185 (Washington, DC, 1978).

fare" objectives: a more equal income distribution and protections against the hazards of old-age, illness, unemployment, and the like.

Without much question, the clearest exemplar of this trend toward the welfare state is Sweden. Sweden, by the mid-1980s, was the first Western economy to have a majority of her citizens dependent on public funds for their livelihood.[12] Public expenditures in the early 1980s were running at around two-thirds of her national income. These expenditures included—beside the usual categories such as defense, police, schools, health, and old-age pensions—a variety of programs addressed to public day-care for children, allowances for raising children, elaborate training programs for unemployed workers, tuition-free college education, and subsidies to private firms in financial difficulties.

Taxes were necessarily very high, by the early 1980s averaging around 60 percent of a full-time male worker's income. The *marginal* tax rate (referring to the percentage taxed out of an additional dollar—or, in this case, krona—of income) rose to 80 percent, or even higher in some cases. Even then, the elaborate welfare programs required an increasing public deficit, reaching in 1982 nearly 10 percent of Sweden's national income.

Was Sweden's experience the wave of the future for the industrial democracies of the West? It seemed so to some observers in the early postwar period, since her private sector remained vigorous and the economy grew rapidly despite the increasing welfare state burdens that were being sustained. With the growing evidence that the command economies were lagging behind, it was easy to imagine a convergence of East and West, with the command economies moving toward market socialism and the capitalistic economies moving toward the welfare state, the similarities between the systems outweighing their differences.

In point of fact, however, this prediction would seem to have been at best only partly correct. As we shall note in the next chapter, the drift toward the welfare state in the United States and most other Western economies slowed down appreciably, and was even partially reversed, during the decade of the 1980s. Sweden herself ran into a number of problems, with the result that numerous books and articles appeared warning of the "crisis" of the welfare state and even proclaiming the "decline and fall of the Swedish model."[13] Sweden did, in fact, take a number of steps to put her economic house in order, including a substantial lowering of her very high tax rates.

But if the drift to the welfare state in the West has slowed down some-

---

[12] This included people on social insurance pensions, employees of the state at both national and local levels, and other predominantly tax-supported groups. See Hugh Heclo and Henrik Madsen, *Policy and Politics in Sweden* (Philadelphia: Temple University Press, 1987), 3–4.

[13] See, for example, Erik Lundberg, "The Decline and Fall of the Swedish Model," *Journal of Economic Literature,* vol. 23, no. 1 (March 1985). For a number of useful essays on Sweden's problems in the 1980s, see Barry P. Bosworth and Alice M. Rivlin, eds., *The Swedish Economy* (Washington, DC: The Brookings Institution, 1987).

what, the collapse of the old command economies of Eastern Europe has, as we have seen, begun to accelerate. Which is to say that if, in fact, "convergence" does occur in the decade of the 1990s, it is very likely to occur much nearer the Western than the Eastern side of the divide.

And what this suggests is that for all its weaknesses, the market mechanism does have a surprising durability, a way of springing back to life when one might least expect it.

SUMMARY

In analyzing the centrally planned or command economy, we begin by going back to Karl Marx, who gave the ideological backdrop for all such economies in the modern world. Marx did not, however, provide a blueprint for economic planning; rather, he provided a detailed criticism of capitalism—because of what he felt to be its class conflicts between capital and labor, its monopolistic elements, and its inherent tendencies to technological unemployment—and he developed an ideology that (when flexibly interpreted) could serve the purpose of Communist revolutions.

A pure command economy must make difficult economic decisions, which often require elaborate institutional arrangements in the modern world. The areas in which problems are likely to occur are: (1) organizing an adequate planning bureaucracy, (2) coordinating economic targets in a consistent manner, (3) making production economically "efficient," (4) securing proper incentives for workers and managers, and (5) setting appropriate goals when consumer sovereignty no longer provides the guidelines.

The Soviet Union provides the longest-lasting approximation to a pure command economy the world has known. This economy produced a very respectable rate of economic growth over the past several decades, in part because of a heavy concentration on capital goods as opposed to consumers' goods. More recently, this economy has been faltering. Consumption has been constrained by heavy investment and defense expenditures, while agricultural production has been weak and GNP growth, in the high-tech era, has declined and even become negative. Through *glasnost* and *perestroika*, Mikhail Gorbachev hopes to reform the economy, presumably increasing the role of markets in its operation.

Whether state ownership and the market mechanism can fruitfully coexist, as in market socialism, is still uncertain. Although the combination is theoretically possible, practical applications in Yugoslavia, Hungary, and China leave the issue undecided. What is clear is that the transition from a command economy to a more market-oriented system, including a greater degree of political democracy, will be very difficult for any country in the Eastern bloc.

During the post–World War II era, the Western world has been generally moving toward increased government participation in the economy, the most advanced example being the welfare state in Sweden. However, the idea that East and West will "converge" toward some point in the middle is increasingly doubtful. Since the drift toward the welfare state has slowed down somewhat in the West and the flight from the command economy has accelerated dramatically in the East, any convergence that takes place seems likely to be very near the Western side of the great divide.

Key Concepts for Review

Marxian critique of capitalism
    Class conflict
    Monopoly
    Crises
Communist revolutions
Central planning
Command economy
Tasks of a command
  economy
    Organization
    Coordination
    Efficiency
    Incentives
    Goals
Soviet economy
    Early rate of growth
    Borrowing technology
    Capital versus con-
      sumer goods
    Extensive growth

Soviet problems
    Declining growth
    Investment and defense burdens
    Agriculture
    Rigidity in the high-tech era
Glasnost and *perestroika*
Market socialism
    Theoretical (Lange model)
    In practice (Yugoslavia, Hungary,
    China)
Welfare state
    Evolution from market economy
    Sweden
    Continued market vitality
Convergence hypothesis

Questions for Discussion

1. Marx predicted an increasing class conflict between capitalists and the workers (proletariat) as the capitalistic system approached maturity. Do you feel that this prediction has been borne out by the American experience over the past century or two? What economic factors may have moderated any tendency toward class conflict in this country?

2. In a pure command economy, what takes the place of the market economy's "consumer sovereignty"?

3. Economic "inefficiency," like unemployment (see Figure 1-6, p. 15), can be represented by a point inside the production-possibility curve, such as *I*. What this point signifies is that the economy in question is not get-

ting the maximum production out of its given resources. Since it is well known that the Soviet economy was highly "inefficient" from the beginning, how can you explain the fact that she did achieve a respectable rate of economic growth for several decades. Illustrate your answer with the following diagram:

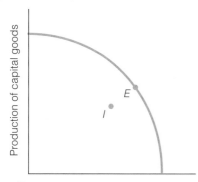

I represents a point of "inefficient" production. Note that, at an "efficient" point, like *E*, we could produce more of *both* capital goods and consumers' goods.

4. Write an essay explaining why the Soviet economy is facing such major obstacles these days. Why did her economic difficulties seem much less evident twenty or thirty years ago?

5. Marx claimed that capitalism would never "evolve" into socialism; it would take a revolution to bring about this result. Applying this logic to Eastern bloc countries, develop the argument that command economies will never reform themselves into market-oriented economies—that is, that only a major cataclysm of one sort or another will produce this result. Examine this thesis critically with respect to the experience of Yugoslavia, Hungary, and China.

6. "The welfare state is fundamentally different from market socialism. The latter is rooted in the historic failure of the command economy, while the former is rooted in the evolution of democratic, market economies." Discuss.

CHAPTER 4

THE MIXED ECONOMY OF THE UNITED STATES

In the two preceding chapters, we discussed forms of economic organization ranging from the market economy at one extreme to the command economy at the other. In the first case, all decisions are made in a highly decentralized fashion by small, private firms and individuals. In the second, the state owns the means of production in the society, and basic decisions are made by central planners who promulgate directives setting various targets for the rest of the economy.

In this discussion, we noted several things: (1) that *pure* market or command economies don't exist in reality; (2) that in each case there has been a drift during the twentieth century toward a modified system that mixes public and private elements, as in market socialism or the welfare state; but (3) that while the movement away from the command model has accelerated drastically in recent years, there has been something of a slowdown in the drift of market economies toward the welfare state.

In this chapter, we will consider the mixed economy of the United States, examining briefly how it has departed in major ways from the market model, but also how the 1980s saw a revitalization of market elements in certain areas of the economy.

GROWTH OF GOVERNMENT IN THE UNITED STATES

When we think of a "mixed" economy, our first thought is usually in terms of the mix of private and government decision making. And, indeed, despite some efforts at retrenchment in the 1980s, the growth of government participation in the American economy remains a salient fact of the past half-century.

Just how rapidly has the public sector of the American economy grown in recent decades? One way of estimating this growth is to take all government expenditures—federal, state, and local—lump them together, and see how they have expanded over time. In Figure 4-1, the top line represents the sum of all government expenditures in the United States from 1939 to 1989. This chart is drawn on a semilog scale, meaning that a straight line would represent a constant percentage increase. The strong upward drift of the curve makes it clear that the public sector has expanded substantially over this period—from about $18 billion in 1939 to about $1.8 trillion in 1989.

To understand the extent of this expansion, however, it is necessary to inspect the figures a bit more closely. In the first place, they are in "current dollars," meaning that they reflect the upward drift of prices over this period as well as the increase in real or physical purchases by government. U.S. prices went up more than ninefold between 1939 and 1989.

Second, we should note that these figures include at least two fundamentally different kinds of government expenditures. In addition to ordinary expenditures on goods and services,[1] they also include "transfer payments." The difference is important. In the case of an ordinary expenditure, the government pays a clerk for his or her services in the Department of Defense or buys a truck or other commodity from a private firm. The payment is for a good delivered or a service rendered. A *transfer payment*, however, involves neither a good delivered nor a service rendered. In a typical form, it simply represents a transfer of purchasing power from a taxpayer to the recipient of the transfer payment. Social Security payments are transfer payments. So are payments for unemployment compensation. So are certain subsidies to farmers under our various agricultural programs. In each case, the key fact is that the government does not produce goods itself or direct private production into certain channels by its orders for goods. The elderly couples on Social Security do not have to provide any services to the government, and they are free to spend their Social Security checks in any way they see fit.

In our present discussion, the relevance of this distinction derives from two considerations: (1) Although transfer payments necessarily involve government intervention in the economy, the degree of that intervention is somewhat less than that of ordinary government expenditures, which represent a claim of the government on the nation's output of goods and services. (2) Transfer payments have grown very rapidly since the early 1950s, particularly in the decade from the mid-1960s to the mid-1970s; they now

---

[1] It should be noted that these ordinary government expenditures include both (1) direct government production—for example, services of policemen and teachers—and (2) government purchases of goods—computers, stealth bombers, and so on—from the private sector.

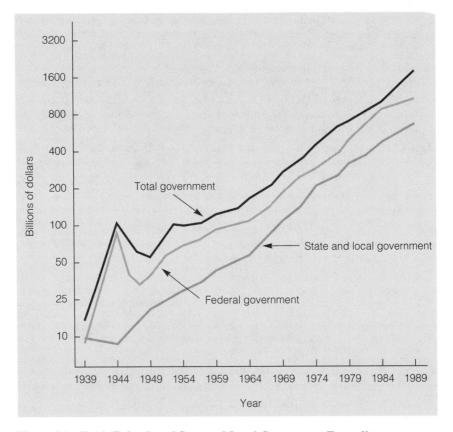

Figure 4-1   Total, Federal, and State and Local Government Expenditures, 1939–1989
SOURCE: *Economic Report of the President*, 1990.

account for about 40 percent of all federal government expenditures. The combination of these two points means that the curves of Figure 4-1 somewhat overstate the increasing impact of government on our economy over this period.

Finally, we should note that while government activity has been growing since 1939, so also has the nation's economy as a whole. What we are interested in most directly is not government expenditures in isolation, but those expenditures in relation to the nation's total output of goods and services. Figure 4-2 represents the total of federal, state, and local expenditures expressed as a percentage of U.S. gross national product.[2] This diagram

---

[2] As mentioned in the last chapter, gross national product (GNP) will be defined in detail in Chapter 6, pp. 103–113. We should note here, however, that since transfer payments do not represent any addition to the goods and services output of the nation, they are not included in GNP.

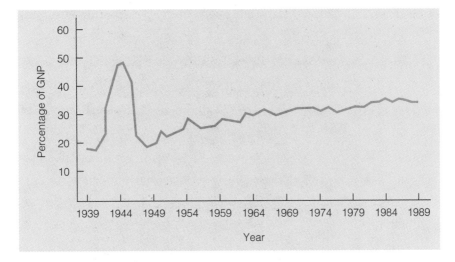

Figure 4-2   Total Government Expenditures as a Percentage of GNP, 1939–1989

makes clear that, in this *relative* sense, the greatest participation of government in the American economy took place not in the 1980s, but forty years before. In 1943 and 1944, at the height of World War II, government expenditures were roughly *half* our total annual national output. There was a sharp cutback immediately after the war and then the beginning of a long upward drift that continued until 1982, when government expenditures reached about 35 percent of GNP. The percentage has remained relatively constant since that time.

CAUSES OF THE EXPANSION OF GOVERNMENT

The reasons for this historic expansion of government activity are varied and complex. In a democracy, one tends to assume that the government grows primarily because of the increasing number of functions that the public wishes its popularly elected representatives to fulfill. Popular sovereignty in the political sphere would be analogous to consumer sovereignty in the marketplace.

This, however, is almost certainly too simple a view of the matter. Taxpayer revolts in many states in recent years suggest that some citizens regard the government not as the executor of their will, but as an adversary to be confronted and contained. Critics of government expansion have begun to stress the government's own role in promoting itself. There is now a vast public bureaucracy in the nation, at federal, state, and local levels, and the self-interest of this bureaucracy might easily appear to lie in expanding its range of functions. It is claimed that while public officials, elected or appointed, may often disagree as to how public funds should be spent, they are unanimous in always wanting more of these funds available.[3]

Thus, we have to qualify the benign view of the government as simply responding to its citizens' wishes. Still, one must also acknowledge that Americans have grown accustomed to many of these expanded government functions. While we may vigorously resist tax increases, we may also resist any cutbacks in our favorite programs. Certain generalizations can be made about the growth of government in the U.S. economy in the modern era:

Traditional Government Roles Cannot Account for the Growth

From the beginning of organized society, government has been assigned certain traditional responsibilities for maintaining order and promoting the common weal. Adam Smith, we recall, gave the Sovereign duties with respect to national defense, the administration of justice, and education. Such traditional functions have, of course, expanded in absolute terms over the past several decades. They cannot, however, account for the substantial growth of government as a *percentage* of GNP during this period. Figure 4-3 shows how the breakdown of federal expenditures has been changing. One traditional expenditure—defense—has declined considerably since the early 1950s despite the defense buildup of the 1980s. Most of the other traditional government expenditure items are included in the "all other" category—for example, justice, general government, agriculture, commerce, transportation, and so on. Clearly, it is not here, but elsewhere, that we would have to look for an explanation of the expansion of government in the American economy.

Important New Functions Have Emerged in Recent Decades

Ever since the 1930s, the U.S. government has assumed certain responsibilities for correcting what are felt to be deficiencies in the workings of a market economy. Such "corrective" actions have, of course, been taken in the distant past as well; however, the increase in scale of such activities marks a qualitative change in the relationship of the government to the private sector. Three broad areas may be noted:

   1. *Stabilizing the economy.* Stable prices and full employment, most economists agree, cannot be guaranteed in a completely unregulated economy. Since the

---

[3] Consequently, a main reason for expanded government could conceivably be our improved ability to collect taxes—an ability that will be enhanced in the future by further advances in computer technology and data processing. See Benjamin Ward, "Taxes and the Size of Government," *American Economic Review* vol. 72, no. 2 (May 1982): 346–50.

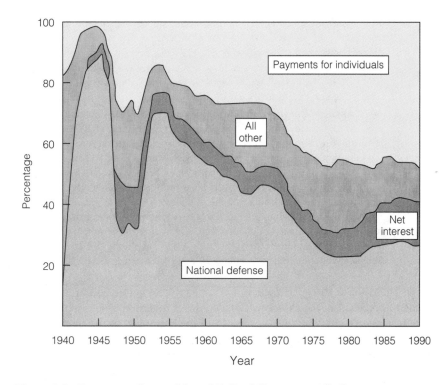

Figure 4-3   Percentage Composition of Federal Government Outlays
"Traditional" federal expenditures (like defense and those included in "all other") cannot account for the expansion of government expenditures in recent decades. The major source of expansion has clearly been in the category "payments for individuals."
SOURCE: Office of Budget and Management, Special Analyses Budget of the United States Government, fiscal year 1990, p. B-7. Adapted by the author.

Great Depression of the 1930s and the passage of the Full Employment Act of 1946, the federal government has assumed major responsibilities for reducing unemployment in the economy and restraining inflationary increases in the price level. Unemployment and inflation will, in fact, be the main subjects in our detailed discussion of the economy in the aggregate, beginning with the next chapter.

2. *Social versus private costs and benefits*. The market does not always place what economists feel is the correct social evaluation on the production of various goods and services. In certain cases, the market may undervalue the good. An example might be the construction of a dam. A firm wants to build a dam on a river but finds that a great many of the benefits of the dam will go to other firms farther downstream. The dam may not be profitable for this firm to build because, although it must bear all the costs, it receives only *part* of the benefits. Yet, if the government were to build the dam, the total benefits to society might

be greater than the total costs. In recent years, more attention has been paid to areas where private production involves *costs* to society for which private parties are not charged. The environmental protection movement, with its emphasis on government regulation to control air, land, and water pollution is based, in principle, on the divergence between private and social costs—a divergence that the market will normally not take into account.

3. *Redistribution of income.* Although private market forces operate efficiently with respect to many problems, few economists would claim that they guarantee an "ideal" distribution of income within the society. Market forces tend to reward the productive. In any given society, however, there will be individuals who, for no apparent fault of their own, cannot be as productive as others; yet, their economic needs may be just as great or greater. The elderly, the ill, the handicapped, the disadvantaged, the uneducated, victims of ethnic or racial prejudice—such individuals are unlikely to receive market-determined incomes that most Americans consider adequate. A great many government programs— Social Security, Medicare and Medicaid, Aid to Families with Dependent Children, and countless others—have been designed to meet these special needs.

These three categories are not completely separable. Take unemployment compensation, for example. This could be regarded as an income redistribution device (transferring income from the employed to the unemployed) or a stabilization program (keeping up purchasing power during a recession). However, the logic behind government action in each of these categories is somewhat different, and their separation allows us to note specifically the spectacular growth in the third category. In Figure 4-3, the item "payments for individuals" includes retirement, unemployment, medical care, food, nutrition and public assistance, and other such programs, most of which have a strong redistributional component. By the early 1980s, over half of all federal expenditures were in this category. This compares to about a quarter of such expenditures in 1960 and less than 20 percent in the pre-War year 1940.

Tax Receipts Have Not Kept Pace with Expenditures

We have been speaking of the expansion of government in the U.S. economy in terms of expenditures, but another measure of government involvement in the economy is in terms of taxes. One might think that these were roughly equivalent measures, but Figure 4-4 shows that, in the case of the federal government, a persistent gap developed between expenditures and receipts from the 1970s on. Federal tax receipts have not kept pace with expenditure growth and, indeed, show very little upward trend over the past 40 years. Numerous cuts in tax rates—in 1964, 1977, 1978, and, most recently, in 1981—have kept total tax receipts at a fairly constant percentage of GNP. Over the whole period from 1951 to 1988, taxes fluctuated in the narrow margin between 17.5 percent and 20.9 percent of GNP.

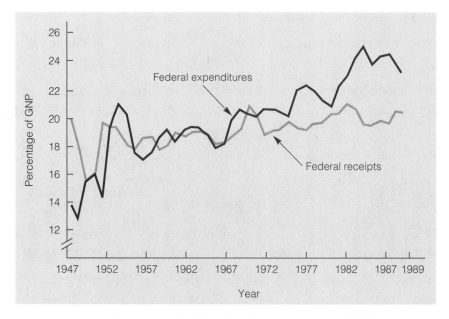

Figure 4-4   Federal Receipts and Expenditures as a Percentage of GNP
SOURCE: Department of Commerce; *Economic Report of the President*, 1989, 1990.
Note: Data are on a national income and product accounts basis.

We have mentioned that a consequence of this diverging behavior of taxes and expenditures has been a substantial increase in the federal debt (but not, we should add, state and local debt; these levels of government have generally moved from deficit to surplus over the postwar period). This is a matter that has attracted much concern and will be studied at length later in this book. (See especially chapter 13.)

For the moment, we simply note the divergence, adding that it is by no means irrelevant to the rate of expansion of the public sector in the U.S. economy. It is widely believed that the Reagan administration in the 1980s expressed its opposition to expanded government *spending* by reducing government *taxes*. The deficit was, in effect, used as a lever to bring down the rate of expansion of the public sector. Opponents of this approach argue either (1) that increased public spending was necessary or (2) that the method of reducing spending by means of heavy deficits is deeply flawed or (3) both of the above. Those who supported the policy, on the other hand, claim (1) that tax revenues as a percentage of GNP, after a dip, are now returning to their prior levels and (2) that the policy worked to at least some degree—that is, that federal expenditures did not increase and, in fact, showed a small decrease as a percentage of GNP after the tax cut of 1981 became effective. Clearly, these are issues we will have to return to later in our study.

AN EXAMPLE OF GOVERNMENT GROWTH—SOCIAL SECURITY

To give an example of an area of government expansion, we can do no better than to glance briefly at our Social Security program, where "payments for individuals" in 1990 were running at around a quarter of a trillion dollars. This sum is virtually certain to increase both absolutely and as a percentage of GNP in the second decade of the next century, when the Baby Boomers begin to retire in large numbers.[4]

The U.S. Social Security program illustrates both the reasons why expanded government has occurred during the past half-century and why some concern has been felt about the rapidity of that expansion. The Social Security Act of 1935 was passed in the midst of the Great Depression, when bank failures, the stock market crash, and massive unemployment put many elderly Americans into desperate economic straits. It did not escape notice, too, that by providing pensions for the elderly, the government might encourage older persons to retire and, thus, reduce competition with younger workers seeking jobs in a badly depressed economy.

The program started on a small scale, with employers and employees each paying only 1 percent of the employee's wage up to $3,000. Little by little, however, the benefits and the employer/employee contributions were increased, and the number of workers covered was also increased. Despite these advances, poverty among elderly Americans remained quite high. In the mid-1960s, for example, the poverty rate among Americans 65 and over was twice as high as that of the general population. In the case of elderly persons living alone, some 40 percent of men and two-thirds of women had incomes below the poverty line.

So the program was further expanded. Quite apart from the health care initiatives of the 1960s (especially Medicare and Medicaid), the pension program itself enjoyed benefit increases in 1968, 1970, 1971, and 1972. These benefit increases came more rapidly than the cost of living was rising and, in the case of the 1972 legislation, involved a "double-indexing" error, which raised benefits far more than anticipated. Coverage, meanwhile, was being extended to a variety of workers (interns, self-employed physicians, ministers, federal employees, and so on), so that what had begun as a partial program was now virtually universal.

Although not the sole factor involved, the expansion of Social Security was, without question, a major reason for the sharply improved position of elderly Americans from the mid-1960s on. Figure 4-5 shows that their pov-

---

[4] The term "social security" is sometimes used in a variety of meanings to cover a number of social insurance and health care programs. We are thinking of it here in the specific sense of two funds: the Old Age and Survivors Insurance Fund and the Disability Insurance Fund (collectively, OASDI). There has, of course, also been a massive increase in government spending on health insurance programs—a matter of some concern for the future.

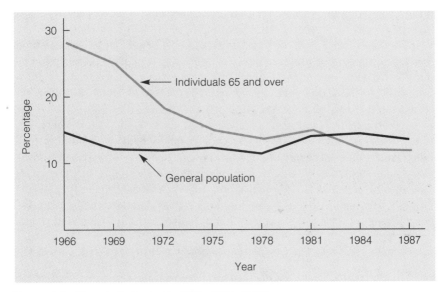

Figure 4-5   Poverty Rates in the U.S., 1966–1987
SOURCE: Bureau of the Census.

erty rate not only fell sharply, but, by the early 1980s, had actually fallen *below* the rate of the general population. Social Security has, in this sense, been a major success, and despite certain reservations that we shall mention below, polls show that it remains an immensely popular program with Americans of all ages.

At the same time that the program was showing such desirable results, it was also running into a major financial crisis. In 1981, the Social Security Trust Fund was within six weeks of being exhausted. In fact, in late 1982, the pension program was kept operating only by borrowing money from the Disability and Hospital Insurance Funds. Suddenly, the general public awakened to two major realizations: (1) that Social Security was not so much an insurance program as a pay-as-you-go transfer program, where current taxes on the working generation are used to finance current payments to the retired generation and (2) that continuing benefit increases were creating what could become an intolerable situation down the road when the Baby Boomers began to reach retirement age. In a word, there really wasn't any significant Social Security Trust Fund—current and past recipients had been receiving far more than they had ever put into the fund—and it looked as though, without such a fund, the future, especially after 2010 or 2015, could pose very serious financing problems.

What has happened to the U.S. Social Security program since the crisis of the early 1980s illustrates the somewhat more equivocal view about the expansion of the public sector that has emerged in recent years. In the first place, legislation in 1983, although it effectively raised Social Security taxes (to a projected 12.4-percent employer/employee OASDI contribution for the year 2000 and later), also took certain steps to *reduce* benefits—a change in the basic direction the program has been following ever since its inception. It did this by delaying a cost-of-living adjustment (COLA) and, more significantly, by introducing a gradual increase in the age at which a retiree becomes eligible for full benefits.

Subsequently, there have been elaborate discussions as to whether future payroll tax increases should be carried out, whether the buildup of a huge Trust Fund—projected under the 1983 legislation—is or is not desirable,[5] and, significantly, whether the program should, at least in some small measure, be privatized. Although a majority of Americans clearly wish the program to remain intact as is, it is no longer considered sacrilegious to discuss alternative structures, even including some partially privatized plans.

GROWTH OF THE MODERN CORPORATION

We have so far been discussing the "mixed" American economy in terms of the changing role of government in the economy. But our economic system departs from the simple market model in more ways than just by having a substantial public sector. We do not have perfect competition either in business or in labor markets, and this requires us to modify the simple laws of supply and demand we developed in chapter 2. Let us now turn to the "mix" of different market structures within the private sector of our economy, considering first business and then labor.

First, a few facts. There are over 16 million business enterprises in the United States. Of these, over 70 percent are *sole proprietorships,* in which an individual puts up the capital and runs the firm. A smaller number (something over 1 million) are *partnerships,* in which a group of people join together to share the profits and financial obligations of an enterprise. Because each partner is liable to an unlimited degree for the debts of his partners, this form is not particularly widespread or significant in its impact.

A third, and highly significant, form of an enterprise is the *corporation.* In this form, the enterprise is a "legal person" that can own property, sell stocks, enter into contracts, etc., and, furthermore, is subject only to *limited liability.* This is to say that the stockholders who own the corporation are *not* liable for the debts of the corporation beyond their original investment. Although the stockholders own the corporation, much of the control

---

[5] In 1990, there was great publicity given a proposal by Senator Daniel Patrick Moynihan to reduce Social Security taxes sharply and forego the buildup of the Trust Fund. Opponents of this proposal argued that the buildup was necessary as a way of increasing national savings to prepare for the large number of Baby Boom retirees after the year 2010.

TABLE 4-1 Sales and Assets of Some Leading American Corporations, 1990

CORPORATION	ANNUAL SALES (in Billions of Dollars)	ASSETS (in Billions of Dollars)
General Motors	126.9	173.3
Ford Motor Company	96.9	160.9
Exxon	86.7	83.2
IBM	63.4	77.7
General Electric	55.3	128.3
Mobil Oil	51.0	39.1
Philip Morris	39.1	38.5
Chrysler	36.2	51.0
Dupont	35.2	34.7
Texaco	32.4	25.6
Chevron	29.4	33.9
AMOCO	24.2	30.4
Shell	21.7	27.6
Procter & Gamble	21.7	16.4
Boeing	20.3	13.3
Occidental Petroleum	20.1	20.7
United Technologies	19.8	14.6
Eastman Kodak	18.5	23.7
USX	17.8	17.5
Dow Chemical	17.7	22.2
Xerox	17.6	30.1

SOURCE: *Fortune Magazine,* May & July, 1990

rests with management, leading to what is often called the *divorce of ownership and control.*[6]

Although there are only two million or so corporations in the United States, their impact is enormous. These two million firms typically account for 90 percent or more of total business sales in our economy. Indeed, the top 500 of large industrial corporations account for nearly half of our total GNP. Table 4-1 shows the sales and assets of some of the leading American corporations in 1989. Large firms do not dominate all industries. In commercial printing, machine shops, and the fur industry, the top few firms account for only a small proportion of total sales; agricultural production is still relatively "unconcentrated"; in service industries and the professions, small units are

---

[6] A famous early study of the modern corporation and its economic significance is A. A. Berle and Gardiner C. Means, *The Modern Corporation and Private Property,* rev. ed. (New York: Macmillan, 1968). See also John Kenneth Galbraith, *The New Industrial State* (Boston: Houghton Mifflin, 1967).

often the order of the day. Still, in many of our basic industries—oil, steel, automobiles, computer hardware, and so on—a few large firms clearly have an enormous impact on sales and performance of the industries in question.

Since the model of the market economy we presented in chapter 2 assumed large numbers of small firms, what can we say about the competitiveness of an economy in which a relatively small number of very large firms play such an important role?

IMPACT OF IMPERFECTLY COMPETITIVE MARKET STRUCTURES

In the real world of today's U.S. economy, we clearly are operating with various forms of *imperfect competition*—monopolistic competition, oligopoly, occasionally monopoly or near-monopoly. When large firms dominate an industry, it is hard to be sure that Adam Smith's "invisible hand" will be sufficient to protect the consumer. As we know, Smith believed that private interest would lead to social harmony, because intense competition among business firms would force them to produce the goods consumers wanted and to sell them at the cheapest possible prices. But if firms are large and few, if they set prices rather than respond to impersonal markets, if they are subject only to limited competition, may we not get examples of excessive profits, reduced outputs, abnormally high prices?

Has the growth of the large corporation seriously compromised the basic competitiveness that is essential to the workings of the private sector of our "mixed" economy?

Different Forms of Competition

Perhaps the first thing to be said in response to the above question is that competition comes in many forms. One of the more striking things about imperfectly competitive market structures is that they involve us in types of competition different from the simple price-and-quantity competition described by our supply and demand curves of chapter 2. In perfect competition, the small business firm simply adjusts the quantity of the product supplied to a market-given price. In oligopoly and monopolistic competition, firms will often engage in significant *nonprice competition*.

> One of the most common forms of nonprice competition in the American economy is competition through *advertising*. Advertising is a kind of competition one would not expect to find in a *pure* market economy, because it involves at least some ability to influence the market for one's product. In advertising, of course, business firms are trying to stimulate or otherwise alter consumer tastes. Where advertising is very pervasive, some critics have come to question the whole concept of "consumer sovereignty," arguing that it is the business interests of the society that shape consumers' tastes to their own purposes. Others argue that advertising is often in-

formative and/or that consumers are now so cynical about advertising claims that they are not easily misled.

Another common form of nonprice competition is what we earlier called *product differentiation*. Instead of trying to compete with other firms by lowering the price of their product, large firms (and sometimes even small firms) can introduce special gadgets, designs, improvements in comfort, appearance, safety, or other features so as to separate off their particular product from that of their rivals in the eyes of the consumer. Again, as in the case of advertising, observers differ about the value of this kind of competition. Product differentiation can give the consumer a more interesting and varied range of choices than is possible in an overly standardized world. Some of the drabness of Eastern bloc markets may have been due to their lack of adjustment to the different preferences of consumers. On the other hand, product differentiation uses up resources for what often seem to be transient, superficial effects of no real value to the consumer.

The first point, then, is that competition often takes on a more complex and varied form under imperfectly competitive market structures than under pure competition.

Price and Quantity Adjustments

Moreover, there is also an important element of price-and-quantity competition even among quite large firms. I may have an absolute "monopoly" over my particular brand name product (Budweiser beer, Bayer aspirin, Chrysler "New Yorker," and so on), but if I set too high a price on this product, I am very likely to lose customers and, hence, my share of the market to my rivals.

In these circumstances, the forces of supply and demand clearly do affect large firms, but they do so in more complex ways. An increase in demand for a general category of products would, under perfect competition, raise prices above costs and bring an expansion of output in that industry. In an oligopolistic industry, the result may be generally the same, though reached by a different route. If firm A raises its price in response to the increase in demand, firm B may decide to stay just below firm A's price, thus capturing some of A's market share. Where we have a few firms dominating the industry, firm A will, of course, be aware of firm B's reasoning, and firm B will be aware of firm A's awareness, and so on. To avoid price wars (which occasionally do break out) and keep their responses to changing demand conditions orderly, oligopolistic industries often resort to a pattern of *price leadership*. This means letting one large (though not necessarily the largest) firm in the industry initiate price changes (the "price leader") and then—by tacit, not open (illegal), agreement—the other firms following along more or less in line with the policy the leader has established.

Firms in these industries also sometimes use pricing on a *cost-plus basis*. Suppose there are changes on the supply side. There has been a big increase in the price of petroleum inputs. Or the unions in this industry have won sharp wage increases. If firms in the industry operate on a cost-plus pricing method, then each of them will have an orderly basis for raising prices when supply conditions change. Indeed, it is relatively so easy for large firms to pass on cost increases to their consumers that some commentators have felt that oligopolistic market structures may contribute to the inflationary tendencies of the present-day American economy.

Is Competition Growing or on the Decline?

Clearly then, there are *some* elements of competition in the business sector of our mixed economy. But are they sufficient? More significantly, are they getting stronger or weaker over time?

This is a difficult question to answer because so many different elements are involved. Historically, the growth of great industrial giants prompted government action in the form of *antitrust* legislation to promote competition. The Sherman Act of 1890 prohibits "every contract, combination in the form of trust or otherwise, or conspiracy, in restraint of trade or commerce"; the Clayton Act of 1914 outlaws business practices that might "substantially lessen competition or tend to create a monopoly." However, with a few notable exceptions (like the breakup of AT&T in 1982), antitrust enforcement has been relatively sluggish in recent years. Does this mean that competition is on the wane?

The answer is almost certainly no, and for at least three reasons:

1. Recent decades have seen a massive increase in *foreign competition* in American markets. We shall be considering the explosive growth in international trade in chapter 16. For the moment, we simply note that those huge firms listed in Table 4-1 are hardly exempt from pressures from abroad; indeed, in some cases, big as they are, they are literally reeling from German, Japanese, Korean, and other Asian competitors.

2. *Deregulation* of certain industries, like the airlines, while it has had certain unpleasant side effects, has probably operated to increase the general level of competitiveness in the U.S. economy.

3. There is no sign that large firms are gaining relatively to smaller firms in the American economy in recent decades.[7] Indeed, *innovation in high technology* is often carried out by relatively small firms. It was, in fact, the absence of small, "start-up" firms that, as we noted in chapter 3, has particularly bedevilled the centrally planned economies of the USSR and Eastern Europe. In a rapidly changing, technologically advancing economy,

---

[7] A measure that is sometimes used in this connection is the *concentration ratio*: the share of an industry's output produced by the four largest firms in the industry. There is no evidence that U.S. concentration ratios are increasing over time, and, in fact, concentration in American industries tends to be a bit lower than it is in other industrialized nations.

older firms, however large, are always subject to competition from ingenious, innovative products of their often far smaller rivals.[8]

In short, just as the growth of the public sector has been somewhat restrained in recent years, the business sector of the U.S. economy has witnessed some revitalization of its market economy elements. Competitive forces are very much in evidence.

UNIONS AND AMERICAN LABOR

Can we say the same with respect to the market for American labor? In a pure market economy, as we know, there are supply and demand curves for factors of production (labor, land, and capital) as well as for products. These factor supply and demand curves are not, of course, the same curves that we would draw for a commodity. When we were talking about washing machines, the demanders were consumers who wanted to buy washing machines for their homes. When we are talking about labor, say textile workers—or welders, or truck drivers, or secretaries, or computer programmers—the demanders are not typically consumers, but business firms that will produce the products we shall ultimately buy. The business firm, in other words, is characteristically a *supplier* of products to the consumer but a *demander* of the services of textile workers or other forms of labor, or land, or capital goods.[9]

In any real-life economy, the smooth functioning of factor supply and demand curves is seldom accomplished in all respects. Many imperfections exist; laborers may not generally know about jobs in other localities or occupations; there may be discrimination by gender or by minority group status; there may be general unemployment in the economy as a whole; the individual laborer faced with the necessity of having some sort of job may be at the mercy of a locally *monopsonistic*[10] employer; and so on.

---

[8] The economist who most emphasized the role of innovation as a force making for business competition was Joseph A. Schumpeter. See chapter 7, p. 128.

[9] Although we cannot explain the derivation of factor supply and demand curves here, a few hints as to their derivation should help make their meaning clear. The *demand curve* for textile workers will ultimately reflect how profitable it is for firms to hire such workers. This, in turn, will be influenced by the consumer demand curve for the textile products produced by these workers and by the productivity of these workers. The *supply curve* for textile workers in a pure market economy will reflect, in the short run, the attractiveness of this kind of work compared with other employment opportunities or leisure for those who possess the necessary skills as textile workers. In the longer run, if the wages of textile workers remain very high, then more young men and women will seek to acquire the special skills required. If textile workers' wages happen to be very low, then in the long run fewer people will head into this line of work. As always, in the pure market economy, equilibrium is reached where the relevant supply and demand curves intersect.

[10] As *monopoly* means a single seller, *monopsony* means a single buyer. In a given locality where there may be only one large industrial firm, the employer of labor in that area may effectively have some monopsonistic control over the labor market.

The particular interference with the "law of supply and demand" that has attracted most attention in the American and other major industrial economies is, however, that due to labor unions. Unions have an impact on many different aspects of the labor market. They have what we may think of as a primary objective—to raise wages for their members—but they bargain collectively about many more issues than this: seniority systems, hours and conditions of work, health and other fringe benefits, methods of production, job tenure, and so on. They are complicated institutions with their own meetings, elections, organizational structures, and often their own political views and political action committees.

If we confine ourselves to the wage-raising objective, we can use supply-and-demand analysis to show how union activity can cause a departure from the market-determined wage.

The basic analysis is presented in Figure 4-6. W_1 is the wage that would obtain if there were no external intervention in the market. The union's objective is to raise the wage to W_2. If it succeeds—and if everything else remains constant (our familiar *ceteris paribus* clause)—then, when the wage rate is raised to W_2, business firms will cut employment from E_1 to E_2. Actually, the measure of unemployment among textile workers would be greater than the difference between those formerly employed and those now employed. The reason is that at the new and higher wage rate, more textile workers' services would be offered than before. (This is what the supply curve tells us.) Consequently, the amount of unemployment is measured by the horizontal distance between the supply and demand curves at the new wage (W_2), or the distance AB.

Figure 4-6   Effects of a Single Union on Wage Rates and Employment
If one union in the economy succeeds in raising its wage (W_2) above the supply-and-demand-determined wage (W_1), the consequences for those workers will be less employment but higher wages for those employed. One must not generalize this effect to the action of unions in the economy as a whole, however, since these curves are drawn on *ceteris paribus* assumptions that do not hold when all unions are acting together.

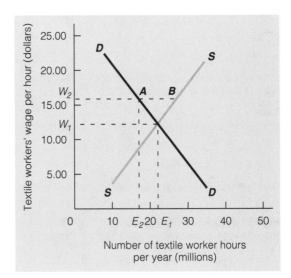

Now, it would seem from this analysis that a main impact of unions in this area of bargaining would be to raise wage rates of their members and to curtail the employment of their members. Indeed, it would seem to be a fairly easy step from this diagram to a general conclusion about inflation and unemployment in the economy as a whole. Because of widespread union activity, it might be argued, the American economy is afflicted with the difficult twin problems of more unemployment than we would like and more inflation than we would like. Not only big business but big labor could be charged with causing, or at least greatly aggravating, these important economic problems.

Such statements, however, involve unacceptable simplifications, and for two reasons:

1. *Labor union activity in the American economy has basically been on the decline for the past 35 years.* In the 1940s and 1950s, union membership represented roughly a third of employed workers; by 1990, that number had fallen to under 18 percent. Figure 4-7 shows both the dramatic rise in union membership from the 1930s to the immediate postwar period and then the almost equally dramatic decline since that time. Unions have always been strongest in certain manufacturing and mining industries, and these industries have sharply declined in employment terms over recent decades. Although unions have made some inroads into service occupations, including government employees, these gains have been minor compared to their losses elsewhere. The new high tech industries have, in general, not been unionized.

What this first point means is that whatever impact unions may have had on national unemployment and inflation in the past, their current influence in these areas is considerably reduced. Indeed, the U.S. labor market provides another example of the recent tendency to retrace our steps and move back somewhat in the direction of a competitive market economy.

2. *We must be very careful in generalizing from the effects of one union acting alone to the collective effects of unions in general.* This second point is particularly important for the analysis we are about to begin in part 2. In general, we cannot say that when one union does something alone, the same results will be achieved for that union as when *all unions together* attempt a similar thing. The relevance of the *ceteris paribus* phrase is particularly important here. When *all* unions are attempting to achieve wage increases, then this clause is no longer appropriate for any one labor market—other things *are* changing. In particular, if all wages go up, this will have an effect on the demand for most products in the economy, and when the demand for products goes up, this, in turn, will have an effect on the demand for labor. We could, in fact, imagine a case where everything more or less canceled out: where there were higher wages in general, higher prices in general (so that the higher wages would purchase the same number of goods in the economy as before), and no change in the employment of workers throughout the economy.

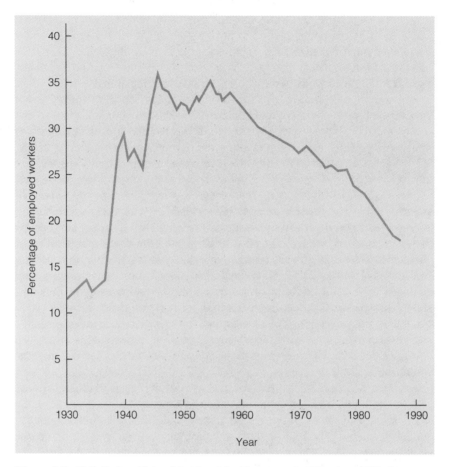

Figure 4-7 U.S. Labor Union Membership, Percentage of Employed Workers
U.S. union membership fell from over 35 percent of employed workers in the mid-1940s to around half that (18 percent) in the late 1980s.

This might seem like an argument against unions, since it would mean (1) that they had not achieved much for their pains but (2) that they had contributed to general price inflation. On the other hand, it can also be used to combat an argument frequently used in the past against labor unions: namely, that by demanding too high wages, they become responsible for large-scale unemployment in the economy.

What we have actually done in the last two paragraphs has been to move on from a particular part of the economy (washing machines, textile workers, and so on) to a consideration of the economy in the aggregate. Thus, we are foreshadowing matters that we shall be taking up in detail beginning with the next chapter.

SUMMARY

The characteristic form of the modern economy is the *mixed economy,* in which both government and the marketplace have important roles and in which various forms of imperfect competition coexist.

In the United States, the public sector has grown substantially in the past half-century; total expenditures of all levels of government having risen from about 20 percent of GNP in the 1930s to about a third of GNP in the 1980s.

The expansion of government has come about primarily through the increase of relatively newer, as opposed to traditional, functions of government. These include the role of the government in (1) stabilizing the economy, (2) correcting discrepancies between social and private costs and benefits, and (3) promoting income redistribution. A central source of government expansion has been the explosive growth of payments for individuals, most of which involve some element of income redistribution.

The Social Security system is an example of recent government growth, the retirement category accounting for around a quarter of a trillion dollars of federal outlays in 1990. The crisis of the early 1980s revealed that Social Security was basically an income transfer program (taxes on the working generation going to support retirees) and that there would be heavy future burdens on the system when the Baby Boomers reached retirement age beginning in 2010. Reforms in 1983 increased Social Security taxes but also reduced some future benefits. Indeed, in general, the 1980s saw a definite pause in the modern expansion of government in the U.S. economy.

The private sector of the American economy is also "mixed," involving a variety of firms, from the tiny sole proprietorship to the giant modern corporation with its billions of dollars of sales and assets. Where imperfect competition exists, it often takes a nonprice form, as when firms engage in advertising campaigns or in extensive product differentiation. Where price competition exists, it often involves complex patterns of price leadership or cost-plus pricing to provide orderly ways of responding to changing demand and supply conditions.

Although competition is more complicated where large firms are involved and although antitrust actions have been fairly minimal in recent years, there is no evidence that large firms are getting relatively larger over time, and, indeed, competition in many oligopolistic industries may have increased recently. Reasons would include increased foreign competition, deregulation, and innovations by relatively small, high tech firms.

American labor is also more complex than the perfectly competitive model, although the influence of union activity has clearly been on the decline in recent years. When we analyzed a particular union's attempt to raise wages, we found that the union might be able to raise the wage, but at the expense of higher unemployment for that type of worker. When one tries to generalize this result to explain overall inflation or unemployment, however, one runs into the limitations of this analysis and enters the world of aggregative economics, which we will turn to in parts 2, 3, and 4.

Key Concepts for Review

Mixed economy
Growth of government in the
    U.S. economy
Transfer payments
New functions of government
    Stabilizing the economy
    Social benefits and costs
    Income redistribution
Expenditures versus taxes
Social Security (OASDI)
Limits to growth of government
    in the 1980s
Forms of business enterprises
    Sole proprietorships
    Partnerships
    Corporations

Imperfect competition
Advertising
Product differentiation
Price leadership
Cost-plus pricing
Antitrust laws
Factors affecting competition
    in the 1980s
    Foreign competition
    Deregulation
    High tech innovation
Labor unions
    Early growth
    Recent decline in members
    Wage/employment effects
    (and limits thereof)

Questions for Discussion

1. Although government tax and expenditure figures give an important indication of the degree of government intervention in the economy, they are not the only measures of government activity. What are some other forms that public intervention might take? Give some examples from the experience of the United States or of other modern mixed economies.

2. Show how in the case of industrial air and water pollution there may be a significant divergence between private interest and social welfare. Does this have any relation to arguments for or against public intervention in these areas? What do you say to someone who argues that the *worst* polluters in recent decades have been governments (as in the case of the Eastern bloc centrally planned economies), not private industry?

3. Explain why Social Security has been described as an income-transfer program. Do you believe that the program will be "there for you" when you retire? Assuming that you had a choice between higher taxes now or lower benefits later, which would you choose?

4. Business firms under pure competition are said to take the price of their product as determined by the impersonal market. Show that this statement

is equivalent to saying that the firm in perfect competition faces a horizontal (perfectly elastic) demand curve for its product:

Quantity

Why is such a demand curve unlikely unless the firm is very small in relation to the industry as a whole?

5. Do you feel that advertising and product differentiation make, on the whole, a positive or negative contribution to the American economy? Explain your answer.

6. Why is it impossible to generalize from the effects of one union acting alone to the effects of all unions acting simultaneously on real wages and employment in the national economy?

7. "During the last decade, the American economy, public and private, has at last begun reversing direction and moving back toward a more competitive, market-oriented economy. Let's hope the new trend continues!"

   Write an essay presenting the pros and cons of the above declaration. Where do you yourself stand on this issue?

PART 2

THE ECONOMY IN THE AGGREGATE: REAL NATIONAL INCOME AND EMPLOYMENT

CHAPTER 5

MACROECONOMICS: AN OVERVIEW

In chapter 4, when discussing American labor, we ran into a difficulty. We found that even if we analyzed one union's actions in a particular market, our analysis would not allow us to draw general conclusions about the effect of unions on the economy as a whole. This is not a special difficulty; it is a general one. It is a very big step, surrounded by pitfalls, to move from the particular union, firm, or industry to the economy in the aggregate. Analyzing the economy in the aggregate, indeed, requires a different point of view.

THE FIELD OF MACROECONOMICS

Economists have recognized this problem by dividing their subject into the two areas we have mentioned earlier: *macroeconomics* and *microeconomics*. The definitions we gave in chapter 1 are repeated below:

Macroeconomics is the branch of economics that studies the behavior of broad aggregates such as national income, total employment and unemployment, or the overall price level.

Microeconomics is the branch of economics that studies the behavior of individual decision-making units, such as consumers, laborers, or business firms.

In parts 2, 3, and 4, we shall be concerned with macroeconomics, or the study of the economy "in the aggregate." The following chapters form a roughly logical progression as we move from a preliminary consideration of

89

national income and employment to the problems of money and prices and, finally, to the difficult theoretical and policy issues involved in an economy, such as our own, where unemployment and inflation often coexist in a tense balancing act that lurches first one way and then the other.

EXAMPLES OF MACROECONOMIC PROBLEMS

To understand this new field, we must first alter somewhat the point of view that we gain almost automatically from our daily participation in economic matters: a view of particular jobs, particular firms, particular industries. We know that it is sometimes hard to find a job, or that some particular business firm may be having troubles; but now we ask, Might the nation sometimes face conditions when businesses in general are failing, when people in general cannot locate work? Actually, the question need not be put pessimistically. We could also ask, Are there times when everyone has work, when labor is in great demand, when profits and wages are both high? The point, of course, is that these questions are about the performance of the economy as a whole.

Now, if we look at the past in our own country or in other industrial countries, we can find many instances to prove that national economies do, indeed, suffer ups and downs in their general economic well-being. All of us know from our reading of American history of the great number of "panics" that have seized our country at one point or another. There were panics in the United States in 1819, 1837, 1857, 1893, 1907, 1914, 1920–1921, and, of course, the "Great Crash" in 1929. Various statistical measures of these ups and downs are also common. In Figures 5-1 and 5-2, we present some diagrams of unemployment in the United States and the United Kingdom at various times in the past. These diagrams measure unemployment as a percentage of the labor force, and they indicate how variable this factor has been historically. The great leap in the unemployment percentage in the United States in the 1930s is a less picturesque, but still telling, way of describing the Great Depression, which we mentioned in our first chapter.

But economies can get out of gear in other ways besides unemployment. In the first chapter, we also talked of the German hyperinflation of the 1920s, when the price level soared to the trillions.[1] This was truly an exceptional incident, but no more exceptional than completely stable prices would be. Almost all industrial countries have had a hard experience with inflation in the twentieth century, and in many less developed countries, rapid inflation is a week-to-week phenomenon. Figure 5-3 shows the general course of consumer prices in the United States since the end of World War II.

---

[1] See Figure 1-1, p. 4.

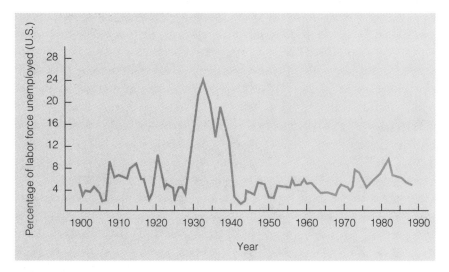

Figure 5-1   Unemployment in the United States   (Percentage of the Labor Force), 1900–1989

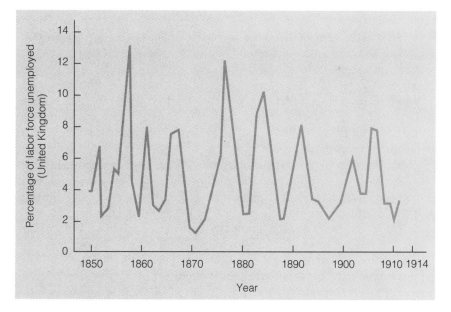

Figure 5-2   Unemployment in the United Kingdom   (Percentage of the Labor Force), 1850–1914

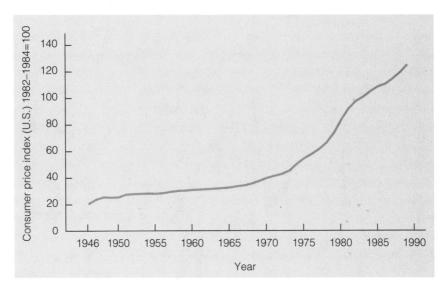

Figure 5-3   Inflation in the United States, 1946–1989   The United States has experienced nothing like the German hyperinflation in the 1920s; nevertheless, like most countries, we have had a general rise in prices during the twentieth century.

We must remember that when we talk about the price *level,* we are talking about something very different from the price of apples or the price of washing machines. When the price of apples alone goes up, our demand curve tells us that we will buy fewer apples because, among other reasons, it will be cheaper for us to satisfy our desire for fruit with, say, peaches and pears. When we talk about the price *level* rising, however, we are referring to a rise not only in apple prices, but in the prices of peaches and pears and washing machines as well.

Similarly, in the case of unemployment, if the wage of electricians goes down, people will turn toward other occupations, and fewer will offer their services as electricians. But suppose there is unemployment in all industries at once. What happens to the wage then? Where do people turn?

These are the heartland questions of macroeconomics. What determines the general level of unemployment? What determines the short-run level of national income?[2] What determines the overall level of prices? These are the problems of the economy in the aggregate.

---

[2] The adjective *short-run* has been inserted here purposefully. The analysis of national income (or total production) that we shall consider in parts 2 through 4 is largely concerned with the utilization of a *given* labor force and productive capacity. In the short run (two or three years), this is a permissible assumption. In the long run, the labor force, the productive capacity, and the economy in general *grow,* and the problem changes. This problem of long-run economic growth will be our principal focus in part 5. Needless to say, there is considerable overlap between these two areas of macroeconomics.

EARLY VIEWS

Our diagram of unemployment in the United Kingdom (Figure 5-2) indicates that macroeconomic problems were around long before the 1930s. What, then, did earlier economists have to say about them? What kind of analysis did they offer?

The truth is that until fairly modern times, the economics profession did not do very well in this particular department, especially when it came to the problem of unemployment. There are some exceptions, but for the most part, prevailing economic theory in the nineteenth century tended either to ignore the problem—that is, to proceed on the *assumption* of a full-employment economy and then to go on to analyze other problems—or to argue that, theoretically, there could not be a general unemployment problem except in a temporary or "frictional" sense. This argument was not simply a personal whim on the part of these early economists; rather, they had certain systematic reasons for believing that an unfettered market economy would automatically solve any short-run aggregative problems. Hence, they could direct their attention to other areas, either to microeconomics or, in the case of the early classical economists, to population growth and other long-run factors.

Say's Law

These systematic reasons are sometimes summarized in what is called Say's Law, after a French economist, Jean Baptiste Say (1767–1832). Say's writings were well known to the eminent British economists of the period such as David Ricardo and Thomas Robert Malthus, whom we mentioned earlier. Ricardo fully subscribed to Say's Law, though Malthus, as we shall see, had serious reservations about it.

Say's Law states that, in the economy as a whole, supply creates its own demand. When we produce goods, according to this law, we create a demand for other goods; consequently, there can be no overproduction of goods in general. Because there can be no overproduction of goods in general, there can be no unemployment problem in general. To put it in different words: Because there is always a market for the goods we produce, there is no overall limit on the number of jobs the society can sustain. If people are unemployed, then it can be only because they make unreasonable wage demands or prefer leisure or are simply in transit between one job and another, searching for the best opportunities available.

The Role of Money

This is simply a statement of the law, not a defense. But Say and Ricardo, and in fact most nineteenth-century economists, also felt that they had a good defense for the law. The defense had two parts.

The first part consisted in relegating "money" to a minor role in the economy:

> They said in effect: Money is just a veil that covers the realities of economic life. Money is simply a medium of exchange. In order to understand what really goes on, let us look at potatoes, steel, wheat, shoes, and so on. Then we will not be deceived by mere monetary changes, and we will reach the fundamental phenomena involved.

They did not say that money had *no* effect on economic life—the money supply, in their view, largely determined the general price-level[3]—but that it had little effect on production or employment. Having put money to one side in this fashion, they went on to their second step:

> They argued: Now look at this real, nonmoney economy. In this economy, when I put a laborer to work producing, say, more potatoes, I am increasing the supply of potatoes, but I am *also* increasing the demand for other goods. What will I use the potatoes for? Either I will consume them myself (my demand is increased), or I will offer them in exchange for some other commodity, say, clothing, and this will mean that the demand for clothing is increased. Either way, the added supply has created an added demand; thus, in general, supply creates its own demand. Hence, there can be no such thing as *general* overproduction or *general* unemployment. Q.E.D.

These arguments are not nonsense. In fact, they can be quite persuasive, and for most of a century, they did persuade most economists that aggregative economic problems could be set to one side.

Early Heretics

Not all economists were persuaded, however. Malthus worried about the problem and remained unconvinced. He saw the possibility that there might be a "universal glut" of commodities in the economy as a whole and that this might lead to widespread unemployment. He tried to argue the point with his friend, Ricardo; but Malthus's own arguments were far from airtight, and Ricardo won out on debating points fairly easily. Marx was another economist who remained unconvinced. As we have already seen, Marx made increasing unemployment an intrinsic part of his analysis of capitalism. This unemployment arose from the technological displacement of labor by machines, but Marx also spoke generally about an overall inadequacy of markets. The capitalistic system, he thought, might produce more goods than it was constituted to absorb. This could also contribute to crises and depressions.

Neither Malthus nor Marx, however, made much of a dent on this part

---

[3] This view is sometimes referred to as the "quantity theory of money." As we shall see in chapter 11, the quantity theory has inspired renewed interest and controversy during more recent times.

of the main body of economic analysis, and it wasn't until the very end of the nineteenth century that really serious thought was given to these problems. Here, special credit should be given to the Swedish economist Knut Wicksell (1851–1926), who anticipated many of the elements in the "revolution" in economic analysis that was soon to take place. The economists of Sweden were, indeed, generally in the vanguard of this particular development, although the major challenge to the then-traditional theory must be attributed to the man we shall turn to now. That man was John Maynard Keynes.

KEYNESIAN ANALYSIS

Keynes (1883–1946), the man, was a most remarkable and versatile figure. He was at one time or another a businessman, teacher, college administrator, high government official, patron of the arts, and, of course, the most famous economist of his age. His wife was Lydia Lopokova, a prima ballerina, and she and Keynes were members of the well-known Bloomsbury group, which included renowned artists such as E. M. Forster and Virginia Woolf. Even in his academic work he was versatile. His first book was on the theory of probability. His economic writings included controversial comment on current issues—like his *Economic Consequences of the Peace,* which made such a stir after World War I—and also highly abstract, theoretical works that are quite incomprehensible to the general public. His great classic, *The General Theory of Employment, Interest and Money* (1936) is in the latter group. It has to be studied hard, and a background in technical economics is required if the reader is to make much headway with it.

Unlike many of his predecessors, Keynes put his emphasis very clearly on the kind of problems we have just been discussing, problems dealing with the *economy as a whole*. His work was fundamentally macroeconomic in approach, meaning that his key variables were total national output, the general level of employment, the price level, and the like. Furthermore, his approach to these macroeconomic problems had five rather significant characteristics:

1. Keynes placed his emphasis on *short-run,* rather than long-run, problems. Writing his *General Theory* in the midst of the Great Depression, he was less interested in the growth of an economy over time than with the full utilization of its labor force and productive capacity at a given time. When asked about this particular emphasis, Keynes made a very simple response: "In the long run, we are all dead."

2. Keynes emphasized the key role of *aggregate demand* in determining the level of national income and employment in the economy as a whole. In part 1, we spoke of supply and demand in particular industries. Keynes spoke of supply and demand in the aggregate. He felt that aggregate demand in a given economy might be high or low in relation

to aggregate supply. In other words, he rejected the theory behind Say's Law that suggested that supply invariably created its own demand in the economy as a whole.

3. He believed that the economy might come to rest at a position of *unemployment equilibrium;* that is, a position where there would be no natural forces operating to restore full employment to the economy. Suppose, he said, that aggregate demand fell short of aggregate supply at the full-employment level. What would happen? According to Keynes, the shortage of demand would mean that businesses in general would cut back on production and jobs. He believed this cutting-back process would go on until an equilibrium of supply and demand had been achieved. But this equilibrium might involve a great deal of unemployment in the economy as a whole. Indeed, Keynes felt that this analysis helped explain why such a phenomenon as the Great Depression could occur in a modern industrial economy.

Points 2 and 3 indicate that Keynes rejected not only the conclusions of Say's Law but, necessarily, the argument that lay behind it. One part of this argument, as we know, was that it was permissible to separate money and prices from the world of goods and services, or, as economists might put it, to divorce *monetary* (having to do with money values) analysis from *real* (potatoes, automobiles, and so on) analysis.[4] This brings us to a fourth characteristic of Keynesian analysis:

4. Keynes attempted to perform what might be called a *synthesis of real and monetary analysis.* More particularly, he argued that "money" was not simply a convenient medium of exchange. He called particular attention to a characteristic of money named "liquidity." By *liquidity,* he meant "command over goods in general." If I have money, I can exchange it for goods or services or bonds or securities in any direction I choose. It is a perfectly generalized way of holding purchasing power. Now, all commodities have some elements of liquidity. When I own a house, I can exchange it for some other goods if I so desire; however, I can never be quite sure what the house will sell for. Similarly, with securities (stocks and bonds), I can quickly turn them into money with which to buy other goods and services; still, it is never quite certain at what price I shall be able to sell them. They are nearly perfectly liquid, but not quite. In short, Keynes said that its perfect liquidity gave money

---

[4] Another term economists sometimes use in this connection is "nominal," meaning "as measured in the marketplace without any correction for prices or inflation." Thus, *nominal wages* would be money wages as they appear on our paychecks, while *real wages* would be those same wages corrected for price changes, say, by the consumer price index. Banks may charge a *nominal interest rate* of 16 percent, but if inflation is 12 percent a year, then the *real interest rate* will be only 4 percent.

an important role in the functioning of the economy. By recognizing this role, he argued, one could explain the possibility of a discrepancy between aggregate demand and aggregate supply in the economy and, hence, the possibility of general unemployment.

5. Finally, Keynes argued that since a market economy could not guarantee full employment by its own devices, it might be necessary to have a greater degree of *government intervention* than had been thought desirable in the past. The government could remedy the problem directly, in the Keynesian view, by affecting aggregate demand by its own purchases of goods and services. On the other hand, it could also influence aggregate demand indirectly by lowering taxes (or raising them if the problem were too much demand) and, thus, stimulating private consumer and business demand. Still more indirectly, the government could affect the level of aggregate demand by altering the supply of money available to the economy. In general, however, the point was that because the market alone could not be counted on to do the job, the government might have to take a more active participating role.

Taken together, these five propositions constituted a major assault on the economic theories prevailing in the 1930s and justified the term Keynesian revolution. This revolution, moreover, was to dominate mainstream economic policies, theories, and even college textbooks for the next four decades. With the possible exceptions of Adam Smith and Karl Marx, no economist in history had quite the impact on his subject that Keynes had.

THE MODERN ASSAULT ON KEYNESIAN THEORY

Not that Keynesian theory was ever free from controversy. In the early years, in fact, Keynes was often (improperly) charged with attacking the capitalistic system in more or less the same manner as Karl Marx had attacked it 75 years earlier. It is closer to the truth to say that Keynes provided a main alternative *to* Marxism. For the approaches of these two economists to the capitalistic system were radically different.

Marx argued that the diseases of capitalism were intrinsic, inevitable, and fatal; they could be removed only by the overthrow of the entire system. By contrast, Keynes argued that the basic features of the capitalistic system could be preserved and its problems eliminated by modifications of that system. The mixed economy—which we actually have in the United States and Western Europe—is the natural heir to Keynesian analysis; but it is anathema to the good Marxist. For if, through modification of the system, one can forestall serious problems from arising and can make the economy "work," then one has completely undercut the ground from the Marxist who believes that things *must* get worse and that "revolution" is the *only* cure.

A much more serious assault on Keynesian theory, however, has been mounted in the sober, often highly mathematical, articles that appear in our scholarly economic journals. Within the past two decades, it has become possible to find economists who, while operating within the *mainstream tradition* of the field, would, nevertheless, deny or seriously qualify each of the five Keynesian propositions we have just listed. To be specific, there are now large numbers and, indeed, whole schools of economists who would argue the following:

1. *The exclusive Keynesian focus on the short run is misleading and often harmful.* Looking at problems and policies only from the point of view of immediate effects can get you into serious trouble, many modern analysts would claim. It may not solve your short-run problems, and, in the long run, those who are not "dead" (for example, our children and grandchildren) may suffer from such a limited focus.

2. *Keynes put far too much emphasis on aggregate demand.* Many would deny that changes in aggregate demand have substantial effects on employment and output over time; some would deny that such changes even have much of a temporary effect. Still others, including the *supply-siders* who came to prominence in the 1980s, argue that attention should be shifted from demand to the factors influencing the supply of output, incentives to work, to invest, and the like.

3. *There is no such thing as unemployment equilibrium.* A few economists appear to go back virtually to the pre-Keynesian, "classical" position that there can be nothing but frictional unemployment even in the short run; a number of others speak of a reasonably low, *natural rate of unemployment* to which the economy will tend to gravitate over time. Perhaps a majority of economists now agree that large-scale unemployment cannot represent an *equilibrium* position, at least unless a number of rather restrictive assumptions are made.

4. *Keynes both underestimated and overestimated the role of money in the economy.* This criticism is particularly associated with Professor Milton Friedman and the so-called *monetarist* school. For the monetarist, it is the stock of money that determines what a country's money national income will be. This gives money a greater role than Keynes allowed, since there are many factors in the Keynesian system that can alter money national income with a given stock of money. On the other hand, the monetarists deny that money has any permanent effects on real income. Thus, in this respect, they claim that the Keynesian synthesis of real and monetary analysis actually overplays the role of money in economic life.

5. *Keynes's analysis of the effects of government intervention was overoptimistic and possibly harmful.* There are many different strands in

this general criticism, but a quite common statement today is that Keynesian-oriented public expenditure and tax policies have tended to lead to a gradual expansion of government intervention over time, with unfortunate consequences for entrepreneurship and creative effort in the private economy. Also, it is said that these policies can lead to an inflationary bias in the economy without, some claim, really solving the unemployment problem.

In short, in the 1980s, Keynesian theory was subjected to an assault the magnitude of which recalls Keynes's own attack on the traditional economics of the 1930s.

THE PROCEDURE WE SHALL FOLLOW

To some degree, the issues between Keynesians and other schools of economic thought reflect changed economic conditions. Keynes wrote during the 1930s in a period of stable or falling prices and massive unemployment. By contrast, post–World War II America has avoided any Great Depression but has seen fairly persistent inflationary pressures. It can be argued that it is a tribute to Keynesian-style policies that the problems of mass unemployment seem to be behind us. On the other hand, it can also be argued that we had to purchase this achievement at an unacceptable price in terms of continuing inflation.

In either event, many things have happened in recent decades that simply do not fit either the Keynesian analysis or his general policy prescriptions. Probably the most striking development was the *simultaneous increase* in both our rate of inflation and our unemployment percentage between the late 1960s and the early 1980s. Keynesian economics, with its emphasis on the manipulation of aggregate demand, faces a very difficult quandary in such a world. In his theory, unemployment is the result of too little demand; inflation, of too much demand. When you have both heavy unemployment and high inflation, Keynesian analysis would suggest that we should both increase and decrease aggregate demand at the same time. Obviously, an impossible situation.

But to say that Keynes did not get everything exactly right is not to say that there is perfect agreement on the correct alternative analysis. Some economists (the "neo-Keynesians") still take Keynes as their point of departure; but others—the monetarists, the supply-siders, or the "new classical economists"—proceed in quite a different way. Moreover, there are considerable differences of opinion on important matters among the members of each group.

What this means is that we cannot avoid controversy in studying today's macroeconomics. It also means that we should be careful to make our own assumptions as explicit as possible. Our procedure will be as follows:

Part 2   The Economy in the Aggregate: Real National Income and Employment. We shall begin our analysis by assuming that prices are constant throughout the period under discussion. We shall show, in a preliminary way, how *real* national income and employment can be determined in such a world. We shall find in the course of this discussion that our analysis is incomplete because it does not deal with changes in the price level or with the role of money in the economy.

Part 3   The Economy in the Aggregate: Money, Prices, and Inflation. We shall now introduce price changes and the money supply into our analysis. This will require us to develop new tools—aggregate supply and demand curves—that determine equilibrium levels for real national income *and* the price level. We shall present at this time two different theories about the way in which the money supply affects the workings of the economic system.

Part 4   The Economy in the Aggregate: Inflation and Unemployment, Problems and Policies. Here, we shall bring our analysis closer to the actual record of economic events in the United States in the past few years[5] and, at the same time, suggest the strengths and limitations of various macroeconomic policy tools. From what we have already said, the reader will understand that we shall not recommend any one particular set of policies but shall try to bring out, as sharply as possible, the assumptions on which different recommendations are based.

S U M M A R Y

We shall be concerned in parts 2, 3, and 4 with macroeconomics, or the economy in the aggregate. Our interest now shifts from the area of individual consumers, firms, and industries to broad questions concerning the level of national income, the general level of employment and unemployment, and the overall level of prices.

The history of modern industrial economies makes it quite clear that there have been fluctuations in the levels of employment and prices in various countries over the past century or two. Early economists (with some exceptions such as Malthus and Marx) tended on the whole to set aggregative problems, and especially the unemployment problem, to one side. They were confident that they could rely on Say's Law to guarantee no major problems.

---

[5] Even here, our analysis will not be completely realistic since we will not yet have taken up (1) the international aspects of macroeconomics and (2) the interaction of our inflation and unemployment policies with the goal of long-run economic growth. We will deal with both these subjects briefly in part 5.

Say's Law depicted a "moneyless" economy in which supply always created its own demand, thus preventing any problems of general overproduction or general unemployment.

In the twentieth century, many economists began to criticize this point of view, and a great theoretical breakthrough was made by John Maynard Keynes. Keynesian theory, heavily macroeconomic in orientation, departed from its predecessors by (1) its emphasis on the short run, (2) its stress on the role of aggregate demand, (3) its acknowledgment of the possibility of under-employment equilibrium, (4) its synthesis of real and monetary analysis, and (5) its emphasis on the role of government in curing unemployment and other aggregative problems.

Early on, Keynesian theory was subject to some doubtful criticisms (for example, the false identification of Keynes and Marx), but in recent years, responsible analysts have questioned much of the basis of that theory. Indeed, between the "monetarists," the "new classical economists," and the "supply-siders," virtually every main point of Keynesian thought has come under assault.

Since there is no general agreement on the correct alternative to Keynesian analysis, the study of macroeconomics today must focus on the acquisition of tools and not on the perpetuation of received doctrines.

Key Concepts for Review

Microeconomics	Aggregate demand
Macroeconomics	Aggregate supply
General unemployment	Unemployment equilibrium
Price level	Real versus monetary
National income	Liquidity
Say's Law	Role of government
Keynesian "revolution"	Critics of Keynesian analysis

Questions for Discussion

1. What is meant by macroeconomics? microeconomics?

2. What are the assumptions behind Say's Law? Show how, given these assumptions, an economy would be able to find markets for an expansion of its total output caused, say, by a sudden immigration of labor from abroad.

3. "The lasting impact of the Great Depression was that it permanently altered the way economists look at their basic subject matter." Discuss.

4. Compare the views of John Maynard Keynes and Karl Marx on the problems facing capitalism and their prospective cures.

5. List the main characteristics of Keynesian thought, and indicate some of the criticisms of his positions a number of modern economists have made.

6. From your reading of newspapers or watching or listening to the news, what do you consider to be three major macroeconomic problems facing the United States today? Do you find that public officials and others generally agree or disagree about the basic way to solve these problems?

CHAPTER 6

THE CONCEPT OF GNP

Having introduced the reader to the general area of macroeconomics, we shall now turn to a concept that is central to this field: the concept of *gross national product,* or GNP. The term GNP is widely used in our daily press, but the concept is somewhat complicated, and it is worth spending some time with it.

TOTAL OUTPUT AND ITS FLUCTUATIONS

The basic idea behind GNP is simple enough. This is one of the important measures economists use when they try to estimate the total output of goods and services produced in the nation over a given period, say a year.

Furthermore, it is apparent that some such concept of total output is indispensable to the field of macroeconomics. For example, we have talked about the Great Depression of the 1930s, but wholly in terms of unemployment. We could just as readily have spoken about a fall in the nation's total output—its GNP—during that period. It is estimated that between 1929 and 1933, the real GNP of the United States fell by nearly 30 percent. Indeed, we should generally expect that when there is heavy unemployment in an economy, its total output of goods and services will fall, or at least will not rise as rapidly as might otherwise be the case.

In Figures 6-1 and 6-2, we have charted changes in the U.S. GNP in two different ways, each diagram bringing out a particular point. The main thing we should note in Figure 6-1 is the pronounced upward trend of our

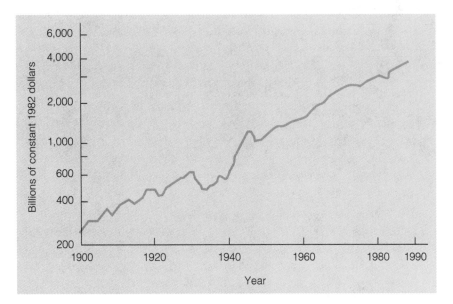

Figure 6-1 U.S. GNP in Constant 1982 Dollars, 1900–1989
SOURCE: *1989 Historical Chart Book*, Federal Reserve Board.

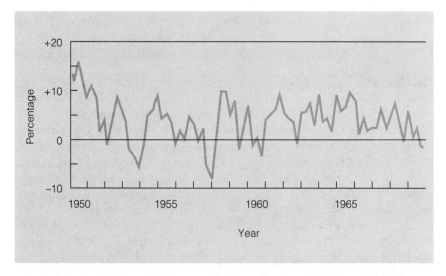

Figure 6-2 U.S. GNP in Constant 1982 Dollars, Annual Growth Rate, 1950–1989 Positive percents mean that real GNP was increasing in those years; negative percents mean that it was declining.
SOURCE: *1989 Historical Chart Book*, Federal Reserve Board.

GNP over the course of the twentieth century: our annual total output of goods and services has increased nearly 16-fold over these 90 years. This long-run growth of total output will be of primary interest in part 5, where we will take up various factors—such as population growth, capital accumulation, and technological change—that bring about long-run gains in a country's productive capacity.

Figure 6-2 brings out a rather different point. It suggests that while this long-run growth has been occurring, there has been also a considerable *short-run fluctuation* in the rate at which that growth has occurred. In some years, GNP growth has been rapid, in others very slow; in some years it has been negative. These negative years correspond with what we call *recessions*. We can see that such recessions occurred a number of times in postwar America—for example, 1957–1958, 1974–1975, the early 1980s, and so on. During these periods, our *actual* GNP was well below our *potential* GNP, the latter being the total output that our economy is capable of producing when our labor force and other resources are fully employed.[1] In 1982, for ex-

---

[1] In terms of our production-possibility curve of chapter 1, "potential" GNP would be at some point like *FE* in Figure 1-6, p. 15.

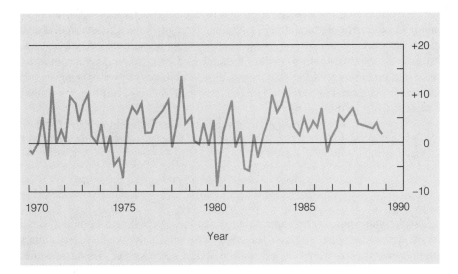

Figure 6-2   (*continued*)

ample, it was estimated that our potential GNP was some $290 billion, or around 9 percent, higher than our actual GNP.

It is these fluctuations of GNP and the gaps between actual and potential GNP that concern us now. Parts 2, 3, and 4 are focused precisely on such questions: What determines our level of GNP in the short run? What determines our level of employment or unemployment in the short run? And what about the price level in the short run? For the most part (though not completely), we shall defer the issue of long-run growth to the last chapters of the book.

MEASURING THE MONEY VALUE OF GNP

Having observed that GNP is an important concept, we now have to ask the more difficult question: Is it a meaningful concept? What is this thing, "total output," and how would we go about measuring it?

The difficulty is an obvious one; in fact, it takes us back to elementary school days. We were told then that we cannot add oranges and apples and pears. But the total output of our economy includes oranges, apples, and pears, *plus* computers, tractors, toy balloons, soft drinks, and several thousand other commodities. How can these different commodities be added together to form a single numerical total?

What is needed is a common denominator, and the common denominator in our particular economy is dollars. Oranges have a price; apples and pears have prices; so do computers, tractors, and toy balloons. What we do is to give a money valuation to the production of each particular commodity, then add up the total of these money values, and this will give us a number in dollars for our total output during the given year. We can call this the *money value of GNP* in that year.[2]

Say that 600 million oranges are produced in the country in a certain year and that the price of oranges is 25 cents each. Then the value of orange output will be determined:

$$25¢ \times 600 \text{ million} = \$150 \text{ million}$$

We can then do the same thing for apples, pears, and computers and come up with money figures for each. We would then add these money figures together to form an estimate of aggregate output. To be specific, suppose there is, in addition to oranges, only one other commodity in our

---

[2] Other names that are given this total are "GNP in current dollars" or "nominal GNP." We shall see in a moment (pp. 109–110) why this total in itself could not give us a good measure of the *real* output of goods and services in the economy.

economy: toy balloons. Toy balloon production is 200 million units a year at a price of 10 cents apiece.

Total output in this fictitious economy might then be defined as equal to

$$P_o \times Q_o + P_b \times Q_b$$

where P_o and P_b are the prices and Q_o and Q_b the quantities produced of oranges and balloons, respectively. In numerical terms, we should have:

Total output $= 25¢ \times 600$ million $+ 10¢ \times 200$ million
$= \$150$ million $+ \$20$ million
$= \$170$ million

It is fairly obvious that what we have done for these two commodities, we could do for the remainder of the commodities in a real-life economy: shirts, missiles, secretarial services. They all have prices and can all be added together in this fashion.

COMPONENTS OF GNP

Having calculated the money value of GNP in this fashion, we can then divide it up into its basic component parts. A common breakdown, and the one we shall be referring to often in the future, is in terms of three main categories of goods and services (see Figure 6-3):

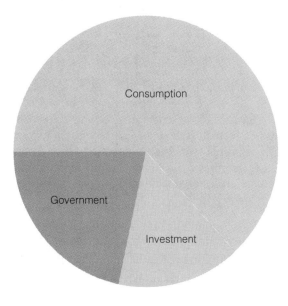

Figure 6-3 Major Components of U.S. GNP These are average proportions of GNP. Remember that they change from year to year, investment being a particularly variable item.

Consumption

There are, first of all, the goods bought by ordinary consumers like ourselves: clothing, food, automobiles, tennis racquets. These include consumer expenditures on services as well as commodities and on durable as well as nondurable consumers' goods. The category of durable consumers' goods has grown very rapidly in recent decades as we have expanded our purchases of automobiles, television sets, stereos, washing machines, and the like. In total, consumption expenditures in the United States currently average between 60 to 65 percent of our GNP.

Investment

Part of the goods produced in the economy each year are funneled back into the productive process either to replace worn-out buildings, machines, and so on or to add to our general stock of capital goods. Gross investment in our economy includes these replacement items and the net additions to our capital stocks.[3] Investment expenditures in the United States may run in the neighborhood of 15 or 16 percent of GNP, though this percentage is subject to a fairly high degree of variability. The term *investment* in the sense we are now using it is different from the kind of investing we do when we buy a stock or a bond. It is better to regard the latter as *financial investment* and to think of *investment* (unmodified) as indicating those goods devoted to building up the real productive capacity of the economy. The main categories of investment expenditure are fixed business investment (machinery, factories, and so on), residential construction (apartments and private homes), and additions to inventories (stocks of products kept on hand to meet orders from other producers or consumers).

Government

The third main category is government expenditures. If we exclude transfer payments—which, as we recall, do not represent government purchases of goods and services—then government expenditures run at around 20 percent of U.S. GNP. These expenditures include state and local as well as federal expenditures. Without transfer payments (which are particularly high at the federal level), state and local expenditures are substantially higher than federal expenditures. The matter is somewhat complicated, however, since there are many large federal grants-in-aid to state and local governments ($116 bil-

---

[3] We shall come to the distinction between "gross investment" and "net investment" shortly (pp. 112–113).

lion in 1989). For our present purposes, the important point to note is that when the government buys goods and services, the demand it provides for total output is exactly analogous to that provided by private investment or consumption purchases.

These, then, are the three main categories by which the total output of the society can be classified: consumption, private investment, and government expenditures.[4] We shall be mentioning each of these categories often in the pages that follow.

COMPARING GNP IN DIFFERENT YEARS

But now it is time to return once again to the basic concept of total output. So far we have shown how economists measure the money value of GNP in a given year using the prices and quantities of the goods produced in that year. But we also want to compare GNP in different years. More than that, we want to show what is actually happening to total output between these years. In this section of our analysis, we are specifically interested in *real GNP*— tons of steel, bushels of wheat—not simply money values. And this poses a problem.

To return to our simplified world of oranges and toy balloons:

In our earlier example (p. 107), we determined that the total output of oranges and toy balloons in our economy was worth $170 million. Let us suppose this was for the year 1980. Suppose someone now comes along and tells us that the combined money value of orange and toy balloon production in 1990 had risen to $340 million. The question is, What can we conclude from this fact? Can we conclude that both orange production and toy balloon production had doubled from 1980 to 1990? Or that if one product less than doubled in quantity, the other more than doubled? Or does the given information actually enable us to conclude nothing at all about the production of oranges and toy balloons in this period?

The correct answer, unfortunately, is the last. We can conclude nothing whatever about orange and toy balloon production in 1990 as compared to 1980 unless and until we know what happened to the prices of these goods during that period. To take an obvious case, suppose the prices of both goods had *quadrupled* in this 10-year period. A rise in total output from $170 million to $340 million would, in this case, represent not an increase in real GNP, but a *halving* of GNP from 1980 to 1990. If, on the other hand, prices had remained absolutely constant, then it would be clear that real GNP was

---

[4] A further important category is *net* exports of American goods abroad. We will mention this category again later on in chapter 16. In the 1980s, we were net *importers,* meaning that this category was negative.

expanding; indeed, if prices are constant, then the changes in the money value of GNP will reflect changes in the real output value of GNP.

MEASURING GNP IN CONSTANT PRICES

The problem thus becomes one of finding some rough equivalent to constant prices when prices are, in fact, changing all the time. The way economists do this is by taking prices for some given year and using these prices throughout the series of measurements of GNP in different years. Thus, you will notice that in the charts of U.S. GNP (Figures 6-1 and 6-2), prices are described as "1982 prices." More generally, we should have to amend our formula for calculating total output to indicate a specific date for the prices involved. Using 1980 prices throughout, our comparison of the total output of oranges and toy balloons in 1980 and 1990 would look as follows:

$$\text{Total Output (GNP)}_{(1980)} = P_{o(1980)} \times Q_{o(1980)} + P_{b(1980)} \times Q_{b(1980)} \quad (1)$$
$$\text{Total Output (GNP)}_{(1990)} = P_{o(1980)} \times Q_{o(1990)} + P_{b(1980)} \times Q_{b(1990)} \quad (2)$$

In this way, by using 1980 prices throughout, the problem of fictitious changes in total output due to mere changes in the price level is removed, and the focus is put on changes in the actual outputs of the goods involved. You should note that the prices and quantities in equation (2) are differently dated; from what we have said, you should be able to explain this fact fully.[5]

Figure 6-4 shows how money GNP and real GNP in the U.S. have behaved in recent years. The much steeper slope of money GNP indicates the inflationary pressures to which our economy has been subject. The two curves cross in 1982 because that is the base year chosen for our "constant prices."

PROBLEM OF DOUBLE COUNTING

Another major problem arises in measuring GNP because many of the goods we produce in a given year are actually already included in the value of other goods being produced.

---

[5] Before leaving the "constant prices" problem, it should at least be noted that when we are making comparisons of GNP over long periods of time, it is by no means easy to handle this problem. Prices are changing not only absolutely, but *relatively* (that is, the price of oranges relative to the price of toy balloons), and when this happens, changes in "total output" do not have an unambiguous meaning. This is one of the reasons that it is so difficult to specify the "welfare" implications of a rise in GNP. Readers who wish to see this point demonstrated numerically can do so by working out question 5 at the end of this chapter.

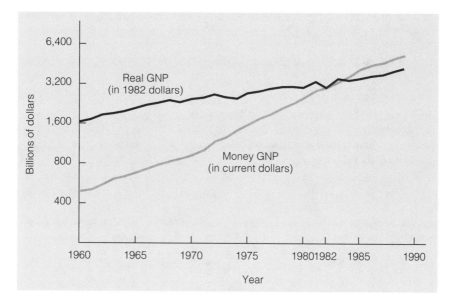

Figure 6-4   Relationship of U.S. Money GNP and Real GNP, 1960–1989   U.S. money GNP rose much more rapidly than real GNP during 1960–1989 because of price inflation.

Suppose we are using all the oranges to produce frozen orange juice. Then we have:

Stage 1	Value of oranges produced (as sold by the grower)	$150 million
Stage 2	Value of canned orange juice (as sold by the canner)	$200 million
Stage 3	Value of canned orange juice (as bought by the consumer from the retailer)	$240 million

The double-counting problem arises here because the $240 million of final output produced includes the value of the oranges and canned orange juice at the earlier stages of production. If we were to add the stages all together, we would get $150 million + $200 million + $240 million, or $590 million. This would be a fictitiously large total because of "double counting."

How does one avoid this problem, given the great number of different industries and different uses for their products in an economy like ours? One way (and the simplest conceptually) is to be careful to avoid all kinds of "intermediate" products when adding up GNP and to concentrate wholly on "final" products in the various lines of production (that is, to count only Stage 3 orange juice at $240 million and to exclude Stage 1 and Stage 2 orange products).

An equivalent, though more roundabout, way of achieving the same result is through what is known as the *value-added* method of calculating GNP. A firm's or an industry's value added to total output is the value of its sales minus its purchases of products from other firms or industries. If we assume for simplicity that the orange growers in our example purchased no inputs from other firms, then we could represent value added at each stage of orange production as follows:

Stage	Value of Sales	Minus	Purchases from Other Firms	Equals	Value Added
1	$150 million		$0		+ $150 million
2	$200 million		$150 million		+ $ 50 million
3	$240 million		$200 million		+ $ 40 million
			Sum of values added	=	$240 million

Note that the sum of the values added equals the value of the final products ($240 million). Prove to yourself that this is not an accident but will necessarily be the case. The ultimate reason, of course, is that in both methods we have scrupulously avoided counting intermediate products.

Before we leave the double-counting problem, however, we should remark on one aspect of measuring GNP where double counting is in fact countenanced. By now, you must have wondered why the *G* (Gross) is always prefixed to this measure of national production. The answer has to do with the way we evaluate the *investment* category mentioned earlier.

> It should be clear that the proper way to evaluate the total output of machines, say, in a given year, would be to take the number of machines produced in that year and to subtract from it the number of machines that have become worn out, obsolete, and have been discarded during the year. Put it this way. We have been using machines throughout the year; when we produce a quantity of new machines, at least some of those machines are necessary to replace those that have become worn out through use; they do not all constitute a net *addition* to our stock of machines.

This is a problem that all businessmen are familiar with: the problem of depreciation and replacement. The difficulty, however, is that really accurate and meaningful depreciation figures in the aggregate are hard to come by, and even hard to define. Hence, economists and government statisticians often include *all* the machines produced in a given year without making the depreciation adjustment. This figure is called *gross investment*. When gross investment is added to consumption and government expenditures, we call the total *gross* national product. If the depreciation of the country's capital stock were estimated and deducted, we would get *net* investment and, correspondingly, *net* national product (NNP).

PRODUCT, INCOME, AND THE "CIRCULAR FLOW"

In a sense, everything we have done so far in this chapter has been a matter of defining terms. Definitions are important in any subject, but now let us try to use our new definitions to gain some important insights into macroeconomic problems. Indeed, with the tools now at our disposal, we can move fairly quickly into actual macroeconomic analysis.

The Basic Equivalence of Output and Income

A useful place to begin this analysis is with the recognition of a fact that we should be able to understand easily now, though it might have been obscure before. This fact is that there is a *basic equivalence between the national product or output of a society and the real national income of that society.* "Annual total output" is really another name for "annual total income," which, in turn, is the sum of all incomes earned in the production of this "total output"; that is, wages, profits, interest, and rents. These are basically two different ways of looking at the same thing.

The simplest way to convince ourselves on this point is to recall our *value-added* method of measuring GNP. At each stage of production, we subtracted from the value of the products a firm sells, the value that it has paid out to other firms for their products. Now the sum of these *values added* is our total "product," but it is also clearly our total "income." For to what uses are these values added put? Because by definition they do not represent sales to other firms, they must represent either payments to the factors of production—wages to labor, rent on property, interest on borrowed funds— or profits to the firm. Indeed, profits can be thought of as being precisely the surplus of value added after payments are made to other factors of production. If we subtract all other incomes from our national product, we get profits as the residual, and profits, of course, are income to someone. Hence, the point is established: national product and national income are equivalent concepts.

Product and Income Concepts

In present-day practice in the United States, we actually have a great number of related, but still distinct, "product" and "income" concepts for use in different connections. If we start with GNP and work downward, we get the following definitions:

$$\text{Gross national product} - \text{Depreciation} = \text{Net national product}$$

$$\text{Net national product} - \text{Indirect business taxes} = \text{National income}$$

$$\text{National income} - \left\{ \begin{array}{l} \text{Retained profits} \\ \text{Corporate profit taxes} \\ \text{Contribution for} \\ \quad \text{social insurance} \end{array} \right\} + \begin{array}{l} \text{Transfer} \\ \text{payments} \end{array} = \text{Personal income}$$

$$\text{Personal income} - \text{Personal taxes} = \text{Disposable personal income}$$

Incidentally, it is only when we come to this last category (disposable personal income) that most consumers actually begin to see the income they have produced.

In the pages to come, we shall use the term *national income* in a less technical sense than in the above definition, as a symbol of the whole family of *total output* concepts. Where a more specific definition is called for, we shall note it explicitly in the course of the analysis.

The Circular Flow

As we think about it, the basic equivalence of income and output in the aggregate is not too difficult to understand. For what determines how much income you and I and our neighbors will have to share amongst ourselves? Ultimately, it has to be what all of us together have produced. Barring special cases where there is aid or personal remittances from abroad, there is simply no other source from which our incomes in the aggregate can emanate.

With this fact clearly in mind, we can illustrate the general workings of a modern economy in a fairly dramatic, pictorial way. Figure 6-5 presents what is sometimes called a *circular flow* diagram. What this diagram does is to picture the macroeconomic process as consisting of two opposite flows: (1) a money-income-and-spending flow and (2) a national-product-and-factor-services flow.

The money-income-and-spending flow is in the inner circle. It shows business firms paying dollars to households for the use of their labor, their land, their machinery. This is the flow of wages, rents, interest, and other incomes. As we follow this flow around the circle, we see that the households pay this money back to the businesses in return for the products they buy from these businesses—oranges and toy balloons, if you will. So the money income flow circulates around as incomes to the public in general, who then spend this income buying the goods that businesses have produced.

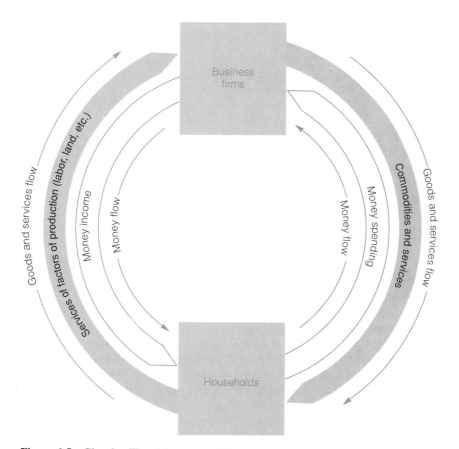

Figure 6-5   Circular Flow Diagram   This is a highly simplified description of an economy in the aggregate. It can serve, however, as a useful point of departure for understanding certain macroeconomic principles.

The national-product-and-factor-services flow goes in the opposite direction (it is made to go clockwise in Figure 6-5, which, of course, is perfectly arbitrary; it is not arbitrary, however, that it goes in the opposite direction from the money-income-and-spending flow). In this circle, we show business firms taking the services of the factors of production—labor, land, and capital—and transforming these into commercially saleable goods, which they then sell to the general public.

HOW MACROECONOMIC PROBLEMS MIGHT ARISE

The circular flow diagram, of course, is a very simplified way of looking at a complex modern economy; yet, even at this stage, we can see intuitively how macroeconomic problems might arise.

Let us try to imagine a case in which these nice smooth flows may not be so smooth after all. For example, let us suppose that consumers in general decide that they wish to *save* (that is, not spend on consumption) a healthy percentage of their money incomes. Businesses, let us say, have paid out $100 million in incomes to households. But the households now decide that they want to spend only $75 million for the goods and services offered by the business firms. They want to lay aside $25 million for a rainy day.

The first question that occurs to us is, Is this really possible? Can we have $100 million going out in the income loop of the flow and only $75 million coming back in the spending loop? The answer, essentially, is no, because incomes are created by customers spending on the products of businesses. What might happen in this case is that business firms might find that they themselves were spending the missing $25 million. They would do this by not selling $25 million worth of the goods they had produced and, thus, automatically accumulating $25 million of added inventories.

This accumulation of added inventories would make the flows come out all right arithmetically, but it would hardly make sense *economically.* Assuming that the firms in the economy had started off with the levels of inventories they needed for smooth production and sales, these *added* inventories would be unwanted and unsought. What they would tell each business firm is that it had produced more of its products than the market would bear. The firm's natural reaction would be to cut back output and employment until it found itself producing just the amounts that its customers wanted.

You should recognize that what we have just done has been to describe what is nothing more nor less than a deficiency in aggregate demand. We recall from the last chapter that Lord Keynes attributed the major causes of depressions to precisely such deficiencies. What we have shown is that one reason why aggregate demand may be too low is that consumer spending may be too low (or, equivalently, consumer saving may be too high).

Still in this preliminary way, we might ask, Can we also describe a situation where aggregate demand is too high? The answer is yes. Let us suppose this time that consumers want to spend all of their incomes on consumption goods (that is, to save nothing). Let us suppose at the same time that business firms, realizing that markets are good and expecting them to continue strong, want to divert part of the national product to investment, either in buildings and machinery or in added inventories. The consumers, then, want to spend the whole $100 million on consumption goods. But business firms want to spend some sum—say $20 million—on investment.

Again, we ask, Is this possible, and if it is possible in some mechanical way, is it economically possible? That is, what will the economic repercussions be?

The answer is that consumer and business behavior in this instance will create a situation in which "something has to give," and that the economic consequences of this behavior would normally be an *expansion* of national output and employment. Essentially, we have $120 million of spending coming around and trying to buy $100 million worth of goods. If we assume that prices are constant (our general assumption at this stage of our analysis), the only way business firms could meet the demand would be by selling off some of their inventories of goods in stock. Now, this would be a good thing from the point of view of the business firm—it would have all these customers clamoring for its goods—but it is not something the firm would simply sit back and watch without doing anything. In particular, the firm would try to increase its employment and output to the point where it could not only meet consumer demands, but also maintain (or add to) its stock of inventories. An excess of aggregate demand, then, would generally lead to a business expansion.

We have moved now from definitions into the beginnings of a theory of national income determination. We have seen that consumer decisions on consumption and saving may be crucial; we have also just seen how business investment decisions can influence the macroeconomic outcome. In short, we are now in a position to move ahead in a systematic way into this important area of modern economics, and this will be our central task in the next chapter.

S U M M A R Y

In studying the modern economy in the aggregate and its short-run fluctuations, we need some measure of annual total output. *Gross national product* (GNP) is such a measure. Its major components are (1) consumption, (2) gross investment, and (3) government expenditures on goods and services.

The common denominator used to make possible the adding together of the various outputs in the economy is the price of each of these goods expressed in money terms. In performing this aggregation of outputs, however, two significant problems arise. The first is the problem of constant prices, or ruling out changes in GNP that derive simply from inflationary (or deflationary) changes in the price level. Our interest in these first chapters on macroeconomics is particularly in changes in the real output value of GNP. To accomplish this end, prices in a given base year are used; for example, "constant 1982 prices." This gives us the important distinction between *money GNP* and *real GNP*. The second problem is that of avoiding double counting in adding up the outputs of different industries in the economy. This may be done by rigorously excluding intermediate products and concentrating on final goods and services only. Or, equivalently, it may be done by the *value-added* method of calculating national income.

The value-added approach has the virtue of bringing out quite clearly the fundamental equivalence of national product and national income. In our society, our real income in the aggregate (wages, salaries, rents, and so on) is nothing but our total production in the aggregate.

This equivalence of product and income leads, in turn, to a circular flow representation of a modern economy. A money-income-and-spending flow, representing households as they sell their services (labor, land, and so on) to business firms and then buy the products of the business firms with their incomes, is matched by an opposite national-product-and-factor-services flow, showing the business firms getting the services of the factors of production and transforming these into useful commodities. With the circular flow diagram in mind, we can begin to understand how deficiencies or excesses of aggregate demand might make their presence felt in the modern economy.

Key Concepts for Review

National income concepts
    Gross national product (GNP)
    Net national product (NNP)
    National income
    Personal income
    Disposable personal income
Components of GNP
    Consumption
    Investment
    Government
Gross versus net investment
Saving

Money versus real GNP
Constant prices
Double counting
Value added
Equivalence of "income" and "product"
Circular flow
Inventories

Questions for Discussion

1. Show the equivalence of the final-product and value-added methods of measuring GNP.

2. Distinguish *financial investment* from *investment* as a component of real GNP. What is the difference between *gross investment* and *net investment?*

3. In a private economy, total output consists of consumption and investment, while total real income consists of consumption and saving. As total output and total income are equivalent, saving and investment must always be equal. However, *decisions* to invest and *decisions* to save are not the same. Is there any inconsistency in saying that saving must always equal investment but that decisions about saving and decisions about investment are often made by different people for different reasons? (*Hint:* Remember the supply and demand diagrams of chapter 2. The quantity of a good bought and the quantity of a good sold must always be equal. However, the decisions of buyers, reflected in the demand curve, are quite different from the decisions of sellers, reflected in the supply curve.)

4. Using the circular flow diagram as a guide, show how a decision of consumers to save more than businesses want to invest can lead to a deficiency of aggregate demand. Show, conversely, how a decision of businessmen to invest more than consumers wish to save can lead to an excess of aggregate demand.

5. In footnote 5 (p. 110), we suggested that an increase in *real* GNP can be defined unambiguously only when the prices of all goods change in the same proportions. If relative prices change and the relative quantities of goods produced change, then the change in GNP will be different depending on what set of prices is used to make the measurement. This is known as the *index number problem*.

   In the following example, determine the percentage change in GNP from 1980 to 1990 as measured (1) in 1980 prices and (2) in 1990 prices.

	1980		1990	
	Oranges	*Toy Balloons*	*Oranges*	*Toy Balloons*
Price	$.30	$.15	$.25	$.30
Quantity	1,000	2,000	3,000	2,500

Which measure—in 1980 prices or 1990 prices—gives the larger change in total output? Can you see why this problem might pose some difficulties for measuring changes in GNP over long periods of time?

CHAPTER 7

NATIONAL INCOME DETERMINATION WITH CONSTANT PRICES

In this chapter, we shall make our first attempt to answer the question, What determines the equilibrium level of real national income? This attempt has to be considered preliminary because we are assuming that prices remain constant throughout our analysis. We are also leaving "money" to one side, assuming for the moment that monetary effects will somehow take care of themselves. These assumptions are, of course, only temporary, and we will drop them in part 3. One other limitation of our present analysis is that we will be concerned mainly with reasonably short periods of time, that is, periods during which the productive capacity of the economy is more or less fixed. We are more interested here in what causes *gaps* between actual and potential GNP than in what determines the *growth* of potential GNP over time.

SOME CLUES TO A SOLUTION

We have already developed a few clues to the solution of this problem. From the last chapter we know the following:

> National income and national product are basically two different ways of looking at the same object. This point led us to the *circular flow* approach to economic life. Businesses pay incomes to the owners of labor, land, and so on, who then use these incomes to buy the goods and services that businesses have produced.
>
> We observed that the three main categories of GNP are (1) consumption expenditures, (2) investment expenditures, and (3) government expenditures.

We showed how a deficiency in one of the spending categories (say, consumer spending) might lead through the circular flow to business troubles and, thus, to a contraction of output and employment. Such a deficiency in the spending flow, we said, was really the sort of thing Keynes meant when he talked about inadequate aggregate demand. If we can show how aggregate demand might fall short, we might have one way of demonstrating how actual GNP could fall below potential GNP.

And this, indeed, will be our procedure in the following pages. We will first determine the factors that influence the three categories of spending: consumer spending, private business investment, and government expenditure. Then, we must "add up" these expenditure items and see whether they will provide us with sufficient aggregate demand to sustain GNP at its full-employment potential level. If they will not sustain full-employment GNP, then we must ask, What *is* the level of national income that can be sustained? When we have answered these questions, our preliminary theory of national income determination will be complete.

We shall follow this suggested structure except for one point. In this chapter, we shall consider the theory of national income determination in a purely private economy—that is, we shall assume that there are no government expenditures or taxes; our only sources of aggregate demand shall be consumer spending and business investment spending. We shall bring government into the picture in the following chapter. This approach, besides being easier to follow, also has the advantage that it enables us to show more explicitly what impact various government policies have on the economy.

A CLARIFICATION—AGGREGATE DEMAND AND SUPPLY

We have been talking loosely about "aggregate demand" and "aggregate supply" as though they were simple extensions of our demand and supply curves for individual commodities from chapter 2. Yet a cautious reader might already have some doubts about this way of speaking. Our microeconomic demand and supply curves of chapter 2 expressed quantity demanded or supplied as a function of the *price* of the commodity. The higher the price, for example, the lower the quantity demanded. But in our aggregate analysis, we are not (for the moment) allowing any higher or lower prices; we are assuming *constant* prices. How, then, can we talk about changes in quantities demanded or supplied?

There is a potential source of confusion here that we should clarify right at the beginning. The reader will recall our earlier discussion of the distinction between movements along a given demand curve and shifts in the demand curve. When the price of a product changes and the quantity demanded increases, that represents a movement *along* a given demand curve. However, this demand curve assumes that a number of other factors affecting demand are held constant: for example, consumers' tastes or consumer incomes (see pp. 22–25). If, say, consumer incomes doubled, the typical demand curve would *shift* to the right, the consumers demanding more of the commodity at each particular price.

What we will be doing in this chapter is to hold prices constant and to consider how aggregate demand and supply vary in response to *other* factors. In particular, we shall focus on changes in aggregate quantities demanded and supplied as national income changes. This will explain why our aggregate supply and demand curves of this chapter bear no resemblance to the individual supply and demand curves of chapter 2. However, when we *do* let prices vary (chapter 9), we will be describing aggregate supply and demand curves as a function of price, and these curves will have more familiar contours.

The two components of aggregate demand in our private economy are (1) consumer demand for the various categories of consumption goods the nation can produce and (2) business demand for goods to invest—that is, to add to the stock of machines, buildings, inventories and other capital goods in the economy. We shall consider these two components of aggregate demand in order.

CONSUMPTION DEMAND

What are the factors that influence consumption demand in a modern industrial economy? Can we generalize about them in any way?

The Income-Consumption Relationship

The most important single generalization economists make about consumer demand states that consumer spending can be usefully related to consumer income. If you wish to know how much a family will spend on consumption, find out what their family income is. If you want to know how much the nation will spend on consumption in general, find out what the national income is. It was with this *income-consumption* relationship that modern macroeconomics began to take form more than half a century ago, and it is still a useful starting point today.[1]

A typical shape for the curve relating consumption to national income is shown in Figure 7-1. In this diagram, you will notice that we have drawn a

---

[1] Keynes himself formulated this relationship in terms of what he called a "psychological law": As an individual's (or society's) income rises, that individual (or society) will spend part, but not the whole, of the increase in income on added consumption. This implies that consumer saving will also increase as income increases.

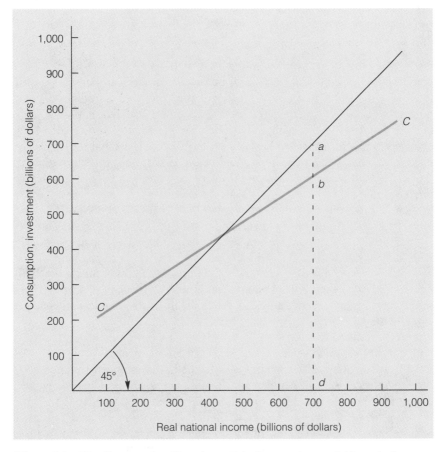

Figure 7-1   The Consumption Function   This diagram shows a fairly typical consumption function. The line *CC* shows how much consumers will want to spend on goods and services at various levels of national income. Understand that any line (for example, *ad*) drawn from the 45° line to the horizontal axis will be equal to national income as measured at the point of intersection with the horizontal axis (in this case, $700 billion). Also understand that the distance *ab* will represent anticipated consumer saving.

45° line from the origin. We shall be speaking about this line again in a moment, but note that along this 45° line, vertical and horizontal distances from the two axes are equal, meaning that the vertical distance is equal to national income. National income, in our simplified economy, can be divided into two components: consumer spending plus consumer saving. If I have a $30,000 income and spend $25,000 of it on consumer goods, then my saving that year will be $5,000. In terms of our diagram, this means that we can calculate saving at any level of income by measuring the distance between the *C* curve and the 45° line.

The Shape of the Consumption Function

The shape of this so-called "consumption function," as we have drawn it, indicates a slightly falling percentage of income devoted to consumption as income increases. At a rather low level of national income ($400 billion), consumption expenditures will equal the whole of national income. At still lower levels—and here we must imagine the nation in a condition of general poverty—people will, in the aggregate, spend more than their entire incomes on consumption. In the economist's phraseology, at very low levels of income, people will *dissave*. They will go to their past savings; they will live on their capital assets, their homes and personal property, without replacing them; they will be consuming, on the average, more than they have actually produced that year. This is a pathological case (though not an unknown case, as there *was* net dissaving in the depths of the Great Depression in 1932 and 1933), and, hence, the more interesting part of the curve lies to the right of $400 billion. In this range, we can see that consumption will continually rise with income but that saving will increase as a percentage of income.

The evidence for this general shape of the consumption function is both macro- and microeconomic in nature. In Figure 7-2, we have plotted out personal consumption expenditures in relationship to disposable personal income in the United States for each year from 1960 to 1989. The shape of the line we have fitted to these data is roughly what we should expect, showing both consumption and saving rising with disposable income.

Another quite different kind of information is provided by microeconomic studies of family spending at different income levels. Thus, we should expect that families with higher incomes will generally save more than families with lower incomes, not only absolutely, but also in percentage terms, and various studies have confirmed this general tendency. A family with a $100,000 income a year will save a higher percentage of its income than one with $30,000 a year. A family with $7,500 a year, at 1990 prices, would *dissave,* on the average.

Complicating Factors

Although the income-consumption relationship is an important starting place for macroeconomics, we cannot accept it without some qualifications. For one thing, the consumption function we have drawn in Figure 7-1 is essentially short run (one or two years), and we know that this curve tends to shift upward over time. At a given level of income, families spent more on consumption in 1980 than they did in 1960, and they will presumably spend still more at that same level of income in the year 2000. Why? Because there were many new products in 1980 that hardly existed in 1960, and we can expect still more product changes by 2000. Even more significant, perhaps, is that we are in a society in which family income, on the average, has historically been rising. Insofar as our consumption expenditures reflect our relative posi-

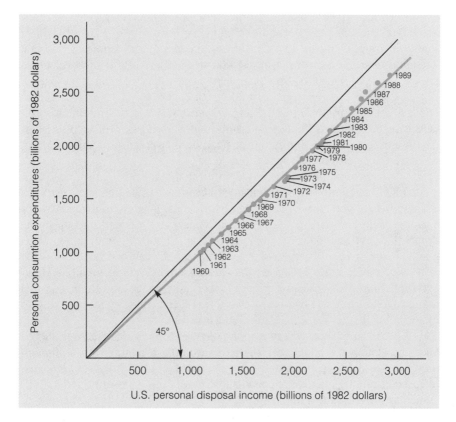

Figure 7-2   U.S. Consumption in Relation to Disposable Income in Constant 1982 Dollars, 1960–1989   In this diagram, we have fitted a line to actual data on consumption in relation to income in the United States for each year, 1960–1989. These data suggest the strength of the income-consumption relationship.

tion in the income distribution, then, if we stay at the same absolute level while other families around us are improving their positions, we may feel *relatively* poorer, and this may lower our willingness to cut consumption and save for the future.[2]

---

[2] Such factors help explain why, when we plot consumption expenditures against disposable income over a number of years (as in Figure 7-2), the percentage of income devoted to consumption does not appear to decrease (nor the percentage of savings to rise) as disposable income increases. What we really have in Figure 7-2 is a *long-run* consumption function, the result of a constant shifting upward of *short-run* curves such as the one we drew in Figure 7-1.

Another complicating factor is that the *kind* of income we receive may influence our saving and consumption decisions. Some economists, like Professor Milton Friedman, have argued that our income is really of two sorts: "permanent income" and "transitory (or windfall gain or loss) income." Saving and consumption patterns will generally be different depending on which sort of income we are talking about.

Even at a given moment of time, there are numerous factors that may make our consumption expenditures higher or lower out of a given level of family income. Compare two consumers, each with an income of $30,000 annually. One has $250 in cash, $1,000 in the bank, $500 of government bonds, and $10,000 of outstanding debt on previous consumer purchases. The second has $650 in cash, $30,000 in the bank, $40,000 in government bonds, $50,000 in stocks, and $400 in consumer debt (last month's credit card balance). Who is likely to consume more out of current income? It is clearly not just income, but the asset position or *wealth* of a consumer that will affect the consumer's spending patterns.

Also, there is the notoriously complicated matter of "consumer senti-ment." Our consumption function does not reflect price changes, yet such changes (as we shall see later on) clearly affect the position of the curve. For example, suppose that I expect prices of consumers' goods to go up in the future. This expectation may convince me that I should buy more now, when goods are relatively cheap, which, of course—if everyone behaves in the same way—will cause increased demand and more future inflation. How-ever, inflation is also a cause of great uncertainty about the future, and this may convince me that I had best be very frugal (increase my saving) now so that I will be better prepared for difficult times ahead.

There are, in short, many complications in this area, and no one should take any statements about the income-consumption relationship as though they were established beyond the possibility of doubt. Still, the view that makes consumption demand depend substantially on the level of national in-come has proved quite a durable one.

Our first question, then, is answered as follows: Consumer spending in a private economy will be largely determined by the level of national income in the general manner described by the consumption function of Figure 7-1.[3]

INVESTMENT DEMAND

We now turn to our second question: What factors will determine the level of investment spending in our hypothetical economy?

The Variability of Investment Demand

The determinants of investment demand are, if anything, even more compli-cated than those that influence consumer demand. Indeed, while economists

---

[3] This discussion of consumption and saving has been limited to household consumption and saving out of personal disposable income. In a fuller discussion, we should have to take into account the fact that business corporations also save and that their savings form an important source for business in-vestment in the modern American economy. These corporate savings arise when businesses pay out less in dividends than their after-tax profits. These retained profits are part of national income but do not go to the consumers as personal income.

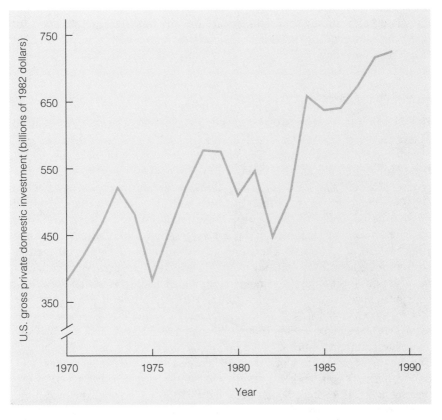

Figure 7-3   U.S. Gross Private Investment in Constant 1982 Dollars, 1960–1989
This diagram suggests the volatility of private investment spending in the American economy.

often stress the relative dependability of consumer spending at a given level of national income, they usually point out the great *variability* of business investment decisions (Figure 7-3). For this reason, changes in investment spending are often seen to be pivotal in causing upswings or downswings in a modern economy.

To appreciate the problem, put yourself in the place of the head of a business firm and ask yourself what factors are likely to influence you in a decision to expand the size of your factory, to add new machines, equipment, and so on. There are a host of obvious factors that you would have to take into account at the outset. Basically, you would be trying to judge the future profitability of the investment. This would involve an assessment of your present position. Are sales good? Is demand for your product high? Is the extra machinery needed to produce more output? But, it would also require an assessment of the future: Are sales likely to expand or contract over the life of the new machinery? Demand may be buoyant today, but does the future look bright or gloomy? In other words, the first thing you would have to do would be to formulate some general opinion about the future market for your particular product. *Business expectations* are a crucial factor influencing investment spending.

Technology and Costs

But it is not just the state of the market that you have to estimate. As the head of a business firm, you would also have to investigate whether there are new productive methods and processes available to you that will make the investment profitable in terms of reducing costs of production or producing an improved product. The kinds of plant, tools, and machinery we have in the economy today are vastly different from what they were fifty years ago, and this is a consequence of the fact that businesses invest not only in more of the "old" machines, but also in replacing "old" machines with "new" machines. Here, we enter the whole area of *technological progress*. If there is an important new invention, for example, this may create a wide range of opportunities for profitable business investment. The great Austrian-American economist Joseph A. Schumpeter (1883–1950) emphasized the pivotal role of new products and new productive methods as stimuli to business investment. He considered the introduction and absorption of innovational advances to be the mainspring of the major fluctuations of a modern economy. The judgment on whether investments in a new line of business or new productive process will work is not a mechanical one; it involves considerable uncertainty, and, indeed, Schumpeter felt that those who took the lead in innovations had to have certain special qualities of character and leadership ability.

Even if you were aware of the future state of demand and also the full range of technological possibilities open to you, however, you still would not have solved the problem of whether or not to invest in a particular factory or piece of machinery. For you would now come up against the problem of financing the new investment. Does your firm have a great sum in the form of retained profits that can be used to purchase the added capital equipment? Or will you have to go to money markets to raise funds from the outside? In either case, the cost of borrowing money—the *interest rate*—would have to be a factor in your decision.[4] If interest rates are high, this will mean that you will have to pay more to borrow money and, consequently, that you will be more reluctant to undertake any vast expansion schemes. High interest rates are often associated with "tight money." It is difficult to get loans from the

---

[4] It might seem that the interest rate would affect your decision only if you had to borrow money from outside, say, take a bank loan, and not if you already had the funds yourself. However, this is not so. If the machine promised you a return of 6 percent a year and you could get 10 percent in a money market fund, would you be likely to purchase the machine? What would you do with your money?

bank, and when one does get a loan, the interest charge is very stiff. In such circumstances, business investment is likely to be considerably curtailed.

In short, we have a whole series of factors that are likely to lead to more or less investment spending in the economy. Current demand for the product, pressure on plant capacity, future expectations, technological progress, the firm's profit position, the rate of interest—all these are factors that may significantly affect this second great component of aggregate demand: business investment expenditure.

We shall return to some of these factors later, especially when we come to our discussion of the economic effects of changes in the rate of interest (chapters 11 and 14). For the moment, however, so that we can get on with our argument, let us simply assume that business investment spending has been determined. Let us suppose that all these various factors have done their work and that the net result has been to give us a level of investment of, say, $100 billion. This is a shortcut, but it will help us get the overall picture in the clearest possible terms.

Very well, then. We have (1) a consumption function (Figure 7-1) relating consumer spending to national income and (2) a given $100 billion of investment demand. How, then, is the level of national income determined?

DETERMINATION OF THE LEVEL OF NATIONAL INCOME

The determination of the equilibrium level of national income takes place basically in the following way:

> We add up the sum of consumer spending and business investment spending at each level of national income and determine whether this sum exceeds the level of national income or falls short of it. If there is an excess, it will mean that aggregate demand exceeds aggregate supply. In this case, forces will be set in motion to produce an expansion of national income. If, however, there is a deficiency, this will mean that aggregate demand is less than aggregate supply, and this will bring about a fall in national income and, with it, of course, a fall in employment.

In short, the root cause of depressions, at least as far as our simplified economy is concerned, is a sum of consumption and investment spending that falls short of national income at the full-employment level.

It is one thing to state the conclusion, it is another to demonstrate it in a convincing way. Actually, there are several approaches, many of which we have already suggested in our various clues along the way. One approach, for example, would be to return to our *circular flow* diagram of the last chapter and to show that households and business firms will be content with what they are doing only when the sum of anticipated consumer spending and planned business investment in the spending flow is equal to the national product flow. We shall leave this approach to be worked out by the reader with two additional hints. (1) It is important to remember the words *antici-pated* and *planned* in the previous sentence. The sum of *actual* consumption and investment expenditures in our private economy *must* equal the national product, because there is no other place for output to go. (2) You may wish to introduce another loop in the diagram, showing part of the output of the economy going directly back to business in the form of business investment. You should then show that there will be overall equilibrium only when an amount equal to this planned investment is drained off from the household spending flow in the form of saving.

$C + I$ Approach

An equivalent, somewhat clearer, approach is to build on the basis of the consumption function diagram (Figure 7-1). In Figure 7-4, we have taken this earlier diagram and made two additions to it:

The *first* addition is the vertical line *FE,* drawn at the level of national income of \$910 billion. This line tells us what national income (Y),[5] or product, would be if all factors of production were fully employed. We could also think of this as what we earlier called *potential* GNP. It should be noted, however, that both of these concepts are less definite than the single straight line would suggest. "Full employment," for example, does not imply that there is literally zero unemployment in the economy. There is always some *frictional unemployment,* as workers leave one job and search for another. There is, in addition, what is sometimes called *structural unemployment:* un-employment that results from major economic changes (say, loss of manufac-turing jobs as the economy turns more to high tech or services production) such that workers who are laid off cannot quickly get back into comparable work or require additional training to do so. What we are really talking about is what might be called a "full employment rate of unemployment," and this is variously estimated by economists today at anywhere between 4 and 7 per-cent of the labor force, numbers which can change over time. (It will depend, for example, on the changing age structure of the labor force, since different age groups normally experience quite different rates of unemployment. Also, the size of the labor force seeking jobs in the labor market is itself a function of economic conditions to some degree.) Hence, we can, if we wish, think of *FE* not as a line, but as a band of a certain width suggesting the range of possible full-employment (or potential) outputs.[6]

The *second* addition is the line $C + I$, which has been drawn above our C curve. The vertical distance between these two lines is \$100 billion. This

---

[5] The reader will notice that we use the symbol Y to represent "national income." This is customary since the symbol I is typically used for "investment."

[6] "Potential GNP" is also sometimes defined in a somewhat more complex way as "the level of GNP consistent with a constant rate of inflation." See our later discussion, pp. 233–234.

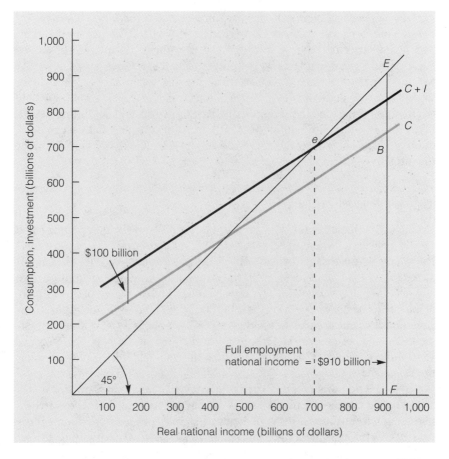

Figure 7-4   National Income Determination   Equilibrium national income will be determined in this private economy at point *e*, where the *C* + *I* curve intersects the 45° line. The equilibrium level of national income in this example will be $700 billion.

represents the amount of planned business investment that we are taking as determined by the host of factors influencing such investment. The vertical distance from the *x*-axis to the *C* + *I* line at each level of national income represents the sum of investment and consumption demand at that level of national income.

Now, this *C* + *I* line is really an *aggregate demand curve,* expressing the demand of businesses and consumers for output at various levels of national income. Since we shall use the term *aggregate demand curve* later on to refer to demand as a function of price, let us be sure to remember that this *C* + *I* curve represents a *curve of aggregate demand for national income as a function of national income.*

What we need now is a curve for aggregate supply as well, meaning a *curve of aggregate supply of national income as a function of national income.* This, fortunately, turns out to require no new addition to our diagram. The aggregate supply curve in this sense is nothing but our 45° line. The value of output at any given level of output includes, besides the payments to the factors of production, the normal profits required to induce business firms to produce that particular output. Thus, at any given level of output—say, $650 billion—the amount of output that business firms will be willing to supply is that same level of output, $650 billion. Which means that we can think of our 45° line as, in fact, the aggregate supply schedule in our current use of the term.[7]

Equilibrium National Income

How, then, will the equilibrium level of national income be determined? The simple answer is: where aggregate demand and aggregate supply are equal! But what exactly does that mean? To see the process involved, let us start out at the full-employment level, or at the national income of $910 billion. We now ask, What is the level of aggregate demand when the economy is fully employed? The answer can, in principle, be read off from the diagram. Consumption demand is equal to the distance *FB*, or about $740 billion. Investment demand, of course, is $100 billion. The sum of the two, therefore, is $840 billion. This is $70 billion less than the value of full-employment national income.

Now, it does not take any very sophisticated analysis to show that this is an untenable situation. Business firms are paying out into the income stream far more than consumers (through their consumption expenditures), and business firms (through their own investment expenditures) are willing to pay back to them. The effects of this will be direct and compelling. If we assume that prices remain unchanged, business firms, in general, will find that they are accumulating inventories of goods beyond the normal stock of inventories needed to carry on their business smoothly. These added inventories represent new investment, but it is unplanned and unwanted investment. Furthermore, it is a kind of investment that each business firm knows how to respond to directly: it will start cutting production and employment. This will be true of firms throughout the economy. There will be general cutbacks in

---

[7] This is something of an oversimplification. For one thing, as we shall see below (p. 134), the 45° line cannot really represent an aggregate supply curve beyond the full-employment potential level of national income. It would be very difficult to "supply" those over-full-employment levels of national income for any sustained period of time. Moreover, the remainder of the 45° line (to the left of full-employment national income) will be an aggregate supply curve only under certain circumstances. We must assume that at each level of national income, our given price level, *P*, assures business firms the normal profits necessary to induce them to produce that output, no more profits and no less. This will be the case, for a given *P*, if wages and other factor costs are also given and if production (until the full-employment barrier) is carried out under conditions of constant cost.

national output and employment. Full-employment national income, in short, has proved unsustainable; employment and income will have to fall.

But how far? Where will the equilibrium level of national income in our economy be? The answer is that equilibrium national income will be at the level determined by the intersection of the $C + I$ line with the 45° line (point e). At this level of national income, aggregate demand will equal aggregate supply. Because the distance between the C curve and the 45° line equals the amount of their incomes consumers wish to save, this equilibrium level of national income is also one at which planned business investment and anticipated consumer saving are equal. In this instance, the amount business firms want to invest and the amount consumers want to save are both equal to $100 billion.[8]

To prove that point e has significance, we must show that levels of national income either higher or lower will not work. We must also show that higher levels will set in motion forces bringing national income *down,* whereas lower levels will set in motion forces bringing national income *up.*

Actually, we have already done half of this by showing the unsustainability of full-employment income and the way in which business firms would react to unwanted inventories of their goods in stock. This logic can be applied to all points to the right of e in our diagram. In each case, there will be some accumulation of unwanted inventories and, consequently, a further reduction of production and employment.

Similarly, we can show that points to the left of e will not work either, though for an opposite reason. Here, the sum of $C + I$ *exceeds* the level of national income (Y). This fact would manifest itself to producers in the form of clamoring buyers who would be trying to purchase more of the firm's products than had been produced in the given period. If, again, we assume

---

[8] Another graphical way of showing equilibrium national income is precisely by showing the intersection of the planned savings and investment schedules. This method is given in the following figure. You should test your understanding of this subject matter by (1) showing for yourself exactly how the figure is derived from Figure 7-4 and (2) analyzing the process of national income (Y) determination (which we have done largely in terms of $C + I = Y$) in terms of savings and investment decisions (or $I = S$).

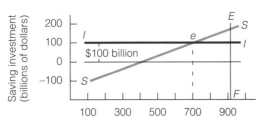

Determination of Equilibrium National Income by Saving and Investment Schedules

Real national income (billions of dollars)

that prices remain unchanged (in this case they would have a tendency to rise), the consequence would be depleted inventories, empty store shelves, unfulfilled orders, and the like. The effect of this, in turn, would be to suggest to business firms that they ought to expand production and employment. In short, at all levels of national income lower than *e*, we would have forces working for an expansion of national income.

Thus, at lower levels, where aggregate demand exceeds aggregate supply, national income will expand; at higher levels, where aggregate demand falls short of aggregate supply, national income will contract; at point *e*, aggregate demand will be just sufficient to match the output the economy is producing, and, thus, there will be no forces effecting any change in the level of national income. Q.E.D.

At point *e*, do we have an equilibrium level of national income? In terms of our present analysis, yes. No household or business firm can improve its situation by an indicated change in its pattern of actions. Do we have general contentment in the economy? Definitely not! Our equilibrium level of national income is short of full-employment income by $210 billion. Translated into employment figures, this amount means that our economy is suffering from massive unemployment. We would be facing, to use a phrase current in the 1930s and revived again in the early 1980s, "poverty in the midst of plenty."

EXCESS DEMAND AND INFLATION

But there is a further possibility to be discussed. Suppose that we have a situation where the *C* + *I* curve intersects the 45° line at a point *beyond* the full-employment level? Such a case is shown in Figure 7-5.

Now, it is clear that we would not normally be able to sustain the indicated level of income because it exceeds full-employment income. What this diagram tells us, therefore, is that when we reach full employment, we still will be faced with a condition of considerable excess demand. The forces for expansion in the economy will still be strong, but, in the short run, there will be no real way in which these forces can be expressed in further expansions of real output. How will they be expressed, then?

Actually, Figure 7-5, with its assumption of constant prices, is of little help in answering this question. Still, it is fairly obvious what that answer must be. The economy depicted in Figure 7-5 will almost certainly be subject to persistent inflationary pressures. Businesses will be trying to expand; they will be competing against each other for labor and other factors of production; wages and money incomes will rise; consumer demands will rise in money terms with the higher money incomes; prices will rise again; and so on.

What we really have here is our first contact with an inflationary economy. This is a rather specific type of inflation that we might refer to as a Keynesian *demand-pull* inflation. Its ultimate problem is an excess of aggre-

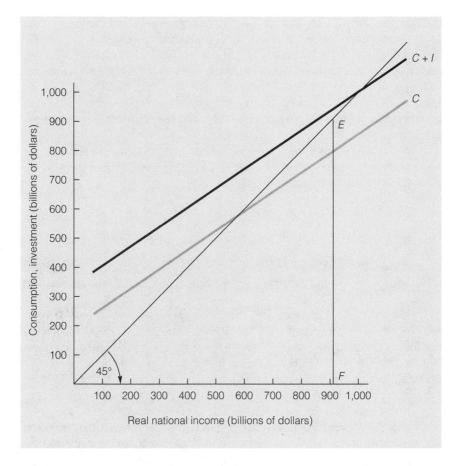

Figure 7-5   A Keynesian Demand-Pull Inflation   When the sum of $C + I$ exceeds full-employment income at FE in our private economy, there will be heavy pressures on prices to rise because of excess aggregate demand.

gate demand at the full-employment level of national income. There are many other types of inflation, and we shall spend a good deal of time discussing them; it should be said, however, that demand-pull *elements* are frequently present in the mix of factors that produce the more complicated kinds of inflation we see in the real world.

WORK TO BE DONE

This chapter has given us an important departure point for analyzing the factors that determine the level of national income in our economy. Needless to say, the conclusions we have reached will have to be modified when we bring "money" into the analysis and when we take explicit account of price changes.

Before we do this, however, it will be useful to show how this present analysis may be extended to a number of important economic problems. We are interested not only in recessions and booms, but in the fact that our economy seems to fluctuate back and forth from one to the other, a fluctuation that is sometimes called the *business cycle*. Also, we want to introduce the third major component of aggregate demand: government expenditures. How will government tax and spending policies influence the equilibrium level of national income?

In our next chapter, therefore, we will develop a number of applications of our present analysis, gaining a better understanding of these tools in the most effective way—by actually using them.

SUMMARY

In this chapter, we have presented the essentials of a theory of national income determination in a simplified private economy, assuming constant prices.

In such a private economy, the main components of aggregate demand will be consumer spending and business investment spending. Consumer spending is related to national income through the *consumption function*. This function tells us that consumers will consume more as their income increases, but that they will also save more. The evidence is that in the short run, saving increases slightly as a percentage of income as income rises.

Investment spending is a function of many different factors, including such important elements as business expectations, technological progress, the amount of profits available for investment purposes, and the cost of borrowing funds, or the rate of interest. Investment spending is, on the whole, a more variable and unpredictable factor than consumer spending. In our simplified analysis, we take a certain amount of planned investment as already determined by the workings of these various factors.

The equilibrium level of national income is determined at the level where aggregate demand equals aggregate supply or, equivalently, where the sum of planned consumption and investment spending equals national income (or output) or, equivalently still, where savings and investment decisions are equated. At levels of national income higher than this equilibrium level, forces will be set in motion to bring about a contraction in output and employment. At levels of national income below the equilibrium level, forces will be set in motion to bring about an expansion in output and employment.

The equilibrium level of national income is not necessarily a full-employment level and, indeed, is compatible with major unemployment in the economy. In the case where aggregate demand exceeds aggregate supply at the full-employment level, we will have persistent upward pressures on the price level. This is Keynesian, or *demand-pull*, inflation.

Before modifying this analysis to take into account "money" and price changes, we will (in the next chapter) apply our tools to the business cycle and government fiscal policy.

Key Concepts for Review

Aggregate demand as a function of national income

Aggregate supply as a function of national income

Consumption function

Consumer wealth

Variability of investment demand

Business expectations

Technological progress

Interest rate

Planned (anticipated) versus actual

   Consumption

   Investment

   Saving

Equilibrium level of national income

Potential level of national income

Full employment

Frictional unemployment

Structural unemployment

Demand-pull inflation

Questions for Discussion

1. State in your own words the basic theory of national income determination as you have understood it from the chapter. On what simplifying assumptions is it based?

2. Define the *consumption function*. What cautions should be kept in mind in employing this important tool?

3. In our analysis in this chapter, we have assumed that all saving is done by households and that all investing is done by businesses. In reality, however, households also invest (for example, building homes) and businesses save (corporate saving now provides a substantial percentage of the funds for business investment in the United States). How might these facts modify the general analysis of national income determination as we have presented it?

4. In the pre-Keynesian era, it was sometimes argued that the main reason for unemployment in the economy was that labor was making unreasonable wage demands. If wages were lower, it was argued, employers would find that they could afford to hire more workers and the unemployment problem would be solved. Do you find this argument satisfactory? If not, why? (*Hint:* Think back to the supply-and-demand curve for textile workers in chapter 4 (Figure 4–6, p. 80). If textile workers and all other workers accepted lower wages, would this be likely to affect the demand curves for textile workers and for other workers? In what direction?)

5. Explain the basics of demand-pull inflation as presented in this chapter. Can you think of any reasons why price increases might start occurring even before full employment is reached?

CHAPTER 8

THE MULTIPLIER, BUSINESS CYCLES, AND ELEMENTARY FISCAL POLICY

In chapter 7, we presented a theory of national income determination with constant prices. In this chapter, we shall apply this theory to important new topics. We shall consider the repetitive ups and downs of a modern industrial economy, usually known as the *business cycle*. We shall also introduce a topic that will be with us frequently in the future: government expenditure and tax policies—collectively referred to as a nation's *fiscal policy*.

But first, we must develop an important tool that derives from our previous analysis.

THE MULTIPLIER

In the last chapter, we indicated that an increase in consumer or business investment spending would raise the level of national income. What we did not specify was how much the rise would be. This is what the *multiplier* tells us.

> The multiplier tells us by how much an increase in spending will raise the equilibrium level of the national income. If a $1 billion increase in spending leads to a $5 billion increase in national income, the multiplier is 5; if the increase is $2 billion, the multiplier is 2.

It is important to stress at the outset that the multiplier is a *general* tool, applying to all categories of spending. So that there will be no mistake about the matter, we will first discuss the multiplier with respect to a change in private investment spending. Later in the chapter, we will illustrate it again with respect to government expenditures and taxes.

Multiplied Effects of Investment

In Figure 8-1, we are in a purely private economy, and we wish to show the effects of a change in investment demand on equilibrium national income. Investment demand was originally $100 billion. But now we imagine that some change has taken place (perhaps there has been an improvement in business confidence, owing to some international development, or perhaps there has been a new technological breakthrough, or perhaps the Federal Reserve System has lowered the interest rate), and planned investment spending has risen to $130 billion. The increase in investment is $30 billion, measured by the vertical distance between $C + I$ and $C + I'$. The effect of this change has been to raise equilibrium national income from $700 billion to $790 billion, or by $90 billion. A $30 billion increase in investment spending has brought about a $90 billion increase in national income. The *multiplier*, then, is 3.

Why 3? The geometrically minded reader will see that the size of this number depends very much on how steep the consumption function (C curve) is. Indeed, everyone can see this in a general way. Imagine that the C curve in our diagram were perfectly horizontal, that is, running parallel to the x-axis. In this case, a rise in investment of $30 billion would raise the intersection with the 45° line by $30 billion only and, consequently, would raise the national income level by only $30 billion. Here, the multiplier would be 1. If we imagined the C curve as very steep, however, we would get the opposite effect. Suppose the curve ran almost parallel to the 45° line; then one can see that even slight changes in investment spending would raise national income by great multiples.

Marginal Propensities to Consume and Save

Thus, we can see that the size of the multiplier in general depends on the steepness of the C curve. But we can be more precise than this. Let us first state our conclusion and then offer two different demonstrations of its validity.

The conclusion is that the multiplier (m) will, in ordinary circumstances, obey the following rule:

$$m = \frac{1}{1 - MPC}$$

where *MPC* refers to the *marginal propensity to consume,* or, geometrically, the *slope* of the consumption function.

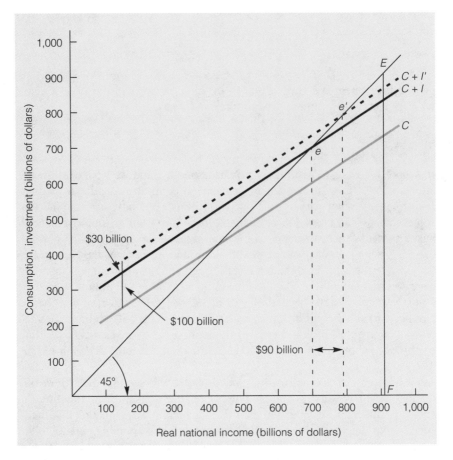

Figure 8-1 The Multiplier The principle of the multiplier is here illustrated in increased investment spending. A $30 billion increase in *I* leads to a $90 billion increase in *Y*.

Figure 8-2 The Marginal Propensity to Consume The marginal propensity to consume (MPC) is equal to the slope of the consumption function, or *BC/AC*. In this case, *MPC* = 67/100, or 2/3.

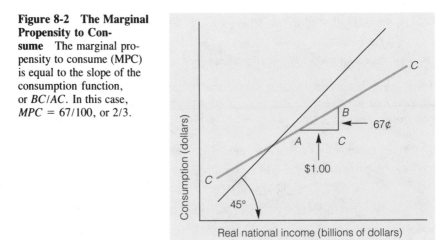

The meaning of this conclusion can be elaborated with reference to Figure 8-2, where we have blown up a small fragment of the *CC* curve. The *marginal propensity to consume* is defined as that part of an extra dollar of income that consumers will wish to spend on consumption. In Figure 8-2, we give an example in which a $1 increase in income increases consumption demand by 67 cents, or roughly, two-thirds. The same result would be obtained if the numbers were not written in but we simply measured distance *BC* and divided it by distance *AC*. This term *BC/AC* is the slope of the *CC* line, meaning that the marginal propensity to consume is the slope of the consumption function. The multiplier in this example can be worked out as follows:

$$m = \frac{1}{1 - MPC} = \frac{1}{1 - \dfrac{BC}{AC}} = \frac{1}{1 - \dfrac{2}{3}} = 3$$

Another way of stating the same conclusion would be in terms of the *marginal propensity to save (MPS)*. The MPS is defined as the part of an extra dollar of income that consumers wish to save. Since the extra dollar of income will be either saved or spent on consumption,

$$MPS = 1 - MPC \text{ (by definition)}$$

This means that we could, if we wished, rewrite the multiplier very simply as:

$$m = \frac{1}{MPS}$$

What we have stated here (but have yet not proved) is that the multiplier in our simplified private economy will be equal to the reciprocal of the marginal propensity to save, or, equivalently,

$$\frac{1}{1 - MPC}$$

When we ask *why* this is so, we come to the matter of proof. Let us show in two different ways why the multiplier will follow this rule.

Reasoning behind the Multiplier

The first is a geometrical demonstration:

Figure 8-3 is simply Figure 8-1 with some additional notation. Say that we have an increase in investment of the amount *b*. The diagram tells us that this leads to an increase in national income of the amount *a*. By definition, then, the multiplier is:

$$m = \frac{a}{b} \tag{1}$$

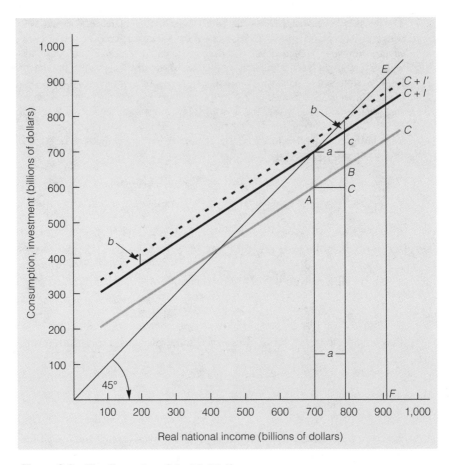

Figure 8-3   The Geometry of the Multiplier

Our 45° line tells us that $a = b + c$; hence, equation (1) can be rewritten:

$$m = \frac{a}{a - c} = \frac{1}{1 - \dfrac{c}{a}} \tag{2}$$

The marginal propensity to consume (MPC), we know, is measured by the slope of the C curve, or $MPC = BC/AC$. Since the investment curves are drawn parallel to the C curve, we can also say that $MPC = c/a$. Substituting for c/a in equation (2), we get:

$$m = \frac{1}{1 - MPC} \tag{3}$$

And this was what we set out to show.

   This geometrical demonstration is useful enough, but it gives us little insight into the economic logic of what is going on. The second demonstration, which we shall take up now, will make this clearer. For it is based on observing what happens at each stage of the game as the increase in investment or other expenditure makes its way through the economy. The *economics* of what happens is essentially this: When a business firm decides to invest in a new factory, it buys products (iron, steel, machinery, and so on) from other people, thus creating *income* for these people. This is in the first stage. But now these people have more income than before, and *they* will want to spend more on consumption. So in the second stage, consumption spending increases. *But not by the whole amount of the increase in income.* That is to say, they will spend part, but will also save part. In particular, the marginal propensity to consume tells us what fraction of this extra income they will want to spend. But then we go on to a third stage. The additional consumer spending (on food, shoes, and so on) creates more income for the producers of food, shoes, and other consumers' goods. This income, in turn, will also be spent in part (determined by the MPC) on consumption. The process repeats itself indefinitely, and at each new stage, further income (though in increasingly smaller amounts) is added to national income.
   Our second demonstration of the theory of the multiplier simply involves adding together all these successive rounds of additionally created income.

   Let us suppose that there is a $100 increase in investment spending and that $MPC = 2/3$. The amount of income created at each stage will be as follows (to the nearest dollar):

Stage 1	$100 (the original added investment)	$(MPC \times \$100)$
Stage 2	2/3 ($100) = $67	$[(MPC)^2 \times \$100]$
Stage 3	2/3 ($67) = $44	$[(MPC)^3 \times \$100]$
Stage 4	2/3 ($44) = $30	$[(MPC)^4 \times \$100]$
Stage 5	2/3 ($30) = $20	
.		
.		
.		
Stage $n + 1$	$(2/3)^n(\$100)$	$[(MPC)^n \times \$100]$

The total of all these stages of added income will be the increase in the equilibrium level of national income. If we use the term ΔY to signify the total increase in national income, then:

$$\Delta Y = \$100 + \$67 + \$44 + \$30 + \$20 + \ldots \quad (1)$$

or

$$\Delta Y = \$100 [1 + 2/3 + (2/3)^2 + (2/3)^3 + (2/3)^4 + \ldots + (2/3)^n + \ldots] \quad (2)$$

or, most generally, where ΔI is the added investment:

$$\Delta Y = \Delta I (1 + MPC + MPC^2 + MPC^3 + MPC^4 + \ldots + MPC^n + \ldots) \quad (3)$$

Because the multiplier is equal to $\Delta Y/\Delta I$, we get:

$$m = (1 + MPC + MPC^2 + MPC^3 + MPC^4 + \ldots + MPC^n + \ldots) \quad (4)$$

Knowing that MPC is less than 1, we can conclude from algebra that[1]

$$m = \frac{1}{1 - MPC} \quad (5)$$

Which, again, is what we set out to prove.[2]

Both these demonstrations prove the same point about the multiplier, but the second is perhaps more vivid in bringing out the economic aspect of what is going on. We must always imagine the successive rounds of expenditures and incomes created by any new act of spending. A business firm invests in an additional typewriter. This creates income for a seller of typewriters, who spends part of her increased income to buy a pair of shoes. This creates income for the producer of shoes, who now buys himself an umbrella. And on, and on, and on, the amounts getting smaller and smaller each time, as part of the added income leaks into added savings. Indeed, it will be precisely when savings in total have increased by the same amount as business investment that the process finally ends. This you can verify by looking at Figure 8-1 again. Note that at the new equilibrium level of national income, saving, like investment, has increased by $30 billion.

BUSINESS CYCLES—PAST AND PRESENT

The multiplier concept can help us to understand an important feature of industrial society: the *business cycle*. First, a few descriptive comments.

In the previous chapter, we discussed ups and downs of business activity (national income, employment, investment, and so on) without, however, trying to relate these movements to each other in any kind of pattern. The concept of a business cycle implies certain recurrent features in these ups and downs. There are common phases in these cycles that repeat themselves over time. There is a cumulative expansion process rising up to a "peak" that, shortly thereafter, gives way to a cumulative contraction process. This contraction process in due course reaches bottom—the "trough" of the

---

[1] The general formula, where $a < 1$, is:

$$1 + a + a^2 + a^3 + \ldots + a^n + \ldots = \frac{1}{1 - a}$$

[2] We are dealing here with what is sometimes called the *instantaneous multiplier*. As every reader will recognize, it would normally take a considerable amount of time for all these successive stages of spending and income creation to occur. In more advanced treatments, the multiplier is often worked out over time in what is sometimes called *period analysis*.

cycle—after which forces for recovery, and renewed expansion, assert themselves. These expansions and contractions (or recessions) are exhibited in a host of different statistical series. There are similar swings in employment, money and credit, investment and output, and stock market and commodity price data. In some cases, these statistical series tend to "lead" (turn down just before the peak and turn up just before the trough) the cycle; in other cases, they "lag" behind; in still other cases they are "coincident."

Historically speaking, the concept of a business cycle in the United States and most other industrial nations has won wide support among economists. Figure 8-4 suggests that these recurrent ups and downs of business activity go back to the pre–Civil War period. Similar charts could be prepared for other economically advanced countries—England, Germany, Canada, Japan, and so on.

Still, this chart, with the wide amplitude it suggests in our historic prosperities and depressions, raises a number of important questions about the business cycle phenomenon.[3]

Just How Regular Are Business Cycles?

Obviously, business cycles are not completely regular. Some expansions are longer than others. Some contractions are shorter. Some peaks are higher, some troughs deeper, and so on. How, after all, are we to compare the Great Depression of the 1930s with the Panic of 1907? These may be of one family, but the sibling differences are clearly enormous. The difficulty of timing cycles is, in turn, a reflection of the fact that very probably more than one kind of cycle is involved. If we have a number of overlapping cycles of different lengths, this would account for a certain amount of apparent irregularity in the data and also might explain why certain recessions are milder than others. (For example, if a downturn of one cycle overlaps with the expansion of another cycle, this might lead to a gentle recession as opposed to a major depression.)

Various economists have suggested that three and perhaps four cycles may be involved: (1) a minor cycle of forty months or so, largely reflective of increases and decreases of business inventories; (2) the major, or ordinary, business cycle, reflecting a whole series of different indices and lasting historically an average of eight or nine years; (3) a construction cycle of perhaps double or more the length of the major business cycle, being particularly ap-

---

[3] Even the drawing of a chart such as Figure 8-4 raises a number of questions. One of the most important of these is the validity of abstracting from the long-run trend in presenting business cycle fluctuations. Business activity in Figure 8-4 is presented as occurring around a horizontal line. In fact, of course, GNP, employment, investment, etc. were all expanding over this century. If, like Schumpeter, you believe that the cycle is an incident of the growth process—that is, that cycles are the *form* that industrial growth takes—then you will object strenuously to this procedure.

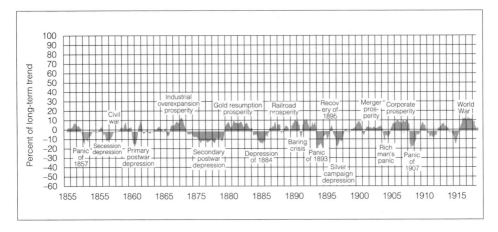

Figure 8-4 Over a Century of U.S. Business Cycles
SOURCE: Adapted from "American Business Activity from 1790 to Today," by The Cleveland Trust Company. Reprinted by permission, Ameritrust Corporation, Cleveland, Ohio.

parent in the building construction trades; and, finally, and more dubiously, (4) long waves of fifty years or more whose upswings—so Schumpeter thought—were associated with periods of major innovations (for example, the industrial revolution, the advent of the railroads, the coming of electricity and the automobile, and so on).

How Much of the Business Cycle Is Caused Externally and How Much Internally?

The degree of regularity (or periodicity) of the cycle is further complicated by the fact that external events—especially wars—are so obviously capable of throwing off the rhythm of a regular cycle, even if we clearly had one. Indeed, the question invariably arises of the relation of external (sometimes called *exogenous*) factors to internal (*endogenous*) factors in the causation of the cycle. Possible views could range from a belief that the ups and downs of Figure 8-4 are simply reflections of wars, gold rushes, good and bad weather (totally exogenous) to an opinion that the whole mechanism is built into industrial society, making, for example, wars and gold rushes themselves a function of the cyclical behavior of the economy (a completely endogenous theory). An intermediate theory might be that shocks to the system do often come from the outside and that they affect the economy but that the economy itself is so constructed that it *reacts* to these shocks in a cyclical way.

We cannot settle these complicated issues here. Suffice it to say that

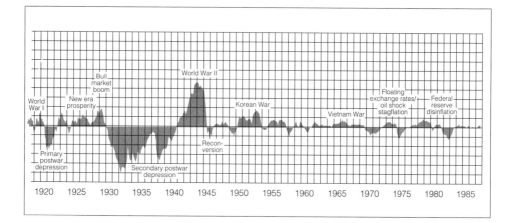

most economists tend to agree that, historically, the structure of the economy has tended to reinforce cyclical behavior in a number of ways. Without denying the importance of huge phenomena like World Wars I and II, these economists would say that there are also certain built-in tendencies for expansions to be cumulative, for prosperities to create conditions that tend to lead to downturns, for cumulative downward forces to develop, and for these situations, in turn, to lead to their own correctives. External factors greatly intensified, most observers would say, but did not create the historical business cycle.

Has the Business Cycle Changed in Recent Years?

At the same time that the majority of economists were agreeing on the existence of important internal mechanisms in the historic business cycle, they would also very probably agree that those mechanisms have changed considerably in the post–World War II period. For one thing, the growth of international trade has meant that no one country's business cycle can be studied in isolation. Also, an important new "external" factor has made its appearance in this period: the existence of governments that are, in one degree or another, committed to "stabilizing" the economy.

Figure 8-5 confirms the impression of most economists that the character of the business cycle has altered in the last four decades. In this diagram,

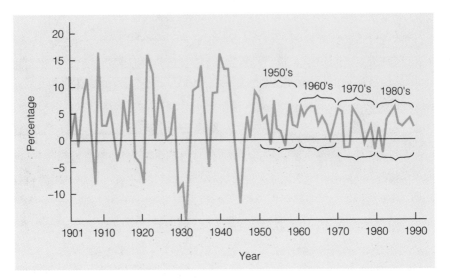

Figure 8-5 Annual Growth Rates of U.S. Real Gross National Product, 1901–1989 The increased stability of the economy in terms of *real* GNP in the last 40 years is shown in this diagram. What is not shown is the increased rate of inflation during this same period.
SOURCE: Adapted and extended by the author from Martin Neal Baily, "Stabilization Policy and Private Economic Behavior," *Brookings Papers on Economic Activity,* vol. 1 (Washington, DC: The Brookings Institution, 1978); *Economic Report of the President,* 1985, 1990.

actual declines in real GNP are indicated when the curve dips below zero (meaning a negative growth rate of GNP). It is apparent that such declines in real GNP have been less frequent and less severe in the past 40 years than they were earlier, even when we consider only the years leading up to, but not including, the Great Depression of the 1930s. Also, the upward leaps in GNP have been moderated. These data could be interpreted as a tribute to the relative effectiveness of modern government stabilization policies[4]—though any self-congratulation on this score would have to be qualified by the recognition that price inflation has notably *worsened* during this same period. In any case, Figure 8-5 strongly suggests that business cycles still exist (they have not become an obsolete concept as some have suggested) but that their amplitude in real terms is substantially less now than it was earlier in the century.

---

[4] Economist Martin Neal Baily has argued not only that government policy has promoted stabilization, but also that the private sector, knowing of the government's policy, has been influenced in ways that promote stabilization. Not all economists agree on this point, however. Some, indeed, have argued that it is only when the private sector *cannot* predict government policy that such policy can be effective. For Baily's argument, see Martin Neal Baily, "Stabilization Policy and Private Economic Behavior," *Brookings Papers on Economic Activity,* vol. 1 (Washington, DC: The Brookings Institution, 1978).

THE MULTIPLIER AND THE BUSINESS CYCLE

Our special interest in the business cycle in this chapter is that it enables us to apply our new tool of macroeconomic analysis. A number of theories of the business cycle involve the use of the multiplier principle.

The fundamental reason for this is that the multiplier helps explain cumulative movements of the economy, either upward or downward; it does so because, as its name implies, movements in any direction tend to have a *multiplied* impact. An increase of $1 billion in investment spending tends to give rise not to a $1 billion increase, but to a $3 or $4 or $5 billion increase in national income.

The multiplier itself, of course, is not sufficient to explain so complicated a phenomenon as the business cycle. But even at this stage of our knowledge of national income determination, we can see how it might be combined with other economic hypotheses to give us real clues as to how cyclical behavior originates. Let us, for example, take a fairly simple idea about investment spending, often referred to in business cycle analyses. The idea is that since investment (whether in machines, buildings, or inventories of goods in stock) represents an *increase* in our capital stock, it will be undertaken by business firms primarily in response to an *increase* in the level of national income. Business firms, in this view, will try to keep their stock of capital and their output in some kind of relatively fixed relationship.

Formally, this principle—sometimes called the *acceleration principle* because, as we shall see, it can speed up a change in any particular direction—can be defined as follows:

Investment is a function of the rate of increase of national income. When income is increasing, investment is positive; when income is decreasing, investment is negative; when income is constant, investment is zero.[5]

Now the acceleration principle can be combined with our multiplier to provide a first approximation view of how an "ideal" business cycle might work. Briefly:

Suppose that, for whatever reason (it could be one of Schumpeter's innovations), business investment increases just slightly. What will happen? The multiplier guarantees us that this increase in investment will lead to a subtantial increase in national income. But an increase in national income is precisely what will lead to a *further* increase in investment. A cumulative process of expansion is now under way. Multiplied increases in national income give rise to further increases in invest-

---

[5] If we call national income Y and the nation's total capital stock K, then the acceleration principle is based on the premise that firms try to keep K/Y relatively constant. This would mean a constant relationship between investment (the increase in the capital stock, or ΔK) and the increase in income (ΔY). Briefly then, the acceleration principle states that $\Delta K = a \times \Delta Y$, where a is a constant. Needless to say, this principle is at best an approximation to a much more complex reality.

ment, which, in turn, give rise to still further multiplied increases in national income.

And the same logic applies to contractions or recessions. Let investment fall, and this will cause a multiplied decrease in national income. But when total output is decreasing, businesses will be reducing their investment and, indeed, *disinvesting;* that is, they will reduce their inventories (remember the minor cycle) and/or let machines and buildings wear out without proper replacement. Thus, we have forces making for cumulative downturns as well as cumulative expansions.

But what of "peaks" and "troughs"? Why don't these cumulative expansions and contractions go on forever? Why do they turn around? Several explanations are possible, but one might go like this:

> The upward expansion can't go on indefinitely, because we run out of labor and other factors of production to keep output growing so rapidly. As we near full employment, the rate of increase of national income has to slow down. But a slowing down of the increase in total output is enough (by the acceleration principle) to bring an actual *decline* in investment. This decline then leads, through the multiplier, to a decline in national income, and we start downward. In other words, a slowdown of the expansion may be enough to turn it into an actual decline. This would explain why the expansion peaks and then turns into a recession.
>
> By the same logic, a slowing down of the contraction might lead to an upward turnabout. This would explain the trough of the cycle and the subsequent recovery. Why might the contraction begin to slow down after a while? There are many possible reasons. Consumers, after a point, might resist any further decreases in their consumption levels (this would reduce the MPC and the multiplier). Similarly, businesses might find it harder to *dis*invest after a time. For example, after inventories are reduced to virtually nothing, there is no further way one can disinvest in inventories. Such factors might explain a slowdown in the rate of decline of national income. And with the powerful multiplier and accelerator behind us, that would be sufficient to get an actual expansion going again.

Thus, we see how these tools of national income analysis can be used to give us insights into so complicated a matter as the business cycle. The multiplier has a wide range of reference over the whole area of macroeconomic phenomena.

INTRODUCING GOVERNMENT EXPENDITURES—*G*

And this range includes the actions of government. To show that the multiplier applies not only to investment (*I*) and consumption (*C*), we must now bring a third major component into our previously private economy: government (*G*). This will be simply an introduction to a topic that will engage our attention in later chapters. To make the analysis as straightforward as possible, we shall deal separately with (1) government expenditures and (2) government taxation.

We begin, then, with government expenditures. In a mixed economy, the government, along with households and private business investors, is purchasing goods and services. What will the effect of this government demand be?

The fundamental answer is that this demand will have precisely the same effect as any other demand. To the business firm producing, say, automobiles and trucks, it makes no essential difference whether the buyers are consumers, other business firms, or the United States government. In each case, the added demand means added sales and added profits.

Because this government demand is to be treated in the same general way as any other demand, we can represent it in our diagram by simply adding it on to our $C + I$ curve, just as, earlier, we added investment spending to our consumption function. Let us pull a number out of the hat. Suppose that in our hypothetical economy, government expenditures for goods and services are running at $50 billion a year. Neglecting the tax side, what will happen?

The answer is given in Figure 8-6, where $50 billion of G has been added vertically to the $C + I$ curves. The consequence is that the equilibrium level of national income has been changed. Before, the equilibrium was at $700 billion; now it is where the $C + I + G$ curve intersects the 45° line, or at $850 billion. As a result of government expenditures, this particular economy is much closer to full-employment national income than before.

In its most primitive form, this is the justification for those who argue that the government ought to act to bring the economy as near as possible to the full-employment level.

We can also see that the multiplier has come into play exactly as in our earlier case of investment spending. $50 billion of G has led to a $150 billion increase in national income; with an MPC of 2/3, the multiplier is again 3. Because we are adding G to our $C + I$ curve in precisely the same way we added I to the C curve, this is very much what we would expect.

GENERAL EFFECTS OF TAXATION—T

We have been discussing government expenditures without discussing government revenues. But we all know that the government taxes as well as spends. What can we say in a general way about the effects of tax policy on aggregate demand and equilibrium national income?

There are many different kinds of taxes, direct or indirect: taxes falling mainly on consumers or mainly on corporations, progressive or regressive taxes, taxes emanating from the federal, state, or local governments, and so on. To keep the argument clearly in mind, we must simplify as much as possible. Let us suppose that the particular taxes that are levied fall entirely on the incomes of consumers. The federal government levies a tax of $30 billion on consumers in the economy. What effect will this have?

What we must do now is to reverse our field—or almost reverse it. G

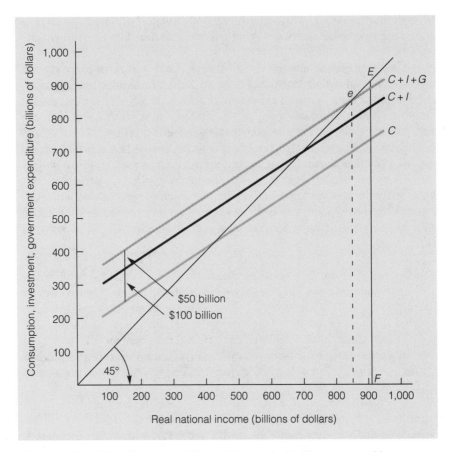

Figure 8-6 Adding Government Expenditures In this diagram, we add government expenditures of $50 billion and get an expansion of national income from $700 billion (without *G*) to $850 billion (with *G*). We have not, however, taken taxes into account at this point in the argument.

added demand, but *T* takes away income that might have added to demand. The effect of *T*, considered in isolation, then, is to reduce aggregate demand and, hence, to put a downward pressure on the economy.

The introduction of a $30 billion tax will lower equilibrium national income. Like government expenditures, taxation will have its effect magnified by the multiplier, but not in quite the same way. This is why we must "almost reverse" our field. There is a certain asymmetry in the effects of *G* and *T*. In particular, the multiplied downward effect of $1 of taxes is somewhat less than the multiplied upward effect of $1 of government expenditures.

To see why this is so, let us show how taxes affect the position of the consumption function in our case of a $30 billion levy. Figure 8-7 indicates, as we would expect, that the consumption schedule is shifted downward by the impact of taxes. At a national income of $600 billion, consumers now have at their disposal only the same amount of income that they previously had at a national income of $570 billion, the difference being the amount of the tax. Hence, their consumption demand at $600 billion will now be the same as it was previously at $570. This is reflected graphically by moving horizontally to the right by the amount of *T* ($30 billion). (You should repeat this argument for other points on the consumption function; for example, the shift between $430 billion and $400 billion national incomes.) The after-tax consumption function (*C'C'*), then, is simply the original consumption function (*CC*) shifted horizontally to the right by $30 billion.

The effect of this shift on equilibrium national income is determined, however, not by rightward movements, but by the *downward* shift of the schedule. It is the height of the *C* + *I* + *G* line that ultimately determines

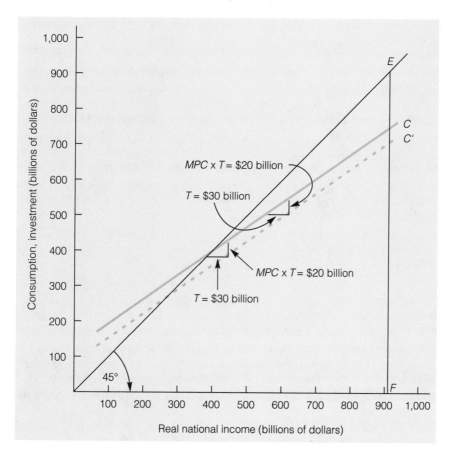

Figure 8-7 Effect of Taxes on Consumption A tax on consumers lowers the consumption function, but not by the full amount of the tax. If *MPC* = 2/3 and the tax is $30 billion, the *CC* curve will shift downward by 2/3 × $30 billion (= $20 billion).

where our equilibrium will be. Now, this downward shift is not $30 billion, but $20 billion. More generally, it is equal to the $MPC \times T$. This is easily seen in graphical terms: the little triangles we have drawn at $600 and $430 billion represent the slope of the consumption function—the MPC—and if the horizontal side of the triangle is $30 billion, the vertical side must be $20 billion. The vertical side, of course, tells us how much the function has shifted downward.

To determine the effect of T on national income, we take this $20 billion and then multiply it by the same factor we used in the case of G; that is, 3. The downward effect of $30 billion of T, therefore, will be $60 billion. This would be in contrast to the upward effect of an equal $30 billion of G, which would lead to a $90 billion increase in national income. We use the same factor (3) in each case, but we use a different starting point: $20 billion in the case of taxes, $30 billion in the case of an equivalent increase in government expenditures.

Why this asymmetry? The economic logic behind these differential effects can best be seen at the very first point of impact of G or T. When the government spends $1 to purchase some stationery for one of its offices, it has created in that very first step an added output (or income) of $1. This income then goes the rounds of consumption and saving, according to the multiplier principle. Now, when the government taxes $1, it lowers consumption demand and income immediately, but not by the full $1. The consumer, had there been no tax, would have *saved* part of this $1; in our case, the consumer would have saved 33 cents. This means that the initial impact of $1 taxes is to cut consumption demand not by $1, but by 67 cents. And this explains why the total effect of a $30 billion tax increase is only 2/3 as great as an equivalent increase in government expenditures ($60 billion as opposed to $90 billion).[6]

G AND T COMBINED—ALTERNATIVE FISCAL POLICIES

Having considered separately the effects on national income of expenditure and tax policies, we can now suggest various alternative approaches to fiscal policy, including those that require a balanced federal budget—that is, where expenditures and taxes are equal. Using Figure 8-6 as our reference point, let us suppose that the government's objective is to increase aggregate demand sufficiently to bring the economy to its full-employment level. From our original equilibrium at $850 billion, we wish to raise real national income to

[6] If the government expenditures are in the form of transfer payments, then the asymmetry between G and T disappears. *Reason:* part of the first dollar of G will be saved, that is, it will not all be used to purchase new goods or services. Thus, in effect, transfer payments can be looked on as *negative taxes*.

$910 billion. Let us examine three different ways of doing this, noting some of the main differences among them.

Increase Government Expenditures, Taxes Unchanged

In Figure 8-8, we have added *G'* to represent the increased government expenditures necessary to bring us to the full-employment level. The multiplier tells us how much the increase in government expenditures will have to be in numerical terms. Before *G'* was added, equilibrium national income was $850 billion. We wish to raise national income to the full-employment level, which is $910, that is, a rise of $60 billion. Assuming, as before, a multiplier of 3, we can find our answer simply by dividing the desired increase in na-

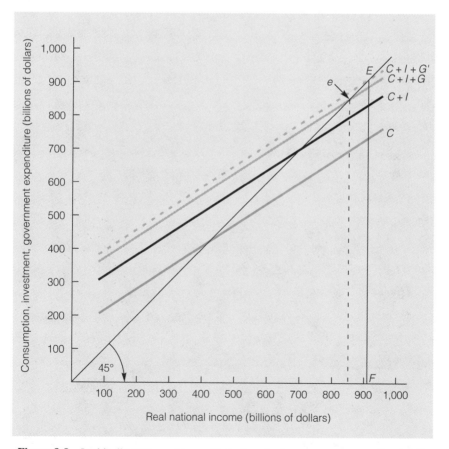

Figure 8-8   In this diagram, we have sufficiently raised government expenditures (*G*) to bring us to an equilibrium level of national income at full employment (assuming no change in tax revenues).

tional income, $60 billion, by 3. This gives us $20 billion, the amount by which we will have to increase government expenditures if we wish to bring national income to the full-employment level.

This method would involve a greater involvement of the government in the economy but a smaller addition to the federal deficit than the next method—tax reduction. It would, by contrast, involve a lesser involvement of the government in the economy but a greater federal deficit than the balanced-budget approach—our third alternative.

Reduce Taxes, Government Expenditures Unchanged

In Figure 8-9, we have left G unchanged but have reduced taxes sufficiently to bring national income to the full-employment level. This objective will

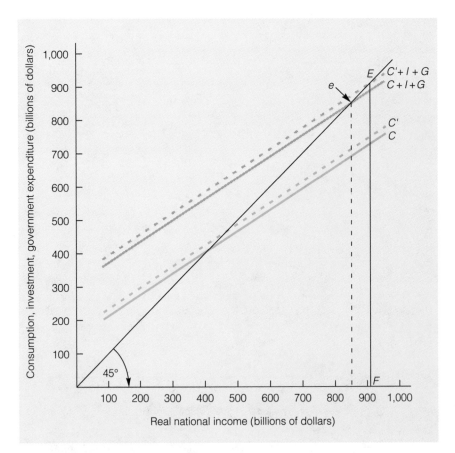

Figure 8-9 In this diagram, reduced taxes (T) have raised the consumption function to reach full-employment national income (no change in G).

require us to raise C to C', or by \$20 billion. From our discussion of taxes, however, we know that this will necessitate a \$30 billion reduction in taxes.

Thus, government involvement in the economy is less than under the expenditure increase policy, but the deficit has been increased by \$30 billion as opposed to \$20 billion.

Balanced-Budget Expansion

The final major route to full employment through fiscal policy is by way of a balanced-budget expansion—that is, increasing expenditures and taxes equally. Such an expansion will lead to some expansion in the economy, although each step forward (increased government demand) will be partially offset by a step backward (decreased private demand because of higher taxes). In Figure 8-10, the increased taxes are shown by the downward shift of C to C'', leaving a greater gap for government expenditures to fill than under either of the other policies.

Incidentally, the principle according to which national income will expand when there are equal increases of G and T is sometimes called the *balanced-budget multiplier.* The size of this multiplier will depend very much on the kind of taxes levied and expenditures undertaken. In our simplified case, however, the balanced-budget multiplier will be 1. That is, an equal increase of G and T will lead to an increase of national income of the same amount. This is essentially because the effects of G and T are the same, except that G has one extra round of impact—the very first—and in this first round, the full amount of government expenditures is added to national income. In our particular case, where the gap between the original level of national income and the full-employment level was \$60 billion, the balanced-budget approach would require a \$60 billion increase in both G and T. (To test your understanding of this matter, figure out for yourself how much of a downward shift in the consumption function has taken place in Figure 8-10). This would involve, as we have said, the greatest direct government involvement in the economy, but it would involve no net addition to the federal debt.

LIMITATIONS OF THIS PRELIMINARY ANALYSIS

Does this preliminary analysis of fiscal policy have any bearing on issues in the real-world U.S. economy? The answer to this question is somewhat complicated. In the early decades after World War II, when faith in fiscal policy was at its height, many economists believed that the above arguments, with minor qualifications, told a basically true story of the effects of fiscal policy on the economy. And there seemed to be some evidence to support this view. In 1964, for example, President Johnson secured passage of what is usually

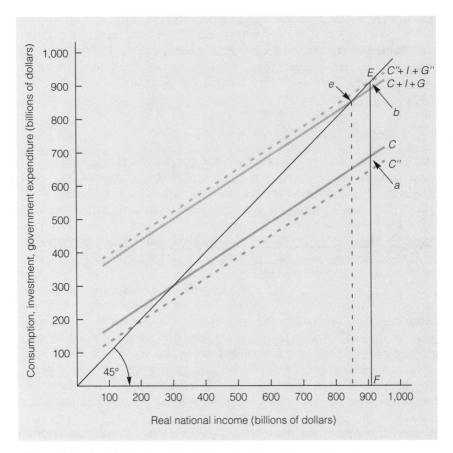

Figure 8-10   In this diagram, G and T have both been increased by the same amount (no increase in the federal deficit) to reach full employment. Taxes will lower C to C'', the distance a. We, therefore, have to increase G by $a + b$ to G''.

called the Kennedy-Johnson tax cut (President Kennedy had urged such action before his assassination) on the simple theoretical premise that cutting T would help revive a stagnating economy—our second method above. Actually, there were some economists at the time (notably John Kenneth Galbraith) who wanted to leave T alone and to increase G instead—our first method. Their argument was that more government spending was needed to meet important social objectives. In either case, however, the logic that we have just outlined offered a major rationale for the proposed policies.

   And the tax cut worked rather well. America did get "moving again," as Kennedy had wished, and the advocates of Keynesian-style fiscal policy invariably cited the 1964 episode as evidence of the basic truth of the kind of G and T analysis we have just presented.

However, fiscal policy was not always so successful as in 1964,[7] and by the 1980s, it had fallen considerably in general esteem. Thus, during the sharp recession of 1982–1983, some economists and a great majority of business executives and politicians were pointing to large federal deficits as one of the main *causes* of the depth of the recession, or at least as a major obstacle to recovering from it. A commonly expressed view went something like this:

> Suppose the government tries to cure a recession by some combination of increased expenditures and reduced taxes. Such actions will increase the public debt. The increase in the public debt will cause the government to compete with private borrowers, leading to an increase in interest rates. An increase in interest rates will cause a fall in investment, housing starts, spending on consumer durables, and the like. This reduction in aggregate demand will cancel out all or part of the expansionary effects of the fiscal policy. Furthermore, if the government tries to avoid borrowing by financing its deficit by creating more money, this will lead to a "printing press inflation"! The cure may be worse than the disease.

The terms of this argument carry us far beyond the simple "constant prices" world in which we have been operating so far. Money, interest rates, inflation—there is no way in which we can begin to evaluate fiscal policy as a cure for recession without entering fully into the complications of a monetary economy. In part 3, beginning with the next chapter, this is precisely what we shall do.

SUMMARY

In this chapter, we have considerably expanded our treatment of national income determination. We have introduced an important general tool of macroeconomics: the *multiplier.* The multiplier tells us by how much an increase in any kind of spending (consumption, investment, government) will raise the equilibrium level of national income. The size of the multiplier in a simplified economy is determined by the *marginal propensity to consume,* or the fraction of an extra dollar of income that consumers will spend on consumption. (The *marginal propensity to save,* by contrast, is the fraction of that extra dollar that consumers will be willing to save, or $MPS = 1 - MPC$.) The formula for the multiplier is:

$$m = \frac{1}{1 - MPC}$$

---

[7] One example of disappointing fiscal policy occurred in 1968, when the government tried to use a tax increase (a tax surcharge) to restrain demand during the Vietnam War, that is, the reverse of a policy designed to increase demand. The problem was that since the tax was regarded as temporary, it did not affect what consumers considered to be their "permanent income" (see chapter 7, footnote 2, p. 125) and, thus, had less than the expected effect on reducing consumption demand.

or, alternatively,

$$m = \frac{1}{MPS}$$

The economic logic behind multiple expansions of national income as spending expands centers on the fact that each stage of spending creates further incomes that, in their turn, lead to further spending, further income creation, further spending, and so on. Each time, however, the amounts added to income are less because part of the income is leaked into extra savings.

With the multiplier concept, we are much better able to understand an important phenomenon: the *business cycle*. Historically, there have been recurrent ups and downs of business conditions in the United States and other industrial nations that seem to show some common features, particularly periods of cumulative expansion leading to "peaks," which are followed by cumulative contractions leading to "troughs," and then recovery. Because of the existence of several different kinds of cycles, because of important external effects like wars, and because of government stabilization efforts in the postwar world, the business cycle is not a perfectly regular phenomenon. However, most economists do believe that certain internal (endogenous) mechanisms in our economy tend to give business conditions a cyclical character. The multiplier, along with other principles such as the *accelerator*, helps us to understand not only the cumulative nature of such expansions and contractions, but also possible reasons for the turning points at the peaks and troughs.

The multiplier concept also enables us to show what the effects of government expenditure and tax policies (collectively, *fiscal policy*) may be under certain simple circumstances:

1. An expansion of government expenditures (*G*) unmatched by an expansion of taxes would lead to a fully multiplied increase in national income.

2. An increase of taxes (*T*) unmatched by *G* would lead to a multiplied decrease in national income, though the total effect would be somewhat less than under point 1 because, in the first round, taxes cut down spending by less than the full amount of the tax. This, in turn, derives from the fact that part of the income taxed away would have been saved anyway.

3. An increase of *G* exactly matched by *T* will normally lead to an expansion of national income, the amount determined by the *balanced-budget multiplier*. Under our simplified assumptions, the balanced-budget multiplier is shown to be equal to 1.

Although the above points represent a preliminary understanding of fiscal policy, we cannot proceed further with this subject without investigating money, interest rates, and inflation. To these topics we turn in part 3.

Key Concepts for Review

Multiplier
Marginal propensity to consume
 (MPC)
Marginal propensity to save (MPS)
Business cycles
  Expansion
  Contraction (recession)
  Peak
  Trough
Exogenous versus endogenous
 factors
Acceleration principle

Fiscal policy
Government expenditures (G)
Taxes (T)
Asymmetry of T and G
Balanced-budget multiplier
Three policies to increase Y
  Increase G
  Decrease T
  Increase G and T equally
Preliminary nature of fiscal policy
 analysis

Questions for Discussion

1. Imagine that there is a change in tastes, resulting in an upward shift of the consumption function by $20 billion at each level of national income. Show how this could lead to an increase of $60 billion in national income if the MPC is 2/3. How much would the increase in national income be if the MPC were 4/5? 1/2? 9/10?

2. Our analysis in this chapter involved a number of simplifying assumptions. Some of the complications that may arise in reality are:
   (a) The MPC falls as the level of national income rises.
   (b) Investment is not a fixed amount, but increases as the level of national income increases.
   (c) Tax revenues of the federal government increase automatically (in the absence of any change in the tax structure) with any increase in national income.

   In each case, explain why these complications may arise. Then show what the general effect of each complication would be on the graphs we have been using in this chapter. Finally, indicate the ways we would have to modify our multiplier analysis to take these effects into account.

3. What is the acceleration principle? Explain how it might combine with the multiplier to account for cyclical activity in an industrial economy.

4. Why is it said that government expenditures and government taxation do not have a perfectly symmetrical effect on the economy? If instead of

ordinary government expenditures we were talking of transfer payments, would this have any effect on your analysis? If so, why?

5. Anticipating our future analysis, suggest some effects that price changes might have on the workings of the multiplier. (*Hint:* Suppose the increased demand that started the multiplier off led not just to increased real output, but to increased prices. Can you think of any way in which these higher prices might make you feel poorer, leading you to cut your demand in real terms, thus lowering the ultimate value of the multiplier?)

PART 3

THE ECONOMY IN THE AGGREGATE: MONEY, PRICES, AND INFLATION

CHAPTER 9

INFLATION AND AGGREGATE SUPPLY AND DEMAND

Until now, except for occasional references to inflation, we have been dealing with national income in constant prices. But prices *do* change, and, indeed, the upward movement of prices in recent years has been a fundamental feature of the United States and the world economy in general. In this chapter, we shall modify our analysis of aggregate supply and demand so that we can take price changes explicitly into account. As we shall see, this will lead us directly into the next chapter's discussion of money and banking. Let us begin, however, by getting a somewhat more definite notion of what modern inflation is and how it affects the public interest.

THE PHENOMENON OF INFLATION

By inflation, we mean any general increase in the price level of the economy in the aggregate. We are so used to such increases nowadays that it comes as something of a shock to us to realize that prices in the United States during the nineteenth century were on a *downward* trend—what we would call *deflation*. From 1814 to 1913, wholesale prices in the United States fell by some 44 percent. Similar decreases took place in other industrial countries such as Britain, Germany, and France. At one point in history, things actually cost *more* in the "good old days"! But not recently. Figure 5-3 (p. 92) showed us that U.S. prices have been rising constantly since World War II. By 1974, inflation had reached "double-digit" levels; in that year, the consumer price index rose by 11 percent. During the next two years, inflation abated somewhat, but then it accelerated again, reaching over 13 percent in 1980 and then declining sharply during the recession of 1982–1983. By the end of the 1980s, it was averaging between 4 and 5 percent a year.

Measures of Inflation

The phrase "general increase in the price level" may mean many different things, depending on what measure of prices is being used. In the United States, there are three main indices of inflation commonly referred to: (1) the consumer price index, (2) the producer price index, and (3) the GNP price deflator. The third index, which reflects the distinction between changes in *real* GNP and changes merely in money, or nominal, GNP, is the most general of these indices. When we talked about GNP in constant prices in earlier chapters, we were referring to this particular price deflator. For special purposes, however, we may be more interested in one of the other two. As consumers, we may have a direct concern about the consumer price index, since this attempts to estimate the cost of living as it affects the average American family. Also, there may be important government benefits or union-management wage contracts tied explicitly to the CPI.[1]

Moderate Versus Runaway Inflation

Even more important, however, is the fact that our definition does not properly distinguish between different kinds of inflation. In the very first chapter of this book, we mentioned the German hyperinflation of the 1920s, when the price index soared into the trillions. Now, this kind of runaway, or "galloping," inflation, with its enormously destructive effect on the whole fabric of society, has to be distinguished from the serious, but very different kind of, inflation that the United States has been experiencing, where prices have roughly tripled in the past 20 years.

Indeed, when we look at the world today, we find quite striking differences in the degree of inflationary pressure in different countries. In the less developed countries, and especially in certain Latin American countries, rapid year-to-year (or even week-to-week) inflation is a common occurrence. In February 1990, for example, Brazil's cost of living went up by 73 percent, the highest monthly increase in the country's history. Over the previous 12 months, the index had risen by 2,751 percent—that is to say, prices had risen over *twenty-eightfold* in one year. Neighboring Argentina was in even worse shape with price increases in early 1990 running at over 80 percent a month. The Argentine currency, the austral, which was trading at 17 to the dollar in early 1989, was trading at 4,800 to the dollar a year later.

---

[1] Remember, for example, our discussion of Social Security indexing, pp. 72–74.

The distinction between runaway, or galloping, inflation and moderate, or "creeping," inflation is clearly important in terms of effects. Runaway inflation can virtually destroy a nation's domestic economy and also its economic relations with other countries. Moderate inflation—which will be our main concern here—is more limited in its harmful effects. Though, of course, one of the important issues of our time is how much of a tendency there is for moderate inflations to accelerate into the more virulent variety.

Anticipated and Unanticipated Inflation

One of the reasons that moderate inflations may be transformed into runaway inflations is that consumers, laborers, and business firms begin to anticipate inflation and to alter their actions on the basis of these anticipations. One can imagine, for example, wage earners trying to keep a step ahead of inflation, demanding wage increases that exceed the current rate of inflation, thus helping to cause that rate of inflation to increase. Here inflation, in a real sense, is feeding on itself. In general, as we shall have many occasions to observe in the next several chapters, it makes a great difference whether we are dealing with inflation that is anticipated or completely or partly *un*anticipated.

EFFECTS OF INFLATION

What are the true costs of inflation? It is sometimes said that while unemployment causes severe hardship for a few, inflation causes hardship for everyone. At various times during recent decades, inflation has been called "the cruelest tax of all," or "America's number one economic problem!"

An Important Misunderstanding

But are such judgments really accurate? There *are* important costs to inflation, yet these strong pronouncements often seem to be based on an elementary misunderstanding of the way economic systems work. The misunderstanding stems from the fact that people may fail to connect the process that raises prices with processes that raise their earnings, with which they will meet these increased costs. They sometimes talk as if every rise in prices impoverishes them by exactly how much less they can buy with a given income. Or they may speak disparagingly about how little a dollar is worth now, failing to ask at the same time how many more dollars per week or per year they and other people now earn.

Such an approach is clearly inadequate. We know from our earlier discussion of the concept of GNP that a rise in the money value of output will also necessarily be a rise in the money value of national income. They are two different ways of looking at the same thing. Figure 9-1 shows that per-

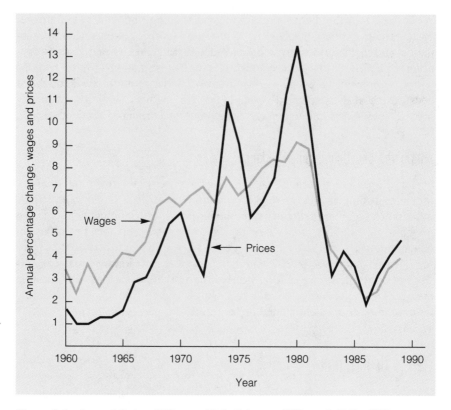

Figure 9-1   Annual Rates of Change, U.S. Prices and Wages,* 1960–1989
In general, money incomes and prices tend to move together. Inflation may directly
impoverish some people, but not everyone.
SOURCE: *Economic Report of the President*, 1990.
* Price changes are for the consumer price index (1982–1984 = 100); wage changes are for
average hourly earnings of private, nonagricultural workers.

centage increases in U.S. prices (as measured by the CPI) and wages (as
measured by average hourly earnings) have generally gone together during
the past three decades. (Actually, wages have gone up substantially more
than prices over the whole post–World War II period, although this has not
been true of more recent years.) To speak of the harmful effects of a general
rise in prices on the assumption that *all* money incomes in the society remain
unchanged is a contradiction in terms.

Changes in the Distribution of Income

Although all incomes may be rising to some degree in an inflation, some income receivers will be gaining much more rapidly than others. The people
who will be hurt are those living on fixed pensions or on the interest from

government or other bonds, or salaried individuals employed by institutions like churches, which may find it difficult to adjust their pay scales to rapid increases in the cost of living. These distributional changes seem particularly unfortunate in that they are quite arbitrary, having nothing whatever to do with the merits of the people involved nor with their relative ability to sustain decreases in real income.

This cost of inflation can easily be overstated, however, since it is by no means clear that these distributional changes particularly benefit the rich as opposed to the poor. Indeed, the group that might seem particularly vulnerable to inflation—elderly widows and pensioners—has been largely protected by increases in Social Security payments, which have exceeded the wage increases of employed persons in recent years. When inflation is *anticipated* in this way, many of its effects on the redistribution of income can be nullified.

Changes in the Position of Creditor, Debtor, Saver

Inflation undermines the value of past savings if these savings are held in a form that represents a fixed claim on money (such as savings accounts, government bonds, life insurance policies, and so on). If the quantity of money in the economy generally is fixed, a rise in prices will lower the *real* value of this money supply. More generally, inflation may alter the debtor-creditor relationship. Creditors suffer because the real value of their credit falls, and debtors benefit because their debts are also falling in real value. Thus, inflation involves not only a redistribution of income, but also a possible redistribution of the stock of wealth in the community.

Again, however, these effects may often be modified, depending on the extent to which they are anticipated. As a creditor, if I know that the real value of the repayment of my loan some years hence will be substantially reduced by inflation, then I will attempt to incorporate an inflation premium in the interest rate I charge on that debt. If inflation turns out to be slower than anticipated, then, in fact, it will be the creditor rather than the debtor who will benefit from inflation.

The Government as Beneficiary

Insofar as debtors do benefit from inflation, the greatest beneficiary in contemporary American society would tend to be the largest single debtor—the federal government. Indeed, some economists have pointed out that statistics on our annual federal government deficits are misleadingly high because they fail to take into account each year's reduction in the *real* value of the existing public debt due to rising prices.[2] Also, the government tends to benefit when

---

[2] This point was stressed by Professor Robert Eisner in his presidential address to the American Economics Association on December 29, 1988. According to Eisner, we should "in effect be including in

taxes are based on nominal, or money, values rather than real values. Suppose I make a *capital gain* of 10 percent on a stock I am holding. If prices in general have gone up by 10 percent that year, then the real value of my stock is unchanged—that is, I am no better off than if I had sold the stock at its original price and there had been zero inflation. In the inflationary case, however, I would have to pay a tax on the gain, meaning that inflation had effectively caused a transfer of wealth from me to the government.

Furthermore, insofar as there is any *progressivity* in our tax structure, this will also tend to favor the government. A progressive income tax is such that the percentage of income taxed rises as the level of nominal income rises. Thus, an inflationary rise in nominal income, without any change in real income, will result in a higher percentage of income being taxed. Our federal income tax is basically progressive in its impact, although the Tax Reform Act of 1986 largely eliminated progressivity for high income (around $250,000 and above) families. In general, the more progressive the tax structure, the more inflation will increase the real value of revenues going to the state.

Production, Planning, and Uncertainty

The effects of inflation, which we have discussed above, while arbitrary and in many ways unfortunate, would not seem in themselves to justify the great alarms many Americans have felt about inflation in recent years, particularly, one might add, when by anticipating and adjusting to inflation (as, for example, by indexing the tax system), one can mitigate many of those effects.

What one should conclude from this is not, however, that inflation is relatively harmless, but that its costs lie less in its distributional effects than in the damage it does to the workings of the economy as a whole. High levels of inflation tend also to be highly *variable* levels of inflation. In general, inflation increases the level of uncertainty in the economy. Planning for the future may be more difficult if tomorrow's prices are substantially and unpredictably different from today's. Many economists feel that the entire efficiency of the market system depends on the possibility of long-term, more or less customary relationships between buyers and sellers, relationships heavily dependent on the use of money as a yardstick and store of value. Inflation upsets these customary relationships, blurs the signals given off by the price system from one sector of industry to another, and requires costly rearrangements that take time, money, and information to set up, which, if the inflation continues or changes direction, then have to be reworked all over again.

---

government revenues the *inflation tax* on the private holders of government securities or the money backed by the central bank holdings of those securities." By his calculations, this inflation adjustment alone reduced the official 1988 federal deficit of $155 billion by $72 billion, or almost half. (Robert Eisner, "Divergences of Measurement and Theory and Some Implications for Economic Policy," *American Economic Review*, vol. 79, no. 1 (March 1989): 5.)

Some economists attributed the slowdown in the rate of productivity increase in the United States in the 1970s partly to these difficulties caused by high inflation.[3]

Furthermore, the very possibility of mitigating the harmful effects of inflation by adjusting our actions, attitudes, and institutions to its existence is likely to intensify the inflationary process. A perfectly "indexed" society may have few harmful distributional effects from inflation, but it is almost guaranteed to have a high rate of inflation. The danger of acceleration from moderate to runaway inflation cannot be ignored.

Finally, we have to recognize that the effort to reduce inflation, or at least to prevent it from accelerating, may involve serious costs. Economists differ on the extent and nature of these costs (matters we shall discuss in later chapters) yet many feel that the sharp recession the American economy experienced in the early 1980s—involving well over 10 percent unemployment—was basically a cost we had to pay to keep inflationary forces from getting out of hand. We shall have many opportunities to discuss the relationship between inflation and unemployment in later chapters.

In short, while the picture is somewhat mixed—inflation certainly does not "impoverish" everyone in the simpleminded way it is sometimes claimed—nevertheless, it is clear that inflation does contribute greatly to the complexity and uncertainty of economic life, adversely affects the production process, has a tendency to accelerate, and is far from costless to control.

AGGREGATE DEMAND AS A FUNCTION OF PRICE

Having made a few comments about the nature of inflation and its effects, we now must begin our analysis of the causes of inflation. We have already taken one small step in this direction when, in chapter 7 (Figure 7-5, p. 135), we spoke of the possibility of a Keynesian demand-pull inflation. As we noted then, however, that kind of inflation represents a rather special case. Furthermore, the tools we were using to analyze national income in constant prices are obviously ill suited to studying inflation, which precisely involves changing prices. What we want to do in the remainder of this chapter is to remedy this defect of our analysis by introducing prices explicitly into our argument. We begin with aggregate demand.

In Figure 9-2, the curve $C + I$ represents aggregate demand in a private economy as a function of the level of real national income at a given price level, P. Our first question may be put as follows: What happens to this curve if the price level is different from P? Suppose we have a higher price level, P'. What effect will this have on the $C + I$ curve?

This question, in turn, can be broken down into two separate questions:

---

[3] We'll return to this issue again in chapter 15, pp. 309–310.

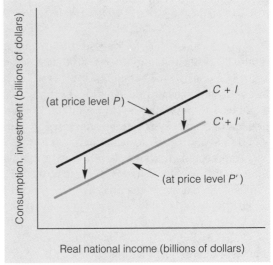

Figure 9-2 At higher price levels ($P' > P$), the $C + I$ curve will shift downward.

(1) What effect will the higher price level have on the consumption function? and (2) What effect will it have on the level of investment demand?

Both these questions require us to bring the money supply of our economy into the analysis. Since we begin our serious discussion of the money supply in the next chapter, the answers we give now will be only preliminary. It will be sufficient for the moment, however, if we can indicate the general direction of the shift in the $C + I$ curve in response to higher prices. Fortunately, the effect of higher prices will generally be to lower both the consumption and investment components of aggregate demand, meaning that the curve will shift in Figure 9-2 from $C + I$ to $C' + I'$.

In the case of consumption, an important reason for the downward shift of demand will be that higher prices will mean a reduction in the *real wealth* of consumers. Take the simplest case, where everyone holds his wealth in money in the bank. Suppose P' represents a price level twice that of P. Assuming everyone's bank balances are unchanged (that the quantity of money is unchanged), then the *real* value of consumer wealth will be halved when prices go from P to P'. For a given level of real income, consumers will feel poorer, and they will want to spend less of their real income. Hence, the consumption function will fall.

Investment demand will also be lower in the high price (P') as opposed to the low price (P) situation. Basically, this decline will take place because higher prices will require the use of more money to carry out the day-to-day business of the economy; there will be less left over to finance investment. In one way or another, this will increase the cost of investing (usually, by a rise in the interest rate, as we shall see later on) and bring I down as well as C. The net effect of the higher price level is shown, therefore, by the shift to $C' + I'$ shown in Figure 9-2.

But how do we get from this shifting of our consumption-plus-investment curve to an aggregate demand curve expressed in terms of prices? We accomplish this task in Figure 9-3. In Figure 9-3(a), we have drawn in a 45° line. Although this 45° line is familiar to us from earlier chapters, we have to say a word of caution about it now:

> The 45° line in this diagram is really a guideline to show us where consumption-plus-investment demand will equal national income. It cannot be used as our new aggregate supply curve for two reasons: (1) we will now want an aggregate supply curve that expresses supply as a function of price—that is, we will be measuring

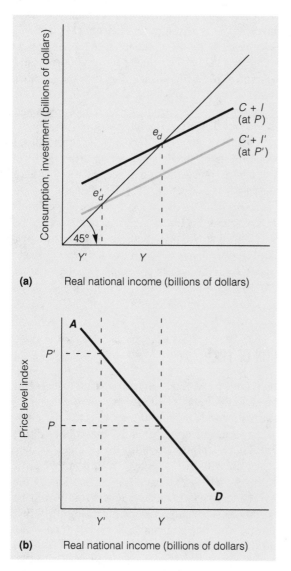

Figure 9-3 Derivation of the Aggregate Demand Curve

the price level on the vertical axis; and (2) we assumed earlier (chapter 7, footnote 7, p. 132) that prices and wages were such that business firms were receiving "normal profits" (no more, no less) at each level of national income. In the next few pages, however, we will be investigating precisely the possibility that profits at any given level of prices and output may be "too high" (leading to an expansion of aggregate supply) or "too low" (leading to a contraction of aggregate supply).

Given the 45° line, we have drawn in a $C + I$ curve and a $C' + I'$ curve and marked their intersections with this line with e_d and e_d', respectively. We use the subscript d to suggest that these intersections represent equilibrium positions on the demand side. Take the point e_d. At this point, where the price level is P and the level of real national income is Y, the demand of households for consumption goods and the demand of business investors for investment goods will exactly be satisfied. If at that price level, P, national income were higher than Y, then there would be excess output that neither consumers nor investors would demand (we are leaving out government for the moment). Suppose, on the other hand, that, at that level of national income, Y, prices were higher than P. This would also mean that there was excess output beyond that which consumers and investors would demand at that price level. Only at the intersection of the $C + I$ curve with the 45° line do we have equilibrium on the demand side at price level P. Similarly, e_d' is a point of equilibrium on the demand side at price level P'.

We present these intersections as points on a demand curve in Figure 9-3(b). This time we are measuring price on the vertical axis and output on the horizontal, as in the case of an ordinary industry demand curve such as we developed in chapter 2. The difference, of course, is that we are now dealing with the price *level* and *national* output, rather than the price and output of a particular industry. Although the reasoning is more complex, notice that the general shape of our aggregate demand curve (*AD*) will be downward sloping to the right. It does, therefore, bear at least a family resemblance to the industry demand curves of our earlier analysis.

AGGREGATE SUPPLY AS A FUNCTION OF PRICE

But what of an aggregate supply curve as a function of the price level? Will it, too, bear a family resemblance to the industry supply curves of chapter 2?

Now, in the case of a particular industry, a higher price for the commodity in question called forth a greater supply, that is, the supply curve tended to slope upward to the right. This higher price for the product—given a certain level of wages and other costs in the industry—meant higher profits, which would stimulate businessmen to expand their production of the commodity. In the longer run, if the profits persisted, new firms would be attracted into the field, and so on. In short, high prices meant high profits, which meant expansion; similarly, low prices meant low profits (or losses) and, hence, a reason to cut back on production.

The above logic has, however, a *ceteris paribus* clause built into it. Basically, we are assuming that the price of this commodity can go up or down with little or no effect on the prices the firms in the industry have to pay for their factors of production, labor, land, and capital. With these other prices constant, a rise in the price of this commodity will mean higher profits. When we are dealing with *national* output and the price *level,* however, such an assumption is no longer valid. When there is a general increase in the price level, this may be accompanied by a general increase in wages, raw material costs, interest payments, and so on, and there is no guarantee that this will be accompanied by higher profits. Prices of commodities, as we know, are basically decomposable into factor incomes plus profits. How can we be sure that higher prices in general will lead to higher profits in general? Wages, after all, may be going up even faster than prices. But if higher prices will not guarantee higher profits, how can we be sure that higher prices will lead to expansions in aggregate supply? In diagrammatic terms, how can we be sure that the aggregate supply curve will have the general shape we have given it in Figure 9-4?

The simple answer is that we *cannot* be sure of this. As we will have frequent occasion to mention in later chapters, one of the main differences separating various schools of modern-day economists is their opinion about the shape and position of the aggregate supply curve and how that curve shifts over time. In order to get a northeasterly sloping aggregate supply curve, we have to find some reasons for believing that higher commodity prices will, at least in the short run, outdistance factor costs—for simplicity, wages. Only in this way will higher prices be associated with higher profits (and lower prices with lower profits) for the economy in the aggregate. There

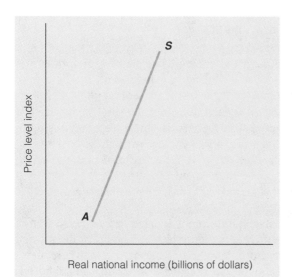

Figure 9-4   A Short-run Aggregate Supply Curve
If factor costs lag behind prices (for example, because of long-run contracts or because price increases are not anticipated), then the short-run aggregate supply curve will slope upward toward the northeast.

are basically two reasons for believing that this may, in fact, be the case in the short run:

> *Reason 1:* The higher level of prices may be unanticipated, meaning that wage costs may temporarily lag behind. In this event, profits will be higher, with higher prices leading to increased aggregate supply in the short run. Another way of putting this is to say that *real* wages may fall with higher prices, meaning that it will be profitable for business firms to hire more labor at the going money wage. Labor has, so to speak, been caught off guard by the higher price level.

> *Reason 2:* There may be long-term contracts that make it impossible to adjust factor costs to price changes, either up or down, except after a certain period of time. In the interim, a higher price will mean lower real wages and incentives to increase employment and production; conversely, a lower price level will mean higher real wages and, thus, an incentive to decrease employment and production. Since labor contracts often cover a period of years (frequently three years), such lags are quite common. Moreover, even individual wage earners or salaried employees do not make continuous and immediate adjustments in their wages or salaries as prices change. Hence, short-run gaps can open up between costs and prices, affecting profits and, hence, the motive for expanding or contracting output and employment.

For these two reasons, we have drawn our aggregate supply curve, *AS*, in Figure 9-4 as sloping upward to the right. This is a subject we will have to come back to again, particularly since the reasoning we have used above is so clearly short run in nature. For the moment, however, we assume that the lags in adjustment are such that a higher price level will generally mean a higher level of profits and, hence, a motive for supplying more output in the aggregate.

EQUILIBRIUM OF AGGREGATE SUPPLY AND DEMAND

Having both an aggregate demand and an aggregate supply curve drawn as functions of the price level, we can now determine the overall equilibrium in our economy. This will be where the two curves intersect (at point $e_{d,s}$ in Figure 9-5), at the price level P_e and the level of real national income Y_e. Notice that this equilibrium is more complete than the equilibrium level we discussed in chapter 7. Then, we assumed constant prices and determined the level of real national income. Now, we determine the level of real national income *and* the equilibrium level of prices. We have moved an important step forward and, in so doing, have developed a tool that permits us to analyze price changes as well as quantity changes in our economy.

It is one thing to assert that equilibrium will occur at the intersection of our two curves, but a rather different matter to have a feeling for the process involved. Let us suppose, therefore, that the price level is somewhere above P_e. Why will this not be an equilibrium situation? On the demand side, this

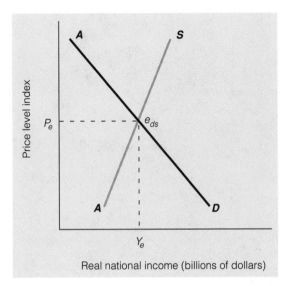

Figure 9-5   Equilibrium of Aggregate Supply and Demand   This analysis enables us to determine the equilibrium level of national income (Y_e) and the equilibrium price level (P_e) at the same time.

higher price level will be associated with a downward shift of our $C + I$ curve (Figure 9-2) and, hence, a lower level of national income demanded (Figure 9-3). At this higher price level, then, the demand for output will be lower than Y_e. Meanwhile, on the supply side, the higher price will mean (by our short-run assumptions) higher profits and, hence, a desire of business firms to expand output beyond Y_e. The quantity supplied will, therefore, exceed the quantity demanded at this higher price level. Now, in chapter 7, when aggregate supply exceeded aggregate demand, the result was an increase in business inventories, and this unwanted acquisition of unsold goods caused businesses to contract production. The same thing happens again now in our more complete analysis—that is, unwanted inventories will start building up—but we will also have downward pressure on prices. (This was part of the picture we could not handle in our constant price world.) Indeed, only when prices fall back to P_e will we get overall equilibrium of both prices and output in the whole economy. "Too high" prices, therefore, lead to a correction back to our intersection at $e_{d,s}$. (The reader should go through the same logic in reverse for the case of a price level below P_e.)

Does this equilibrium level of national income, Y_e, coincide with full-employment national income? Not necessarily, or at least not as far as anything we have yet said is concerned. In Figure 9-6, we show a situation in which the equilibrium level of national income, Y_e, clearly falls short of full-employment potential national income, *FE*. According to this analysis, we still have the possibility of massive unemployment such as occurred in the 1930s, which was a main purpose of Keynesian theory to explain.

In a preliminary way, however, we might ask, Aren't there *any* natural forces that might move this economy closer to the full-employment level,

Figure 9-6 Unemployment Equilibrium Since Y_e is below full-employment (*FE*) national income in this diagram, the economy could still be facing Keynesian-style mass unemployment. Critics, however, suggest that by bringing money wages down, we might be able to shift the aggregate supply curve to the right, either partly or wholly remedying the problem.

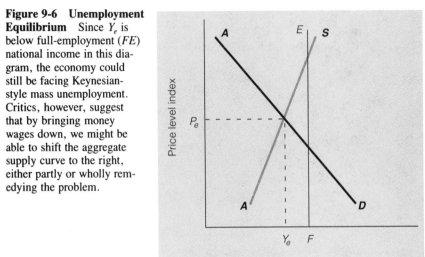

from Y_e toward *FE*? Clearly, an argument could be made that there are such forces. Suppose that, with massive unemployment, laborers throughout the economy decide that they are willing to work for lower wages. The lowering of wages, for any given level of prices, will mean higher profits and, therefore, a motive for expanding output. Technically, a lower level of wages will mean an outward shift of the aggregate supply curve. We could, indeed, imagine this curve shifting farther and farther to the right with each lowering of wages until full-employment equilibrium was reached.

With this picture in mind, many critics of Keynesian economics claimed that his theory really worked at all only if you assumed that money wages were rigid—that is, the reason people were out of work was simply that they wouldn't allow money wages to fall to an appropriate level. Labor, in a sense, was simply pricing itself out of the market.

Whether we approve or disapprove of it, such behavior on the part of labor may be fairly common. Labor unions, feeling that unemployment is temporary whereas wage cuts may be permanent, may, indeed, resist any downward revisions of their wage rates. So Keynes might simply have replied that, like it or not, the assumption of rigid wages (at least in a downward direction) was more realistic than an assumption of perfectly flexible wages.

Keynes's main response, however, was a different one. He said that while *lower* wages might help move the economy toward full employment, the process by which one got to lower wages might actually cause an opposite effect. *Falling* wages would be accompanied by *falling* prices, and these, in turn, might have such a damaging effect on business *expectations* that aggregate supply might be adversely, rather than positively, affected.

This last point is worth noting. Whether a valid response to the critics or not, it brings home the important difference between a "low" or a "high" something and a "falling" or a "rising" something. Even more important, it emphasizes the role of expectations in this whole area of macroeconomics. How expectations are formed and whether they are "rational" or "irrational" turns out to be the key to many economic puzzles, though it also creates a few puzzles of its own.

We will get into such problems again later on, but now we must attempt to fill a gap that has become obvious during the course of this chapter. We were forced to bring in the subject of money when we were constructing our aggregate curves, yet, in fact, we have not even said "officially" what money is. In the next two chapters, we shall repair this omission, defining the nature of money and explaining some of the controversies about its role in the economy at large.

S U M M A R Y

Inflation is the economist's term for a general rise in prices, though there are many different measures and kinds of inflation: some anticipated, some unanticipated, some very rapid, others (like that of the United States in recent years) more moderate (though U.S. inflation did have a period of acceleration in the late 1970s).

The harmful effects of a moderate inflation are sometimes overstated by those who fail to realize that rising prices and rising incomes (wages, salaries, profits, and so on) are not separable phenomena. However, even a moderate inflation, especially if unanticipated, is likely to have some undesirable effects on the income distribution, the position of creditors versus debtors, the finances of the government versus the private sector, and the like. Probably even more serious is the fact that rapid inflation tends to be variable inflation, and this increases the general uncertainty of economic planning and may have serious effects on the productivity of the economy. Also, there is the danger that moderate inflations may tend to accelerate unless controlled; these controls, moreover, may involve serious costs to the economy.

In order to begin the analysis of inflation, one must abandon the constant price assumption of part 2 and introduce curves of aggregate demand and supply expressed as functions of prices. Other things equal, a higher price level will mean a lower level of consumption and investment demand. Higher prices will mean lower real wealth for consumers and, thus, bring a downward shift in the consumption function. A higher price level will also, for a given quantity of money, reduce the funds available for investment (for example, by raising interest rates), thus lowering the investment schedule as well. Thus, the aggregate demand curve will tend to slope downward in a southeasterly direction.

The short-run aggregate supply curve, like an ordinary industry supply curve, is likely to slope upward in a northeasterly direction; the logic behind this shape is, however, somewhat more complicated in the aggregate case. A higher price level will mean more profits (and, therefore, a reason to expand production) only if factor costs—for example, wages—lag behind the higher price level. In the short run, this may often be the case if the higher prices are not anticipated in advance and/or there are fixed contracts that keep wages and salaries from increasing as rapidly as prices. We shall return to the question of the shape and position of the aggregate supply curve, particularly in the long run, later on.

Given both an aggregate demand and aggregate supply curve, we can now determine simultaneously both the level of national income *and* the price level. This equilibrium level of national income is not necessarily at full employment, though there are those who argue that employment can be improved if labor accepts lower wages, thus shifting the aggregate supply curve to the right. This controversial question we shall also return to later.

Key Concepts for Review

Inflation
Deflation
Measures of inflation
   Consumer price index
   Producer price index
   GNP price deflator
Moderate ("creeping") inflation
Runaway ("galloping") inflation
Effects of inflation
   Income distribution
   Creditor versus debtor
   Production, planning, and
     efficiency

Anticipated versus unanticipated
   inflation
Aggregate demand as a function of the
   price level
Aggregate supply as a function of the
   price level
Price changes and
   Consumer real wealth
   Investment demand
   Lagging factor costs
Long-term contracts
Equilibrium of national income and the
   price level

Questions for Discussion

1. Distinguish between the harmful effects of a runaway inflation and a moderate inflation. Why might a moderate inflation tend to be cumulative? Does American experience in recent years suggest to you that we are or are not moving toward a runaway inflation?

2. "Inflation is an even worse threat to our economic well-being than depression; for whereas depression impoverishes only some of us, inflation impoverishes us all." Discuss.

3. Explain why inflation, particularly high and variable inflation, might have negative effects on a nation's productivity.

4. Explain why a higher price level, other things equal, might lead to (a) lower consumer demand and (b) lower investment demand.

5. Give the reasons for thinking that the aggregate supply curve may slope upward in a northeasterly direction. How do these reasons differ from those we might apply to a supply curve for an individual firm within the economy? Using your answer as a basis, discuss the following statement: "Although macroeconomics and microeconomics are ultimately related, one does require a slightly different approach for each field."

6. Does the equilibrium of our aggregate supply and demand curves necessarily bring us to full employment? If not, are there any forces tending to do so? What might be some of the counterforces?

C H A P T E R   10

MONEY AND BANKING

One of the paradoxes of the field of economics is that most of its subject matter is quite familiar to the man in the street (who, indeed, often has strong views on economic issues!) and yet may be decidedly puzzling to those who have spent a lifetime studying it. One reason the "experts" have so much difficulty with what are apparently commonplace matters is that economic issues are ultimately embedded in human history; they are subject, therefore, to the mysteries of human psychology and also to considerable change and variation over time. No better example of this paradox can be found than the subject of *money*. Everyone is familiar with money. The subject has been studied by economists since ancient times; yet, in fact, there is to this day no *general* agreement among economists as to the precise impact of money on the workings of our economic system. Indeed, when it comes down to specifics, even the *definition* of money seems to keep changing, almost on a month-to-month basis.

WHAT IS MONEY?

Despite these difficulties, the experts do have a number of useful things to say on this particular subject. Economists often distinguish three important functions that money serves: (1) *a medium of exchange* (money is acceptable for exchanges against all different types of commodities), (2) *a measure of value* (prices are quoted in money), and (3) *a store of value* (savings may be kept in the form of money for future purchases). If someone puts to us the question, What is money? our answer might be: any thing, object, or commodity that serves these functions. Notice that this answer is rooted in human psychology from the beginning. Money can only be money if it is accepted by people as money. You may think your beads and shells are money, but if I and other people will not accept them in exchange for goods generally, then you'll obviously have to rethink the whole subject.

The Inconvenience of Barter

Suppose there is no thing, object, or commodity that serves these functions, can an economic system still exist? I will not accept your beads and shells; you will not accept my buffalo hides; neither of us will accept John Doe's live cattle. Can we still get along? The answer is yes, but with great difficulty, and a realization of this difficulty is an appreciation of just how useful money truly is. Imagine that we are in a barter economy in which there is no generally accepted money, and yet we must trade with other people to get the goods we want. In my workshop, being handy at these things, I have produced a cassette recorder; however, I already have a cassette recorder, and what I really need is a tuxedo. My problem is to find someone who has a tuxedo for sale but, at the same time, happens to want a cassette recorder. This requirement is what economists usually call a *double coincidence of wants*. It clearly imposes tremendous waste and inefficiency on the economic system. When money, as often seems to be the case, causes great difficulties in our economy, we must not lose sight of its enormously important role in facilitating efficient transactions throughout the system.

Any Commodity Can Serve as Money (and Probably Has)

Not all commodities serve equally well as money, but the role of money is so important to the economic system that, under appropriate conditions, almost any commodity can be adapted to a monetary use. Historically, many different commodities have served in this capacity in different cultures and times, including paper, gold, other metals, beads, shells, hides, and cattle. In an article written just after World War II, R. A. Radford, a British economist, described the elaborate use of cigarettes as currency in a prisoner of war camp. In the POW camp, cigarettes served all the functions we have mentioned above. Prices, for example, were generally quoted in terms of cigarettes, rather than in terms of particular commodities that might be bartered against each other. But cigarettes also suffered from some difficulties in serving as money. For one thing, like gold coins in the hands of a deceitful sovereign, they could be "clipped" or, more likely, "sweated by rolling them between the fingers so that tobacco fell out." More serious was the fact that they were a very desirable commodity in their own right. Radford notes that when Red Cross packages (the main source of the supply of cigarettes) failed to arrive, the smokers were likely to take over the money supply of the nation.[1] Despite these problems, it was still better to have cigarettes as money than no money at all.

Evolution of Money over Time

Although any commodity *can* serve as money, there has been a very significant evolution in the direction of more efficient monetary instruments over time, an evolution that is still continuing today. In the old days, gold, silver, and other metals were often chosen in preference to other commodities because they had a number of desirable properties: they were limited in quantity and availability, had some useful value of their own, were durable, and were easily divisible. Paper currency was a further improvement in terms of convenience and efficiency. It could, moreover, be issued in the form of gold or silver certificates so that, in principle, paper simply served as a convenient surrogate for the previous metals. As paper currency became acceptable in its own right, it became possible to sever its ties to its metallic base. In the early years after World War II, for example, the U.S. Treasury was ready to buy and sell gold at a fixed rate of $35 an ounce; in mid-1973, however, the last remaining tie of the dollar to gold was severed. As far as one can judge, the complete divorce of our currency from a gold base had no effect whatever on the acceptability of U.S. currency as a general medium of exchange. Meanwhile, currency itself has long since been displaced as the main source of money in our economy by deposits in banks and other financial institutions. This source, too, has been going through a vigorous evolution in recent years.

MONEY AND THE BANKING SYSTEM

Most money in the American economy today is not in the form of currency, but in the form of bank deposits. A couple of decades ago, it was relatively easy to describe the deposits that were components of our money supply, since they consisted basically of ordinary checking accounts—what we call *demand deposits* (that is, deposits subject to withdrawal on demand). Today, however, there is a plethora of different kinds of accounts, not only in banks, but in other institutions as well. These range from the negotiable order of withdrawal accounts (NOW accounts), which pay a low interest rate and are sometimes included in a category called "other checkable deposits," all the

---

[1] R. A. Radford, "The Economic Organization of a P.O.W. Camp," *Economica*, vol. 12 (1945).

way to our various credit card accounts, where we have credit limits that determine how much we can withdraw and where we pay a charge for the advances made.

Students sometimes feel that their checking accounts are not really the equivalent of money because occasionally personal checks (say, in a strange town) are not accepted as money, whereas cash would be. However, reflection should convince us that what is being doubted here is not the value of the deposit behind the check, but whether such a deposit does, in fact, exist. Doubts about accepting a check disappear once it is certain that "the money is in the bank to back it up"—that is, that the person presenting the check has the necessary deposit in the same name.

Fractional-Reserve Banking

It is true that a bank must occasionally redeem checking deposits in currency. But the central fact about modern banking is that the bank does not need to back up its checking deposits with an equivalent amount of cash and currency, but only with a fraction of that amount. We operate on a system of *fractional-reserve banking*. Withdrawals and deposits generally tend to cancel out. In the ordinary course of business, as some employers are withdrawing funds, say, to meet their payrolls, employees will be depositing their paychecks from other firms. Only a relatively small fraction of checking deposits needs to be kept on hand to meet excesses of withdrawals over deposits at any given time. In point of fact, the main reserves that commercial banks hold today are those that they are legally required to hold. Only a portion of these cash reserves are actually held in the bank in the form of *vault cash;* a larger amount is held in the form of deposits with *Federal Reserve banks*.

Measures of Money

Table 10-1 shows us various components of the money supply as of November 1989. Notice that we refer here to money as a *stock*. A *stock* of something—number of pairs of shoes, books on our shelves, cans of soup, or whatever—is the quantity of that item that we have at a *moment of time*. It is in contrast to a *flow* of something, which measures the quantity of something over a *period of time*. Income and output concepts are flow concepts—so many dollars per week or month, so many bushels of wheat per year, and so on. To measure the money stock, however, we do not need a period of time, but only a date. Since we sometimes use the term "money" loosely to refer to "income"—for example, "How much money did you make last year?"— we have to be very careful to avoid confusion here.

We see from Table 10-1 that demand and other checkable deposits (including NOW and certain other accounts) totaled $562.3 billion and were

TABLE 10-1 Measures of U.S. Money Stock,* November 1989 (Billions of Dollars)

Components of Money Stock (Selected)

Currency	$ 220.3
Demand deposits	279.0
Other checkable deposits	283.3
Savings deposits	409.4
Small-denomination time deposits	1,131.2
Large-denomination time deposits	560.0

*Overall Measures of Money Stock***

M_1 (currency plus demand deposits, other checkable deposits, travelers' checks)	$ 790.0
M_2 (M_1 plus savings deposits, small time deposits, money market deposit accounts, certain money market mutual funds, other)	$3,198.9
M_3 (M_2 plus large time deposits, money market fund balances [institution only], other)	$4,047.3

SOURCE: Adapted from Board of Governors of the Federal Reserve System, *Federal Reserve Bulletin* (February 1990): A 13–14.

*Seasonally adjusted.

**Various measures of money (M_1, M_2, and so on) tend to merge with each other near the margins. There are also near-monies (for example, U.S. government bonds) that are for some purposes (though not for all purposes) similar to money. Except when otherwise specified, we shall think of money as M_1, or, very roughly, "transactions money."

over two and a half times greater than currency ($220.3 billion). These categories together (plus the small category of travelers' checks) comprise one definition of money, M_1. M_1 is sometimes referred to as *transactions money*, since the funds involved are usually being employed to carry out the day-to-day business of life, as opposed to being set aside for savings and other future uses. Other definitions of money, however, include a broader group of instruments. M_2 equals M_1 plus certain time and savings deposits and money market funds. M_3 equals M_2 plus large-denomination time deposits and certain other balances, including money market mutual funds available only to institutions.

The fact is that we are on a spectrum here. Money market deposit accounts and mutual funds, included in M_2 but not M_1, clearly are often used for transactions purposes. At the other end of the scale, there is little to distinguish savings accounts and time deposits from a variety of *near-monies*—say, Treasury bills or government bonds—which are not officially included in our money definitions. In general, in this textbook, we shall think of "money" as being M_1, unless otherwise specified. There will be occasions, however, when we will find other definitions of greater use. No matter which definition we employ, however, we must never forget that money cannot be identified with *folding green* or pictures of American statesmen. The banking system is crucial to our money supply, and *deposit creation* is at the heart of the banking system's role in the economy.

THE BALANCE SHEET OF AN INDIVIDUAL BANK

Deposit *creation?* That may sound rather illegal, or at least questionable. Are not checking deposits created by our depositing "money" in a commercial bank? Surely, a commercial bank cannot simply create these deposits out of thin air?

A Simplified Balance Sheet

The answer to this kind of question requires us to look at the balance sheet of a typical commercial bank, simplified for the purposes of our analysis.[2] We include three items:

1. *Cash.* Cash is listed as $200,000. We can think of this as currency held by the bank to meet occasional excesses of withdrawals over deposits. Because we operate with a fractional-reserve banking system, a bank does not need to hold in the form of cash (or in the form of reserves with a Federal Reserve bank) the full amount of its deposit liabilities. Not all depositors come rushing in for their funds at once. While some come in demanding cash, others are depositing cash. This particular bank has $200,000 set aside for such contingencies.

2. *Loans, investments, bonds.* Our second asset item is listed as $800,000. Here, the bank is engaged in making loans or buying bonds or other securities in order to earn income in the form of interest. These are the interest-earning assets of the bank, and they are, of course, an essential feature of the commercial banking system.

3. *Checking deposits.* On the liability side, we have $1 million worth of checking deposits. These deposits are called liabilities because they are owed by the bank to its depositors. It would be through the creation of more of these checking deposits that this commercial bank would be

---

[2] A more detailed balance sheet would include many other items. For example, among the bank's assets we would clearly want to include the buildings and equipment it owns. The liability side would include time and saving deposits as well as checking deposits. Also, on the credit side of the ledger would be the item *net worth.* This is essentially the value of the bank's assets after the claims of creditors are allowed for. The bank *owes* some part of its assets to its depositors—that is, they can come and claim these assets under specified conditions. What is left, the net worth, is what the bank itself *owns:* the original capital paid in by stockholders plus surplus and undivided profits.

able to "create money," if it in fact could accomplish such a miracle. But can it do so?

Simplified Balance Sheet of a Commercial Bank

January 1, 1990

Assets		*Liabilities*	
Cash	$200,000	Checking deposits	$1,000,000
Loans, investments, bonds	$800,000		

A Monopoly Bank Example

Let us first imagine circumstances in which the bank clearly could create more checking deposits—without any miracle or even any risk to its share-holders or other depositors. Suppose that it were the only bank on an isolated island, or that for some other reason it had a monopoly on all the banking business in a particular area. Suppose further that everyone in this area used the banking system for all their money payments. It might be very awkward to use literally *no* cash (for example, to write out a check for a bus ride or the evening newspaper), but assume that the need for coin and currency is trivial. Basically, all payments of any size are made by check, and all these checks are drawn on one monopoly bank.

We imagine, now, that a business executive comes to the bank and wants to borrow $50,000. A vice president of the bank, forgetting that the bank already has checking deposit liabilities of $1 million and cash assets of only $200,000, agrees to the loan. She adds to the bank's assets the $50,000 loan and to the bank's liabilities $50,000 of checking deposits in the name of this particular executive. There is now $50,000 more money in this economy than before.

Does this mean that the vice president has been reckless? On the contrary, she has been all too conservative. For, on our assumptions, not only is the new position tenable, but the bank is earning more income (through the interest on the added $50,000 loan), and the reserve cash of $200,000 hasn't even been touched. Nor will it be touched under our special assumptions. When the business executive wants to use this money to hire workmen to build, say, an addition to his factory, he will pay these workmen by a check drawn on his account with our bank. The bank, receiving these checks for deposit, will simply deduct the total amount from the business executive's account and add it to the workers' accounts. Eventually, when the loan is due, the business executive will have sold additional products to consumers who will pay him by their checks, thus building up his checking deposit account again. When he actually pays off the loan, the bank will simply cancel the $50,000 on the asset side and his $50,000 of deposits.

Bank's Balance Sheet after New $50,000 Loan

Assets		Liabilities	
Cash	$200,000	Checking deposits	$1,050,000
Loans, investments, bonds	$850,000		

We can now see why this bank vice president has been conservative. She should have loaned out not $50,000, but $100,000 or $500,000. Or $10 million, if she could have found a sufficient number of creditworthy customers. Under our assumptions, there is no limit whatsoever to the amount of new checking deposits—and, hence, additional money—this bank could, in principle, create.

The Position of the Ordinary Bank

Now, this situation is unrealistic as a description of a modern American commercial bank for three reasons: (1) there are some demands for currency in our system—no bank could operate on the assumption that the public would never want to increase its holdings of cash in the least amount; (2) commercial banks are required to hold certain percentages of their checking deposits in the form of cash or reserves with the Federal Reserve System—that is, there is a *legal reserve requirement;* and (3) no bank in this country, however big, is so isolated or as much a monopoly as the bank in our example—funds can be withdrawn from one bank and put into some *other* bank. This means that all the checks will not come back to one bank; hence, there can be a *net* withdrawal of funds instead of everything just "canceling out."

This last point is rather crucial. Indeed, it is clear that a small bank operating in a big system simply could not hope to "create money" in the way our isolated monopoly bank did. When it created the $50,000 checking deposit for the borrower, it would have to recognize that when the latter drew checks on this account, the chances are that they would be deposited in other banks (or, at least, that only a small fraction would come back to this bank). Deposits in other banks would create claims on the bank that it would meet by transferring cash to these other banks. Hence, its $200,000 cash *would* come under assault. An undue expansion of loans and investments by this bank *alone* could, indeed, be reckless behavior.

MULTIPLE CREDIT CREATION THROUGH THE SYSTEM

What a small, single commercial bank cannot accomplish by itself, a system of such banks can. In fact, the banking system can operate very much as our earlier "monopoly" bank did. The first bank that creates the $50,000 loan (and $50,000 demand deposits for the borrower) is subject to a net withdrawal of cash as the borrower starts using the loan. But this cash goes to another bank that now finds its deposit-creating ability enhanced. It, too, is subject to a net withdrawal when it increases its loans; but this, in turn, means more cash for a third bank, and so on.

   This process has to be followed through with some care if we are to understand it properly. To make our example a bit more realistic, let us at this time formally introduce a legal reserve requirement of 20 percent. Suppose that the actual demands for increased cash and currency by the public are trivial but that to guard against possible dangers, the federal authority (in the United States, it would be the Federal Reserve System) requires that every bank in the system keep a cash holding of $20 for every $100 of checking deposits it creates. We shall proceed sequentially through the following case:

>   All banks in the system are "fully loaned up" at the outset; that is, their cash reserves are equal to exactly 20 percent of their checking deposit liabilities. Then, suddenly, a widow withdraws $100,000 of cash from under her mattress and deposits it in her neighborhood bank.

The Process of Multiple Credit Expansion

1. $100,000 is deposited in Bank A.

Bank A	Assets	Liabilities
(Before $100,000 is deposited)	$200,000 Cash	$1,000,000 Checking deposits
	$800,000 Loans and investments	
(After $100,000 is deposited)	$300,000 Cash	$1,100,000 Checking deposits
	$800,000 Loans and investments	

Bank A now lends out $80,000, and its balance sheet becomes:

Assets	Liabilities
$220,000 Cash	$1,100,000 Checking deposits
$880,000 Loans and investments	

Addition to checking deposits in first round = $100,000

2. The $80,000 loaned out by Bank A is now deposited in Bank B.

Bank B	*Assets*	*Liabilities*
(Before $80,000 deposit)	$200,000 Cash	$1,000,000 Checking deposits
	$800,000 Loans and investments	
(After $80,000 deposit)	$280,000 Cash .	$1,080,000 Checking deposits
	$800,000 Loans and investments	

Bank B now lends out $64,000, and its balance sheet becomes:

Assets	*Liabilities*
$216,000 Cash	$1,080,000 Checking deposits
$864,000 Loans and investments	

Addition to checking deposits in second round = $80,000

---

3. The $64,000 loaned out by Bank B is now deposited in Bank C.

Bank C	*Assets*	*Liabilities*
(Before $64,000 deposit)	$200,000 Cash	$1,000,000 Checking deposits
	$800,000 Loans and investments	
(After $64,000 deposit)	$264,000 Cash	$1,064,000 Checking deposits
	$800,000 Loans and investments	

Bank C now lends out $51,200, and its balance sheet becomes:

Assets	*Liabilities*
$212,800 Cash	$1,064,000 Checking deposits
$851,200 Loans and investments	

Addition to checking deposits in third round = $64,000

In the next round, Bank D will be able to lend out 80 percent of $51,200, or $40,960; in the next round, Bank E will be able to lend out 80 percent of $40,960, or $32,770; and so on.

The total addition to checking deposits (ΔCD) when all the rounds are completed will be:

ΔCD = $100,000 + $80,000 + $64,000 + $51,200 + $40,960 + $32,770 + . . .

ΔCD = $100,000 [1 + .80 + $(.80)^2$ + $(.80)^3$ + $(.80)^4$ + . . . + $(.80)^n$ + . . .]

$$\Delta CD = \$100,000 \left(\frac{1}{1-.80} \right)$$

ΔCD = $100,000 (5) = $500,000

To show: that the banking system can now create substantial additional money beyond this $100,000, in particular, that it can create an additional $400,000. In total, there will be $500,000 of checking deposits created in response to the $100,000 cash deposit—or a 5-to-1 ratio.

By following the balance sheets above, you will see exactly how this happens.

Notice that this process resembles the action of the national income multiplier of chapter 8. We increase *C, I,* or *G* by $1 and get a $3 or $4 increase in national income. In the case of multiple credit creation, we get $1 more in cash reserves and $5 more in checking deposits, or money. Actually, in formal terms, the processes are very similar, the role of the MPS in the multiplier (remember that $m = 1/MPS$) being played in the case of credit expansion by the legal reserve requirement. Thus, assuming that all banks lend out all their funds up to the legal requirements, we would get, where ΔM equals the addition to the money supply, ΔR equals the new reserves, and *LR,* the legal reserve requirement:

$$\Delta M = (1/LR) \, \Delta R$$

The term $1/LR$ can be thought of as the *money creation multiplier,* or the *credit creation multiplier.* In this case, it would be 1/.20, or 5.

If we consolidated all these balance sheets and looked at the process before, during, and after the expansion had taken place, it would look like the situation shown in the table below. The total cash reserves of the member banks have gone up from $2,000,000 to $2,100,000. As a consequence, and on the assumption that each bank at each stage of the game lends out any excess reserves that come its way, the checking deposits in the system have gone up from $10,000,000 to $10,500,000—that is, in total, there has been a $500,000 expansion of the money supply.

Consolidated Commercial Bank Balance Sheets

If we assume that there are ten banks in the system, each with a balance sheet identical to those we have been describing, then we have:

1. Consolidated balance sheet before $100,000 cash deposit:

Assets	Liabilities
$2,000,000 Cash	$10,000,000 Checking deposits
$8,000,000 Loans and investments	

2. Consolidated balance sheet immediately after $100,000 cash deposit:

Assets	Liabilities
$2,100,000 Cash	$10,100,000 Checking deposits
$8,000,000 Loans and investments	

3. Consolidated balance sheet after multiple expansion of credit has taken place:

Assets	Liabilities
$2,100,000 Cash	$10,500,000 Checking deposits
$8,400,000 Loans and investments	

LIMITATIONS OF THE CREDIT MULTIPLIER

The main weakness of the foregoing description of multiple credit creation is that it makes the process seem too mechanical. It suggests that, given the reserve requirement and the reserves in the banking system, we can determine simply and arithmetically what the nation's money supply will be. One reason this impression is misleading is that the nature of the money supply changes over time as new financial mechanisms (NOW accounts, money market funds, and so on) are developed. We have mentioned this point before.

Equally important, however, is that the expansion of the money supply in response to a change in the system's reserves is in no way automatic. It requires bankers who are willing to lend and borrowers who are willing to borrow. In very depressed times, these conditions may not be fulfilled: bankers may prefer to retain excess reserves than to lend money for doubtful investments; business firms may have little interest in borrowing for investment purposes when their plants and machinery are already operating with idle capacity. It is important to recognize such limitations on the credit multiplier, for, otherwise, we would tend to assume that the government or its central bank could alter the nation's money supply virtually at will. In fact, the process is a good deal more complicated than this. The proof is that although the U.S. government has sometimes focused considerable attention on controlling the money supply in recent years, the actual money supply figures have always managed to produce their share of surprises.

THE FEDERAL RESERVE SYSTEM

Still, the government can and does try to influence the money supply and its rate of growth; in the United States, the basic agency for handling *monetary policy* is the Federal Reserve System. This system (usually called the "Fed") was established in 1913, during the presidency of Woodrow Wilson, and is divided into twelve districts, each of which has its own Federal Reserve bank (see Figure 10-1). Much of the authority of the system, however, resides in Washington, where the Fed's board of governors is located. This board of governors is composed of seven members, appointed by the president, with the approval of the Senate, for fourteen years. One of these members serves as chairman for a four-year term. The Fed's economic influence is so great that in the early 1980s, some observers considered then-Fed chairman, Paul Volcker, to have more power to affect the nation's economy than any other single individual, including even the president himself!

This comment about Volcker suggests, as does the length of the board members' terms, that the Fed exerts an *independent* influence on the U.S. economy. Indeed, this is true and a matter of some controversy. Fourteen-year terms mean that most members of the board of governors will outlast a one-term president and often a two-term president. The Fed chairman's term is shorter, but it does not coincide with the president's—that is, a new administration is likely to be dealing with a Fed chairman appointed by the previous

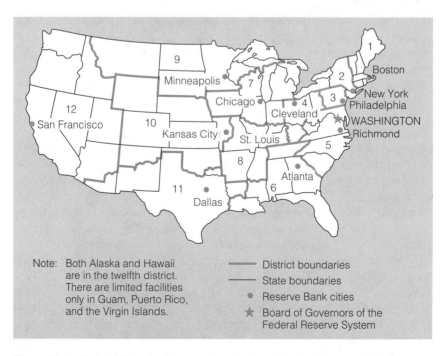

Note: Both Alaska and Hawaii
         are in the twelfth district.
         There are limited facilities
         only in Guam, Puerto Rico,
         and the Virgin Islands.

——— District boundaries
——— State boundaries
●   Reserve Bank cities
★   Board of Governors of the
     Federal Reserve System

Figure 10-1   Federal Reserve System: Boundaries of Federal Reserve Districts

president, often of a different political party. Many people feel that this independence is a good thing, representing another example of the principle of the separation of powers, already exemplified in the executive, legislative, and judicial branches of government. Others consider it intolerable that a nonelected body should exert such economic influence.

To a certain extent, there is a natural conflict built in between the Treasury Department and the Federal Reserve Board in that the former, generally, would like low interest rates (to keep the federal deficit down), while the Fed, at least during inflationary periods, may want to raise interest rates to restrain aggregate demand. Officially, this problem was solved forty years ago in the famous (to economists) Accord of 1951, affirming the Fed's autonomy. Yet high interest rates continue to bother elective officials. In the early 1980s, when the economy was in a deep recession and the Fed was maintaining high interest rates, there were moves afoot in Congress to prescribe the policies that the Fed must follow. In 1990, with the economy showing signs of sluggishness, some public officials were suggesting that the Fed might want to ease up a bit more than it seemed inclined to do. Despite all this, however, the Fed has managed to maintain a high degree of independence, both in good times and bad.

The Fed has a number of functions and is sometimes called a "banker's bank." In the case of our widow with $100,000 in cash to deposit, the bank that received this deposit would not hold most of it in cash, but would deposit it with the Federal Reserve bank in its region. The money would then become part of the reserves that the bank is legally required to hold against its checking deposits. The Federal Reserve bank may also make loans to commercial banks in much the same way that these banks make loans to companies and private citizens. One function of the Fed, however, has no analogy in the case of private banks: the issuing of currency. If you look at a dollar bill or a twenty-dollar bill or a bill of any denomination, you will see printed across the top "Federal Reserve Note." The Fed has other functions too—supervising member banks,[3] serving as a clearinghouse for checks, and so on—and, of course, regulating the nation's money supply. It is in this last connection that the Fed attempts to fulfill what is, in fact, its *major* role: contributing to the macroeconomic stability of the American economy.

TOOLS AVAILABLE TO THE FEDERAL RESERVE SYSTEM

Basically, the Federal Reserve attempts to alter the country's money supply (and/or interest rates, as we shall discuss later on), by altering the legal re-

---

[3] Not all commercial banks in the country are members of the Federal Reserve System, though the larger ones are. Legislation in 1980 largely eliminated the distinction between member and nonmember banks, making reserve requirements virtually universal.

serve requirement or by making more (or fewer) reserves available to the member banks. An important group in this connection is the Federal Open Market Committee, which is composed of the seven members of the board of governors plus five representatives of the district Federal Reserve banks (always including the New York bank). The three main tools available to the Fed are the following:

Altering the Legal Reserve Requirement

A fairly obvious way for the Fed to influence the quantity of money in the economy would be to change the legal reserve requirement. It could either raise or lower the requirement, depending on whether it wanted to decrease or increase the money stock. Suppose it wanted to expand the money supply and, therefore, cut the reserve requirement from our hypothetical 20 percent to, say, 18 percent. If all banks were fully loaned up at the beginning of the operation and remained loaned up after the change, then the shift in our consolidated bank balance sheets would look like this:

Consolidated Commercial Bank Balance Sheets

---

1. With legal reserve requirement of 20 percent:

Assets	*Liabilities*
$2,000,000 Cash	$10,000,000 Checking deposits
$8,000,000 Loans and investments	

2. With legal reserve requirement lowered to 18 percent:

Assets	*Liabilities*
$2,000,000 Cash	$11,111,111 Checking deposits
$9,111,111 Loans and investments	

We have increased our checking deposit money from $10,000,000 to $11,111,111 (= $2,000,000/.18), or by $1,111,111.

Although conceptually simple, changing reserve requirements, which are currently set at 12 percent for most checking deposits and 3 percent for most time deposits, is a fairly cumbersome method for increasing or decreasing the money supply. Unless very small and frequent changes were instituted, the effects might be larger than were called for. In any event, this method of altering the money supply has been used only infrequently in the past.

Altering the Discount Rate

As the Fed is a banker's bank, it can also lend money to member banks to augment or replenish their reserves if they are running short. The rate of interest it charges member banks for such loans is called the *discount rate*. By lowering the discount rate, the Fed would, in effect, be making reserves available to its member banks on easier terms. This action would also, in principle, lead to a multiple expansion of the money supply. The discount rate is also significant because it is often considered a signal of what the Fed's monetary policy is going to be. In October of 1982, for example, the Dow-Jones industrial stock average increased over 100 points, largely on *rumors* that the Fed was going to lower the discount rate from 9½ percent to 9 percent! Interestingly, when the Fed finally did lower the discount rate from 9½ to 9 percent (in November 1982), the stock market showed no reaction (actually, it *fell* slightly the next day); the change had been completely anticipated already. Another example of the significance of expectations in economics!

Open-Market Operations in Government Securities

Although the above two methods are important in theory, the most significant way in which the Fed has historically influenced the money supply in this country has been by open-market purchases and sales of government securities. Essentially, if the Fed wishes to *increase* the money supply, it will *purchase* government bonds on the open market. If it wishes to *reduce* the money supply, it will *sell* government bonds on the open market. The way this works is, as we should expect, through the effect of these actions on member bank reserves. In the particular case of a purchase of $100,000 in government bonds, we may imagine that the Fed buys these bonds directly from a member bank. In this case, the member bank's balance sheet will be affected as shown on the sample balance sheets below.

The key change here is the increase in reserves to $300,000. Assuming a 20-percent legal reserve requirement, this means the member bank now has excess reserves of $100,000 that it can lend to businesses and other investors. This $100,000 will now go the rounds of the other banks in the system, each of which will in turn increase its loans and investments. The net effect will be an increase of the money supply by—in a "fully loaned-up" system—$500,000.

Member Bank Balance Sheet before Open-Market Operation

Assets		*Liabilities*	
Reserves in Federal Reserve bank	$200,000	Checking deposits	$1,000,000
Loans, investments, bonds	$800,000		

**Member Bank Balance Sheet after Federal Reserve Bank
Purchases of $100,000 Government Bond**

Assets		*Liabilities*	
Reserves in Federal Reserve bank	$300,000	Checking deposits	$1,000,000
Loans, investments, bonds	$700,000		

As we think about this method of increasing the money supply by open-market operations (or, indeed, by either of the other methods), we can hardly avoid observing its immediate effects on the economy. How does the money supply get expanded when the Fed engages in open-market purchases of government bonds? Basically, by the expansion of loans and investments by the member banks in response to the increase in their reserves above the required level. Indeed, it would not seem illogical to suggest that the commercial banks, having these excess reserves, might even offer loans to businesses on more favorable conditions, that is, at lower interest rates.

With these last comments, we are moving directly into a question that is of enormous significance to the whole of macroeconomics: What exactly *is* the impact of changes in the money supply on the economy? It is to this important question that we will address ourselves in the next chapter.

SUMMARY

Money may be defined as any commodity or instrument that is generally accepted as (1) a medium of exchange, (2) a measure of value, and (3) a store of value. The nature of monetary instruments has undergone a major evolution over time, an evolution that is still continuing today. The most common form of money in the American economy today is not cash and currency, but deposits in commercial banks.

We operate on a *fractional-reserve banking system,* meaning that commercial banks need to hold in the form of cash (or reserves with the Federal Reserve System) only a fraction of the value of their checking deposit liabilities. Given the widespread use of the banking system, it is possible for banks collectively to "create money" by extending credit to a multiple of the value of any new deposit. Basically, the *credit creation multiplier* may be derived from the formula:

$$\Delta M = (1/LR)\, \Delta R$$

where ΔM equals the addition to the money supply, ΔR equals the new reserves, and LR, the legal reserve requirement.

In the United States, the Federal Reserve System performs many important banking functions and has a special responsibility for regulating the money supply (and/or interest rates) so as to promote macroeconomic stability. The main instruments the Fed uses to promote this objective are (1) altering the legal reserve requirement (for example, lowering the requirement if the Fed wishes to expand the money supply), (2) altering the discount rate (the rate the Fed charges member banks for loans to replenish their reserves), and (3) open-market operations in government securities (Fed purchases of government securities would increase bank reserves; sales of government securities would have the opposite effect).

Neither the credit creation multiplier nor the Fed's control of the money supply can be treated as simple, mechanical processes. Ultimately, we are dealing with business firms and bankers who must decide when and where and how much lending and borrowing to undertake, decisions affected by the state of the economy generally.

Key Concepts for Review

Money
  Medium of exchange
  Measure of value
  Store of value
Stock of money versus flow of income
Barter
Double coincidence of wants
Transactions money
Checking deposits
  Demand deposits
  NOW accounts
Savings, time deposits
M_1, M_2, M_3

Near-monies
Bank balance sheet
Fractional-reserve banking
Deposit creation
Money (credit) creation multiplier
"Fully loaned up"
Federal Reserve System
"Banker's bank"
Legal reserve requirement
Discount rate
Fed open-market operations
  Purchases ($M \uparrow$)
  Sales ($M \downarrow$)

Questions for Discussion

1. Define *money*. What are some other forms, beside money, in which people might hold their wealth? Rank the various assets you have listed according to their degree of nearness to money.

2. Suppose that an individual, having come to distrust the banking system, withdraws his $5,000 demand deposit from a commercial bank and buries

the $5,000 in a hole in his backyard. Will this have any effect on the money supply of the economy? Follow through the steps involved.

3. Banks sometimes keep "excess reserves" on hand. Why, in general, would they be reluctant to do so? Why might they, nevertheless, decide to do so from time to time?

4. Explain why Federal Reserve banks are sometimes called "banker's banks."

5. What are the three main tools that the Fed may use in the operation of monetary policy? Explain briefly how each might be used if the Fed wished to bring about a contraction of the money supply.

CHAPTER 11

THE ROLE OF MONEY IN THE ECONOMY: TWO VIEWS

In this chapter, we shall try to show how money can be brought into the aggregate demand and supply curve analysis by which we determine national income and the price level. More accurately, we shall present two views on this matter: the Keynesian (or "post-Keynesian" as some would say) view and the monetarist view. The monetarist view, once a minority position particularly associated with Professor Milton Friedman, then of the University of Chicago, gained numerous adherents in more recent years and must now be treated as part of the economic mainstream. Incidentally, we might state in advance that this chapter contains both some good news and some bad news. The good news is that we can find ways of looking at the Keynesian and monetarist doctrines in which they do not seem to be seriously contradictory. The bad news is that neither doctrine seems adequate for the special problems of our age.

SYNOPSIS OF THE KEYNESIAN VIEW

In the last chapter, we showed how in the American economy the Federal Reserve System might act to change the quantity of money. Our question now is, How do changes in the quantity of money work their way through the economic system to affect such variables as the price level, real national income, and employment? The Keynesian position (with many variations that we will ignore) can be summarized as follows:

1. Changes in the quantity of money have relatively little effect on the price level unless we are at, or very near, full employment, in which case their effect may be wholly on the price level.

2. Whether changes in the quantity of money have much or little effect on the level of real national income and employment will depend on the strength of the factors linking the money supply to these real variables. These links are given in propositions 3, 4, and 5 below.

3. An increase in the quantity of money, *ceteris paribus,* will generally cause a fall in the interest rate.

4. A fall in the interest rate, *ceteris paribus,* will generally cause an expansion of business investment demand.

5. An expansion of business investment demand, *ceteris paribus,* will generally cause an expansion of real GNP and employment.
(The reverse of these propositions is also claimed: that is, that a fall in the quantity of money will tend to raise interest rates, inhibit investment, and cause a fall in real income and employment.)

Let us take up these three links in order.

THE MONEY SUPPLY-INTEREST RATE LINK

We start with the first link, which purports to show how the quantity of money achieves its point of entry into the economic system. In the Keynesian view, a change in the money supply causes other economic effects largely through its impact on interest rates.

Demand for Money

Let us begin by considering the demand for money. Given the functions of money discussed in the previous chapter, there are many reasons why people might want to hold their wealth in the form of money. Economists sometimes distinguish two (or more) motives: (1) a *transactions motive*—people need to hold a certain amount of money in the form of currency, demand deposits, or checkable NOW deposits simply to carry on the everyday transactions of life, such as paying bills, meeting weekly payrolls, and so on; and (2) a *liquidity motive*—people sometimes prefer to hold money rather than interest-bearing assets like bonds or stocks because they fear that bond or stock prices might fall and they will lose some of the capital value of their assets; also they may hold money because they are waiting for a better moment to jump into the bond or stock market.

What the basic Keynesian analysis says is that while the transactions demand for money is largely influenced by the volume of transactions that are being carried on in the economy—roughly by the size of money national income—the liquidity motive is heavily influenced by the rate of interest. It is through the liquidity demand that most post-Keynesians find the crucial money supply-interest rate link. If the interest rate is low, people in the economy may find that their desire to hold money for liquidity purposes is quite high. A low rate of interest means, first, that there is relatively little cost to holding one's wealth in the form of money—one is not losing an opportunity to make a large income through holding interest-bearing assets. It may also mean, second, that the price of bonds is expected to fall. The reasoning here requires us to understand that a *low* rate of interest is really the same thing as a *high* price for bonds. Ten dollars a year on a bond that sells for $100 is an interest rate of 10 percent; $10 a year on a bond that sells for $50 is 20 percent. When the interest rate is lower—when, say, a $50 bond goes up in price to $100—then people may expect that this high bond price is due to come down. In this case, they may prefer to hold their wealth in the form of money rather than buy the bond.

By the same logic, the liquidity motive for holding money is likely to decrease when interest rates are high. Low bond prices seem a bargain; and, of course, the return for parting with one's liquidity in terms of high interest is greater.

The general conclusion Keynes and his followers drew from this was that the amount of money that people wish to hold for liquidity purposes will vary inversely with the interest rate. Indeed, Keynesians went beyond this and argued that there might be a thing called a "liquidity trap." At very low rates of interest (high bond prices), the risk of buying bonds might be so great and the return for giving up money so low that people might hold any additional money given to them in the form of money. They could not be induced to use the money to buy bonds or other assets at these low rates of return. They would simply add to their cash balances.

The Liquidity Preference Curve

These comments may be summarized in a diagram (Figure 11-1). Assuming a given level of real national income (Y_o) and a given level of prices (P_o), we have, then, a given level of money national income (nominal GNP). We can say, therefore, that the transactions demand for money will be a certain amount (OT_o) independent of the level of the rate of interest. The liquidity demand for money, however, will vary inversely with the rate of interest, meaning that the curve will slope downward to the southeast. If the quantity of money in the economy, as determined, say, by the Federal Reserve System, is M_o, then everything will be in equilibrium when the interest rate is at i_o. At higher rates of interest, people

Figure 11-1   Demand for Money at a Given Level of National Income (Y_o) and Prices (P_o)   Curve DD represents the demand for money in an economy at different interest rates, given a certain level of real national income (Y_o) and prices (P_o). If the quantity of money in the economy is given (M_o), then the rate of interest will be i_o.

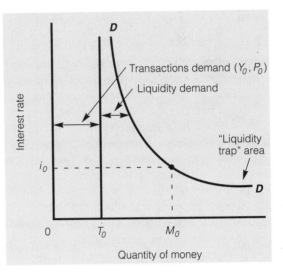

would want to hold more bonds; this would cause them to bid up the price of bonds; this would bring a fall in the rate of interest. Conversely, at lower rates of interest than i_o, people would want more liquidity; they would sell their bonds, bringing down bond prices and raising the rate of interest.

To test your understanding of this process, you should explain why a money supply smaller than M_o would bring a higher interest rate.

Figure 11-1 also displays what we have called a "liquidity trap." You will notice that at the far right, the DD curve becomes horizontal. What this means is that any further increases in the quantity of money will have no effect in lowering interest rates. What such a trap might mean for a country's monetary policy we shall consider later on in chapter 14. In terms of our present analysis, it means that at certain low levels of interest rate, the quantity of money really doesn't affect anything in the Keynesian system. The links between the money supply and the rest of the economy are broken off right at the beginning.

THE INTEREST RATE-INVESTMENT LINK

Assuming that there is *some* effect of an increased money supply on the interest rate, we can bring our second link into play: A fall in the interest rate, *ceteris paribus,* will generally cause an expansion of business investment demand.

Our previous point was about the *causes* of a change in interest rates; this point is about the *effects* of such a change. What is the logic behind the interest rate-investment link?

We have already discussed this matter briefly in chapter 7, when we were listing some of the factors that influence investment demand (pp. 126–129), and again in chapter 9, when we were explaining shifts in aggregate demand at different price levels (pp. 171–174). There are two further comments we should make here, however.

Ordinary Versus "Financial" Investment

The first comment is really a clarification and has to do with ascertaining the *direction* in which changing interest rates move the level of investment. There is a potential possibility of misunderstanding here, largely because of the different ways we use the term "investment" in everyday discourse. It is most important now to recall our earlier distinction between "financial" investment (buying a stock or a bond) and ordinary business investment (building a new factory, adding to one's inventories of goods in stock, and so on). The reason for this special caution is that the effect of changes in the rate of interest will be very different—in fact, ordinarily in opposite directions—depending on which kind of investment one has in mind.

To make this point clear, let us consider "financial" investment first. From the point of view of "financial investors," a high rate of interest is a good thing. The issue before investors is not whether or not to build a factory, but whether or not to buy a bond. If the interest rate is high, this will not discourage financial investors from buying a bond; on the contrary, it will make them eager to do so. At 10 percent, they get $10 a year by putting $100 into a bond. At 15 percent, they get $15 a year from the same $100. In certain circumstances, this difference may induce them to buy an extra bond or two. The point is that for "financial investors," the interest rate appears as a *payment to a lender* for the use of the money lent.

It is just the reverse when we come to investment in the ordinary sense in which we have been using the term—that is, the actual adding of new productive capacity to our economy. For when we talk about this kind of investment, we are approaching everything from the point of view not of the lender, but of the borrower. To say that the interest rate has gone up is nothing but to say that the *costs* of borrowing have gone up. As the head of a business firm, you wish, say, to invest in a new machine that costs $100,000. You go to the bank to finance this purchase with a loan. If the bank charges you 10 percent on the loan, then you will have to pay out interest charges of $10,000 a year on the machine. If the rate is 15 percent, you will have to pay out $15,000 a year. It may be that the machine will be just profitable to you at 10 percent, but not profitable at 15 percent and decidedly *un*profitable at 19 or 20 percent. A high interest rate, then, is not an encouragement, but a definite *dis*couragement as far as ordinary business investment is concerned.

This clarification should make it apparent that the direction of changes in investment in this second sense will be in the opposite direction from changes in the rate of interest. A high interest rate will tend to discourage investment. A low interest rate—meaning that the costs of borrowing are low—will tend to foster higher levels of investment. Which, of course, is what our second link asserts.

The Shape of the Investment Demand Curve

We now ask, How *great* an effect on investment will changes in the interest rate have? This leads to our second comment on the interest rate-investment link. For if the *direction* of the effect is now perfectly clear, it is equally important to determine the *magnitude* of the effect.

Now, the Keynesians, on the whole, tended to play down the size of these effects. The problem, as they saw it, was that so many different factors influence business investment, with the interest rate being only one of them. We have mentioned some of these factors before: business expectations, plant capacity, technological progress, amount of retained profits, and, of course, the interest rate. One could argue that if, say, business expectations are sufficiently pessimistic, or if the economy is already suffering from excess capacity, then it may be that investment will stay small, no matter how enticingly low the interest rate may be. Conversely, if certain remarkable new products or processes are available for investment, business firms may be difficult to discourage, no matter what the costs (within limits) of borrowing.

A technical way of describing this is to say that investment demand may, for wide ranges of different interest rates, be *interest inelastic*—that is, the percentage change in investment for a given percentage change in the interest rate may be quite small.[1]

An *investment demand curve* displaying this feature is shown in Figure 11-2. The amount of investment (*I*) business firms are willing to undertake does increase with lower interest rates (*i*) as we would expect; however, the percentage increase is rather slight. Thus, a substantial percentage reduction in the interest rate (from 14 to 10 percent) brings only a few billion dollars increase in investment. Generally, Keynesians seemed to feel that the investment demand curve would have this shape.[2]

---

[1] For a discussion of the concept of *elasticity*, see pp. 25–28.
[2] That this is not a universal view of the effect of interest rates on investment we should recognize immediately. The recession of 1981–1982, for example, was attributed by many, perhaps most, economists to the strongly negative effect of high interest rates on business investment spending and also on consumer spending on houses and automobiles and other consumer durables. Again, in 1990, many economists believed that the sharp recession in the U.S. housing industry was largely due to high interest rates. We shall return to these points later on.

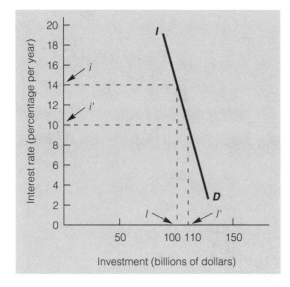

Figure 11-2   An Investment Demand Schedule
In the past, Keynesians had a tendency to think of this schedule as relatively inelastic—that is, a fairly large percentage change in interest rates (from 14% to 10% here) might bring only a rather small percentage change in investment demand (from $100 to $110 billion).

THE INVESTMENT-GNP LINK

The final link in our chain provides the connection between changes in investment demand and changes in real GNP. We have discussed this link in earlier chapters, but now we want to place it in a more definitely Keynesian context.

The Shift in the Aggregate Demand Curve

The general way in which an increase in investment demand will shift our aggregate demand curve is shown in Figure 11-3. In Figure 11-3(a), we show the rise in the $C + I$ curve to $C + I'$, as investment rises from I to I'. Figure 11-3(a) is drawn for a given price level, P. The increase in real income demanded as a result of the increased investment is, at price P, from Y to Y'. This gives us a point on our new aggregate demand curve, $A'D'$—Figure 11-3(b). When we do this for all possible price levels, we will get the full curve $A'D'$. The increase in investment demand has shifted our aggregate demand curve to the right.

To get from this shift in the aggregate demand curve to the new equilibrium level of real GNP, we have to specify what kind of aggregate supply curve the Keynesians employed. Before doing that, however, we should note that the Keynesians were somewhat pessimistic that any very great shifts in the aggregate demand curve could be brought about by changing the quantity of money. This is particularly true in the case of depressions, where an ex-

Figure 11-3 Changes in the Money Supply and Aggregate Demand In Figure 11-3(a), for a given price level (P), an increase in the money supply from M to M' raises investment from I to I'. In Figure 11-3(b), increases in investment demand will shift the aggregate demand curve to the right at each price level.

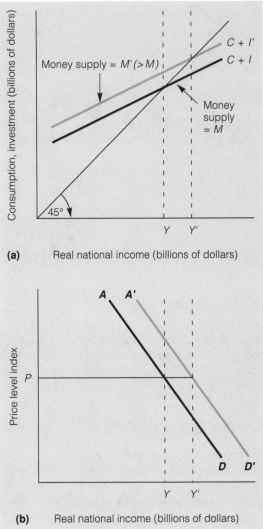

panding money supply might run into the obstacles of a liquidity trap and/or inelastic investment demand, meaning that to produce the final result—a shift of *AD* to *A′D′*—might be difficult, or even impossible, using monetary measures alone.

The Shape of the Aggregate Supply Curve

Finally, we add an aggregate supply curve to our analysis, and we can answer the question, What will the new equilibrium level of real GNP be? The an-

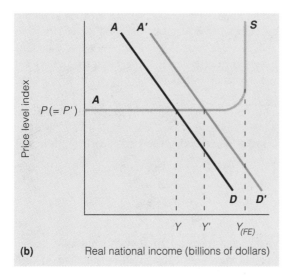

Figure 11-4 New Equilibrium of Aggregate Supply and Demand Note the special shape of this Keynesian-style aggregate supply curve (*AS*).

(b)   Real national income (billions of dollars)

swer can be read off from Figure 11-4. If the end result of an increasing money supply, a falling rate of interest, and an increasing investment demand is to shift the aggregate demand curve from *AD* to *A'D'*, then our new equilibrium level of GNP will be at *Y'*. Incidentally, we have also determined the price level: it remains the same in this diagram, that is, $P = P'$.[3]

The above statements follow if we assume that the aggregate supply curve has the shape we have given it in Figure 11-4. We have drawn *AS* so that it is perfectly horizontal until quite near the full-employment (Y_{FE}) level of income, at which time it rapidly shoots upward and becomes perfectly vertical. What does this shape mean? Essentially, it means that when there is an increased demand for their products at a time of general unemployment and excess capacity, businesses will respond wholly in terms of increasing production and employment at a given price level. It is only when they begin to hit bottlenecks, either of labor or plant capacity, near full employment that the increased demand is reflected in increasing prices. We might imagine that money wage rates are basically fixed while there is unemployment in the economy. If production expands more or less at constant cost, then any increase in aggregate demand that is reflected in the least rise in prices will tend to increase profits and cause an

---

[3] We use the phrase "end result" of an increasing money supply in this paragraph to suggest that the process is slightly more complicated than shown in Figure 11-4. As income increases from *Y* toward *Y'*, this will cause an increase in the transactions demand for money, meaning that only part of the original increase in the money supply can enter into the liquidity sphere. Thus, the ultimate lowering of interest rates and the increase of investment will be less than it might at first seem. In the monetarist view, indeed, as we shall see below (pp. 214–216), virtually *all* the increase in the money supply will get "soaked up" by increased transactions demands.

expansion of output. At or near full employment, however, expansions of output may occur only at substantially increasing cost; also, the bidding of firms for labor may be expected to send money wages up. At this point, then, the increases in aggregate demand are more and more reflected in changes in the price level and, presently, when the curve becomes vertical, completely in price level changes.

Now, any good Keynesian, or certainly any *post*-Keynesian, economist would modify this account in numerous details. However, it will serve us as a fair representation of the main thrust of Keynesian doctrine, at least for purposes of contrast with the theories of the monetarists.

A SYNOPSIS OF THE MONETARIST VIEW

We can set out the main propositions of monetarism in a list analogous to the one we presented for the Keynesian view. This presentation relies heavily on the statements of the Nobel Prize-winning economist Milton Friedman, whom we have already identified as the leading monetarist thinker.[4] Four propositions should be noted:

1. Changes in the quantity of money largely determine the money value of GNP (nominal GNP), or $P \times Y$, where P is the price level and Y is the level of real income.

2. The effects of changes in the quantity of money on real GNP (Y) are very short run. The main effect of money supply changes is on prices, P.

3. Increases in the quantity of money may lead to short-run declines in the rate of interest, but in the long run, they are likely to lead to increases in the nominal rate of interest.

4. If the nominal rate of interest is corrected for expected inflation, so that we are talking about the *real* rate of interest, then money supply changes are unlikely to have any clear or permanent effect on the rate of interest. This means, in turn, that money supply changes are unlikely to have any long-run effects on the other real variables in the system: real investment, real national income, real wages, and employment.

Let us now inspect the logic that lies behind these very non-Keynesian-appearing propositions.

---

[4] For a fairly concise statement of Friedman's views, see Milton Friedman, "The Role of Monetary Policy," *American Economic Review* 58, no. 1 (March 1968) and Milton Friedman, *Money and Economic Development: The Horowitz Lectures of 1972* (New York: Praeger Publishers, 1973).

THE QUANTITY THEORY OF MONEY

One way of looking at monetarism is as a new and sophisticated version of a *pre*-Keynesian theory, a theory that dates back at least to the eighteenth century: *the quantity theory of money.* This theory can be expressed in terms of the following equation:

$$M \times V = P \times Y$$

As before, M is the money supply, P is the price level, and Y is the level of real income; the new term is V. V is the *income velocity of money.* It is meant to measure the number of times the average dollar bill or checking deposit circulates through the economy during a given period of time in exchange for final output. In particular, it is defined as:

$$V = \frac{P \times Y}{M}$$

In words, the income velocity of money is defined as nominal (money) national income in a given year divided by the total of currency and checking deposits available on the average during the course of that year.

This definition raises a possible source of confusion about the quantity theory equation; namely, the equation appears to be true by virtue of the meaning of the term "income velocity." $MV = PY$ becomes a truism that tells us nothing whatever about the real world. This is quite correct, and what it means is that in order to get a proper theory about the role of money in the economy from the equation, we have to make some further statements about its terms. In the old days, the quantity theorists said, first, that on the whole, national income in real terms (Y) was largely determined by real factors— the size of the labor force, amount of capital, technology, and so on. These factors would alter over time, but very slowly, and, in any event, they would not be affected by the quantity of money in any serious or enduring way.

Second, they argued that V—the rate at which money turned over— could also be regarded as largely fixed by institutional circumstances, such as banking practices or the ways in which businesses make wage payments and other disbursements of funds. Consider, for example, how one institutional circumstance—the payment period for salaries—affects the quantity of money I might want to hold on the average and, consequently, the rate at which the money supply turns over. At an after-tax salary of $24,000 a year, if I am paid by the month and spend my salary steadily during the course of that month, I will, on the average, hold $1,000 in my bank account. (*Reasoning:* I get $2,000 at the beginning of each month and reduce this to $0 by the end of the month, averaging a $1,000 balance during the month.) If, by contrast, I am paid by the week, my average balance will be less than a quarter of $1,000, or something less than $250. The velocity of circulation is, thus, more than four times as great for weekly as opposed to monthly payments, other things equal. Now, if one considers that the only motive for holding money is the transactions motive, and if the way in which these transactions are carried out is institutionally determined, then V will be pretty well a constant.

The consequence of these propositions was, for the quantity theorists, that changes in M affected only P. We are in the world of full-employment economics. It is more or less assumed that Y is at or, except for frictional disturbances, very near full-employment Y. Changes in the money supply? These will only affect prices, and, in fact, if the assumptions of the quantity theorists are accepted, then the monetarist position we have outlined above would clearly be valid.

HOW PREDICTABLE IS V?

One way of framing the difference between the Keynesian and monetarist view, then, would be in terms of their attitudes toward V. Insofar as the monetarists follow the old quantity theory, they would seem to be arguing that V is at least reasonably constant. A further development of this view might be that although V can hardly be expected to be constant—particularly considering all the banking and other institutional changes affecting our money supply in recent years—nevertheless, V is quite predictable. It will tend to increase at a certain reasonably constant rate over time. If we know this rate, then we will still be able to look at the money supply as the primary determinant of money GNP.

The Keynesians, by contrast, would argue that V is not only quite variable, but that these variations are systematically related to changes in the interest rate. If i is low, they say, the velocity of circulation of money will fall because people will want to hold more money for liquidity purposes. At a higher i, V should also be higher. Another reason for expecting a higher i and a higher V to go together is because they are both affected by *inflationary expectations*. If you expect prices to rise sharply in the future, then you will usually demand a higher interest rate for lending out your money (and borrowers will be willing to pay a higher interest rate for the funds that they borrow) than if you expected prices to remain constant. Thus, high inflationary expectations normally go with high nominal interest rates. But they also go with high income velocity. If you expect prices to rise in the future, you will want to get out of money into real goods—that is, buy today rather than wait for tomorrow. In short, V will go up because people accelerate their purchases of real goods.

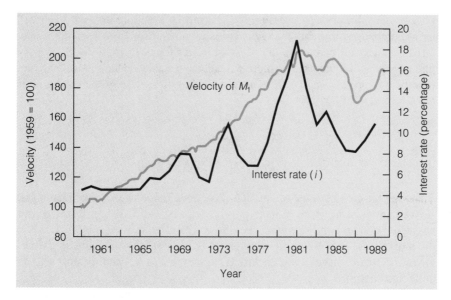

Figure 11-5   Velocity of Money (M_1) and the Interest Rate   Although the velocity of M_1, generally varies with the interest rate (measured by the prime rate), the fit is by no means perfect.
SOURCE: Board of Governors of the Federal Reserve System.
Note: Data are quarterly.

So what is the answer, then, in point of actual fact? Does *V* remain constant and/or reasonably predictable over time? Or is it highly sensitive to interest rate changes?

Unfortunately, as in many economic matters, it is very difficult to settle this question by statistical measures, partly because external ("exogenous") changes keep upsetting things (for example, you may suddenly have an oil cartel quadrupling energy prices or Iraq invading Kuwait or communism collapsing in Eastern Europe), but also because, as we have said, banking practices and useful definitions of the money supply keep changing.

If we think in terms of M_1 money, Figure 11-5 shows that *V* has certainly not been constant over recent decades. However, for a good part of this period, until around 1981, *V* was increasing at a relatively stable rate, leading many monetarists to claim that their basic approach was still sound. But then, in the 1980s, all this changed, and *V* (of M_1) became erratic and unpredictable.

Figure 11-5 also shows that in a very general way, there has been some relationship between changes in *V* and changes in *i* (here measured by the prime rate charged by commercial banks). Roughly speaking, while *V* was rising from the 1960s to 1981, so also was the prime rate; thereafter, both were falling. This is more or less what Keynesians would expect. The key phrases here, however, are "roughly speaking" and "more or less"; the "fit" between changes in i and changes in V is obviously far from perfect. Monetarists, moreover, can claim that if we shift our focus from M_1 to M_2, we can find a concept of money that exhibits a much more stable velocity in the long run. (See below, pp. 273–274.) In short, simple empirical tests of the two theories remain somewhat inconclusive.

MONETARIST ANALYSIS OF THE AGGREGATE DEMAND CURVE

Although we cannot come to any definitive conclusions about the behavior of V, we can show how the monetarist view can be expressed in terms of our aggregate demand and supply curves. In the Keynesian world, an increase in the money supply is likely to bring about only a rather small shift in the aggregate demand curve; the monetarists, however, argue that this shift will be quite substantial.

For one thing, they deny the importance, or even existence, of the "liquidity trap" under ordinary circumstances. In general, in the monetarist world, when people get money in their hands, they will find some way of spending it. The transactions motive tends to dominate. This means that changes in the money supply will definitely have an effect on aggregate demand and will not be cut off, as they may be in the Keynesian world, virtually at the source.

Secondly, an increase in the money supply will affect spending in a monetarist world not just through the interest rate effects on investment, but also through its effect on consumer wealth. We have actually touched on this point before, when we were considering the effect of changes in the price level on our consumption function, (p. 172). We said there that for a given quantity of money, a higher (or lower) price level would lower (or raise) the real value of the monetary wealth of consumers, causing the consumption function to shift downwards (upwards). Now, an increase in the quantity of money in the economy at a given price level has many of the same effects as a fall in the price level in the economy with a given money supply. In both cases, the total real value of the money wealth of the citizenry has increased. Some of this increase in cash balances individuals may use to buy bonds, bringing down the rate of interest and causing investment spending to increase. But consumers may also increase their consumer spending as well. They may buy more houses, cars, clothing, food, entertainment, what have you. Thus, in the monetarist world, an increase in the money supply affects all categories of spending. For this reason, we can expect a greater shift of the aggregate demand curve for any given change in the quantity of money than we would get in the Keynesian world.

MONETARIST ANALYSIS OF THE AGGREGATE SUPPLY CURVE

It is because of their view that changes in the money supply bring large changes in aggregate demand that monetarists are often associated with the notion that "Money matters a great deal" or, even, that "Money alone matters!" However, their position cannot be fully understood until we also say something about the aggregate supply curve. When we do this, we come to realize that there are definite limits on the power of money in the monetarist system.

If the Keynesian-style aggregate supply curve was virtually horizontal through most of its range (Figure 11-4), the monetarist aggregate supply curve tends to be virtually vertical. Certainly, this is true for the intermediate and long run. Figure 11-6 shows a fairly typical monetarist aggregate supply curve. It also shows how the final equilibrium of national income and prices will change when there is an increase in the money supply that causes a shift in aggregate demand from AD to $A'D'$.

Now, the first thing to note about this diagram is that it is consistent with what we described earlier as the first two propositions of monetarism. That is to say, a change in the money supply has produced a substantial change in nominal GNP, and virtually all this change is in the price level, with very little effect on real income.

The second thing to note about Figure 11-6 is that equilibrium real GNP can only vary within a very narrow range. Does this mean that the monetarists believe that our economy can be at equilibrium only at full employment or at some level fairly close to full employment? The answer is a

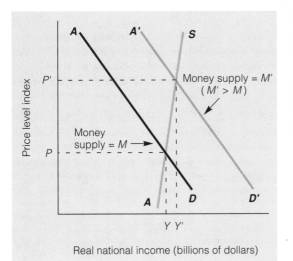

Figure 11-6 A Monetarist View of Money Supply Effects In contrast to the Keynesian world (Figure 11-4), the monetarists claim that changes in the money supply bring (at least in the long run) large changes in prices (from P to P') but little effect on real income.

qualified yes. They argue that there is a *natural rate of unemployment*. The exact definition of this natural rate is a matter of some complexity, as we shall discuss in the next chapter. The term often carries the connotation of a rate of unemployment such that there will be no tendency for inflationary pressures in the economy to increase. As a definition, this is not exactly equivalent to what we think of as the full-employment rate of unemployment. It is clear, however, that most monetarists do not consider the natural rate of unemployment to be a *high* rate of unemployment—that is, they would not consider large-scale Keynesian unemployment to represent an equilibrium situation.[5]

But if there is an increase in aggregate demand, won't this have some effect on output and employment? According to the monetarists, very little, though there may be some short-run effects that are quickly reversed. Consider first the situation with respect to wages and profits. If there is an increase in the money supply leading to a shift in aggregate demand, this will lead, in the very first instance, as in the Keynesian world, to a slight upward pressure on prices. This upward pressure on prices will, for a given money wage rate, bring a lowering of *real* wages and an increase in profits. The result in the Keynesian system will be an immediate expansion of output and employment. Such an expansion also begins to occur in the monetarist world, but it is very short lived. Real wages fall below their equilibrium level; wage earners quickly become aware of this; they demand higher money wages; real wages soon return to their original level, thus reducing profits back to *their* original level and removing the motive for output expansion; meanwhile, at the nominal level, both wages and prices rise. The increased quantity of money will be, so to speak, "soaked up" in carrying out transactions for the higher level of nominal GNP due to the higher price level.

Similarly with interest rates. In the first instance, some of the increase in the money supply may go into increased cash balances to satisfy the liquidity motive. This will bring about a fall in interest rates. However, the fall in interest rates will stimulate economic activity, leading ultimately (as we have just stated) to a higher nominal GNP, so that the new addition to the money supply will once again be used up for transactions purposes. Not only that, but *if* these increases in the money supply keep coming, so that continuing price rises become the expected situation in the economy, then the net result will be a *higher nominal interest rate* than the one with which we began. This is because borrowers and lenders will begin correcting the nominal interest rate for inflation. If prices are rising at 10 percent per year, a lender may insist on getting, say, 15-percent interest rather than the 5 percent he was

---

[5] They reject Keynesian unemployment equilibrium because it will not represent equilibrium in the market for labor. Unless one simply assumes fixed or rigid money wages, unemployed workers will have reason to bid down the money wage rate. Thus, the system has not come to rest, that is, to an equilibrium position; there will be strong deflationary pressures in such an economy.

accustomed to getting when prices were constant. The borrower, for his part, may be quite willing to pay this higher nominal interest rate (actually, the *real* rate has remained the same, at 5 percent) since he expects the prices of his products and his nominal profits to keep rising in the future. One of the most striking of the monetarists' contentions is that persistent increases in the money supply will characteristically lead not, as the Keynesians predicted, to lower nominal interest rates, but to *higher* nominal interest rates. Meanwhile, in the monetarist world, the real rate of interest, like the other real variables—national income, employment, and so on—have been left little changed by the whole exercise.

But what about history? What about the Great Depression of the 1930s? Can the monetarists deny that there were massive falls in employment and output following the "crash" of 1929? Can they deny that these problems with *real* economic variables lasted a whole decade? Where was the "natural" rate of unemployment then?

The monetarists cannot, of course, claim that these events did not happen; what they can do is claim that they did not represent any kind of equilibrium condition. In fact, Friedman himself seems to attribute what he calls the "Great Contraction" to perverse actions on the part of the government and especially the Federal Reserve System. According to Friedman, the Fed followed highly deflationary policies from 1929 to 1933, sharply reducing the money supply and, in general, throwing a monkey wrench into the operation of the entire economic system. The implication: the economy would have returned much more quickly to its natural equilibrium had not these disruptive actions by the monetary authority taken place.

A RECONCILIATION AND A SERIOUS PROBLEM

For the nonmonetarist, the above explanation seems inadequate to account for the scale and persistence of the Great Depression. At a minimum, he is likely to feel that the monetarist's "short run," during which serious problems can occur, may be far too long for comfort, certainly for the comfort of unemployed workers and their families.

At the same time, the Keynesian view of macroeconomic problems also seems seriously deficient. The most prominent group of Keynesians made their predictions known at the end of World War II. They expected a serious postwar depression and a strong, persistent, and probably increasing tendency toward mass unemployment and below-capacity real GNP over the ensuing decades. They were, in fact, known as the "stagnationists."[6] Yet, the

---

[6] Their best-known representative was the distinguished Keynesian economist Alvin Hansen, a Harvard professor who influenced many students who later became distinguished economists in their own right.

postwar recession in the late 1940s proved surprisingly mild, and the American economy—as well, of course, as the Japanese and many European economies—set off on a high-employment growth spree for the next quarter of a century. If the monetarist view seems inadequate to cope with the Great Depression, the Keynesian view seems equally inadequate to explain the persistent prosperity of the late 40s, 50s and 60s.

Considering the different circumstances during which they were conceived, it is not surprising, perhaps, that the Keynesian and monetarist theories address themselves to basically different problems. Indeed, this very fact suggests the possibility that the two theories might be combined. The monetarist view might be applied to the normal or even "natural" state of the economy, while the Keynesian view might be used to explain why serious departures from the natural condition occur.

Such a "reconciled" theory might go roughly as follows:

> The ordinary historical condition of the economy is to be at or fairly near the full-employment (loosely defined) level. An economy operating in this range will generally find that changes in aggregate demand mainly affect prices; short-run declines in GNP and employment will tend to be self-correcting; the main danger to this economy will be inflation, but since inflation is largely determined by the quantity of money, it should not be too difficult to control. However, (the "reconciled" theory might go on), there can be times when the economy gets seriously off the track. Perhaps it is some "external" factor: bad policies, war, and so on. In such an economy, the normal recuperative powers may be seriously weakened. Business firms facing excess plant capacity may hesitate to invest, no matter what encouragements are offered; consumers, fearing possible unemployment, may hesitate to spend; the liquidity motive may become exceptionally strong. Once sufficiently "off the path," so to speak, it may prove very difficult to get back on.

In short, monetarist theory could be applied to the ordinary, prosperous, slightly inflationary modern economy, while Keynesian theory could be used to explain the possibility of occasional (there have been other *near*-Great Depressions in the past) economic disasters and, especially, their persistence and intractability. Both parties, on such a view, could simply shake hands and stop fighting altogether. This is the good news mentioned at the beginning of this chapter.

The bad news is that even such a happily "reconciled" theory seems inadequate to the experience of the last two decades. During the 1970s, we had neither a prosperous, full-employment, somewhat inflationary economy (the world of the monetarists), nor a generally depressed, high-unemployment, noninflationary economy (the world of the Keynesians). Instead, *both* inflation and unemployment were rising on the average during the decade. Meanwhile in the 1980s, we had essentially the reverse experience: the rate of price inflation in 1989 was far below what it had been in 1980 or 1981, but so also was the unemployment rate.

In consequence, new schools of economic thought were developing to challenge both the Keynesians and the monetarists. Some, like the *supply-siders*, thought that both theories put too much emphasis on what was happening to aggregate demand, to the neglect of supply factors. Another school of economists, the *rational expectationists* (sometimes called the *new classical economists*), raised a question as to whether any government policies, whether of a Keynesian or monetarist slant, seriously affected the actual workings of the economy.

In short, when we come closer to the real world in the next few chapters (part 4), we shall have to introduce some important qualifications to the analysis we have developed thus far.

SUMMARY

In this chapter, two views of the role of money in the economy are discussed and compared.

The *Keynesian* view sees changes in the money supply affecting the economy through three links: (1) a money supply-interest rate link (an increase in the quantity of money will tend to lower the rate of interest); (2) an interest rate-investment link (a lower rate of interest will tend to increase the volume of business investment spending); and (3) an investment-GNP link (an increase in investment will tend to raise the level of real GNP). Thus, in a depressed economy, one would try to expand the money supply in order to raise GNP and lower unemployment.

However, the Keynesians feared that the money supply-interest rate link might be weak in a depressed economy (an increased quantity of money might simply feed into the "liquidity trap") and that the interest rate-investment link might also be weak (faced with poor expectations and excess productive capacity, businessmen might have an interest-*inelastic* demand for investment). Under these circumstances, changes in the money supply might have very little effect on real GNP. As far as the price level is concerned, changes in the quantity of money would have little effect in the Keynesian system, except when the economy was at or near the full-employment level.

According to the *monetarist* view, virtually all the effects of changes in the quantity of money—certainly all long-run effects—are on the price level and other "nominal" (as opposed to "real") economic variables. If we take the quantity theory of money as a starting place, using the equation $M \times V = P \times Y$, we can specify conditions under which changes in M will affect only P. Thus, if we are operating in a basically full-employment world, where real GNP is largely determined by factor supplies and technology and where the velocity of money is institutionally determined, then money supply changes will only affect prices, leaving the real variables (real GNP, unemployment, the real interest rate, and so on) largely unaffected.

Empirically speaking, V is not constant; nor do the monetarists claim that it is. What they do claim, in contrast to the Keynesians, is that changes in *M* will have large effects on the aggregate demand curve (they reject the "liquidity trap" idea and emphasize the effect of increased money supplies on all categories of spending), and also that these changes will not have much effect on real variables. This second point can be shown in terms of the aggregate supply curve. While the Keynesians tend to see this curve as near-horizontal through most of its range (except, of course, in the vicinity of full employment), the monetarists tend to see it as near-vertical through most of its range.

A "reconciled" theory might state that the monetarist view is appropriate to the normal, prosperous, somewhat inflationary modern economy, while the Keynesian view best applies to an economy that, for whatever reason, has seriously gotten off the track into a depression. Unfortunately, neither view seems fully adequate to the American economy of the last two decades, where increases, or decreases, in inflation and unemployment have often gone together. In part 3, therefore, we will have to consider a more complex view of the economy, including the somewhat newer approaches of the *supply-siders* and the *rational expectationists*.

Key Concepts for Review

Quantity of money (M_1, M_2)
Interest rate
Bond price ↑, interest rate ↓
Investment demand
Three Keynesian links
  Money supply-interest rate
  Interest rate-investment
  Investment-GNP
Transactions motive
Liquidity motive (preference)
Liquidity trap
Ordinary versus "financial"
  investment
Interest-inelastic investment demand

Monetarism
$M \times V = P \times Y$
Income velocity of money
Quantity theory of money
Aggregate supply and demand
  Keynesian
  Monetarist
Natural rate of unemployment
"Reconciled" theory
Simultaneous increases (decreases)
  in inflation and unemployment
Supply-siders
Rational expectationists

Questions for Discussion

1. State the three links through which the Keynesians relate the quantity of money to the level of real national income. Explain the logic behind each of these links. Assuming that the monetary authority (in the U.S., the Fed) decides to *decrease* the quantity of money in the economy, trace the effects of this action as it works its way through the economic system.

2. Define the *transactions motive* and the *liquidity motive* for holding money. What is meant by a possible *liquidity trap?*

3. Why is there said to be an inverse relationship between the interest rate and the price of bonds? Suppose that we have a given stock of money in the economy and a given number of bonds but that people want to hold more money and fewer bonds. What will happen? Will the price of bonds change? the interest rate?

4. Define the income velocity of money (V). Why is it often said that the equation $M \times V = P \times Y$ is simply a truism (that is, true by definition)? Under what assumptions does this equation represent a *theory* about the effect of money on the economy?

5. The monetarists are sometimes criticized for believing that "money alone matters." In what sense does money play a larger role in the monetarist world than in the Keynesian world? In what sense is the role of money in the monetarist world very limited?

6. Express the differences between the Keynesian and monetarist views through the use of aggregate supply and demand curves. How might these two theories be "reconciled"? Why has such a "reconciliation" brought little joy to most economists in recent years?

THE ECONOMY IN
THE AGGREGATE:
INFLATION AND
UNEMPLOYMENT,
PROBLEMS AND
POLICIES

CHAPTER 12

FURTHER ANALYSIS
OF INFLATION AND
UNEMPLOYMENT

In parts 2 and 3, we provided a basic analysis of national income, unemployment, and inflation and of the tools of fiscal and monetary policy. In part 4, we must deepen this analysis so that it comes closer to capturing important features of the real-world U.S. economy. We must also specify more carefully the actual problems that face the policymaker who wishes to use the fiscal and monetary tools we have introduced.

In this chapter, we shall focus primarily, although not wholly, on problems, while in the next two chapters we shall deal mainly with policies. The problem that particularly engages our interest here is the relationship between inflation and unemployment. No problem in short-run macroeconomics[1] has attracted more attention than this relationship; furthermore, the analysis of the inflation-unemployment relationship has been changing radically over recent decades. We shall see why in a moment.

DOES LESS UNEMPLOYMENT MEAN MORE INFLATION?

If one ever watches the Financial News Network (FNN) or other business programs on cable television, one has the immediate impression of an American economy constantly poised between a run-up of inflation on the one hand or a run-up of unemployment on the other. A typical statement would be:

---

[1] Although our focus in parts 2, 3, and 4 is on relatively short-run problems, we shall find in this and the next two chapters that we frequently have to take longer-run problems into account. Thus, we will be anticipating some of the analysis we will discuss explicitly in part 5.

"Well, if tomorrow's unemployment figures show an increase in unemployment, then the Fed won't have to worry about inflation and it'll be ready to ease up on interest rates and the money supply." Or, of course, the opposite, if unemployment is expected to fall. One of the paradoxes of these programs is that the analysts almost invariably seem to imply that bad news for the economy is good news for the stock market. The reason is that higher unemployment is thought likely to bring an easier monetary policy, which is likely to bring lower interest rates, which, in turn, are believed to be good for the stock market.

Whether accurate or not, these analyses seem to take for granted that more unemployment will be associated with less inflation and less unemployment with more inflation. But is this true in fact?

The Phillips Curve

We ourselves have already implied that there is some truth to this view in chapter 8, when we noted the difference between pre–World War II and post–World War II business cycles. We used to have greater fluctuations in the *real* economy (including unemployment) in the old days, whereas now we have a lesser unemployment problem but stronger inflationary tendencies. Some economists have argued that we have, in fact, substituted inflationary problems for unemployment problems between the two periods.

The possibly inverse relationship between unemployment and inflation goes back well into the nineteenth century. In Figure 12-1, we present the pioneering effort in this area by the economist A. W. Phillips, who studied changes in inflation (more specifically, changes in the money wage rate) in relation to unemployment for the United Kingdom from 1861 to 1913. The whole class of curves relating price or wage rate changes to the unemployment percentage are now called *Phillips curves*. It is apparent that in this early study, higher rates of wage inflation were associated with lower levels of unemployment, and vice versa.

U.S. Experience, 1960–1970

This was also the experience of the United States through most of the 1950s and 1960s. In Figure 12-2, labeled "A Tale of Three Decades," if we look at Figure 12-2a, we see that during the first of those decades, there is at least a general tendency for unemployment and inflation to be inversely related. A few years seem a bit out of line—1970, for example—yet we would hardly expect an ironclad relationship when so many different factors operate on an economy at any moment of time. Still, we could draw a curve "fitted" to these points that would look not unlike the Phillips curve of Figure 12-1.

Another interesting feature of this period is that if we look at the path of change over the specific years involved, it is in the direction of greater inflation and lesser unemployment, a point we shall return to in a moment.

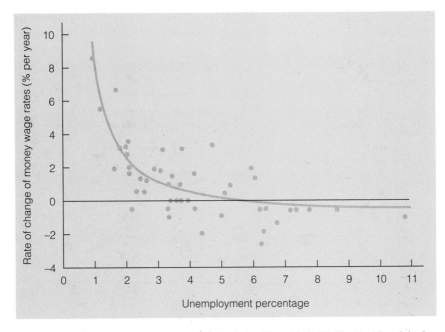

Figure 12-1   Phillips Curve for the United Kingdom, 1861–1913   In this original study of wage changes in relation to unemployment, higher rates of inflation tended to go with lower rates of unemployment, and vice versa. Each dot in the diagram represents the inflation (wage) rate and unemployment rate for one year.
SOURCE: A. W. Phillips, "The Relation Between Unemployment and the Rate of Change of Money Wage Rates in the United Kingdom, 1861–1957," *Economica* (November 1958): 285.

The Supply and Demand Basis of the Phillips Curve

In a general sense, the inverse relationship between these two great macro-economic variables is what we might expect from our previous aggregate supply and demand analysis. With this analysis, we can suggest how a Phillips curve might be derived. Let us suppose for the moment that our aggregate supply curve is fixed and that we are faced with different levels of aggregate demand. In Figure 12-3, we have drawn in three different aggregate demand curves for our given supply curve *AS*. The movement from *AD* to *A'D'* involves a new equilibrium at price level *P'* and real GNP at *Y'*. Let us suppose that *P'* is 5 percent higher than *P* and that *Y'* represents the level of national income when unemployment is at 9 percent. What we have then, roughly, is 5-percent inflation associated with 9-percent unemployment.

Contrast these percentages now with what happens when aggregate demand increases from our original *AD* to *A"D"*. The price level goes up to *P"*, and national income goes up to *Y"*. Let us suppose that *P"* is 10 percent higher than *P*. What about *Y"*? Whatever *Y"* is, it will be, in our diagram, greater than *Y'*. (This is because the aggregate supply curve is sloping up-

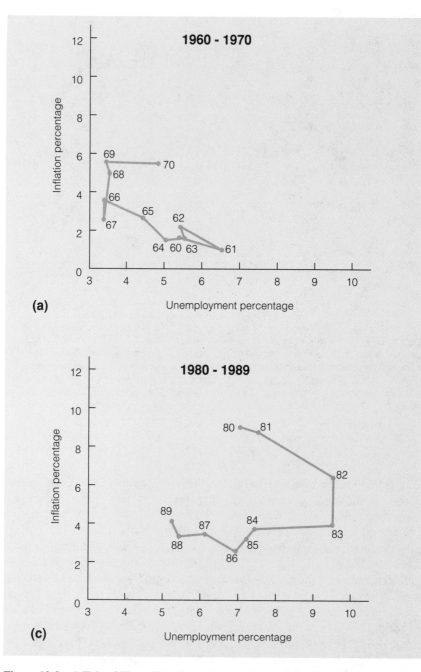

Figure 12-2   A Tale of Three Decades   The changing relationship of inflation and unemployment in the U.S. economy is clearly shown in these diagrams.
SOURCE: *Economic Report of the President*, 1990.
Inflation percentage = percentage change in the GNP price deflator.

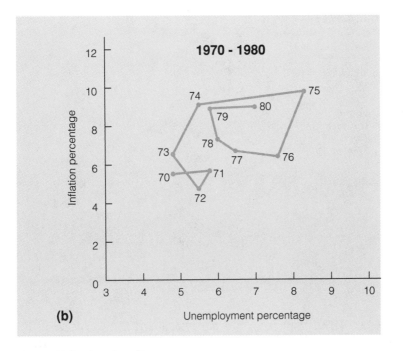

Figure 12-2   (*continued*)

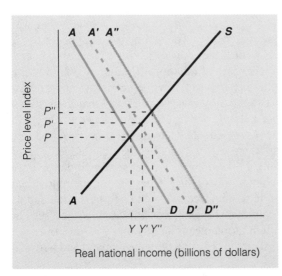

**Figure 12-3   Supply and
Demand Basis for the
Phillips Curve**   In this diagram, a higher rate of inflation ($P''/P > P'/P$) will be
associated with a lower rate
of unemployment ($Y'' > Y'$,
meaning that a higher proportion of the labor force is
employed at Y'').

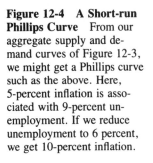

Figure 12-4   A Short-run Phillips Curve   From our aggregate supply and demand curves of Figure 12-3, we might get a Phillips curve such as the above. Here, 5-percent inflation is associated with 9-percent unemployment. If we reduce unemployment to 6 percent, we get 10-percent inflation.

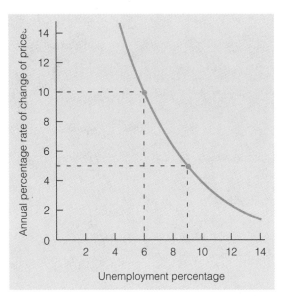

ward to the left.) This implies that unemployment at Y'' is lower than at Y'. The latter rate was 9 percent; let us suppose that the new rate is 6 percent. Thus, we have a 10-percent rate of inflation associated with a 6-percent rate of unemployment. When we plot these numbers out (Figure 12-4), we see that they suggest the familiar shape of a Phillips curve. We call this a "short-run Phillips curve" since, among other things, we are holding the AS curve constant.

The Inflation-Unemployment Trade-off

One should notice already that these diagrams suggest a problem that was unfamiliar in a strictly Keynesian world. The policymaker appears to be faced with a dilemma: If you want to cut down the rate of unemployment, you will have to live with a higher rate of inflation. If inflation gets too high to be endured, the only way to cure it is to throw the economy into a recession. During the 1960s, it was agreed by many economists that there was a *trade-off between inflation and unemployment.* This seemed a cruel choice to have to face since, as we have just noted, such a trade-off is not required in a strictly Keynesian world. In that world, with its nearly right-angled aggregate supply curve (recall Figure 11-4, p. 209), you get serious inflation only at or very close to full employment. Hence, if you have more unemployment than seems tolerable, you can feel quite free to expand aggregate demand as much as needed to raise the employment level; price inflation will be zero or very moderate. Similarly, high inflation means simply that you have overshot the full-employment mark. Just cut back your aggregate demand and you will be all right.

Thus, the first blow to economists in the postwar era was to realize that they might not (or at least not easily) be able to get both full employment and price stability; they might have to sacrifice one or the other. And much worse was yet to come.

THE TRADE-OFF GETS WORSE

The deterioration of our unemployment-inflation trade-off in the 1970s is easily seen by comparing Figure 12-2(b) with Figure 12-2(a). Virtually the entire set of 1970s points is located to the northeast of the 1960s points—that is, *both* inflation *and* unemployment were rising over the whole course of these two decades. In 1960–1961, unemployment averaged under 6 percent and inflation under 1.5 percent; in 1979–1980, unemployment had risen slightly to around 6.5 percent while inflation had soared to 9 percent (or higher, depending on the index used). Economists at this time were fond of using the term "the misery index," which measured the sum of the inflation rate and the unemployment rate. Roughly, our national "misery" doubled between the beginning of the 1960s and the end of the 1970s.

In considering the many factors responsible for this change over a 20-year period, we have to relax our "short-run" assumptions a bit. This will require us to examine shifts in the short-run aggregate supply curve and the development of a longer-run Phillips curve. It will also mean a brief detour into the world of rational expectations, a subject we mentioned in the last chapter.

SHIFTS IN AGGREGATE SUPPLY AND PHILLIPS CURVES

In our analysis of the inflation-unemployment trade-off in the 1960s, we held our aggregate supply curve constant. But if the aggregate demand curve is allowed to shift, we also have to entertain the possibility of shifts in the aggregate supply curve.

Changes in the Costs of Production

In general, anything that changes the cost of producing goods will affect the position of the aggregate supply curve. One kind of shift that customarily takes place in a growing economy is *favorable* in terms of the dilemma we have just been discussing. In the long run, technological progress will tend to increase the productivity of the factors of production—that is, it will permit a greater level of output from a given quantity of inputs, or, alternatively, it will require fewer inputs for a given level of output. Now, the effect of this productivity increase is to keep shifting the aggregate supply curve to the right. At a given price level and wage rate, the money costs of producing a given quantity of output will fall while revenues remain constant. This will create added profits, meaning that equilibrium will be reached only at a higher level of output for that given price. Thus, the supply curve will shift outward, leading, other things equal, to deflationary pressures on the economy. (Remember our discussion of *falling* prices during the nineteenth century; Schumpeter explained these falling prices precisely in terms of the effects of technological progress.)[2]

The aggregate supply curve will also shift if the money costs of the inputs of the productive process change. We will shortly come upon a clearcut (and *un*favorable) example of this in terms of energy prices in the 1970s. But also, of course, money wage rates can change. Since inflation in the modern world has often been described in terms of a "wage-price spiral," we have to look at this matter more closely.

Expected Versus Actual Inflation

To do this, let us recall that when we first drew an aggregate supply curve sloping upward toward the northeast, we explained that higher prices might lead to higher output supplied because they would not be matched by equal increases in factor costs—let's say wages. Prices go up; this catches people off guard since prices were stable (or, more realistically, rising less slowly) before; also, there are contracts holding wage increases to a certain pattern over time—these contracts cannot immediately be adjusted. There is, thus, a period when wages and other factor costs lag behind prices, creating a higher profit margin and a reason to expand production. This was our basic explanation for the northeasterly slope of our short-run aggregate supply curve.

Ignoring fixed contracts for a moment and concentrating solely on expectations, we can frame this process in terms of a gap between *actual* and *expected* inflation. Wage rates, let us suppose, are bargained for on the basis of the expected rate of inflation. If actual inflation exceeds this expected rate, a profit margin and, hence, an expansion of output and employment will occur. This expansion, however, will last only as long as the profit margin continues to exist, and this, in turn, will last only as long as the expected rate of inflation is below the actual rate. As soon as expectations catch up with the facts, output and employment will contract back to their original levels; the new situation will differ from the old only in having a higher rate of inflation. What we have described above amounts to nothing but a shift of our short-run aggregate supply curve upward (or to the left). The process is suggested in Figure 12-5. Suppose there has been an increase in aggregate demand from *AD* to *A'D'*. Now, in the first instance, the rise in prices is not fully matched by the rise in factor costs (actual inflation exceeds expected inflation), and output is expanded along the short-run aggregate supply curve, *AS*. Short-

---

[2] We will have a fuller discussion of technological progress in relation to the growth of the economy in part 5 of this book (see especially pp. 306–311). As mentioned earlier, we are presently dealing with problems on the borderline of the short run versus the long run.

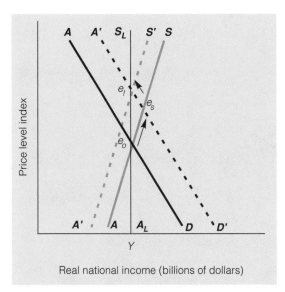

Figure 12-5   A Vertical Long-run Aggregate Supply Curve   An increase in aggregate demand may, in the first instance, take us to a new equilibrium at e_s. When expectations adjust to higher prices, however, the aggregate supply curve shifts to the left, and we go to a long-run equilibrium at e_l—the same level of real national income with which we began.

run equilibrium, at e_s, involved higher output and less unemployment but higher inflation than where we started from (e_o). Now, expectations catch up with realities: wage demands go up; *real* wages, which have temporarily fallen, rise back again; the additional profits disappear, and the economy moves from e_s to a longer-run equilibrium at e_l. The long-run aggregate supply curve that would emerge in such a context (barring other long-run changes such as technological progress and so on) would, therefore, be a vertical line, A_LS_L. Shifts in aggregate demand would, in the long run, affect only the rate of inflation and not the level of output and employment.

A Long-run Vertical Phillips Curve

Now, the consequence of a vertical long-run aggregate supply curve is a vertical long-run Phillips curve. The supply curve A_LS_L tells us that equilibrium real GNP is a constant, and this implies (for a given technology) a constant equilibrium level of employment and unemployment. Any attempt to depart from this level of unemployment will simply lead to higher or lower rates of inflation. To put it in terms of an assertion quite common among economists in recent years: *There is no long-run trade-off between inflation and unemployment.* The trade-off we thought we had discovered in the 1960s is, it is claimed, only a short-term phenomenon, and any policy based on choosing less of one evil at the expense of the other is wholly misguided.

The Natural Rate of Unemployment

If the long-run Phillips curve is vertical (Figure 12-6), then it means that there is a certain equilibrium level of unemployment, largely impervious to

Figure 12-6 The Long-run Phillips Curve A vertical long-run aggregate supply curve (Figure 12-5) will lead to a vertical long-run Phillips curve. This implies no long-run trade-off between inflation and unemployment.

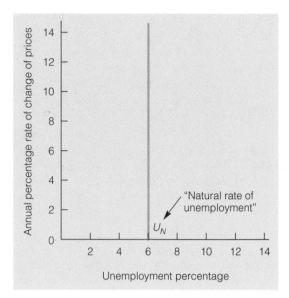

changes in aggregate demand. This rate is equal to U_n, which stands for the *natural rate of unemployment*. We mentioned this concept briefly before when we were discussing monetarism; now we can give it a somewhat clearer meaning. The natural rate of unemployment is usually taken to signify that rate of unemployment below which inflation will have a tendency to accelerate. Or, to put it slightly differently, any attempt to decrease unemployment below its natural level will simply cause a more rapid rate of inflation. The increasing rate of inflation is necessary to keep the actual rate above the expected rate. In the case we have just presented in Figure 12-5, the rise of the actual rate of inflation above the expected rate permits us to increase output and employment above the natural rate to e_s. To *stay* there, however, we would have to increase aggregate demand and prices still further; otherwise, we would simply slip back to the new equilibrium at e_1. Only the natural rate of unemployment is compatible with a constant rate of inflation.

The natural rate of unemployment is also often identified with what might be called the "full-employment rate of unemployment."[3] We may re-

---

[3] This is not always the case, however. The late Otto Eckstein, for example, distinguished the "natural rate of unemployment" from the "full-employment rate of unemployment" and distinguished *both* from the "noninflationary rate of unemployment." (Otto Eckstein, *Core Inflation* [Englewood Cliffs, NJ: Prentice Hall, 1981], pp. 102–104.) In general, our definition in this text will be the equivalent of what is sometimes called the "nonaccelerating inflation rate of unemployment," or "NAIRU," as it is frequently referred to in the literature. From our present point of view, perhaps the main thing to keep in mind is that all of these concepts involve relatively low rates of unemployment—that is, users of the concepts do not consider it a "natural" (or equilibrium) condition when there is massive general unemployment as contemplated in the Keynesian analysis.

call from chapter 7 (pp. 130–131) that "full employment" does not imply literally zero unemployment, but rather the existence of only frictional unemployment (as workers between jobs search for other opportunities) and structural unemployment (as changes in our industrial technology or other factors cause shifts in the kinds of employment available in the economy).

If the economy is appropriately competitive, and the adjustments of the short-run aggregate supply curves are as we have shown them in Figure 12-5, then the rate of unemployment defined in terms of maintaining a constant rate of inflation and the full-employment rate of unemployment should be at least roughly the same rate. However, the economy is not always perfectly competitive, as we know. Also, there is great disagreement among economists as to how rapidly the adjustments to the natural rate of unemployment will take place.

RATIONAL EXPECTATIONS THEORY

The speed of adjustments to the natural rate of unemployment is, in fact, a major issue when we enter the ultramodern (and still controversial) world of the *rational expectationists* (or *new classical economists*). What we have just presented is an argument to the effect that there is no long-run trade-off between inflation and unemployment. In the world of "rational expectations," there is no such trade-off even in the short run. These economists claim that not only the long-run but also the *short-run Phillips curve is vertical!*

Such a position implies that there is no systematic gap between expected and actual inflation, even in the short run. Another way of putting this is to say that the actors on the economic scene—laborers, business executives, consumers, and so on—have *rational expectations* about the future state of the economy. Workers are not regularly misled into accepting, say, lower-than-usual real wages because they fail to foresee the extent of the inflation that lies ahead. Sometimes they may expect too low a rate of inflation, but at other times they will expect too high a rate. In either event, they will not go on regularly making the same mistake over and over again. Similarly, in the case of business firms, they will not regularly pay labor too high a real wage because they have overestimated future inflation. Sometimes they will, in fact, overestimate future inflation; at other times, however, they will underestimate it. The central fact is not that everyone's expectations are always exactly fulfilled, but that they are rationally formed. Businesses, labor, consumers make their forecasts on the basis of the known economic facts and a reasonable understanding of how the economic system functions. They will not always be right, but they will not make systematic errors of judgment. There will be random errors only. Furthermore, they will form their expectations quite quickly and flexibly on the basis of current inflation. For that reason, even in the short run, the actual rate of unemployment will not depart much, or for very long, from the natural rate.

This theory seems to put quite a burden of understanding on the man in the street—it is by no means clear that economists themselves do not make systematic forecasting errors about the future of the economy!—and it also ignores a number of contractual and other lags that are likely to slow down the adjustment of economic expectations to economic realities. Thus, a majority of economists find it necessary to modify this rather extreme position. We can, however, notice one very happy feature of a world in which the theory of rational expectations is valid: The government could halt inflation simply by announcing (and being believed!) that it was going to halt inflation. Knowing what the government was going to do and how it would affect the economy, everyone would quickly adjust to his or her new situation. Inflation would be stopped, and, furthermore, there would be no temporary cost in terms of increased unemployment. Unemployment would simply stay at its "natural" rate throughout. Although this analysis does seem quite unrealistic, it will help explain what we will later notice as a tremendous emphasis on *credibility* in the government's macroeconomic policies in the early 1990s.

INCREASING "MISERY"—WHAT HAPPENED IN THE 1970s?

Returning now to our worsening experience with unemployment, and especially inflation, from the mid-1960s through the end of the 1970s, we now ask what caused this unfortunate departure from our previous experience? Among the main factors many economists cite are the following:

Supply Shocks

During the decade of the 1970s, the American economy was subject to a number of what have been called "shocks" whose ultimate effect was to bring a substantial deterioration in the inflation-unemployment relationship. Many of these shocks adversely affected the supply side—that is, caused the aggregate supply curve to shift to the left—and many of them had international ramifications. A drop in the exchange rate of the dollar in the early 1970s raised the price (in dollars) of imported raw materials and other goods required by industry. In 1972–1973, poor agricultural harvests in the U.S., combined with the sale at subsidized low prices of more than a billion bushels of wheat to Russia (called the "Great Grain Robbery"), sent food prices soaring. Then, of course, the biggest shocks of all were the explosion of energy prices in 1973–1974 and again in 1979–1980 engineered by the Organization of Petroleum Exporting Countries (OPEC). In 1970, the world price of a barrel of light Arabian oil was $1.80; by 1982, even with an emerging "oil glut," the price of this same barrel of oil exceeded $30. In one year, 1973–1974, oil prices more than quadrupled.

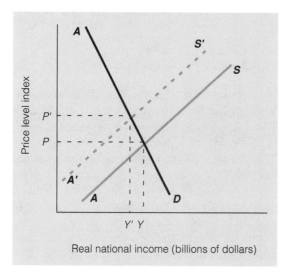

Figure 12-7   Effect of Supply Shocks   A supply "shock"—for example, the increase in price of some vital import like petroleum—will cause our aggregate supply curve to shift toward the left. Increasing unemployment *and* inflation will be the result.

The immediate effect of such shocks, as we mentioned above, is to shift our short-run aggregate supply curve to the left, as in Figure 12-7. The reason for this shift is that for any given price level, these supply shocks increase the costs of the factors of production and, therefore, lower profits. Take the case of the explosion of oil prices. All industry is dependent to some degree on energy in the form of oil, and in the United States, a substantial amount of that oil is and has been imported from abroad. When the dollar price of oil is increased, the cost of producing a wide variety of products also increases. To continue the same rate of output, therefore, the producers will require higher prices for their products. Alternatively, if prices for their own products remain unchanged, they will cut back production and employment. In other words, our short-run aggregate supply curve will shift to the left.

Note this important point: *When an increase in inflation is caused by an increase in aggregate demand, there is a tendency for output to go up and unemployment down. When, however, the cause is an unfavorable shift in aggregate supply, we get not only more inflation, but also reduced output and, hence, increased unemployment.*

Which, of course, is exactly what we did have during the 1970s.

This shifting of the supply curve to the left because of these various shocks could, in principle, have been offset by technological progress, which, as we have already noted, tends to shift the aggregate supply curve favorably—that is, to the right. For a variety of reasons—including the effects of higher energy costs, but also other factors that we shall discuss in part 5—the rate of improvement in productivity of American labor during this period declined quite sharply. Whereas the improvement in productivity during the 1950s and 1960s was of the order of 2 to 3 percent per year, in the 1970s, it fell well below 2 percent, and in the years 1974, 1978, 1979, and 1980, it was negative.[4]

Adverse Effects on the Demand Side

While these unfavorable supply effects were taking place, there were also some unfavorable developments on the demand side as far as inflationary pressures were concerned. These developments, many economists believe, were the result of the actions of the federal government. The first development occurred in the late 1960s, where we have already noted the tendency toward higher levels of inflation in the U.S. economy. It was essentially the failure of the government to raise taxes sufficiently to pay for the Vietnam War, which was occurring simultaneously with the launching of a number of Great Society social programs. Economists of almost all persuasions are agreed that the resort to large-scale deficits to finance an unpopular war was, from an economic point of view, a serious mistake.

The second mistake, or series of mistakes, on the part of the federal government is more debatable. Many economists believe, however, that the general fiscal and monetary policies of government during the late 1960s and 1970s were too expansionary on the average. According to the critics of government policy, the attempts to stimulate aggregate demand during periods of recession were ultimately self-defeating. These demand-stimulation tactics seemed to work at the time—that is, output and employment were expanded—but they left a residue of generally increased inflationary pressures. This meant that each successive recession became more difficult to "cure" in this fashion. Each time around, the inflationary cost became greater. By the same token, to reduce this new and higher level of inflation back to some reasonably moderate level would have involved increasingly high costs in terms of unemployment.

The Increasing Inflationary Bias of the Economy

The foregoing comment suggests what is, in fact, the view of many economists: that an increasing inflationary bias was being built into our economy during these years. That our economy does have certain structural features that make for this inflationary bias has been widely recognized in the post–World War II era. As we pointed out in part 1, the American economy is not in any sense a pure market economy. Large oligopolistic firms have, within limits, the power to set prices independent of the laws of supply and demand. Labor unions, similarly, can agitate for higher wages, even in the presence of

---

[4] By "productivity" here, we mean output per hour of all persons engaged in the private business sector. (See below, pp. 308–309.)

considerable unemployment in their industry. If these price- and cost-raising activities happen to be validated by expansionary government macroeconomic policies, then the possibility of high levels of inflation, even when there is substantial unemployment, cannot be denied. Furthermore, the government can also be a direct contributor to this built-in inflationary bias, since numerous pieces of government legislation—trade and tariff protection, agricultural price supports, minimum wage laws, and so on—have the effect of institutionalizing such a bias.

During the late 1960s and 1970s, the inflationary bias of the economy, augmented by the supply shocks and government policies, appears to have become embedded in business, labor, and consumer expectations. It was expected that inflation would continue at high levels, and people increasingly conducted their economic affairs on this premise. What this meant, in effect, was that the amount of unemployment that would be necessary to *reduce* the rate of inflation was growing to ominous levels.

THE TURNAROUND OF THE 1980s

As it proved to be. If we now look at Figure 12-2(c), the first thing we notice is the unemployment disaster (or near-disaster) of the early 1980s. In 1982 and 1983, U.S. unemployment rose to levels not seen since before our entry into World War II. For those economists who argue that there is no trade-off between unemployment and inflation, whether short run or long run, this period poses an enormous problem. For it seems abundantly clear that this deep recession—caused largely by the government's macroeconomic policies— was a major factor in the second striking feature of this diagram: the dramatic reduction in inflationary pressures in the economy between 1980–1981 and 1983–1986. By 1986, inflation, which had been rising fairly steadily for two decades, plunged to its lowest levels since the mid-1960s. There were undoubtedly numerous factors involved—for example, supply "shocks" were favorable in this period, with the dollar rising in value sharply in the early 1980s (when inflation was plummeting), making our imports cheaper in dollar terms; oil prices after OPEC II plunged in real terms; unions were declining in strength and numbers, with the breaking of the air-traffic controllers' strike in 1981 signifying the government's hostility to large wage increases; and so on. Still, in all, few economists doubt that a *major* factor in the collapse of inflation in the early 1980s was the sharp increase in unemployment that immediately preceded it.

So apparently a trade-off does exist after all, or at least so it strongly appeared in the early 1980s. Furthermore, the *late* 1980s would also seem to give support to the trade-off concept. If one looks at the curve from 1986 to 1989, one finds it quite reminiscent of the curve traced out in the early 1960s. Unemployment and inflation are both a bit higher in the later period, but not by much,[5] and there is the same gentle drift toward somewhat lower levels of unemployment at the expense of somewhat higher levels of inflation. The trade-off appears to be reviving even in this period of rather undramatic changes.[6]

What do those who argue against the trade-off concept have to say about all this, particularly the dramatic break in inflation wrought by the sharp recession of 1981–1982? Their basic answer probably has to be that although it might have taken a little time, we did not really have to go through such a sharp recession as we did, that natural forces would have brought down inflation as long as the government did not continue following highly expansionary fiscal and monetary policies. Businesses would have had to moderate their price increases and laborers their wage demands once the government ceased validating them with its expansionary policies. Unemployment might have risen a little temporarily, but nothing like what occurred during the 1981–1982 recession. In other words, the natural rate of unemployment would have remained largely unchanged, and the departures from it could have been kept to a minimum.

The issue, then, is to some degree one of differences of opinion about timing. How rapidly and rationally do economic participants adjust to changes in economic conditions? For many, and perhaps most, economists, these adjustments are believed to take time. In particular, once inflationary expectations—whether originally due to supply shocks, demand-management policies, collective bargaining agreements, or any combination of these or other factors—get embedded in the system, they may be very difficult to dislodge. In an ideal world, the trade-off of inflation and unemployment may disappear completely. In our more ordinary, human circumstances, it remains a problem to be coped with and certainly watched with care as the economy evolves.

And if this is true of anyone, it is certainly most true of our fiscal and monetary policymakers, to whose complex tasks we turn our attention in the next two chapters.

SUMMARY

The relationship between inflation and unemployment has been undergoing major changes, both in fact and in theory, during the past three decades.

---

[5] It isn't really clear that unemployment in the late 1980s is higher than that of the 1960s, or, rather, it depends on what measure one wishes to use. There has been a substantial increase in the labor force *participation rate* between the two periods. Thus, if we look at the employment-to-population ratio, we actually find it to be higher in the late 1980s than it was in the 1960s.

[6] Although the late 1980s were a period of rather "undramatic" changes, the 1990s started off very differently. The 1990 invasion of Kuwait by Iraq and the subsequent turmoil in the Middle East suggested the possibility of a new round of supply shocks similar to (or perhaps much more dangerous than) those of the 1970s. Even before any physical shortages of oil could be felt, gasoline and heating oil prices in the United States rose sharply, and analysts uniformly worried about a return to the problems of our earlier energy crisis—increasing inflation *and* increasing unemployment.

The common view in the 1960s (and still a popular view today) was that there is a trade-off between inflation and unemployment—if we wish to get less of one we have to put up with more of the other. This view was supported empirically by the Phillips curve analysis of wages and prices in the United Kingdom and by the behavior of inflation and unemployment in the United States in the early postwar period. Analytically, this view was suggested by aggregate supply and demand analysis. With a fixed short-run aggregate supply curve sloping upward to the northeast, changes in aggregate demand will tend to decrease (increase) unemployment at the same time that they increase (decrease) inflation.

This view was seriously challenged by the experience of the 1970s, when there was a sharp worsening on the unemployment and, especially, the inflation fronts. Several factors explained this changed picture. First, there were a number of supply "shocks" (like OPEC-engineered oil price hikes), which meant a shifting upward (to the left) of the aggregate supply curve. These unfavorable shifts, unlike demand shifts, normally lead to an increase in *both* unemployment and inflation. Second, there was the question of government policies dating back to the 1960s—the failure to increase taxes to pay for the Vietnam War and generally expansionary macroeconomic policies—which led to increased inflationary pressures from the demand side. And, finally, there was a general rise in inflationary expectations as businesses, labor, and consumers began to make decisions based on the assumption of continually rising prices.

At the same time, economic theorists were showing that the supposed trade-off between inflation and unemployment was more a short-run than a long-run phenomenon. It depended on temporary gaps opening up between actual and expected inflation. In principle, an increase in aggregate demand would raise both prices and employment, but when employment was raised above its natural rate, this would only be until expectations could catch up with the facts, whereupon employment would be reduced back to its natural rate again. Rational expectations theorists went even further and argued that there would not even be a short-run trade-off between inflation and unemployment since participants in economic life would not make systematic errors in their judgment of future trends. These theorists argued that not only the short-run but the long-run aggregate supply curve and Phillips curve would be vertical at the natural rate of unemployment (or output).

The experience of the 1980s involved an apparently sharp trade-off between unemployment and inflation as the recession of 1981–1982 brought 20 years of gradually accelerating inflation to a halt. Although it could be argued that natural forces might have brought down inflation without the pain of a major recession, the realism of such relatively pain-free adjustments was brought into question. In the late 1980s, as in the 1960s, slowly rising inflation and slowly improving employment were occurring simultaneously and being nervously watched by all concerned.

Key Concepts for Review

Phillips curve
  Short run
  Long run
Inflation-unemployment trade-off
Aggregate supply curve
  Short run
  Long run
Expected versus actual inflation
Rational expectationists
  (new classical economists)

Vertical Phillips curve
Vertical aggregate supply curve
Natural rate of unemployment
Full-employment rate of
  unemployment
Supply shocks
Inflationary bias in the U.S.
  economy
Sharp recession of 1981–1982

Questions for Discussion

1. Describe for someone unfamiliar with the facts how the relationship between unemployment and inflation in the United States changed over the years 1960–1989. What major events would you single out as necessary for an understanding of this pattern of change?

2. Using Figure 11-4 from the last chapter as your guide, show what a Keynesian-style Phillips curve would look like.

3. Draw a Phillips curve showing a short-run trade-off between inflation and unemployment. Why is it that many economists who accept a Phillips curve of this shape for the short-run claim that there is no long-run trade-off between inflation and unemployment. What would the long-run Phillips curve look like on this hypothesis? Describe the process by which short-run Phillips curves of one shape give rise to a long-run Phillips curve of quite a different shape.

4. Since you have just shown (in question 3) the process by which a short-run Phillips curve of one shape gives rise to a long-run Phillips curve of a different shape, how can the rational expectationists claim that both curves are of the same shape (vertical)? Does their logic seem realistic to you?

5. Following the second OPEC-engineered oil price rise in 1979–1980, there was an oil supply "shock" in reverse—that is, in 1982–1983, petroleum prices were falling worldwide. Use aggregate supply and demand curves to show how these falling energy prices might affect both unemployment and inflation in a heavy-importing country like the United States.

6. "Despite what the theorists say, when inflation takes root, the only way you can break its back is by throwing the economy into a painful recession—or worse." Discuss.

CHAPTER 13

FISCAL POLICY AND
THE NATIONAL DEBT

If one concentrates on the "misery index" (the sum of the unemployment and inflation rates), which we mentioned in the last chapter, then one would have to give exceptionally high marks to the macroeconomic achievements of the Reagan administration of the 1980s. The improvement from the 1970s to the later 1980s was dramatic and unequivocal (see Figure 12-2, p. 000). The argument of some critics that a similar achievement could have been accomplished without the economic and personal losses of the recession of 1981–1982 remains unproved, and is at least doubtful.

In point of fact, however, Reaganomics, as it was commonly called, has been seriously criticized on a number of grounds. Some of these criticisms have more to do with microeconomics than macroeconomics, especially those concerned with the distribution of income, poverty, possible deficiencies in the social "safety net," the effects of deregulation, and the like. But two of the most severe criticisms are focused on heartland issues of macroeconomics. The improvements on the inflation-unemployment front during these years were achieved, it is claimed, only at the expense of (1) a horrendous escalation of the national debt and (2) a disastrous rise in our international balance of payments deficit. Both these deficits, it is said, will come back to haunt us in the future.

In terms of the ever-shifting definitions of "liberal" and "conservative" in economics, there is a fine irony in this situation. For it always used to be the liberals who said that there was little or nothing to worry about in the national debt, while the conservatives were forever spending sleepless nights agonizing about it. But it was under the most conservative administration of the postwar era that our national debt exploded, and it was the liberals who were spending the sleepless nights worrying about the matter.

How serious are these so-called "twin deficits"? We shall postpone consideration of the trade deficit until part 5, but in this chapter, we shall look closely at the national debt and the subject of fiscal policy in general. Have we, in fact, been mortgaging our children's futures?

ELEMENTARY FISCAL POLICY REVISITED

Changing attitudes about the national debt are not the only source of irony in recent years. In the heyday of Keynesian analysis in the first two decades or so after World War II, fiscal policy was considered the principal weapon by which the twin goals of full employment and price stability were to be achieved. In an inflationary economy, we were to increase taxes and/or decrease government spending. In a depressed economy, we were to cut taxes and/or expand government spending. How far we had come from this position by the early 1980s may be indicated by the fact that many business executives, Wall Street economists, and politicians were attributing the high levels of unemployment of that period to the federal deficit. What a few years before would have been considered an expansionary fiscal policy was now being criticized for its contractionary effects! Although few academic economists would have accepted this verdict, the fact is that a changed climate of opinion was everywhere in evidence. At the annual meeting of the American Economic Association in late 1981, Columbia University economist Edmund S. Phelps announced that the preceding year had seen "the efficacy of fiscal policy . . . shaken to its foundations." [1]

To see what has been happening here, let us return to our own preliminary analysis of fiscal policy as spelled out in chapter 8. We were dealing then with a world in which the price level was constant and where we were operating in the range of real national income somewhere below the full-employment level. We left the monetary aspects of the economy deliberately vague. An increase in government expenditures in this economy (from G to G' in Figure 13-1 [a]) would lead to a fully multiplied increase in real national income (from Y to Y'). The multiplier, we recall, would be equal to the reciprocal of the marginal propensity to save ($1/MPS$). If MPS was, say, one-third, then the multiplier would be 3, and a given increase in G would lead to a threefold increase in Y and, hence, a substantial increase in employment.

Alternative policies were also discussed. Reducing taxes on consumers would raise the consumption function and cause an expansion of output and

---

[1] Edmund S. Phelps, "Cracks on the Demand Side: A Year of Crisis in Theoretical Macroeconomics," *American Economic Review*, vol. 72, no. 2 (May 1982): 378.

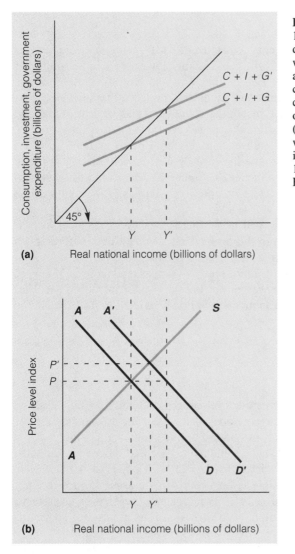

Figure 13-1 In Figure 13-1(a), we have the standard Keynesian multiplier with an increase in G to G' and Y to Y'. When price changes are taken into account, part of the expansion of G goes into higher prices ($P' > P$ in Figure 13-1[b]), while real national income increases less (Y' in Figure 13-1[b] is lower than Y' in Figure 13-1[a]).

employment by that route. Since taxes were seen to have a somewhat smaller negative effect on spending than the positive effect of government spending on goods and services, it was also shown that the government could expand national income with a balanced budget expansion of both G and T.[2] The multiplier in this case, under certain assumptions, would be 1.

---

[2] Recall that this differential effect of government spending and taxes only holds in the case where the government spending is for goods and services. Where government *transfer payments* are con-

FISCAL POLICY AND PRICES

One way of approaching the changed status of fiscal policy in recent years is to show how various factors will considerably lower the simple multiplier for government spending we used in chapter 8 and have displayed again in Figure 13-1(a). A major amendment we have to notice is that increased government spending will, in a typical case, raise prices as well as output and employment. If we could assume that prices would remain at their original level, we would get the full multiplier of Figure 13-1(a). When, however, prices are allowed to change, the increased government spending is partly "wasted," as it were, in price increases. Figure 13-1(b) shows us what happens in terms of our aggregate demand and supply curves. The given increase in government expenditures will lead to a rightward shift in our aggregate demand curves; the net effect will be an increase in the price level from P to P' and a smaller increase in the level of real income than before. Y' in Figure 13-1(b) is smaller than Y' in Figure 13-1(a).

In a sense, Figure 13-1(b) represents two strikes against fiscal policy as compared to Figure 13-1(a). We get not only a smaller increase in real income than expected, but also an increase in prices, which, in itself, would be considered a negative effect.

MONETARY EFFECTS

The degree to which an increased level of government spending leads to merely nominal effects (price) as opposed to real effects (output, employment, and so on) will depend, of course, on the shape and positions of the aggregate supply and demand curves and the factors that influence their shifting over time. One obvious factor that has to be considered is the way in which this government spending is financed. We are assuming for the moment that we have increased G to G' without any increase in taxes. This means that the government will have to borrow—issue bonds—to finance its additional expenditures. There will be an increase in the federal debt.

There are many complexities involved in analyzing different methods of financing the federal debt. Bonds may be sold to the general public, to commercial banks, to the Federal Reserve banks (another branch of the government!), and so on. The two extreme cases are where the financing of the debt involves no new money creation (where the bonds are sold directly to the public) and where the bonds are all bought by newly created money (the bonds are purchased by the Federal Reserve System).

---

cerned, the positive effect of government spending is cancelled out by the negative effect of taxes— that is, the multiplier is zero.

The second method is often called the "printing press" method in that one arm of the government simply creates the money that bails out another arm of the government. The way it works, technically, is that the Treasury sells the bonds to the Fed, which pays the Treasury by increasing the Treasury's deposit account with the Fed. For a $1 billion purchase of bonds, the balance sheet of the Federal Reserve bank is altered as follows:

FEDERAL RESERVE BANK BALANCE SHEET

1. The Treasury is credited with a $1 billion deposit at the Federal Reserve bank:

Assets	*Liabilities*
+ $1 billion government bonds	+ $1 billion U.S. Treasury deposits

2. The Treasury spends the money, and the individuals who receive it deposit it in their commercial banks. The commercial banks thereby increase their reserves at the Federal Reserve bank:

Assets	*Liabilities*
+ $1 billion government bonds	+ $1 billion member bank reserves

These member bank reserves are, we recall from chapter 10, the foundation on which a multiple expansion of the money supply can take place. Thus, in contrast to the case where the bonds are sold to the public, this method does involve an expansion of the money supply.

The task of increasing or decreasing the money supply in this fashion is really a part of monetary policy, which we shall discuss in the next chapter. We can say here, however, that insofar as an expansionary fiscal policy puts pressure on the Fed to increase its purchases of government bonds, then to that degree fiscal policy is making the flexible exercise of monetary policy more difficult. Historically, the differing needs of the Treasury and the Fed have come into conflict more than once, a notable case being just after World War II, when the Fed wanted more freedom to fight inflation and the Treasury wanted to assure itself a purchaser of its bonds at low interest rates. (See above, p. 195.)

For the moment, however, let us assume the bonds are purchased by the general public and that there is no increase in the economy's quantity of money. In this case, the government is competing with private borrowers in the credit markets, and we would expect a tendency for interest rates to rise. This rise in interest rates will have at least some negative effect on the level of business investment and also spending on consumer durables. As national income expands, moreover, there will be a need for more money for transactions purposes, and this will put further pressure on interest rates to rise. This increasing pressure on interest rates will take place, even if there is no rising price level as a result of the expanded government deficit; if prices rise, of course, this will also have the effect of increasing the amount of money needed for transactions purposes. With a given supply of money, rising prices, thus, will also lead to an upward pressure on interest rates.

If we go back to Figure 13-1 again, we can see the mechanism by which the effects we have just been discussing will reduce the multiplier. What happens is that the expansion of G to G' in Figure 13-1(a) is offset to some degree (how big a degree we'll discuss in a moment) by declines in C and I. This means that even at constant prices, the new equilibrium level of Y' will not be as great as that shown in the diagram. If the multiplier was 3 before, it will be less than 3 when these effects have been taken into account.

Translated into Figure 13-1(b), this means that there will be a smaller shift to the right of the aggregate demand curve than before. This shift will, of course, lead not just to added output, but also to higher prices. Thus, the new equilibrium level of real income will not only be less than the Y' shown in Figure 13-1(a), but also below the Y' shown in Figure 13-1(b).

INDUCED INVESTMENT

But won't the expansion of national income, however small, have some *favorable* effects on investment as well? Businesses undertake investment ultimately in order to produce output. Low levels of production will be discouraging to business investment since they already have "excess capacity." Higher levels of production will make additions to capacity—investment— more desirable and potentially profitable.

There is little doubt that this factor must be taken into account and that its general impact is in the opposite direction from the two factors we have just discussed; those factors led to a *decrease* in the multiplier as shown in Figure 13-1, while this new factor would lead to an *increase* in the multiplier. We can show the impact of this so-called *induced investment* (that is, induced by the increase in the level of national income) in a diagram by having the rate of investment increase as the level of national income increases. This is done in Figure 13-2. The distance between the C curve and the $C + I$ curve increases as we move to the right with higher levels of national income. Other things equal, this will increase the steepness of the slope of the combined $C + I + G$ curve. The reader should convince himself that a steeper slope will, in fact, mean a higher value for the multiplier.[3]

---

[3] This discussion may remind the reader of the "accelerator," which we mentioned in chapter 8, pp. 149–150). The mechanism of induced investment, as presented here, is not exactly the same as

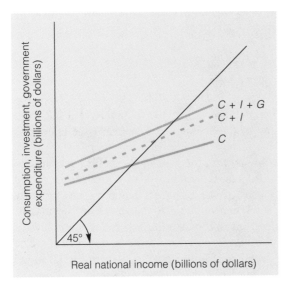

Figure 13-2 Induced Investment If an expansionary fiscal policy leads to an increase in GNP, then one positive effect might be to cause "induced investment"—that is, I increases as Y increases.

TAX EFFECTS

Although we are considering the case where G is increased with no change in tax policy, it is unrealistic to assume that we can have an expansion of either real or nominal GNP without taxes increasing automatically along the way. A fixed tax *policy* in this case will lead to increased tax *collections*. This will hold even if that tax policy involves no progressivity—that is, if taxes are set, say, at a constant percentage of income, no matter what the level of income. Since taxes have historically been based on nominal income rather than real income, the increase in taxes takes place if the increase in nominal GNP is wholly due to prices and involves no increase in real income at all. In the more realistic case where the tax structure is at least mildly "progressive," then, of course, the increase in nominal GNP due to increased government spending will tend to increase taxes by a greater percentage than the percentage increase in GNP.

What this means is that we have another offset to the government spending multiplier displayed in Figure 13-1(a). Suppose it works out that each additional $1 of government expenditures leads, through the expansion of income, to an increase of 40¢ in taxes. Clearly, this will lead to a substantial reduction in the net value of the multiplier for increased G. The advantage, of course, is that not all the new G will require additions to the national

---

the accelerator in that the former depends on the *level* of national income while the latter depends on the *rate of change* of national income. However, there is clearly a strong family resemblance between the two mechanisms. The both tell us that investment will be strongly affected by the relationship of income to productive capacity.

debt. A significant fraction of the expanding expenditures will be offset by the automatic increase in tax revenues.

HOW FAST HAS THE NATIONAL DEBT GROWN?

We have mentioned the national debt once or twice in the above discussion, yet, as we said at the beginning of the chapter, it is precisely the enormous expansion of the national debt in recent years that has worried so many people. In fact, it is accurate to say that the size of the public debt has so preoccupied the minds of presidents and members of Congress in recent years that fiscal policy, as a means of stablizing the economy, has virtually disappeared as a policy option. When public officials speak of the macroeconomic implications of federal tax and expenditure policies these days, a dominating issue is the effect of these policies on the national debt.[4] The overwhelming objective—in principle if not in practice—seems to be to get to a balanced budget as soon as humanly or politically possible.

Are such concerns justified? How fast has the national debt grown in recent years? Let's first look at a few facts.

On the surface, at least, the facts seem overwhelming. The total interest-bearing public debt in the United States at the end of December 1989 had reached over $2.93 trillion. Since a substantial proportion of this debt was held by government agencies, a more relevant figure is probably the public debt held by private investors. In 1989, this was $1.95 trillion, or approximately $7,800 for every person, or $31,200 for every family of four in the nation.

Furthermore, this huge debt has been accumulated at an extremely rapid pace, especially since 1975. Figure 13-3 shows the sharp upturn in our public debt during World War II, followed by nearly 30 years in which the debt barely rose at all, and then the explosion in the late 1970s and throughout the 1980s. Figure 13-4 shows what has been happening to the excess of federal expenditures over federal revenues during the decades of the 1970s and 1980s. These charts, many critics feel, should be placed next to the inflation-unemployment diagram (Figure 12-2, p. 228) before we congratulate ourselves too heartily on the macroeconomic achievements of recent years.

Whether this view is justified or not, we shall consider in a moment.

---

[4] Even when President Bush was making his "no new taxes" ("read my lips") pledge in the 1988 presidential campaign, he was very conscious of the budget deficit problem. His position on taxes was defended on the grounds (1) that to achieve a balanced budget we should reduce spending rather than raise taxes and (2) that low tax rates will stimulate economic growth, which will have at least some effect in raising tax revenues later on. When it became apparent in 1990 that the budget deficit would be even larger than previously anticipated, the deficit problem went to center stage immediately, and the president publicly expressed his willingness to reconsider his no-tax pledge. About the two arguments that prompted the original pledge, we will have more to say later in this and the next chapter.

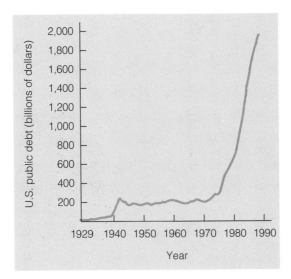

Figure 13-3   The U.S. Public Debt, 1929–1989 This chart measures the U.S. public debt held by private investors (that is, excluding government agencies). As is obvious, it has grown extremely rapidly in recent years.

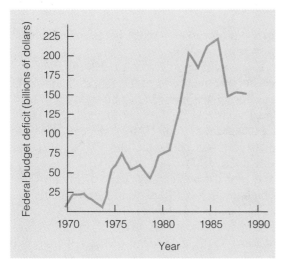

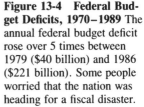

Figure 13-4   Federal Budget Deficits, 1970–1989 The annual federal budget deficit rose over 5 times between 1979 ($40 billion) and 1986 ($221 billion). Some people worried that the nation was heading for a fiscal disaster.

Under any circumstances, however, it has to be noted that Figures 13-3 and 13-4 paint an overly dramatic view of the deterioration of our fiscal condition. For one thing, they are measured in current dollars (rather than constant dollars) and, thus, incorporate the huge inflation we have experienced over these years. Furthermore, they do not take into account the substantial growth in our real GNP during these same years. At the personal level, the burden of our debts (say, for our home mortgage or our credit card expenses) has to be measured in relation to our income if it is to be meaningful to us.

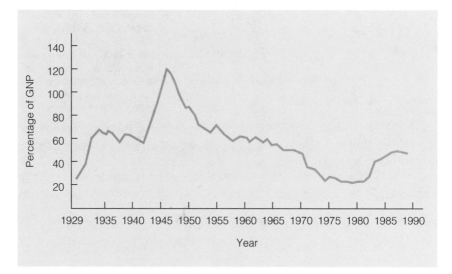

Figure 13-5   U.S. Public Debt as a Percentage of GNP, 1929–1989

Similarly, the burden—whatever it proves to be—of the public debt has to be measured against our national income, or GNP.

When we make this measurement (Figure 13-5), a rather different picture emerges. Suddenly it turns out that the period of the greatest public debt burden in the United States was during and immediately after World War II. At the end of the 1980s, although there had been a clear increase in the debt as a percentage of GNP during that decade (from 23 to 37 percent), we were still below the level of the 1950s and well below the mid-1940s, when our public debt was greater than (exceeded 100 percent of) our GNP.

Furthermore, although our annual federal budget deficits (Figure 13-4) seem to have remained fairly high in the late 1980s—and have regularly exceeded the proclaimed targets of the 1985 Balanced Budget Act[5]—nevertheless, one again gains a somewhat different perspective by relating these deficits to GNP. Between 1983 and 1989, the federal deficit fell from 6.1 percent of GNP to 2.9 percent. Although this is not unqualifiedly good news,[6] it does suggest that the more harrowing tales of national fiscal irresponsibility are a bit exaggerated.

---

[5] This is the so-called Gramm-Rudman-Hollings Act (sometimes referred to simply as Gramm-Rudman) passed by Congress in December of 1985. Since the targets of the act have generally not been met and since the Supreme Court struck down one of its key provisions, it seems clear that the legislation has not accomplished all that it intended. That it has had *some* effect on reducing the deficit, if only psychological, seems likely however.

[6] It can be argued that the deficits of the late 1980s, although lower as a percentage of GNP than that of 1983, really should have been *much* lower—that is, because unemployment was so much higher in

Finally, we should remember that the annual federal deficits are over-stated in *real* terms since they fail to account for the fact that inflation is regularly reducing the real value of each $1 of federal debt (see chapter 9, p. 169). Actually, one can go further than this and suggest that the officially measured federal deficits badly overstate the true increase in *national* indebtedness since (1) they do not include state and local budgets, which have, in total, been running surpluses ever since the late 1960s, and (2) they make no allowance for the fact that certain federal expenditures lead not just to the accumulation of indebtedness, but also to the accumulation of capital assets. It is one thing to spend money on, say, health care for the very elderly, which, however desirable, brings no productive return, and another thing to spend it on, say, bridges and highways, which add to the nation's stock of productive capital. The *net* deficit, according to some economists, should clearly exclude both items, as well as be adjusted for inflation. The result of all these adjustments, according to economist Robert Eisner, whom we quoted in chapter 9, would, in 1988, have transformed a measured federal deficit of $155 billion into an actual total government *surplus* of $42 billion! Although other economists remain unconvinced (appropriately dividing government expenditures between consumption and capital formation is quite perilous), it is clear that extreme statements about the gargantuan proportions of our public debt should be avoided by any serious student of the subject.

NATIONAL DEBT—ALARMS AND FACTS

It should be evident by now that public discussion of our national debt frequently takes on an overly alarmist tone. Let us first put some of the more obvious alarms to rest and then go on to point out some of the real burdens of the debt.

Public Versus Private Debt

One common concern about the expansion of the national debt may be put this way:

> The federal government is no different from any private individual. Everyone knows that a private individual cannot keep accumulating indebtness all the time. Consequently, the federal government should (or must) reduce the size of the public debt.

1983. Economists sometimes speak of the *high employment budget*—that is, what the budget surplus or deficit would have been had the economy actually been near the full-employment level. The high employment deficit, so measured, was greater in the late 1980s than in the recession years of the early 1980s. It can be argued, therefore, that fiscal policy was perversely more expansionary during our prosperous years than in our recession years.

This argument is, in part, a throwback to the view that Adam Smith expressed in his famous declaration: "What is prudence in the conduct of every private family can scarce be folly in that of a great Kingdom." And, indeed, this is part of the problem with the argument, because Smith's statement is clearly untrue in a number of important circumstances. To take a couple of obvious examples: It is clearly prudent for a private individual to refrain from printing money, but does that mean that it is folly for the national government to print money? It is prudent for a private individual not to take the law into his own hands, but are we then to conclude that it is folly for the state to maintain a police force and a legal system? And so on. The point is that the actions of the state and the actions of private individuals are often regulated by different principles, and argument by analogy from one to the other is filled with pitfalls.

In the particular case of the public debt, moreover, there is at least one feature that distinguishes it from the debt of private individuals. When I owe a debt to you, I owe it to an external party. The proper analogy in the case of the nation as a whole would be a debt owed to some foreign country, or an *external debt*. Insofar as our public debt is held by foreign parties—a matter we'll come to in a moment—then the analogy does hold. But the overwhelming majority of our public debt is held by Americans, and, indeed, we could imagine hypothetical circumstances in which the holders of government bonds and the payers of taxes were identical individuals, in which case it would be literally true that "we owe the debt to ourselves."

There is an even deeper flaw in this argument, however. This is the incorrect assumption that private parties don't keep accumulating indebtedness over time. Of course they do. Private mortgage debt (excluding mortgages held by federal agencies) doubled in the decade of the 1980s and, in total, was larger than the entire federal debt held by the public. Add other consumer credit and our huge corporate debt and you have a multiple of government debt at the present time. Nor is this surprising. We all know that businesses regularly issue bonds to finance new ventures and expansions; in a growing economy, we expect such indebtedness to increase over time. This is also true of households. We do pay back debts as they come due, but in the meanwhile, we incur new debts. While we are paying off our car loan, we are also taking out a mortgage on a new house and buying a washing machine and dryer on the installment plan. Thus, whatever folly (or prudence) there is in the government accumulating debt over time, there is the same folly (or prudence) being exercised by private individuals every day of the year.[7]

---

[7] It has been argued by some economists that the increase in corporate indebtedness in the 1980s was potentially a *greater* economic problem than the increase in the public debt. This is because (1) much of this corporate debt was taken on not to invest in new ventures or added plant and equipment, but to finance mergers and leveraged buyouts and to reduce equity capital and (2) when interest costs rise very high (as they have for many firms) their vulnerability to financial difficulties and bankruptcies

National Bankruptcy

But perhaps it *is* folly for private and public parties to keep accumulating debt. In the case of private individuals or corporations, such actions can lead to bankruptcy. May we not face a similar situation with our public debt? Thus, the following worry is often expressed:

> All debts must ultimately be repaid, and so it is with the public debt. The debt has grown so large now that to repay it would place enormous burdens on the economy. Under these circumstances, further increases in the debt will lead us to national bankruptcy.

Again, the analogy with private parties is an error, since the government can always guarantee the payment of its debt by simply printing money to do so. After all, U.S. bonds promise redemption in dollars, which the government can always supply. Private firms or individuals faced with bankruptcy simply do not have this option.

The whole question of having to "pay back" the debt is basically fanciful in any event. As we have just seen, private and corporate debts keep growing over time—in aggregate, they are never "paid back." Nor will the public debt. Furthermore, it cannot be claimed that the debt has shown unprecedented growth relative to our ability to sustain it—our GNP. On the contrary, as Figure 13-5 demonstrated, our debt was far greater in this relative sense in the late 1940s and 1950s. If we managed to survive the expansion of debt that took place during World War II, it seems highly unlikely that we are seriously threatened by the far less burdensome expansion that has taken place since.

Burdening Future Generations

But perhaps the problem is that we are adding burdens to those—like the financing of World War II—that we have never really paid for:

> By increasing the public debt, we are putting the burdens of the present generation off onto the shoulders of future generations. We are saddling our children or our children's children with financial responsibilities that really ought to be borne by ourselves now.

As we shall indicate presently, there are some definite future burdens arising from our public debt. In the sense in which this worry is often conceived, however, the possible shifting of burdens from present to future is

---

increases in hard times. According to Harvard economist Benjamin M. Friedman, the greater financial "fragility" of American corporations may make it much more difficult for the Federal Reserve System to control inflation in the future. (Benjamin M. Friedman, "Financial Fragility and the Policy Dilemma," *Challenge,* [July/August 1990]: 7–16.) See below, chapter 14, footnote 6, p. 271.

quite limited. Take World War II for example. Did we, in fact, pass the fundamental economic burdens of World War II on to later generations? The fact is that we needed the guns, tanks, planes, and ships then, not later. Subject to a qualification we shall mention presently, the resources had to be used and were, in fact, used in the 1940s. Imagine a fully employed economy operating on its transformation (production-possibility) curve.[8] If it wants to produce more of one commodity (armaments), it must give up some of the other commodity (civilian production). When a war effort of the magnitude of our own in the 1940s is involved—50 percent of our national income was going to defense purposes at one point—then the basic costs must be sustained when they occur (by the current generation) and not in the future.

REAL BURDENS OF THE DEBT

Having shown that our current deficits are not quite as large as some critics imagine and that some worries about the national debt are unduly alarmist, we must not go to the other extreme and imagine that there are no burdens to the debt. As we entered the 1990s, virtually all economists in the nation felt that it was desirable to reduce the debt to at least some degree. What are some possibly valid grounds for worrying about a growing national debt?

National Debt in Relation to the Size of Government

One of the oldest and most popular worries against the expansion of the national debt is that it makes it easier to expand the overall role of government in the economy. This is not an alarmist argument, but a perfectly reasonable one; though, of course, one's ultimate judgment depends on how one feels about having more or less government in the economy. The argument itself is simple: Taxes are unpopular and growing more so every year. If the government had to raise taxes to finance each and every new expenditure, it would subject these new expenditures to the most careful scrutiny. Financing these expenditures through increases in the national debt is far easier. Since gov-

---

[8] See chapter 1, p. 15. Of course, it may be said that when we entered World War II, we were far from being a fully employed economy. This is quite true, and it is also true that the economic sacrifices (not speaking, of course, of the tremendous human sacrifices) of the war in terms of actually "giving up things" were minimal. In a fundamental sense, we financed the war by taking up the tremendous slack in our economy—that is, moving out to the production-possibility frontier—and also by pushing the curve outward. This, however, is not an argument against debt financing as opposed to the major alternative: total reliance on increased taxation. Indeed, it seems highly doubtful that without some debt financing we could have moved out so quickly to the production-possibility frontier. The huge burdens of taxation would have made mobilization on this scale very difficult. Hence, while it is not right to say that the debt postponed the fundamental burdens of the war, it is fair to give debt financing some credit for easing the pains of the war effort at the time it occurred.

ernment politicians and bureaucracies may have their own built-in expansionary motives (see chapter 4, pp. 67–74), giving them an unrestricted national debt is like giving safecracking tools to a burglar, or a box of matches to an arsonist.

To say that this is a reasonable argument is not, of course, to say that it is by any means universally accepted. Critics of the Reagan administration, for example, argued that the large tax cuts the administration launched in the early 1980s plunged the nation into debt in a vain attempt to cut government spending. The counterargument is that by opposing *both* taxes *and* a growing debt, the administration did, in fact, slow down the growth of government spending from 1982 on. Those who felt that there was a *need* for more government spending during this period naturally reject this argument altogether.

The Increasing Interest Burden of the National Debt

More universally accepted is the fact that the debt creates a burden in terms of increasing interest costs. As Figure 13-6 shows, interest payments on the federal debt have risen sharply as a percentage of GNP, from 1.30 percent in 1973 to 3.23 percent in 1989, or about two and a half times. The burden of these interest payments can be exaggerated, since (1) they should really be discounted by the rate of inflation (recall that inflation constantly reduces the real value of each dollar of national debt), and (2) like the debt itself, the interest payments are "owed to ourselves" for the most part. Still, there is a definite burden involved for two reasons:

1. Approximately 20 percent of our national debt is now held by foreigners. This means that interest payments on this part of the debt go

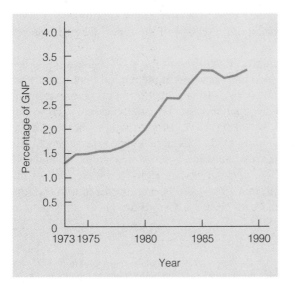

Figure 13-6   Interest Payments on the Federal Debt as a Percentage of GNP, 1973–1989   As a percentage of GNP, federal interest payments on the debt have increased from 1.30 percent in 1973 to 3.23 percent in 1989.

out of the country and become part of the international trade deficit, itself a subject of great concern in the 1990s.

2. Although we may owe most of the debt to ourselves in a general sense, there will usually be some transfer of income from taxpayers to bond-holders, who will generally not be the same individuals. Also, there is the general problem that taxes are believed to diminish economic incentives to work, save, and invest. Higher interest payments requiring higher taxes may reduce those incentives, leading to lower GNP or a reduced rate of growth of GNP.

No one believes that these interest burdens are in any way unsustainable in the American economy at the present time, but they do represent a definite cost of the debt, and one which has grown over the past decade and a half.

Saving, Investment, and "Crowding Out"

Although the above points carry some weight, they do not really explain the virtual unanimity of opinion among economists about the desirability of reducing our federal deficits. The main reason may be stated as follows:

> Federal deficits tend, other things equal, to reduce national saving and investment and, ultimately, to reduce future economic growth. Since the United States is already suffering from relatively meager domestic savings and weak productivity growth, and since the demands on our future GNP may be very heavy as the Baby Boom generation retires, it is highly desirable to reduce the deficit as rapidly as possible.

As a February 1990 report of the Congressional Budget Office put it simply and succinctly: "The purpose of reducing the deficit is to increase national saving, which can spur economic growth and capital formation."[9] It is no accident that this statement occurs in a section of the report labeled "Social Security Projections."

We may look at this matter in two different ways. We have already described the mechanism by which an expansion in the federal debt might lead to higher interest rates, which could cause a reduction in private investment spending (pp. 247–248). This phenomenon is usually called "crowding out," implying a competition between the government and businesses for the limited amount of loanable funds made available by private savings. Although, in principle, there can also be some induced investment if added G causes an expansion of GNP—what might be called "crowding in"—this effect will likely be very small in a close-to-fully employed economy, as the U.S. was in the late 1980s and early 1990s. "Crowding out" is thus seen to

---

[9] Congressional Budget Office, *Reducing the Deficit, Spending and Revenue Options: Report to the Senate and the House Committees on the Budget,* part 2, February 1990, 5.

be the dominant effect, and this is regarded as very serious since (1) personal savings have been running at quite low levels in recent years, and (2) the need for the nation to save and invest for the upcoming retirement years of the Baby Boom generation is widely recognized.

Now, we have to pause here a moment to note that this picture is complicated when we allow *foreign* investment to enter our analysis. What has actually been happening in the United States in recent years is that foreign savers have been coming in to provide the funds to allow our investment level to remain relatively high. Our federal deficit has, thus, indirectly been a major factor in our international trade deficit. In analyzing the burdens of the federal deficit, therefore, we would have to say that it is largely responsible for the increasing foreign ownership of American industry and real estate that has occurred during the past decade. This is a matter we must defer until chapter 16 (see pp. 328–333).

Restricting ourselves to our domestic economy only, another way of looking at the matter is this: We have government spending and private investment $(G + I)$ to provide for on one side, and taxes and savings $(T + S)$ available to finance them on the other. If government spending is greater than taxes, this means that our investment will have to be less than our savings. In symbols:

$$G + I = T + S$$

When the government runs a deficit, this means that

$$G > T$$

which, in turn, means that

$$I < S$$

For a given level of domestic savings, a federal deficit will result in a reduced level of investment.

A major argument—indeed, *the* major argument—most economists levy against our continuing deficits is that they tend to reduce U.S. investment at a time when, more than normally, we need to be engaged in capital formation for our national future.

WHERE DOES FISCAL POLICY STAND IN ALL THIS?

The last few paragraphs make it clear that in order to evaluate the national debt issue fully, we shall have to get into questions about the international economy and also about the relationship of capital formation to long-run economic growth. These subjects we will take up in part 5.

For the moment, however, returning to our somewhat shorter-run concerns, we can ask, Where does fiscal policy, as an economic stabilizing tool, stand today? In the foregoing discussion, we seem almost to have lost sight of the relationship of this policy to the issues of unemployment and inflation, with which we have been centrally concerned.

In answering our question, the first thing we should do is to distinguish between *discretionary fiscal policy* and the so-called *automatic stabilizers.* The former refers to actions taken specifically to alter government spending and taxes in response to short-run changes in the economy's unemployment or inflationary condition. The latter refers to changes in taxes and spending that occur with changes in economic conditions independent of any specific government actions. When GNP falls in a recession, tax receipts automatically go down; also, certain welfare payments, farm subsidies, and unemployment benefits go up. The opposite occurs when GNP and prices are rising. These "automatic" changes tend to be "stabilizing"—that is, they tend to keep aggregate demand from falling too sharply in recession periods and from rising too rapidly in inflationary times.

Economists differ about the importance of these automatic stabilizers, but on the whole, they have a rather good press among the professionals. The real debate over fiscal policy is over *discretionary* policy. And here there has been a massive change in attitude over the years. From being the *primary* economic stabilization tool during the reign of Keynesian economics, discretionary fiscal policy is seldom even mentioned in this connection in the early 1990s. There are two reasons for this:

1. *Fiscal policy is much weaker as a stabilization tool than the early Keynesians thought; indeed, some economists argue that it is almost completely impotent in this context.* When the various limitations on the multiplier that we discussed earlier in this chapter are taken into account, it becomes apparent that changes in government spending or tax policies may have much less effect on, say, raising the level of employment in the economy than our elementary fiscal policy discussion suggested. Indeed, if we take seriously the possibility that the long-run aggregate supply curve (as well as the associated Phillips curve) is a vertical straight line (see above, pp. 232–234), then fiscal policy in itself becomes incapable of altering the level of employment or real GNP in the economy.

Let us consider what we might call the *extreme monetarist position* (analogous to the *extreme Keynesian position* represented by Figure 13-1[a] above). In analyzing an expansion of G, the extreme monetarists would make the following points:

a. If the increase in G is accompanied by an increase in the national debt ("no new taxes") and the debt is financed by the creation of new money, then there will be an upward shift in the aggregate demand curve. This shift, however, will lead only to higher inflation and to no change in output or employment.

b. If the increase in the debt is financed by borrowing from the public and no new money is created, then "crowding out" will be the dominant effect. The net result will be:

(1) no shift in the aggregate demand curve,

(2) no change in either real GNP or the price level, and

(3) an increase in the government share of GNP as the government "crowds out" private investors and consumers.

c. If the government finances the increased G by added taxes, then the ultimate result will be the same as b.[10]

This position is suggested by Figure 13-7. Because the aggregate supply curve is vertical, changes in aggregate demand can have no real effects on output and employment. Where expansionary fiscal policy is accompanied by an expansion of the money supply to finance the debt, the aggregate demand curve will shift from AD to $A'D'$, causing a general rise in the price level. When there is no such expansion of the money supply, then the added G will simply crowd out an equivalent amount of I and C. This means that there will be no shift in the aggregate demand curve—AD will remain where it is. (To show the increase in government in the economy in this case, the reader should go back to Figure 13-1[a]. When G goes up to G', he should draw in a $C + I$ curve and then lower this curve by the amount of the increase in G. This will leave the intersection of the new $C + I + G'$ curve with the 45° line at the same level of real income as before. The only difference will be that the proportion of G to C and I has increased.)

If, like some new classical economists, one believes that even the *short-run* aggregate supply curve (and Phillips curve) is vertical, then this transition to a larger government share in the economy will simply be more rapid, but with the same end result.

2. *Fiscal policy is an awkward stabilization tool and, in any event, has basically been preempted by other objectives.* Added to the fiscal policy pessimism suggested by the above analysis, there are a number of considerations that argue that frequent changes in government spending and tax policies are very cumbersome ways to try to stabilize the economy. Public works projects launched in a recession may just begin to come to fruition (and add to aggregate demand) as the economy is heating up again. Tax increases or tax cuts designed to stabilize the economy may be regarded as essentially temporary and have very little effect on spending out of "permanent income."

Even more seriously, there is the strong possibility that we may view government spending and tax policies not from the point of view of stabilization, but with reference to wholly different objectives. Indeed, the discussion

---

[10] To which most monetarists would be likely to add that any policy that increases the government's share of the economy is a "bad" thing since there is already "too much" government in the picture.

Figure 13-7   Extreme Monetarist Position   If an increasing G is financed by an expansion of the money supply, it will cause a shift in the aggregate demand curve (to $A'D'$). According to the extreme monetarist doctrine, this will have no effect on output, but only on prices. If G is financed *without* an increase in the money supply, neither output nor prices, but only the size of the public sector, will be affected.

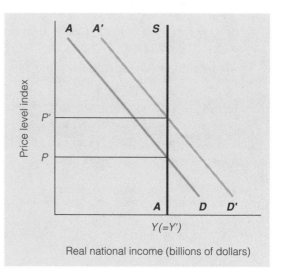

of the national debt that we have just concluded arrives at the view that the big thing now is to get the debt down so that we can increase national saving and investment and the growth of future GNP. From this vantage point, the only question is which way is best to reduce the debt—lowering spending or raising taxes. Fighting shorter-run hazards like unemployment or inflation hardly seems to enter into the debate.

Of course, a serious recession (or inflation) could change attitudes on these issues. Still, the experience of recent years has made many economists skeptical of the value of fiscal policy, even when unemployment seems too high. It has even been argued that such a policy tends essentially to be *destabilizing*. We try to correct a rate of unemployment that we consider too high via an expansionary policy. This leads not only to higher inflation, but to higher expectations of inflation. Now, inflation seems out of control; we decide we have to employ a contractionary fiscal policy. But we now have built in higher inflationary expectations and patterns of behavior; to get inflation back to its original rate, we may have to impose even *more* serious unemployment costs on the economy; and so on.

Which is to say that, at best, most economists do not expect any great miracles from fiscal policy in the American economy of the 1990s. To monetary policy, and other policy options, therefore, we turn our attention in the next chapter.

SUMMARY

A closer look at the multiplier analysis of elementary fiscal policy (first presented in chapter 8) reveals a number of problems. A given increase in G is likely to have a smaller impact on real national income than previously suggested because: (1) some of this impact is likely to result in higher prices, raising nominal rather than real GNP; (2) the government's need to borrow to finance its deficits will cause interest rates to rise and, thus, cause a fall in C and I; and (3) tax revenues rise as nominal GNP rises, taking away some of the impetus of the added G. These factors may be offset to some degree by the fact that any expansion of real GNP that occurs is likely to have some positive effect on I via the route of induced investment. Whether "crowding out" or "crowding in" effects are dominant may be dependent on the state of the economy, "crowding out" becoming dominant the nearer the economy is to being fully employed.

An aspect of fiscal policy that has caused great alarm in recent years has been the rise in the public debt as government expenditures have exceeded tax revenues. Some of this alarm is based on exaggerations of the true size of the federal debt. When corrected for inflation and other factors, and especially when viewed as a *percentage* of our GNP, the federal debt seems less alarming than some observers have believed. Also, false or incomplete analogies to the debts of private parties, or misunderstandings about the future burdens of present expenditures, have added little to our understanding of the problem. Still, debt financing can be opposed because it may lead to an undue expansion of government activity, to interest rate burdens, and to a reduction of national saving and investment. It is this last factor that explains why most economists, looking ahead to the retirement of the Baby Boom generation, feel that we should actively seek to reduce our public debt.

This focus on the long-run, savings-and-investment implications of the debt has drained away much of the former Keynesian-style emphasis on fiscal policy as a stabilization tool. Although automatic stabilizers are generally thought to be somewhat helpful, discretionary fiscal policy has fallen out of vogue in recent years and is held by some, like the extreme monetarists, to be of little (or even negative) value in stabilizing the economy. The closer the aggregate supply curve (long run or short run) is to being vertical, the less effect fiscal policy will have on real GNP or employment. In such a world, the main effect of increasing G will be simply to expand the role of the government in the economy relative to C and I.

Key Concepts for Review

Fiscal policy
Modifications of the multiplier
   Price effects
   Interest rate effects
   Taxes
Induced investment
"Crowding out"

Size of the U.S. public debt
   Absolute
   Relative to GNP
Public versus private debt
Internal versus external debt
Future burdens of the debt
Saving and capital formation

Automatic stabilizers

Discretionary fiscal policy

Extreme positions
  Keynesian
  Monetarist

Vertical and aggregate supply and Phillips
  curves

Change in attitudes toward fiscal policy

Questions for Discussion

1. Using Figure 13-1 as a starting point, show how the simple multiplier analysis of chapter 8 must be modified to take into account the following possibilities:

   a. Increases in aggregate demand may affect the price level as well as the level of real income.

   b. Increases in government borrowing may cause pressure on the supplies of loanable funds available to the private sector.

   c. Increases in GNP due to an expansionary fiscal policy may increase tax revenues, thus reducing the impact of added G.

   d. A successful fiscal policy could lead to induced investment.

2. What are automatic stabilizers? Using Figure 13-1 again, how would you illustrate the effect of such stabilizers graphically?

3. Write an essay on the pros and cons of having a constitutional amendment prohibiting any further increases in the national debt. Would you personally support such an amendment?

4. Looking at Figure 13-1(a), show how you would represent the extreme monetarist contention that an increased G that involved no increase in the money supply would have no effect on the level of real national income. By what logic do monetarists support this contention?

5. According to the Congressional Budget Office (CBO), "the purpose of reducing the deficit is to increase national saving, which can spur economic growth and capital formation." In commenting on this quotation (p. 258), we said, "It is no accident that this statement occurs in a section of the report labeled 'Social Security Projections.'" What basis is there for the CBO's statement? What is the meaning of our comment on it?

C H A P T E R   14

MONETARY POLICY: SUPPLY-SIDE AND OTHER OPTIONS

The decline of the role of fiscal policy as a stabilization tool was indicated in the spring of 1990, when, in the face of a sluggishly growing economy with signs of rising unemployment, there was a loud demand in Congress that President Bush vacate his "no new taxes" pledge and support a tax increase. Raising taxes when we might be on the verge of a recession? Not long ago, that would have been considered economic heresy!

Which is another way of saying that in the macroeconomic area, attention has definitely shifted from fiscal policy to monetary policy as a way of stabilizing the economy. Since monetary policy itself is far from being difficulty free, there has also been a surge of interest in policies that, in one way or another, try to affect aggregate supply in a favorable way. At the extreme, these other policies, as held by what are usually called supply-siders, promise more than they have yet been able to deliver. At the same time, emphasis on the supply side of the economic equation has increased for virtually all economists.

Indeed, it can be argued that the shift in emphasis from an almost exclusive preoccupation with the demand side to a more balanced appreciation of demand *and* supply factors is one of the two main changes in economic policy-making that have occurred since the heyday of the Keynesians in the 1950s and 1960s.

LONG-RUN VERSUS SHORT-RUN MONETARY POLICY

Arguably, the second of the two great changes in policy-making that have occurred during this period is a general shift to longer-run policy approaches as opposed to short-term or "fine-tuning" measures.[1] This shift is by no means complete in practice, though it is increasingly emphasized in the public statements of our prominent economic policymakers. Certainly this is true in the area of monetary policy.

One of the reasons for the shift from short-run to long-run considerations is that, like fiscal policy, monetary policy may be faced with unacceptable, or at least very painful, short-run choices. The difficulty is endemic to any policy that operates primarily on the demand side. In the late 1970s, for example, we faced both high inflation and high unemployment. If we were to work on the unemployment problem, we would be inclined to increase the money supply and lower interest rates. This expansionary policy, however, can be expected to worsen inflation in the short run. The contrary is also true for a contractionary policy to fight inflation: there will presumably be at least some negative short-run effects on the unemployment front. (In the early 1980s, there were indeed large unemployment effects of a tight money policy as we know.) Although the situation of the late 1970s and early 1980s was especially difficult, the problem remains even in the early 1990s. Would the Fed tighten or loosen? Forecasters could not agree because inflation seemed to be heating up slightly, yet at the same time, economic growth (and employment growth) was definitely slowing down.

Also, monetary policy, like fiscal policy, can affect future expectations. If, for example, it is believed that at the least sign of weakness on the unemployment front the Fed will backtrack on its antiinflation policies, then these policies may be rendered largely ineffective, requiring more stringent measures—and harder choices for the Fed—in the next go-round.

What this means is that the increased interest in monetary policy in the last decade or two has relatively little to do with confidence in monetary policy for the purposes of short-run economic stabilization. It is, rather, based on the possible virtues of a longer-run approach. These virtues are derived from two widely (though not universally) shared beliefs: (1) that in the long run, there is no serious trade-off between unemployment and inflation and (2) that in the long run, inflation is essentially a monetary phenomenon—that is, that substantial inflation cannot persist over time unless it is "accommodated" by parallel increases in the money supply. These two points raise the possibility, in its extreme form, of completely ignoring the short run and focusing exclusively on the long run. According to the second point, such an approach *could* halt inflation in the long run; according to the first point, this

---

[1] One could probably add a third major development to the two mentioned, although there would be considerable controversy about it. It would be a declining overall faith in the ability of the government to manage the economy in the areas of inflation and unemployment, and something of a renewal of faith in the self-adjusting capacities of the marketplace. This is hardly a universally shared view, however.

reduction in inflation would have *no* long-run effect on unemployment. Further, it could be argued that this approach is not as callous toward short-term sufferings as it might seem. The reason: each short-term problem would become easier to handle as time went on. This contrasts with an active month-to-month or quarter-to-quarter monetary policy, which might easily *worsen* the inflation-unemployment trade-off over time.

RULES AND TARGETS

Following through with the above logic, one can argue that the long-run approach favors certain operating procedures for the Fed in carrying out its policies:

Rules Versus Discretion

One way to express the long-run approach is by avoiding discretionary policy moves by the Federal Reserve Board and formulating a *fixed rule* of some kind by which its actions are to be dictated. Nobel economist Milton Friedman has been a longtime advocate of such a rule. In a famous exchange way back in 1969, Keynesian Walter Heller, in urging a discretionary monetary policy, commented: "Let's not lock the steering gear into place, knowing full well of the twists and turns in the road ahead. That's an invitation to chaos." To which Friedman replied: "When you start talking about cars driving along a road, and whether you want to lock the steering wheel, well that's a good image. . . . But metaphors or similes are to remind you of arguments; they are not a substitute for an argument." The reason he favored a fixed rule, he added, was that his studies of the monetary history of the United States convinced him that with such a rule, we could have "avoided all the major mistakes" we made.[2]

Of course, a fixed rule and a constant policy are not necessarily the same thing; it may take considerable discretion in the interpretation of rules to maintain a steady overall course. We shall return to this point in a moment. Nevertheless, the advantage of a fixed rule, particularly if it is well-publicized and scrupulously followed, is that it can serve to convince businesses and the public that the Fed means business over the long haul. Having faith that the Fed really *does* intend to bring down inflation is undoubtedly one of the main factors lowering inflationary expectations. And this, in turn, can lower the unemployment costs of bringing down the inflation rate to any

---

[2] Milton Friedman and Walter W. Heller, *Monetary versus Fiscal Policy: A Dialogue* (New York: W. W. Norton & Company, Inc., 1969), 30–31, 77.

given level. (Indeed, on a pure rational expectations hypothesis, we recall, such faith would tend to bring down inflation immediately with no cost in additional unemployment at all.) To instill such faith requires some measurable and widely published monetary term to be used as a target.

Money Supply Versus Interest Rate Target

But what target is to be chosen? According to 1990 Fed Chairman Alan Greenspan, the "ultimate objective of economic policy is to foster the maximum sustainable rate of economic growth."[3] According to the above analysis, however, the only way monetary policy can really contribute to this objective is through its effect on the price level.[4] Unfortunately, there is no switch that the Fed can directly turn off or on to change prices. Thus, it has to find some intermediate target to achieve its desired goal.

During most of the 1950s and 1960s, the variable chosen was interest rates. This was natural since, as we recall, in Keynesian theory it is largely through the interest rate that changes in money exert their effects on the economy. However, the increasing rate of inflation during the 1970s made this variable increasingly unreliable as a measure of the effect the Fed was actually having on the economy. An important reason for this was that in an inflationary period, a large gap can open up between nominal interest rates, or the interest rates actually quoted in the marketplace, and real interest rates, which are nominal interest rates corrected for the expected rate of inflation (see chapter 11, pp. 216–217).

In Figure 14-1, we show the huge gap that opened up between these rates in the 1970s as compared to the 1960s as the U.S. inflation rate accelerated. It is especially interesting to note that while the nominal rate (measured here by the 3-month Treasury bill rate) was generally rising during the 1970s, the real rate was frequently *negative*. This made it very difficult to judge from the nominal rate alone whether monetary policy was effectively "easy," "tight," or somewhere in between.

As the monetarists gained influence during these years, the emphasis shifted to a money supply target. According to the quantity theory, as we know, the quantity of money is supposed to bear a fairly regular relationship to nominal GNP ($P \times Y$). In 1975, Congress adopted a resolution asking the Fed to report on its target rates of growth for the money supply ("the monetary and credit aggregates"), and in 1978 this request was made mandatory

---

[3] Statement by Alan Greenspan to Senate Committee on Banking, Housing, and Urban Development, 2 February 1990, in *Federal Reserve Bulletin*, vol. 76, no. 4 (April, 1990): 215.

[4] Cf. statement by Donald Kohn, Director of the Fed's Division of Monetary Affairs: "Along with others at the Federal Reserve, I believe that the price level is the only variable that over the long run is under the control of the central bank." In *Federal Reserve Bulletin*, vol. 76, no. 1 (January 1990): 1.

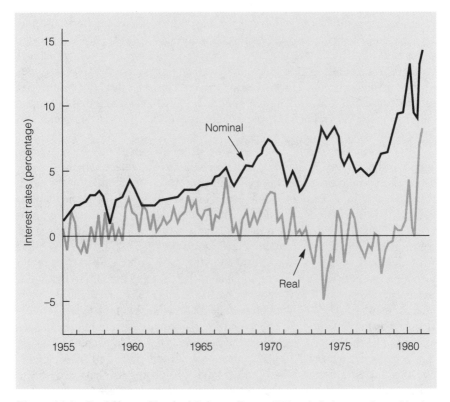

Figure 14-1   Real Versus Nominal Interest Rates   When inflation accelerated in the 1970s, a huge gap opened between nominal and real interest rates. This made it more difficult to use an interest rate target for monetary policy than it had been in the 1950s and 1960s. (The interest rate here is measured by the rate on 3-month Treasury bills.)

by law. From 1979 to 1982, the Fed paid particular attention to the growth of the monetary aggregates—M_1 in particular, but also M_2 and M_3 to a degree. This was, in fact, the period when the back of the 1970s inflationary spiral in the United States was broken, with, of course, an attendant serious recession. Under any interpretation, monetary policy, guided by then-Chairman Paul Volker, has to receive a large part of the responsibility and/or credit for what happened during those three years.

DIFFICULTIES WITH RULES AND TARGETS

With the important victory (at least for the time being) over accelerating inflation it might seem that the fixed-rule, money-supply-target approach would

have become institutionalized as the permanent U.S. stance on monetary policy. In point of fact, however, as noted by the late Arthur Burns in his last
paper in 1987, "by the early 1980s, it appeared that monetary policy had lost
its moorings in both interest rates and monetary aggregates." He gently described the new approach as "eclectic." [5] What happened was that neither set
of targets seemed to work very well in practice, with the result that the application of any clear and orderly rule of operation became increasingly elusive.
The difficulties included:

1. *Gyrations of interest rates.* One danger of focusing on the money
supply is that the Fed may effectively lose control over what happens to interest rates. It would be nice if the Fed could control *both* variables at the same
time, but this is impossible, since every time the demand for money shifts,
the relationship between the quantity of money and the interest rate will also
change. Thus, in focusing on a money supply target, the Fed runs the risk of
very unsettling gyrations in the interest rate as the demand for money shifts.
And, indeed, this clearly happened during the 1979–1982 episode, when the
prime rate went from 20 percent down to 11 percent and then up to nearly 22
percent in the space of less than two years. Furthermore, *real* interest rates
also zoomed up and down with unprecedented speed. What made this so wor-
risome was that interest rate effects may be particularly severe in certain specific areas of the economy. Residential housing is a notable example. During
the recession of the early 1980s, housing starts in the U.S. fell *by over half,*
and this during a period when the demand for housing as charted by basic
demographic factors was expected to be quite strong.

2. *Constant policy versus fixed rules.* Another problem with framing a
monetary rule in terms of a money supply target is that the relationship between the target and the ultimate objectives—say relatively stable, noninflationary growth of GNP—may change over time. This clearly happened in the
case of M_1 in relation to nominal GNP during the 1980s. If we look back at
Figure 11-5 (p. 213), we find that the income velocity of M_1 was rising over time
at a reasonably steady rate between 1960 and 1980, and then suddenly this rise
reversed itself. Any rule that had factored in this long-run rise in velocity into the
relationship between M_1 growth and nominal GNP growth would have proved
widely off the mark. And, in fact, it did prove so in the early 1980s. In the face of
lower than expected velocity (an increase in the liquidity demand for money) in
1982, the Fed decided to accept above-target money growth during the first and
second quarters of that year. To have stayed with its previous targets would have
meant a tighter monetary policy than intended. Indeed, by the end of that year,
the Fed had effectively abandoned M_1 as a target variable.

---

[5] Arthur F. Burns, *The Ongoing Revolution in American Banking* (Washington, DC: American Enterprise Institute for Public Policy Research, 1988), 48. Dr. Burns was the Fed chairman from 1970
to 1978.

The general point is clear: A constant policy may often require a *change* in the rule that implements that policy as circumstances alter over time.

3. *Changing institutional circumstances.* And circumstances clearly do change over time. Burns's last paper, just referred to, is titled *The Ongoing Revolution in American Banking,* and there is little doubt that substantial institutional changes have made it increasingly difficult to find *any* monetary target that remains fixed long enough for it to be properly aimed at. The period of the 1980s saw vast changes in our banking system as a result of deregulation and financial innovation. With NOW accounts and countless varieties of money market funds entering on the scene, the old distinction between transactions money and money held as a store of wealth began to disappear. Meanwhile, banks often sold off their mortgage and other loans in a process called "securitization"; the junk bond market further blurred the distinction between stocks (equity) and bond (debt) instruments; the savings and loan institutions were going through a massive crisis; and, finally, the great expansion in international transactions has meant that investors can treat assets denominated in dollars and those in foreign currencies virtually interchangeably. The point is that these, and other changes, were constantly altering the economic significance of each given money supply category, rendering it uncertain whether its target rate of growth should be raised, lowered, or abandoned altogether.[6]

Interest rates, meanwhile, had their own complications as targets. Besides the real-versus-nominal problem, there was the increasing possibility that interest rates at any given moment of time reflected not just expectations about the future of the economy, but also expectations about what the Fed was about to do. International constraints were apparent here too: if a high interest rate policy were adopted, for example, this might have the effect of attracting foreign capital, raising the value of the dollar vis a vis foreign currencies, and, thus, punishing American exporters whose goods would become more expensive for foreign customers to buy.

Again, a fixed rule would run you into serious trouble if it were expressed in terms of a target that itself was highly variable.

4. *The problem of hitting the target.* Finally, even if the target remained fixed and the relationship of the target to ultimate economic objectives remained relatively stable, the Fed still had the problem of actually hitting the target. The Fed, we recall, basically operates by altering the reserves of the commercial banking system, not the money supply directly. The latter requires the actions

---

[6] Another problem for monetary policy raised by institutional changes in the 1980s was the overall increase in corporate indebtedness, which we mentioned in the last chapter (footnote 7, p. 254). Insofar as the increase in the ratio of debt to equity capital in U.S. corporations has raised their interest costs and made them more vulnerable to economic recession, it may become increasingly unlikely that the Fed will be willing to allow recessions to occur. According to economist Benjamin M. Friedman, a "no recession" policy (required to prevent large-scale corporate bankruptcies) may well lead to "accelerating inflation." Under any circumstances, this corporate debt problem may create still another constraint on the effective exercise of monetary policy.

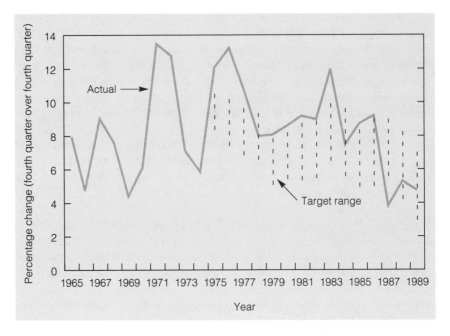

Figure 14-2   Actual and Target M_2 Growth
SOURCE: Board of Governors of the Federal Reserve System.
Note: Target ranges are only set for 1975 and on.

of banks and borrowers, who through the familiar processes of credit creation (pp. 190–193, above) transform the reserves into money. And the existence of this further link means that the Fed may aim very well but still miss not only a specific target, but even a fairly broad *range* within which the growth of the target variable is theoretically to be confined. Figure 14-2 shows how the Fed has managed with respect to M_2 since it began targeting this aggregate in the mid-1970s. In eight of the fifteen years recorded, it missed the entire target range. And if the diagram makes it seem as though it didn't miss by too much, the reader should note that while the target varied only a few percentage points between 1983 and 1987, the *actual* growth of M_2 was *three times as great* (12 percent versus 4 percent) in the earlier year as in the later one. At a minimum, we have to accept the fact that monetary policy is less than an exact science at this stage of our knowledge.

MONETARY POLICY FOR THE 1990s

Having said all this, we should not go to the opposite extreme and conclude that monetary policy, like fiscal policy, has been so diminished in practical importance as to leave us largely helpless before the vicissitudes of inflation and unemployment. On the contrary, the achievements of that policy in at least helping to keep inflation under better control should be acknowledged. And the following, more positive points should be noted to counteract the negatives listed above:

1. *The emphasis on a long-run approach to monetary policy has not been weakened by recent experience.* In fact, it has probably been strengthened. This is to say that most of the problems we have noted above involve complications in applying monetary policy in the short run. If we take a longer-run perspective, it becomes more possible to make the necessary adjustments in defining our targets and their ranges than if we are operating on a quarter-to-quarter or even year-to-year basis. We may even be able to hit our targets in this longer-run sense even though we are missing them on almost every given occasion. Thus, in Figure 14-2, the *good* news is that actual M_2 growth did slow down over the entire targeting period, and this, in fact, was what the Fed was striving to achieve.

Perhaps even *better* news is given in Figure 14-3. Having seen the enormous variability in the velocity of M_1, we may be all the more impressed to see the relative stability in the velocity of M_2. In the short run, M_2 velocity is still fairly variable and may be more sensitive to interest rate changes than in the past. Thus, an "eclectic" short-run approach that includes both attention to other variables (the interest rate, the price level, the level of GNP, and the like) and a readiness to alter short-run targets for M_2 growth may be appropriate. At the same

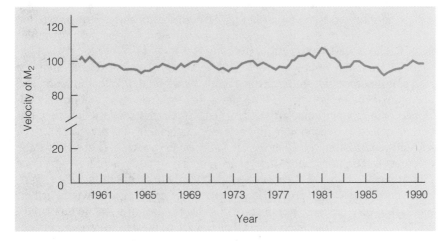

Figure 14-3   Income Velocity of M_2 (First Quarter, 1959 = 100)   Although M_2 velocity does show definite short-run fluctuations, it has been remarkably stable over the past 30 years on average.
SOURCE: Board of Governors of the Federal Reserve System.
Note: Data are quarterly.

time, targeting M_2 growth over a longer-run perspective may be highly desirable. The 1990 Council of Economic Advisers concludes:

> Research at the Federal Reserve and elsewhere shows that the velocity of M_2 has been essentially stable over the long run. M_2 could serve therefore as an anchor for price stability and as a basis for a credible, systematic long-run monetary policy. That is, as long as there are no signs of *permanent* shifts of M_2 velocity, the Federal Reserve would do well to commit to eventually maintaining *long-run* growth of M_2 consistent with expansion of the economy's potential to produce.[7]

Needless to say, if these conditions were met, then the Fed might well achieve its Holy Grail of long-run price stability, or zero inflation.

2. *Awareness of the crucial importance of credibility.* Another positive sign is a growing awareness of the need for the Fed to achieve credibility in whatever policy it undertakes. Advances in economic theory, including the work of the rational expectationists, have made it clear that what businesses and the public *believe* to be Fed policy will have a substantial bearing on the actual effectiveness of that policy. One of the disadvantages of the short-run, fine-tuning, stop-and-go approach is that people may believe that the Fed's determination to achieve any given goal—say to lower inflation—will buckle under pressure. In general, such beliefs will increase the *costs* of achieving that goal. Practical experience during the tough years of the early 1980s also supports this view. Although the recession was painful, it turned out in the end to be a lot less painful than many observers had predicted once businesses and the public became convinced that Chairman Volker and the Reagan administration would actually carry through with their antiinflation efforts, even when heavy unemployment was involved.

Credibility, then, is important, and, more significantly, is recognized to be important. Fears that the Fed will not "stay the course" when troubles arise should be less damaging in the future.

3. *Monetary policy, along with fiscal policy, may have an important role in promoting long-run growth.* Finally, we should note that inflation and unemployment are not the only variables that macroeconomic policy is concerned with. As our quote from Chairman Greenspan suggested, a very important objective of economic policy is sustainable long-run growth. This is a subject we will discuss further in part 5, but it very much overlaps with some of our considerations here. Insofar as monetary policy is able to promote long-run price stability, then most economists believe it will make a significant contribution to improving our real rate of economic growth. Furthermore, it is very probably possible to alter the *balance* of fiscal and monetary policies so that we do much better than we are at present in promoting economic growth. Essentially, this would involve reducing our fiscal deficits so as to increase national saving and lowering our real rate of interest so as to

---

[7] *Economic Report of the President,* 1990, p. 86.

promote investment. An appropriately long-run view of *both* fiscal and monetary policies, then, could undoubtedly increase their positive contribution to our national well-being.

INCOMES POLICIES

Given that monetary policy, even at its best, involves the problem of all demand-side approaches—at least some short-run conflict between expanding employment and restraining inflation—the postwar era has seen a number of other approaches to macroeconomic stabilization in this country and abroad. Very commonly employed in the early postwar years in the United States and still somewhat popular in Europe are wage-price policies, or *incomes policies* as they are known to economists. Essentially, these policies try to operate directly on the wage and price decisions of business and labor, restraining increases in nominal values in the economy independent of the state of the economy's aggregate demand.

In the extreme form of wage-price controls, an incomes policy was applied in the United States during World War II in conjunction with a certain amount of actual rationing of scarce goods. It was reasonably successful in restraining inflationary pressures during a period when, according to the normal laws of supply and demand, prices and wages could have gone through the roof. However, most economists believe that the success of the policy was due to the limited time during which it was applied and the special circumstances of war during which civilian belt-tightening and other restraints took on a patriotic urgency. Even then, the policy was far from flawless, and a black market did develop to some degree.

After the war, the United States went through a series of quasi incomes policy approaches, which mainly amounted to the government urging business and labor to observe restraint in their wage and price decisions. This "jawboning" method involved the publication of such things as wage-price "guideposts," "inflation alerts," even President Gerald Ford's WIN buttons ("Whip Inflation Now!"). The idea always was to keep wage increases fairly close to the rate of increase of labor productivity so that price increases could be held within a fairly narrow range, say 2 or 3 percent per year. At one time or another, this approach was used by Presidents Kennedy, Johnson, Ford, and Carter, and with the same basic result: whenever serious upward pressure on wages and prices developed, the guidelines collapsed. Fundamentally, *urging* inflation to stop didn't work.

But then trying to *compel* inflation to stop didn't work either. For this was tried under President Nixon, first with a 90-day wage-price freeze, which Nixon announced to the nation with much fanfare in a television broadcast on August 15, 1971, as part of his "new economic policy." This was followed by Phase 2 (mandatory controls remained), Phase 3 (very loose regulation), Phase 3½ (another freeze), Phase 4 (easing of controls), and finally—in April 1974—the dismantling of the entire program. The succession of these different "phases" suggests, in itself, that the program never really found quite the right way to attack the problems it had set out to solve. The verdict most economists give to the effort is that insofar as wage and price increases were somewhat restrained during the control period—as they probably were—the nation simply paid the price in higher inflation in subsequent years. And it was, of course, during the late 1970s and early 1980s that our inflation reached its peak.

Meanwhile, economists—or at least some economists—were coming up with their own pet version of an incomes policy, the so-called tax-based incomes policy, familiarly, TIP. The basic principle of TIP is to use taxes or subsidies to penalize (or reward) those who fail to follow (or do follow) some specified set of wage-price guidelines. The primary emphasis may be on either taxes (the stick) or subsidies (the carrot). Thus, for example, if a corporation agreed to a wage increase above the guideline, it might have its corporate income tax rate raised according to some suitable formula. Good behavior on the part of corporations could be rewarded by tax reductions. Or the whole thing might be done in the form of increases or decreases in a payroll tax, thus bringing home to labor the consequences of excessive wage demands.

The basic logic behind *all* these incomes policies is that inflation becomes more and more serious as inflationary *expectations* increase. If one can break the pattern of rising wages and prices through a freeze, controlled increases, voluntary restraints, or tax and subsidy incentives, then one can hopefully break the back of inflationary expectations and, thus, remove a major driving force behind the inflation itself. To this general approach, TIP simply adds the concept that to accomplish this end, one should work with economic incentives, rather than trying to control or stifle them.[8]

The TIP approach has, however, attracted very little interest in government circles or in the minds of the public at large, and, indeed, in the early 1990s, the appeal of incomes policies of any sort seems to be vanishingly low. Partly this is because, although a desire for zero inflation does undoubtedly exist, the country has developed a certain tolerance for inflation of the 4- to 5-percent variety. Partly it is because most Americans have become aware of the complexities that develop when the government gets too intimately involved in detailed decision making in the economy, especially when this involvement attempts to force serious departures from market-determined prices. Partly it is just because of past history—voluntarism doesn't seem to have worked, but then compulsion doesn't appear to have worked either.

Indeed, in light of the experience of the 1971–1974 period, it is prob-

---

[8] For a discussion of this point, see Henry C. Wallich, "Tax-Based Incomes Policies," chap. 5 in Henry C. Wallich, *Monetary Policy and Practice* (Lexington, MA: D.C. Heath and Company, 1982), chap. 5.

able that any form of serious wage-price controls would work *even less effectively* now than they did then. Why? Because in view of this earlier experience, it would be virtually impossible to convince anybody that the controls would be more than temporary. But if we believe that they are only temporary, controls will completely lose their one possible advantage: substantially reducing long-run inflationary expectations.

SUPPLY-SIDE POLICIES

Incomes policies, if they were workable and did not have substantial costs attached to them, would be a nice complement to policies, like monetary policy and fiscal policy, that affect the economy from the demand side. If we could administratively hold wages and prices constant, then we could manipulate demand through fiscal or monetary measures and happily reach our full-employment potential without having to worry about inflation. In rejecting income policies, we are not, however, left with no alternative policies. For we could focus our attention on shifting not the aggregate demand curve but the aggregate supply curve.

It is only repeating what we already know (p. 231) to say that a favorable shift in the aggregate supply curve, as in Figure 14-4, involves no intrinsic conflict between employment and price stability. On the contrary, such shifts, if they can be accomplished without incurring other offsetting costs, will tend to promote both higher employment and lower prices, even in the short run.

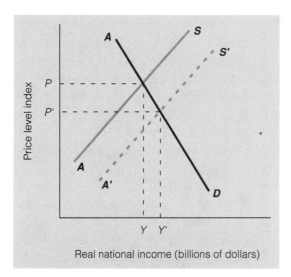

Real national income (billions of dollars)

Figure 14-4   A Favorable Shift in the Aggregate Supply Curve   If we can engineer a favorable shift in the aggregate supply curve, we do not face any conflict between employment and price stability, even in the short run. This possibility helps explain the recent appeal of supply-side policies.

The Optimistic "Supply-Siders"

Because of this attractive feature, supply-side policies, especially those involving various forms of tax cuts, became very popular in the late 1970s and 1980s. Many economists feel that they became somewhat *too* popular, that is, that their advantages were overstated and their costs considerably understated. In this connection, it is desirable to distinguish between "supply-siders," in quotation marks, and the general run of modern economists, virtually all of whom favor giving serious attention to the shape and position of the aggregate supply curve.

The "supply-siders" (in quotes) we can define, without too much inaccuracy, as those economists who believe that in the present, or recent, state of the American economy, cuts in tax *rates* will involve little or no costs in terms of tax *revenues* and, indeed, may well *increase* overall tax revenues.

This position is particularly associated with the Laffer curve, named after its originator, Arthur B. Laffer, a professor of business economics at the University of Southern California. In Figure 14-5, we represent the tax rate on the *y*-axis and total tax revenues on the *x*-axis. We see the obvious point that at a zero rate of taxation, tax revenues will be zero. We also see the reasonable proposition that at 100-percent taxation, tax revenues will again be zero. Who would want to earn income if it were totally appropriated by the government? In between, total revenues are positive, and there is some point, *m*, where tax revenues are at a maximum. At all points above this tax rate, a lowering of the tax rate will bring increased total tax revenues. This is ultimately because reductions in very high tax rates will have the effect of inducing people to work harder, save and invest more, and, in general, earn

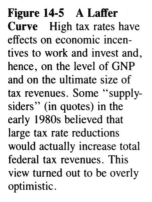

Figure 14-5   A Laffer Curve   High tax rates have effects on economic incentives to work and invest and, hence, on the level of GNP and on the ultimate size of tax revenues. Some "supply-siders" (in quotes) in the early 1980s believed that large tax rate reductions would actually increase total federal tax revenues. This view turned out to be overly optimistic.

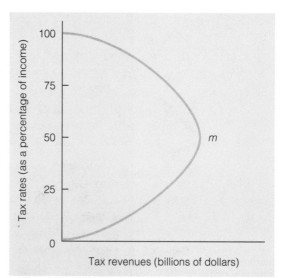

more income, which can then be taxed. Insofar as lowering tax rates reduces tax avoidance (failure to report income and so on), then this will be an added factor to increase revenues with lower rates.

This analysis is believed to have had considerable influence on the decision of the Reagan administration to propose substantial tax cuts in the early 1980s, for it was argued that the United States, not only as a theoretical possibility but in actual fact, was above point m on its Laffer curve. In 1981, Congress enacted a cut in income tax rates of 5 percent in 1981, a further 10 percent in 1982, and a final 10 percent in 1983. It also voted a further reduction in tax bracket rates in 1986. As the discussion of a possible new round of tax legislation began in 1990, no one in the United States was subject to an income tax rate of more than 33 percent, a quite low rate among all industrial nations.

Whether these tax cuts were advisable or inadvisable is a matter on which honest individuals differ. That they were not the panacea that the "supply-siders" envisaged is fairly obvious. Federal tax revenues did, in fact, fall, not rise, after the tax cuts, and, as we know, the early 1980s saw the emergence of the large federal deficits that have created the substantial increase in our national debt. Indeed, in terms of general analysis, it seems obvious that one cannot treat large changes in tax rates as though they will affect *only* the supply side. Most economists believe that the tax changes of the 1980s also shifted the aggregate demand curve to the right; in principle, such demand shifts could cancel out the favorable price effects of the associated supply shift.

More to our immediate point, one cannot ignore the possible *negative* effects of these tax cuts on the supply side itself. In the absence of the predicted Laffer effect, and in the absence of associated cuts in government spending (and this part of the Reagan proposals fared less well than did the tax side), large government deficits emerge and act as a form of *dis*saving for the nation as a whole. Thus it is that, from a *supply-side* point of view, many economists in 1990 were advocating *raising* taxes in order to promote a higher level of national saving and investment—ultimately to shift the aggregate supply curve to the right.

Examples of Supply-Side Policies

While the "supply-sider" view is a minority one among economists, it is also accurate to say that the influence of supply-side (without quotes) thinking has become much more prominent in economics in recent years. We conclude this chapter (and part 4) with a brief examination of the advantages and disadvantages of supply-side policies.[9]

---

[9] As we move into these supply-side considerations, we tend to move closer to the factors that promote long-run economic growth, a subject we shall consider in more detail in part 5. The following paragraphs can, in fact, be thought of as serving as a "bridge" between parts 2–4 and part 5.

Supply-side policies try to affect aggregate supply favorably by (1) increasing the supply of effort and work from the labor force, (2) increasing incentives to save and invest, and (3) increasing the rate of technological progress.

A major purpose of the early 1980s tax cuts we have just been discussing was to increase the work effort of our population. The focus of efforts to increase labor hours is usually on cutting the *marginal* tax rate, that is, the tax on an extra dollar of income. If we work harder or put in an extra hour of work, how much of the additional income will the government take away from us in taxes? Supply-side advocates hope that if marginal rates are lowered sufficiently, the labor supply effects will be large. Other policies that might be advocated to promote increased labor supply would be to restructure or repeal the minimum wage law and to reduce unemployment insurance benefits. It is argued that a main effect of the minimum wage law is to increase unemployment among teenagers who can be profitably employed only at wages below the required minimum. Another effect is to raise the wage rate of those unskilled workers who do get hired. In the case of unemployment benefits, it is argued that high benefits (relative to the wages that could be earned in productive employment) extend the period during which workers remain unemployed, perhaps as much as one extra week for each week of coverage.

As far as the second objective—raising the rate of saving and investment—is concerned, there are countless supply-side ideas that have either been proposed, adopted, or, in some cases, adopted and then repealed in recent years. On the investment side, the main focus, as in the case of labor supply, is on reducing taxes that are believed to dampen the level of investment. General cuts in *corporate income taxes* would presumably affect investment favorably by (1) allowing firms to increase their retained earnings as a source for expanding investment and (2) making investment more attractive to firms by reducing the taxes on income which that investment will produce. More specific measures can also be taken. One of the features of the 1981 tax reform was an accelerated cost recovery system (ACRS), usually called *accelerated depreciation*. The purpose of accelerated depreciation is to increase investment incentives by lowering the immediate tax burden of new investment. The higher the percentage of the value of a machine one can write off—that is to say, the shorter the period over which the machine can be depreciated for tax purposes—the lower the taxes will be in the machine's early years. Another specific measure is encouraging investment through the so-called *investment tax credit,* a mechanism that would allow businesses to deduct from their general tax liabilities a certain percentage of the cost of the investment goods that they purchase. This credit, which had been around since the 1960s, was actually one of those eliminated in the 1986 tax reform.

A major debate in the early 1990s was over the fate of *capital gains* taxes. When anyone purchases an asset and resells it at a later date, the difference between the sales price and the original purchase price is a capital gain (or loss). Many people object to taxes on capital gains for the simple reason that many of such gains are nominal and not real, that is, result from general inflation. If, for example, one buys an asset for $1,000 and resells it in ten years for $2,000 while the price level in general has gone up by a factor of 3, one has actually sustained a real loss on the asset and, yet, is also required to pay taxes on the nominal gain. Supply-side advocates feel that lowering, or even abolishing, taxes on capital gains would encourage individuals and businesses to increase their investments (and also be more fair at the same time). Capital gains taxes have gone up and down over recent years, and in 1990, President Bush's strong advocacy of capital gains reductions faced equally strong opposition from many members of Congress.

On the saving side, many proposals have been offered to increase the general level of saving in the nation, the most extreme of which would focus taxation away from income *per se* to consumption. Also, one could shift the balance from *direct taxes* (taxes, like the income tax, that are levied on people) to *indirect taxes* (taxes that are levied on economic activities). For example, an increase in *sales taxes* would generally punish consumption and reward saving. Less drastic measures would reduce taxes on interest and dividend income to encourage additional savings. One could also expand the availability of *IRAs* (Individual Retirement Accounts), which allow individuals to shelter part of their savings from income taxes. Like capital gains taxes and the investment tax credit, IRAs have had something of a bumpy course in recent years, being promoted strongly in 1981 and then restricted in 1986.

Finally, a supply-side approach would tend to favor all actions that might promote technological progresss. These could include increased government commitments to education and to research and development (R & D) activities. It could also include providing subsidies or tax reductions to business firms to encourage private R & D activity.

Some Possible Disadvantages of Supply-Side Measures

Since the objectives of most supply-side measures seem so commendable, and since they do apparently avoid some of the defects of demand-side policies, it may seem puzzling that in the case of several measures listed above we have noted that supply-side stimulants (like, say, reduced capital gains taxes) were subsequently reversed or repealed. There are actually many reasons for these subsequent actions, amounting overall to the sad truth that most of these measures also have certain accompanying disadvantages. Four categories of such disadvantages are:

1. *Effects on the federal budget.* Almost all of these measures involve tax cuts of one kind or another (and, in a few cases, like greater spending on education and research, increased federal outlays). Since the assurances suggested by the Laffer curve have not, in general, been validated, this means

that these measures tend, for the most part, to add to the federal budget deficit at a time when a major effort is underway in the United States to reduce this very deficit. As we have already mentioned above, this effort is premised on the belief that a reduction in the deficit is necessary for *supply-side* reasons, that is, to promote national saving and investment. Hence, in the absence of corresponding federal spending cuts, supply-side-motivated tax cuts can paradoxically have certain negative effects on important supply-side objectives.

2. *Demand-creating effects.* The attractive picture of supply-side effects presented in Figure 14-4 leaves the aggregate demand curve unchanged. But if tax cuts do create increased budget deficits (that is, are not counterbalanced by spending cuts), then they will almost certainly also shift the aggregate demand curve outward. This is again a point we have mentioned in connection with the tax cuts of 1981–1983. As far as inflation is concerned, then, the general question becomes, Which is the bigger effect of a tax reduction—its supply-side effect or its demand-side effect? The reader should draw in a new aggregate demand curve in Figure 14-4, labeled $A'D'$, showing how, with a big enough shift in aggregate demand, a supply-side tax cut could actually end up *raising,* rather than lowering, the price level.

3. *How big are the supply effects?* Whether the supply or demand effects dominate will depend in part on how large the supply effects are likely to be. Roughly speaking, the more enthusiastic the proponent of the supply-side approach, the larger these effects are believed to be. In point of fact, the analysis of labor and capital supply in response to tax reductions is quite complicated. Take, for example, a reduction in the marginal tax rate on a worker's income. Is this really guaranteed to encourage him to work harder or longer hours? Not necessarily. Because of the lower marginal tax rate, an extra hour of work does bring him more income and, thus, increases the cost to him of an hour of leisure. On the other hand, the tax reduction makes him richer overall (in terms of take-home pay), and, being richer, he may actually prefer to buy more leisure, that is, to work less.[10] In short, it is very easy to get carried away by promises of large supply-side effects when, according to most studies, these effects tend to be fairly modest.

4. *Negative income distribution effects.* Finally, we should note a generic difficulty with most of these supply-side proposals: they tend to reward the productive and the well-to-do directly, while their possibly favorable effects on the unproductive and poor are more roundabout and less certain. Without question, one of the main reasons for congressional opposition to

---

[10] Economists have terms for these two different effects: (1) the *substitution effect,* and (2) the *income effect.* These two effects also come into play when we try to determine whether an increase in the reward for saving (either through a tax reduction on savings, or, say, an increase in the interest rate on savings accounts) will actually end up raising or lowering the rate of savings. For discussion of these two effects, see my *Economics and the Private Interest.* In press.

major capital gains tax cuts in 1990 was that the direct benefits of such taxes go overwhelmingly to upper-income individuals. This is also true of tax cuts on corporate income, interest and dividends, business investment, and so on, as well as of any shift from direct and income taxes to sales and consumption taxes, since the poor, in general, consume far more of their income than the well-to-do. In terms of saving and investment, this difficulty is virtually impossible to avoid since these activities in America are carried out either by relatively wealthy individuals or by corporations owned by relatively wealthy individuals. The same problem is inescapable when we come to labor supply, since any attempt to reward the productive is almost certain to punish the unproductive. Should we cut unemployment benefits? Possibly yes if we wish to get workers back to work as quickly as possible. Definitely no if we wish to provide certain minimum standards of material well-being and simple dignity for the unemployed.

In short—to sum up—there has unquestionably been a shift in policy emphasis in recent years, a shift we shall comment on again in part 5 in our discussion of long-run growth. The long-neglected supply side is now recognized as an equal partner with the demand side in terms of effects on our macroeconomic objectives. At the same time, while supply-side measures can be helpful in many instances, they are, like fiscal and monetary policies before them, no panacea for all our ills. There is no escaping the necessity for studying each measure in terms of all its (usually rather complicated) dimensions.

SUMMARY

The relative decline in the role of fiscal policy as an economic stabilization tool has led to increased interest in monetary policy and also to supply-side and other policy alternatives. In the case of monetary policy, this modern interest has generally focused more on the long run than the short run. This focus is based on widely held beliefs that in the long run, there is no significant trade-off between unemployment and inflation and that—also in the long run—inflation is essentially a monetary phenomenon.

This longer-run approach has also prompted some economists (Milton Friedman being a notable example) to advocate rules versus discretion, and the targeting of money supply aggregates, rather than interest rates, in the application of monetary policy. Although monetary fine-tuning is very difficult and although interest rates have some objectionable features as targets (for example, the gap between nominal and real rates), it must not be thought that the fixed rule-money supply target approach is without its serious problems. These difficulties include (1) gyrations of interest rates, (2) the need to change rules to maintain a constant policy, (3) financial innovations that complicate any given set of targets, and (4) the difficulty the Fed faces in actually hitting any given targets.

However, monetary policy, with a good deal of credit due it for the breaking of inflationary expectations in the early 1980s, emerges as a still-important policy tool. A long-run approach using M_2 (the velocity of which has been fairly stable over time) as an anchor, giving due emphasis to the credibility of policy measures, and adjusting to the needs of long-run growth promises to continue to have merit in the 1990s.

Still, other policies have their place as well. Incomes policies, which attempt to operate directly (either through persuasion or control) on wages and prices, have declined in popularity in recent years in the United States. However, there has been something of a tilt toward the supply side among most economists. A minority of economists are "supply-siders" (in quotes), who generally expect that one can cut tax rates without sacrificing (and possibly increasing) total tax revenues.

More common is the view that some measures should be taken to increase labor supply, raise saving and investment levels, and promote technological change—the object being to achieve favorable shifts in the aggregate supply curve. Examples of possible supply-side measures of this nature are cuts in marginal income tax rates, corporate tax rates, and capital gains taxes; special investment-promoting measures like accelerated depreciation and investment tax credits; taxes focused on consumption rather than investment and special tax shelters, like IRAs; and government spending to promote education and R & D, or tax reductions to promote private R & D.

While many of these measures may prove worthwhile, supply-side policies generally face a number of difficulties because of their negative effect on the federal budget, their demand-creating effects, their uncertain supply-creating effects, and their sometimes adverse effects on the distribution of income. No panacea, then, such measures, nevertheless, are important additions to the modern policymaker's kit of tools.

Key Concepts for Review

Monetary policy
    Long run versus short run
    Rules versus discretion
    Interest rates versus money
        supply
Real versus nominal interest
    rates
Gyrations of interest rates
Deregulation and financial
    innovations

Hitting the target range
Velocity of M_2
Credibility
Monetary-fiscal balance
Demand side versus supply side policies
Incomes policies
    Jawboning
    Wage-price controls
    Tax-based incomes policy

"Supply-siders"   Specific measures to
Laffer curve   Increase labor supply
Tax cuts of 1981–1983   Raise *I* and *S*
Marginal tax rates   Promote technology
                              Disadvantages of specific supply-side measures

Questions for Discussion

1. What is the theoretical basis for proposing that the Fed adopt a long-run, well-publicized, fixed-rule monetary policy? What are some of the difficulties that the attempt to apply this policy have encountered in practice? To what degree, if any, does this proposal still make sense to you?

2. In 1987, the late Arthur Burns described the Fed's monetary policy as "eclectic," a term many would still apply in the early 1990s. What meaning do you give this term in this context? Why have certain past interest rate or money supply targets failed to retain their special roles? Apart from interest rates and monetary "aggregates," what targets might the Fed also be looking at in judging whether to tighten or ease monetary policy at any given time?

3. Why do commentators on monetary policy today almost universally emphasize the concept of "credibility"?

4. In one of his rare jokes, when President Nixon was told that freezing wages and prices was like "trying to walk on water," he replied that, in fact, "you *can* walk on water—when it's frozen." Evaluate not the joke, but the U.S. experience with freezing, controlling, or trying to jawbone wages and prices down during the postwar era. Why have some economists supported the TIP idea?

5. Explain why economists have begun to emphasize the supply side in recent years and why some may have become perhaps a bit too enthusiastic.

6. Take several specific examples of supply-side measures (for example, cuts in marginal income tax rates, investment tax credits, abolition of capital gains taxes, and so on) and show how each measure (a) might help push the aggregate supply curve to the right and (b) might produce other effects that are considered less desirable.

GROWTH AND THE WORLD ECONOMY

CHAPTER 15

MODERN ECONOMIC GROWTH

In part 5, we shall expand our economic analysis in terms both of time and space. We shall consider the factors that have made for the remarkable growth of the American economy over the past century or two. We shall also place our economy in its international context, showing how trade, dependence on foreign resources, and competition from abroad have affected our domestic economy. Finally, in the last chapter, we shall journey (if somewhat tentatively) into the future. What are the problems and prospects facing the rich and also the poor nations of the world in the years ahead?

It should be readily apparent that there is no deep line of separation between these issues and those concerning inflation, unemployment, and national income, which have occupied us in parts 2, 3, and 4. Indeed, a characteristic of recent developments in the field of economics is a recognition that these macroeconomic problems cannot be treated in a purely "short-term" way, but must be viewed from a long-run vantage, and also in an international setting. We have seen many examples of this already. Supply-side economics inevitably focuses on the growth of output over time. Emphasis in fiscal and monetary policy has shifted toward the longer run. As far as international effects are concerned, there is the complex interrelationship between our domestic fiscal deficit and our international trade deficit—the so-called "twin deficits"—that we have already run into. Both deficits, of course, are related to our rate of capital accumulation and long-run growth.

In the present chapter, we shall take a broad historical and theoretical view of the processes of economic expansion over time.

A BRIEF HISTORY OF MODERN ECONOMIC GROWTH

"Modern economic growth," the title of this chapter, suggests that what we are dealing with is a relatively new phenomenon. In a country like the United States, we are likely to take the process for granted because rapid growth has been a customary feature of our personal experience. In a broader historical perspective, such rapid growth is decidedly "modern," and, indeed, it is unprecedented.

The Beginnings of Modern Growth

The beginnings of the process are usually dated in terms of the English industrial revolution of the late eighteenth century. This dating is necessarily somewhat arbitrary. England had been making substantial economic progress for at least two centuries before the revolution occurred. Furthermore, even this earlier progress was dependent on the general expansion of the European economy, which had its roots back at least as far as the tenth or eleventh century. Historians, eager to prove the essential continuity of the British experience, are easily able to find antecedents for virtually every change that took place in the economic structure of late-eighteenth-century England.

Still, the concept of a genuine revolution is not altogether arbitrary. For it was only in late-eighteenth-century Britain that certain distinctive features of what we think of as "modern growth" appeared unequivocally on the scene. For the first time in the history of mankind, a nation began to produce an output of goods and services that was regularly expanding at a rate far in excess of its rate of population growth. We can put this even more strongly. The industrial revolution in England was accompanied by a marked acceleration in the rate of population growth. To have *matched* this growth of population with an equal growth of production would have been achievement enough by any previous historical standard; to have *exceeded* it so that output *per capita* was also growing rapidly was something basically new in historical experience.

And this is what we mean by "modern economic growth":

> Modern Economic Growth is a sustained, relatively regular, and rapid increase in a nation's real GNP, and especially in its real GNP per capita.

It is this kind of growth that was born in Britain in the late eighteenth century.

Some Characteristics of the Industrial Revolution

This birth process had many different aspects. Some of them were clearly favorable and were so regarded by the more perceptive observers of the time.

This was particularly true of the rapid development of new technologies of production. Economically useful inventions were being developed and applied at what, earlier, would have been considered an astonishing rate. There were improvements in virtually all branches of industry—in cotton textile production, in iron and steel, in pottery making, even in agriculture. The greatest single invention of the period was probably James Watt's steam engine (1769). This invention came to affect many different branches of industry and was important in giving durability to the growth process as it continued on into the nineteenth century. It was not, however, the "cause" of the industrial revolution, because the process of technological change was general and pervasive, and, indeed, the revolution was well under way before the steam engine made its impact felt.

Some other aspects of the birth process were clearly unfavorable. This period saw the development and spread of the factory system and, in consequence, a substantial dislocation of the traditional British way of life. It was a period that witnessed great distress among certain groups in society—children employed in the new cotton mills, craftsmen displaced by new techniques of production, rural villagers and squatters dispossessed of their lands. Indeed, these unpleasant features of the transformation of English society were so pronounced that the leading economists of the early nineteenth century (especially Malthus and Ricardo) took a very pessimistic view of the future. They convinced themselves that society was heading toward a dismal "stationary state" in which the great mass of people would be buried in poverty.

As it turned out, their specific analysis was wrong.[1] As a consequence of the industrial revolution, Britain jumped economically far ahead of all her rivals. By the middle of the nineteenth century, she was far and away the outstanding industrial nation in Europe. She was called, and indeed was, the "workshop of the world."

The Process Spreads

This was the beginning, but then the process spread far beyond the British Isles. The United States was already very much embarked upon the growth race before the Civil War. Germany began making major strides in the second half of the nineteenth century. Russia was a very "backward" economy through most of the nineteenth century, but then, in the 1890s, she began to make her move. It is an interesting fact of history that the Russian Revolution of 1917 came not when the Russian economy was deteriorating, but after two decades of quite substantial economic progress under the Czars.[2]

---

[1] "Wrong," that is, about the future prospects of an industrializing economy like that of Britain. But Malthusian-Ricardian fears still have relevance to some of the less developed countries of today.

The process went beyond the boundaries of Europe and the United States—to Canada, Australia, and, rather remarkably, to Japan. The astonishing rate of growth of the Japanese economy since World War II was made possible ultimately by the groundwork that Japan laid in the late nineteenth and early twentieth centuries. Indeed, this early achievement is really more astonishing than the later one. Japan had to face all kinds of obstacles—poor natural resources, heavy density of population, a culture largely isolated from the industrial world of Europe, relatively meager assistance through foreign investment—and yet she still managed to have an industrial revolution of her own beginning in the 1870s and 1880s. The Japanese experience, to this day, remains a particularly fascinating one for those who wish to understand the underlying causes of modern growth.

The process spread, but not everywhere. The underdeveloped world—most of Asia, Africa, Latin America—poses a problem we shall return to later. But wherever the process did spread—Europe, North America, Australasia, Japan—the countries involved began to experience a new and dramatic expansion of their real GNP and their real GNP per capita.

GROWTH TRENDS IN THE UNITED STATES

The expansion of output per capita in these various countries was accompanied by a transformation of their entire pattern of economic life. Before examining some of the causes of this phenomenon, let us sketch out a few of the elements of this transformation, using the American economy as our example. The trends we will now describe, though differing in detail from one country to another, are fairly typical of the modern growth process in general.

Population Growth

Figure 15-1 shows the massive increase in American population over the past 190 years, from 5 million or 6 million to 250 million and still growing. Population increase was more rapid in the United States than in most of the industrial nations during this period (because of special circumstances, including, of course, heavy immigration from Europe), but an increasing population is a characteristic feature of a growing economy, especially in the earlier stages of growth.

---

[2] Though, of course, Russia was still very far behind the economically advanced countries of Europe and North America. Even in 1928, when she began her first five-year plan, Russia's per capita industrial output was probably only 5 to 10 percent of that of Britain.

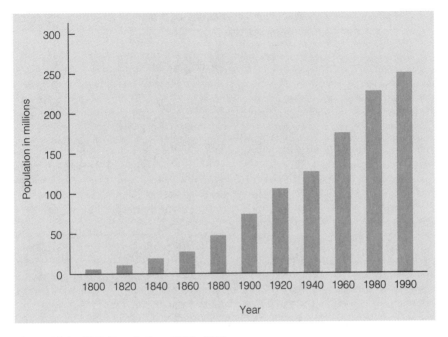

Figure 15-1   U.S. Population, 1800–1990
SOURCES: Bureau of the Census; U.S. Department of Commerce.

Increase in Life Expectancy

One of the causes of our substantial population increase was a sharp increase in life expectancy during this period, as Table 15-1 shows. In the economically advanced countries, increases in life expectancies have been reflective of the overall growth process in the dual sense that growth brings higher standards of living and material comfort and that growth is also accompanied by considerable improvements in medical technology.

Urbanization and Changing Occupations

The growth process has transformed the United States from a largely rural to a predominantly urban society (see Table 15-2). At the beginning of the nineteenth century, the characteristic American worker was a farmer. Over the course of the century and a half since, the occupational structure of the American labor force has changed drastically. There has been an enormous decline in the number of farm families and farm workers. This has been accompanied by a substantial rise in the percentage of the labor force in manufacturing and construction and an even more dramatic increase in the percentage of the labor force in the professions, commerce and finance, gov-

TABLE 15-1 Increasing Life Expectancy in the United States

Year	Average of Male and Female Life Expectancies at Birth*
1850	39.4 years
1878–1882	43.6
1890	43.5
1900–1902	49.24
1909–1911	51.49
1919–1921	56.40
1929–1931	59.20
1939–1941	63.62
1949–1951	68.07
1954	69.6
1967	70.5
1979	73.8
1986	74.8

SOURCES: Elizabeth W. Gilboy and Edgar M. Hoover, "Population and Immigration," in *American Economic History,* ed. Seymour Harris (New York: McGraw-Hill, 1961); *U.S. Statistical Abstract,* 1978, 1981, 1989.

*For years 1850, 1878–1882, and 1890, life expectancies are for Massachusetts only.

TABLE 15-2 Urbanization in the United States

Year	Percentage of Population in Urban Areas	Year	Percentage of Population in Urban Areas
1800	6.7	1900	39.7
1820	7.2	1920	51.2
1840	10.8	1940	56.5
1860	19.8	1960	69.9
1880	28.2	1980	73.7

SOURCE: *U.S. Statistical Abstract,* 1973, 1978, 1981.

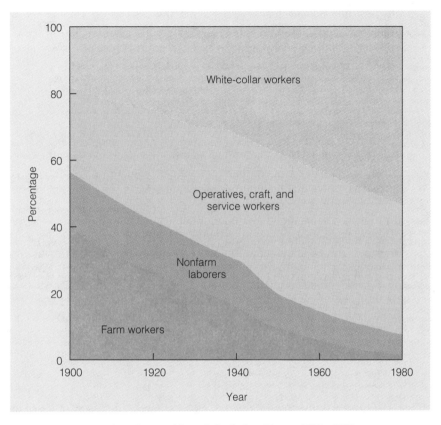

Figure 15-2 Changing Composition of the Labor Force, 1900–1980
SOURCES: U.S. Department of Labor; U.S. Department of Commerce.

ernment service, and other so-called service occupations. Within industry as a whole, there has been a steady movement away from "blue-collar" to "white-collar" positions, as shown in Figure 15-2.

More Leisure Time

The standard workweek has been falling steadily over the past century: in the 1870s, the average was about 67 hours per week; by 1920, it had fallen to 46 hours; by the late 1980s, the average number of hours per week of non-agricultural wage and salary workers had fallen below 39. Individuals now enter the work force later in life than they did in the past, and despite increasing life expectancies, men are retiring at younger ages, thus giving them far more leisure after retirement. Although women are now spending many more hours in the labor force than they once did, the combination of a shorter workweek, reduced housework due to appliances and other technological advances, fewer children, and more years spent unmarried may also have meant more leisure time for most women, even during the past 20 years.[3]

Increasing Education

Today, the average American—man or woman—has far more formal education than he or she did in 1900. The number of years of schooling per member of the population over fourteen and per member of the labor force both increased substantially since the turn of the century. In 1900, only about 7 percent of all children ever attended college. By the late 1940s, the figure had already risen to around 20 percent. Table 15-3 shows the rapid increase since 1940 in the percentage of Americans 25 and older who have completed (1) four years of high school and (2) four years of college. This, of course, is not to say that all is well with the U.S. educational system at this point in time. Low educational standards are a matter we shall return to later (see p. 350). Still, in terms of a broad historical sweep, educational levels have clearly risen in the United States during the process of economic growth, as they have in all the developed nations of the world.

Growth in Output Per Capita

Finally, we come to the trend in output per capita itself. In terms of long-run figures, Professor Raymond Goldsmith has estimated the growth of U.S. real GNP per capita from 1839 to 1959 at 1.64 percent per year. Angus Maddison has pieced together a series for U.S. Gross Domestic Product (GDP) per capita dating back to 1820.[4] He found that over this span of nearly 170 years, U.S. output per capita grew at a rate of 1.8 percent per year. Using a somewhat different measure (real national income per person employed), Edward Denison found that the U.S. growth rate from 1929 to 1982 was 1.5 percent per year.[5]

---

[3] This is the conclusion of a careful study by John P. Robinson, Director of the Americans' Use of Time Project, Survey Research Center, University of Maryland. See his "Time's Up," *American Demographics* (July 1989): 32–35. For an opposing judgment on this issue, see Arlie Hochschild, with Anne Machung, *The Second Shift: Working Parents and the Revolution at Home* (New York: Viking, 1989).

[4] GDP includes output produced within a country's borders, no matter who owns the production units; GNP is the product attributable to the country's citizens, wherever they are located. For Maddison's estimates, see Angus Maddison, *Phases of Capitalist Development* (New York: Oxford University Press, 1982), 167–68.

TABLE 15-3 Increasing Education
in the United States

Year	Percentage of Persons 25 Years and Older Who Have:	
	Completed 4 or More Years of High School	Completed 4 or More Years of College
1940	24.5	4.6
1950	34.3	6.2
1960	41.1	7.7
1970	52.3	10.7
1980	66.5	16.2
1987	75.6	19.9

SOURCE: *U.S. Statistical Abstract*, 1989.

Are these rapid rates? The numbers may seem rather small, but by any past historical standard—that is, prior to the industrial revolution—they are extraordinary rates indeed. Take, for example, Goldsmith's estimate of 1.64 percent per year. A compound interest table will reveal that such an annual rate of increase implies a roughly fivefold increase every century. The median level of family income in the United States in 1988 was something over $32,000 (in 1988 dollars). If we actually succeed in continuing at a 1.64-percent annual expansion for the next century, then in 2088, the median family income in the United States will be over $165,000, and this in terms of *1988 prices and purchasing power!* Is this unrealistic? Possibly, but as Figure 15-3 shows, it is actually less than the rate of increase we have already experienced in the present century. It is this extraordinary multiplicative power of apparently modest increases in output per capita that makes it clear that modern economic growth is a fairly recent historical phenomenon. Had it been going on long at these rates, we would be far richer than we are now.

This, then, is the story of modern growth as exemplified in the American experience. We live longer now, we are a much bigger nation, we live in cities or suburbs instead of on the farm, we work at industrial and service occupations rather than agriculture, we are much better educated on average, we enjoy an increased productive power that dwarfs anything in past history,

[5] Edward Denison, *Trends in American Economic Growth, 1929–1982* (Washington, DC: The Brookings Institution, 1985), 30.

Figure 15-3   Growth in U.S. Per capita GNP in Constant 1982 Dollars, 1900–1987   In less than a century, output per capita in the United States has increased more than fivefold. SOURCE: *Historical Chart Book,* Federal Reserve Board, 1989.

*Measured as a percentage of per capita GNP in 1982 (= 100).

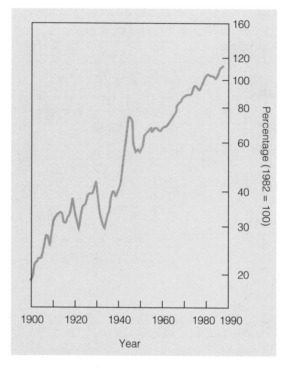

and at the same time, our leisure has been significantly increased. And all this is directly attributable to, or is in large part a reflection of, the phenomenon of modern economic growth. This is not to say that we are happier now—even an affluent society can have very deep problems—nor is it clear that this process can continue indefinitely, for modern growth seems, at least to some observers, to have unacceptable environmental costs. But, without question, it does mean that our entire way of life has been transformed in what, historically speaking, is a very short period of time.

MAJOR FACTORS IN MODERN GROWTH

So far we have been concerned with description. Now we must turn to analysis.

Growth and Aggregate Supply and Demand Curves

One way to organize our analysis of the growth process would be in terms of our aggregate supply and demand curves. What happens over time is that both these curves will tend to shift to the right. Depending on whether the shift of the aggregate demand curve or the aggregate supply curve is the greater, growth in GNP will be accompanied either by inflationary or deflationary pressure, respectively. U.S. growth in the post–World War II era has been unequivocally of the sort shown in Figure 15-4(a), with rising prices regularly accompanying expanding output. However, deflationary growth has actually occurred historically—for example, U.S. wholesale prices were much lower in 1900 than they were in 1800—and this is shown in Figure 15-4(b), where the shift in the aggregate supply curve more than counter-

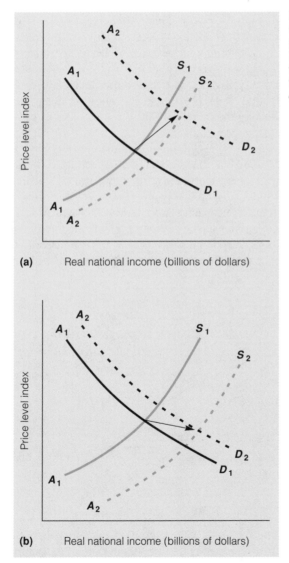

Figure 15-4   Different Growth Patterns   Although post–World War II U.S. growth has been inflationary (a), U.S. growth in the nineteenth century was deflationary (b).

balances the shift in the aggregate demand curve. Much of the impetus for supply-side economics, which we discussed in the last chapter, arises from the desire to promote price-lowering, or at least relatively noninflationary, growth as in Figure 15-4(b). (See also below, pp. 277–283.)

Growth and the Production-Possibility Curve

Looking at growth in real terms, we could represent it by a continual shifting outward of our production-possibility curve. In year one, we have to choose between various determinate amounts of, say, food and steel. In year two, we can have more of both commodities. A possible path of choices is indicated in Figure 15-5, where our hypothetical society is seen to be choosing relatively more steel and relatively less food as it becomes richer. This reflects the relative shift toward manufacturing industry and away from agriculture that we observe in all economically advancing societies after their industrial revolutions. Later on, we might put "goods" on one axis and "services" on the other and show a path reflecting the increasing shift toward services production at later stages of economic growth.

We can also use this diagram (as we did in our discussion of the Soviet economy, p. 49) to illustrate some of the *choices* that affect the rate at which the production-possibility curve shifts outward. If we use all our income today for luxuries and "riotous living" (consumption), then we will not be accumulating additional productive capacity (investment) for tomorrow. If instead of consuming champagne and caviar we use part of our output to build a factory, we will have a higher potential output next year. If instead of spending our nights dancing we study how to become engineers, we will be

Figure 15-5 Growth shifts the production-possibility curve outward. A society may follow the path indicated by line *ABC*. Food production is increasing absolutely, but steel production is increasing much more rapidly. Later in the growth process, the service industries will typically show the fastest growth.

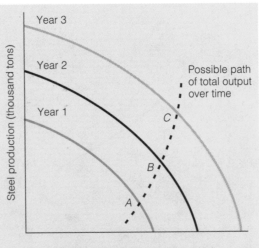

more productive workers next year. As a consequence of such choices, our production-possibility curve will shift out more rapidly, meaning that we may have more consumption (champagne and caviar) and more leisure (for dancing) in the future.

Classification of Growth Factors

This brings us to the question of the *causes* of modern economic growth. This question is a very large one because growth is such a pervasive phenomenon that virtually no aspect of our socioeconomic and political organization is irrelevant to it. The general *type* of economy is obviously extremely important. We have noted that while the command economy may have certain advantages (heavy capital accumulation) at certain stages of the growth process, it may produce economic basket cases later on. Even in a market economy, however, there is always an underlying assumption that the state is strong enough to guarantee the rights of property and the orderly administration of justice. But in many societies, past and present, such an assumption is unjustified: property is destroyed, lawlessness is unchecked, civil strife is the order of the day. In such a society, it may be necessary to build up the political preconditions for stability before modern economic growth can even begin.

Faced with such a wide range of influences, the economist must be somewhat selective. In general, the economic analysis of growth has centered around three main variables:

1. Population growth and expansion of the labor force
2. Capital accumulation
3. Technological progress

Broadly speaking, the expansion of the labor force and the stock of capital are thought of as increases in "factor inputs," while technological progress sums up many elements that contribute to "increased output per unit of input." These are clearly catchall terms, and there are many interrelationships among them, as we shall note as we go along.

POPULATION GROWTH

The effects of population growth on modern economic growth are not easy to predict in all circumstances. In general, an increase in population will bring about an outward shift in a society's production-possiblity curve for the simple reason that it will bring more laborers into the economy and, hence, a greater productive capacity. But modern economic growth involves an increase in output *per capita*. Will the increase in population bring about a proportionately larger or smaller increase in total output? If the increase in total output is proportionately larger than the increase in population, we will have an increase in output per capita. If the increase in total output is proportionately smaller than the increase in population, we will have a decline in output per capita.

The simplest view might seem to be that an increase in population, everything else unchanged, would bring about an equivalent expansion of total output and, consequently, would leave output per capita unchanged. Double the number of laborers, and you double the productive potential of the economy. This simple view, however, ignores certain aspects of the picture that may either inhibit or enhance the output-creating effects of population increase.

Population and the Law of Diminishing Returns

One of the major factors that has been ignored is the famous *law of diminishing returns*. We have already mentioned this law in connection with the analysis of the supply curve in chapter 2. To repeat our earlier definition:

> The *law of diminishing returns* states that in the production of any commodity, as we add more units of one factor of production (the "variable" factor) to a given quantity of other factors of production (the "fixed" factors), the addition to total product with each subsequent unit of the variable factor will eventually begin to diminish.

The operation of this law with respect to population growth is shown in Figure 15-6. Our commodity in this case is "total output," and our "variable"

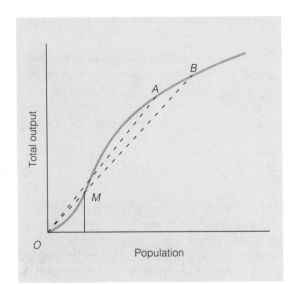

Figure 15-6   The Law of Diminishing Returns   A graphical representation shows that as we increase population (holding natural resources and capital stock constant), total output eventually begins to increase at a diminishing rate. As we move out from point *A* to point *B*, there is a fall in output per capita.

factor is population. What is the "fixed" factor (or factors)? Essentially, it is the whole group of other means of production, natural or man-made, that cooperate with labor in the production of total output. If population increases while the society's natural resources and stock of capital remain fixed, each laborer will, on the average, have less land, minerals, and so on, and fewer tools, machines, and so on, to work with than before. The law of diminishing returns says that this will eventually lead to a declining rate of increase of total output. This happens in our diagram after point M, where it can be seen that the total output curve, while still rising, is rising at a diminishing rate. Sooner or later, this is likely to lead to a decline in output per capita. In our diagram, for example, output per capita declines as we move out from point A to point B. (Why? Because the slope of the line OA or line OB is measured by total output divided by population. As these lines become less steep, it means that output per capita is falling.)

The *significance* of the phenomenon of diminishing returns in the real world is likely to be great or small, depending on a number of other factors. The worst possible situation is a very rapid rate of population increase combined with a very slow rate of capital accumulation and a heavy density of population in relation to land and other natural resources. In this case, each laborer has markedly less capital and land to work with and is likely to add very little to total output. The best possible situation is plenty of land and other natural resources, a rapidly growing stock of machinery and other capital goods, and a relatively less rapid growth of population. Here, there is very little pressure on our "fixed" natural resources, and each laborer has more machines and tools to help him do his work.

Economies of Scale

To complicate the matter further, however, we must now add that there may also be certain *offsets* to the law of diminishing returns. This is why we used the adverb *eventually* in our statement of the law. For as an economy expands, there may be certain *economies of scale* that develop.[6] Large-scale production may, in many instances, be more efficient than small-scale production. A larger economy as a whole may permit an increased specialization of economic functions, or *division of labor* as it is sometimes called. This is a matter that was greatly stressed by Adam Smith nearly two centuries ago. The point is that while an increase in population may be putting pressure on the other factors of production, it is also, to some degree, increasing the

---

[6] Technically speaking, *economies of scale* may be said to exist when, having increased all the factors of production in a certain proportion, total output increases in a *greater* proportion. If you double both the quantity of labor and the quantity of machines and thereby get more than double the previous output, you have *economies of scale*.

"scale" of the economy as a whole. In an economy with a fairly abundant supply of natural resources, this scale effect may actually dominate over the diminishing-returns effect for long periods of time.

What this discussion brings out is that the effect of population growth in contributing to, or inhibiting, modern economic growth will depend very much on how, when, and where it occurs. In the history of the United States, our rapid population growth was much less of an obstacle to achieving an increase in per capita output than it might have been in other countries because we were a very sparsely settled nation throughout the nineteenth century. On the whole, it probably contributed to an *increase* in our output per capita during this period. By contrast, even a slower rate of population growth was a serious problem for late-nineteenth- and twentieth-century Japan, and, indeed, the Japanese have been very vigorous and effective in bringing their rate of population growth down. When we come to modern underdeveloped countries in chapter 17, we shall see further evidence of the importance of the context in which population growth occurs. In some of these countries, the rapid increase of population probably constitutes the major single obstacle to achieving modern economic growth.

CAPITAL ACCUMULATION

It is evident from what we have been saying about population growth that the accumulation of machines, tools, factories, and so on is also an important factor in a nation's economic growth.

Supply-Creating Effects of Investment

In speaking of *capital accumulation* we are speaking of the same phenomenon we were in earlier chapters when we referred to *real investment*. These are equivalent terms, and they both mean adding to society's stock of physical means of production over a given period of time. Our emphasis now is on the longer run, however, and this emphasis has two main consequences.

First, the shift from the short run to the long run tends also to be a shift from the *demand-creating* effects of investment to its *supply-creating* effects. These supply-creating effects of investment have frequently been ignored for short-term purposes. The original Keynesian theory assumed that the additions to capital stock in a year or two were too small to have any major impact on the size of that capital stock and could safely be ignored. Meanwhile, the demand-creating effects of investment (for example, through the multiplier) during that same short period would be substantial. Modern supply-siders criticize this Keynesian emphasis on demand even in the short run; when it comes to the long run, however, *all* economists are agreed: The main purpose and effect of investment is to create new productive capacity. The supply side dominates.

Second, the relative shift from the demand side to the supply side means an almost complete reversal of our view of the relationship between investment and consumption. In terms of the creation of demand, *I* and *C* are on quite an equal footing—we simply add them together to get our aggregate demand curves. When it comes to the creation of supply, however, they are opposites, or at least tend to be competitors. In the long run, we are likely to ask, How can we *cut* consumption so that the society will save more and, thus, be able to increase its investment in more machines, buildings, factories, and so on? *C,* in this case, is seen as the alternative to *I,* and the distribution of today's production between the two will have a substantial effect on tomorrow's productive capacity and output.[7]

Capital Accumulation and Output Per Capita

The effects of capital accumulation on economic growth can be analyzed in much the same general terms as the effects of population growth. If natural resources and population in the society remain constant while the capital stock continually increases, then we should expect "diminishing returns" to capital, except insofar as they are offset in the early stages by whatever economies of "scale" the increased capital stock makes possible. There is one significant difference, however. When population growth is attended by diminishing returns, we face a decline in output per capita (in Figure 15-6, as we move from *A* to *B*). In the case of capital, however, diminishing returns means not that output per capita is declining, but only that it is increasing at a slower rate for any given amount of investment. Insofar as additional capital is still increasing total output, then, for a given population, the effect will be *some* (even though a diminishing) *increase* in output per capita. (This follows simply from the fact that output per capita is defined as total output divided by population.) Unlike population growth, then, the increased accumulation of capital will always have at least some favorable effect on the growth of output per capita.

A few decades ago, most economists gave capital accumulation pride of place among the factors producing economic growth. And, indeed, every economically advanced country in the world has witnessed an extraordinary

---

[7] Both points in this section have to be somewhat qualified. We certainly cannot ignore the demand-creating effects of investment in the long run. An interesting question for more advanced students is to determine the long-run path along which the aggregate supply and demand for output will be in equilibrium. Investment is clearly involved on both sides of this equation, even in the long run. Also, it is not true that consumption is always competitive with investment. While this may be true in a full-employment economy, it will not necessarily be true in an economy with idle labor and unused productive capacity. In such an economy, an increase in *C* could easily lead to an increase in *I* as well.

expansion of its capital stock since the industrial revolution. This expansion has been far more rapid than the expansion of population, with the result that workers in these countries have regularly had more machines and tools to assist them in producing increasingly high levels of output. In the United States, for example, the amount of capital per worker increased by an average of over 2 percent per year from 1870 to 1978.[8] This has clearly been a major factor in promoting our continuing high rate of growth.

Still, the constant increase of capital relative to population, without changes in any other factor, would doubtless have encountered diminishing returns a long time ago, with the result that our output per capita should have been increasing ever more slowly as time went on. That this has *not* happened seems to be attributable to the fact that the growth in our capital stock has regularly been accompanied by a process of technological change. It is this third major factor that has, indeed, occupied a very special place in growth analysis in recent decades.

TECHNOLOGICAL PROGRESS

Population growth and capital accumulation both involve increases in the supplies of our factors of production; by contrast, *technological progress* is concerned with the new and different ways in which we utilize our basic factors of production.

The Meaning of Technological Progress

A working definition of technological progress might go like this:

> We attribute to *technological progress* in the broadest sense those increases in output that cannot be accounted for by the increase in our inputs alone. Technological progress involves new knowledge and the application of this new knowledge to economically useful ends. It may occur through the development of new kinds of machinery, an increase in the skills of the labor force, a reorganization of the productive process, or through the development of new products hitherto unknown. In any case, the emphasis is on doing things in new and different ways as compared to times past.

Technological progress, in this broad sense, has been a characteristic feature of the growth process since the British industrial revolution. From the

---

[8] A. Maddison gives these estimates of annual growth rates of U.S. nonresidential fixed capital stock per man-hour, 1870–1978: 1870–1913, 2.6 percent; 1913–1950, 1.9 percent; 1950–1973, 2.9 percent; 1973–1978, 1.8 percent. (Maddison, *Phases of Capitalist Development*, 109.)

spinning jenny and steam engine of the eighteenth century to electricity, synthetics, atomic energy, and computer technology in our own, there has been a
virtually unbroken line of major innovations in our methods of production.

In recent years, economists have been attempting to separate out the
effects of technological progress on growth from the effects due to the increases in factor inputs (labor and capital). In practice, this is very difficult to
do. For one thing, new techniques of production may become effective only
when they are embodied in new productive capacity. To develop the technology of the railroad is one thing; to make railroads economically effective is
something else again, requiring large investments of capital. In general, the
expansion of our capital stock and the expansion of our technological knowledge have gone hand in hand, and difficult interpretive problems arise when
one tries to separate them. For another thing, there are some "investments"
that are intended precisely to expand the technological know-how of the society and the ability of the society to absorb technological advance. Consider
education, for example. If a person or firm devotes time and money to
education or research, they are making an investment that may lead to the
development of new technology or to an increased ability to operate the new
technologies as they come into being. This process is very similar to ordinary
capital accumulation, except that we are dealing not with physical capital but
with *human capital*. We are saving and investing not in new machines, but in
new knowledge. Again, the borderline between capital accumulation and
technological progress may become blurred.

The Special Significance of Technological Progress

The above points are well worth keeping in mind because they are important
qualifications to a general conclusion of some significance that economists
have developed in recent years. The conclusion is this: If we try to evaluate
the effect of technological progress as opposed to capital accumulation on the
rise in output per capita in the American economy, we find that over most of
the twentieth century, technological progress is the more important factor. In
his study of the period 1929–1982, for example, Denison found that the annual growth of U.S. national income per person employed of 1.48 percent per
year could be decomposed into two contributions: a "total factor input" contribution of 0.47 percentage points and an increased "output per unit of input" contribution of 1.1 percentage points. He estimated the contribution of
increased capital per worker to be only 0.30 percentage points, whereas increased education per worker accounted for 0.40 percentage points, and advances in knowledge (plus otherwise unclassified factors) accounted for 0.65
percentage points. Even when *total* national income (as opposed to national
income per capita or per person employed) is analyzed, Denison found that
increased output per unit of input contributes almost as much as does the

combined contribution of capital accumulation and the increased employment of labor.[9] Broadly speaking, then, technological progress does seem an especially important element in the growth process.

This hypothesis—and it is no more than that because of the great difficulties of isolating and measuring "technological progress"—nevertheless, has some interesting implications. One point it suggests is that the growth process is best understood as a continuing development into new areas rather than as a simple quantitative expansion of what we already have. This makes sense intuitively. Consider the products we buy today. How many of them were in existence or even had equivalents 100 years ago?—the automobile, telephone, television, household applicances, electric lights, synthetics, plastics, personal computers, VCRs, and so on. And this is quite apart from the technological progress involved in finding new methods for producing "old" products. Think of the agricultural revolution in this country over the past century. Now, less than 3 percent of our population not only feeds us, but sustains exports to the outside world. Growth, in other words, is not just more tools or more people to use the tools, it is new products, new methods, new approaches—nothing less than a continuing revolution in our day-to-day lives.

Another important implication is that the factors that stimulate technological progress may be particularly important in maintaining a country's rate of growth. Education and research, the acquisition of new skills, general literacy, on-the-job training—all these ways by which a society prepares its members to discover, develop, and apply new knowledge may have economic implications of the first magnitude.

THE GREAT PRODUCTIVITY QUESTION

This chapter's description of American growth and the factors behind it may seem overly upbeat, considering that we have just been through a period when a major question was how to explain America's great productivity slowdown. By *productivity* here, we mean a measure of output per worker hour, or total output divided by the number of hours worked in the economy. Figure 15-7 indicates the nature of the problem. Annual U.S. labor productivity increase not only declined from the immediate post–World War II period (as we might expect), but actually showed negative values in a number of years in the 1970s and early 1980s.

---

[9] Thus, Denison found that of the annual growth of U.S. national income in 1929–1982 (averaging 2.9 percent), about 51 percent is accounted for by capital accumulation (19 percent) plus growth of the employed labor force (32 percent). The rest comes mainly from advances in knowledge (28 percent) and increased education per worker (14 percent). (Denison, *Trends in American Economic Growth*, 30.)

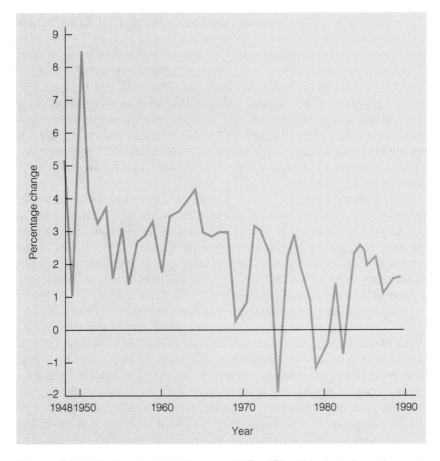

Figure 15-7   U.S., Productivity Changes, 1948–1989   This chart shows the year-to-year increases (+) or decreases (−) in U.S. labor productivity over the past 41 years. Productivity here is measured by output per hour of all persons engaged in the business sector.
SOURCE: *Economic Report of the President*, 1990, tab. C-47.

(The reader may wonder why this break with past experience does not really show up in our per capita GNP diagram in Figure 15-3. A major reason is that over the period from 1970 to 1989, the proportion of our population employed was growing sharply, from 58.0 percent to 63.3 percent. The U.S. economy was thus doing extremely well in terms of creating new jobs—38.7 million new civilian jobs over this 20-year span—though less well on the productivity per worker front.)

What accounts for this unfavorable performance of labor productivity? Denison, whose studies of long-run growth we have referred to, wrote an entire book discussing the slowdown from 1973 to 1979, and he concluded:

"No single hypothesis seems to provide a probable explanation of the sharp change after 1973." [10] Technology expert Edwin Mansfield of the University of Pennsylvania considered that changes in the composition of the labor force, in the growth of the capital-labor ratio, in pollution and other safety and health regulations, in increasing energy prices as a result of OPEC, in general inflation, and in the rate of innovation all played a part in the matter, but he concluded: "The unfortunate truth is that we do not know how much of the decline is due to each of these factors." [11] The 1970s and early 1980s were, of course, a rather peculiar period in the American economy generally, with inflation and unemployment rising simultaneously. Did high inflation, with all its attendant uncertainties, have anything to do with the productivity slowdown? Some think so. [12]

The large question, of course, is whether the experience of the 1970s and early 1980s is an omen of future retardation in the historic American growth rate. No one can answer this question with any certainty. Some economists have argued that productivity increase is intrinsically slower in the services industries than in the goods-producing industries and that the increasing proportion of the labor force now engaged in the production of services could retard our overall growth rate in the future.

In contrast, other economists suggest that this is too pessimistic a view. Productivity specialist John Kendrick, for example, argues that official estimates of GNP significantly understate our rate of economic growth. The reason is that in a number of service sectors, lacking a hard output measure, government statisticians use labor inputs as a proxy measure for output. Such a method effectively assumes *zero* labor productivity increase in these industries. Kendrick believes that this and other measurement problems have led us to exaggerate the recent productivity slowdown, or if not that, at least to underestimate our entire economic growth rate during the past 40 years. [13]

Furthermore, as Figure 15-7 indicates, from 1983 on, there has been something of a bounceback of U.S. productivity growth. Considering that the immediate postwar period showed exceptionally vigorous economic growth in the United States (after the setback of the Great Depression), current productivity figures do not look that bad.

---

[10] Edward F. Denison, *Accounting for Slower Economic Growth* (Washington, DC: The Brookings Institution, 1979), 145. Denison's 17 explanations include changes in the advance of knowledge (slowing down of R & D expenditures, decline of Yankee ingenuity, and so on), changes in government taxes and regulations (pollution regulations, increased paperwork, and so on), and a very large miscellaneous category (energy prices, inflation, decline in the work ethic, and so on).

[11] Edwin Mansfield, "Technology and Productivity in the United States," in *The American Economy in Transition* ed. Martin Feldstein, (Chicago: University of Chicago Press, 1980), 593–96.

[12] This view is taken by Peter K. Clark, "Inflation and the Productivity Decline," *American Economic Review,* vol. 72, no. 2 (May 1982): 149–54.

[13] John W. Kendrick, "The Economy's Even Better than It Looks," *Wall Street Journal,* 14 October 1989.

Which is not to say that we may not face serious problems ahead. There is, after all, the whole question of the environmental impact of modern growth to be considered, an issue we will be raising in our final chapter. On the whole, however, we have to say that so far, there is no incontestable evidence that the great, creative industrial and technological impulse born in the industrial revolution of the eighteenth century has yet begun to peter out. In total, the period since the end of World War II has seen a truly remarkable transformation in all the industrial nations of the world.

SUMMARY

In this chapter, we shift our attention from the relatively short-run analysis of national income, inflation, and unemployment to the problem of long-run growth. There are, of course, many respects in which short-run and long-run analyses are intertwined.

Modern economic growth involves a continuing, relatively regular, and rapid increase in real GNP per capita. It is a decidedly new phenomenon from the historical point of view. The great breakthrough was the English industrial revolution of the eighteenth century, when new techniques and the reorganization of production produced (1) considerable social dislocation and (2) the beginnings of an expansion of production that substantially exceeded the increasing rate of population growth of the period. Britain was for a time the "workshop of the world," but soon the United States, Continental Europe, Russia, Japan, Australia, and other countries joined in.

The experience of the United States, though special in a number of ways, nevertheless indicates some general features associated with the modern growth process. These features include population growth, increased life expectancies, urbanization, the decline of agriculture in national income and employment relative to manufacturing and especially to the service industries, increased leisure time, higher levels of education, and, of course, a continuing expansion of output per capita. Simple arithmetic shows that apparently small annual increases in output per capita—of the order, say, of 1 percent or 2 percent per year—lead over time to surprisingly massive increases in family incomes.

Economic growth may be either inflationary or deflationary, depending on whether the greater shifts are in the aggregate demand or aggregate supply curves. Growth will involve an outward shift in the production-possibility curve, with the usual path being from agriculture to manufacturing to services. Of the many factors that produce economic growth, economists tend to focus on three major variables: population growth, capital accumulation, and technological progress.

Population growth may have either positive or negative effects on the level of a society's output per capita, depending on whether the law of diminishing returns is offset by other factors, such as economies of scale. In general, population growth will be an obstacle to the achievement of modern economic growth if it is very rapid, is accompanied by relatively little capital accumulation, and takes place in an already densely populated society. By contrast, in the United States, where our problem in the nineteenth century was the sparsely settled nature of the country, population growth may have had a favorable effect on the growth of output per capita.

By *capital accumulation* we mean what we earlier referred to as "real investment," except that now our attention is focused less on the demand-creating than on the supply-creating (capacity-creating) side. Capital accumulation is clearly a factor favorable to the rise in output per capita, though this rise in output per capita may be at a diminishing rate if the capital stock is growing in relation to population and natural resources and if no other elements in the picture change.

Technological progress involves changes in the quality and in the utilization of our basic factor inputs. It involves new things—new skills, new methods of production, new products, and so on. Modern studies have suggested that technological progress is a particularly important factor in economic growth, accounting for more of our increased output per capita than the accumulation of more capital per worker. These studies have to be qualified in a number of important ways, but they do make sense intuitively when we think of the novelties that modern growth has brought during the past century or more.

The great productivity slowdown in the United States in the 1970s and 1980s remains something of a mystery, although numerous factors—including labor force changes, energy price increases, general inflation, governmental environmental regulations, and many other factors—may have played a part. It is possible, however, that productivity advance in the services sector may be underestimated.

Key Concepts for Review

Modern economic growth
Industrial revolution
Characteristic growth trends
    Population growth
    Increased life expectancy
    Urbanization
    Agriculture, manufacturing,
      services
    Leisure
    Education
    GNP per capita

Inflationary versus deflationary growth
    (aggregate demand and
    supply)
Shifts in the production-
    possibility curve
Major factors in growth
    Population and labor force
    Capital accumulation
    Technological progress

Population growth
    Law of diminishing returns
    Economies of scale
Capital accumulation
    Supply- versus demand-
        creating effects
    I as an alternative to *C*
    More capital per worker

Technological progress
    New products and methods
    Advances in knowledge
    Education and human capital
Importance of technological progress
Labor productivity
Productivity slowdown
Vigor of overall post–World War II
    growth of industrial nations

Questions for Discussion

1. Define *modern economic growth*. Indicate some of the changes in the structure of a society that usually accompany the growth process.

2. Discuss various possible favorable and unfavorable effects of population growth on the rate of growth of output per capita.

3. "The problem with short-run national income analysis is that it focuses too much on the demand-creating side of investment and neglects the capacity-creating side." Discuss.

4. It has been said that an industrial revolution is nothing more nor less than the process by which a country that has been saving and investing 5 percent or less of its GNP begins to save and invest 10 or 12 percent of its GNP. What arguments do you think could be made for and against this proposition?

5. In the early twentieth century, the Austrian-American economist Joseph Schumpeter gave a central role to *innovation*—the introduction of new methods of production and new products into the economy—in the growth process. How has modern analysis tended to verify Schumpeter's basic intuition? Schumpeter also characterized the growth process as one of "creative destruction." Does this term seem apt to you?

6. List some of the factors that may have been responsible for the slowdown in U.S. productivity increases in the period 1973–1982. Why do some economists feel that the slowdown may be somewhat less than the numbers suggest?

CHAPTER 16

INTERNATIONAL
BALANCE OF PAYMENTS

We ended the last chapter with a reference to the remarkable transformation of all the industrial nations of the world in the post–World War II era. In no area of economics has this transformation had more impact than in the field of international trade. The economic interconnections among nations have grown immensely closer in recent decades. In the United States, for example, we cannot even discuss that major subject of interest—the federal deficit—without being immediately drawn into a discussion of what seems to be a wholly different subject—our international balance of payments deficit. In point of fact, these "twin deficits" are deeply intertwined, as is our domestic savings-and-investment performance with the behavior of foreign savers and investors and, indeed, as is the American economy and the world economy in virtually every dimension.

In this chapter, we extend our analysis to the international sphere, emphasizing especially the macroeconomic aspects of our international balance of payments.

TRADE AND THE AMERICAN ECONOMY

The first point to emphasize is, quite simply, that foreign trade *is* important to the American economy. To those who have witnessed the flood of foreign cars and electronic products into this country in recent years, this may seem an obvious point. The fact is, however, that such a statement could not have been made, or at least would have been made with much less emphasis, 20 or

30 years ago. At that time, one would have been inclined to say that U.S. trade was, because of the size of the American economy, very important to other countries but of much less importance to the United States itself. Except for a few strategic commodities, we could, it seemed, have done without trade altogether.

The Expansion of U.S. Trade

All this is now changed. Since foreign imports are obviously all around us, let us look at trade from a different point of view: How important is *export* production to American businesses and workers? Figure 16-1 shows the dramatic expansion of U.S. exports of goods and services from 1950 to 1989. In constant 1982 dollars, our exports increased almost 10 times, from $59.2 billion to $587.6 billion. This represents not only a striking absolute increase, but also an increase relative to our rapidly growing GNP. In current dollars, our exports of goods and services rose from 5 percent of GNP in 1950 to 12 percent in 1989.

The composition of our trade also changed substantially during this period. The United States has seen a large expansion in its exports of agricultural goods, chemicals, capital goods, and military goods. At the same time, it has experienced equally large, or larger, increases in its imports of oil, automobiles, electronics, textiles, and consumer products generally. It is hard to realize today, but from 1925 to the mid-1950s, the United States was a net exporter of fuels and lubricants; we were a net exporter of automobiles until 1968.

The Changed Status of the United States

Despite the great growth of our trade, the *relative* importance of the United States in the world economy has declined substantially during these postwar decades. At the end of World War II, the United States was the dominant industrial producer in the world, actually accounting for over 60 percent of the world's manufacturing output. The rapid reconstruction of Europe and Japan, followed by various "miracles" of modern economic growth and the spread of the process to newcomers like Taiwan, Korea, Singapore, and Hong Kong (the so-called *NICs,* or "newly industrialized countries"), changed all this. The U.S. share of the world's manufactured goods exports fell from 29 percent in 1953 to 13 percent in 1976, that is, by more than half. By 1990, the United States had simply become one of three major trading centers in the free world, the others, of course, being Western Europe and the Pacific nations centered around Japan.

This change in status also has been reflected in the altered position of the dollar. At the end of World War II, the dollar was *the* key currency in

Figure 16-1   U.S. Exports of Goods and Services in Constant 1982 Dollars, 1950–1989   U.S. exports have expanded even more rapidly than our fast-growing GNP in the postwar era. Imports, of course, have expanded even more rapidly than exports.
SOURCE: *Economic Report of the President*, 1990. tab. C-21.

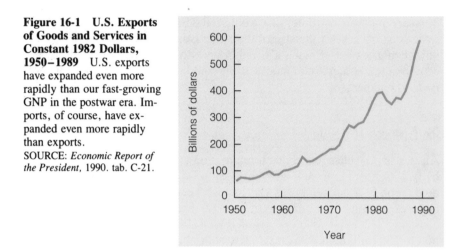

international trade, and the world was suffering from an acute "dollar shortage." The dollar is still an extremely important trading currency, but it no longer has the kind of invulnerability it once possessed. Thus, for example, in 1971 and again in 1977–1978, we had not "dollar shortages," but "dollar crises." Also, the dollar has shown enormous fluctuations with respect to other currencies, now rising, now falling in value. Between 1967 and 1989, for example, it lost over half its value relative to the German mark and nearly two-thirds its value relative to the Japanese yen.

The Fundamental Benefits of Trade

The last comment suggests—as everyone who ever reads a newspaper knows—that it has not been altogether clear sailing for the United States in world markets in recent years. Indeed, our balance of payments problems have been such that voices have been raised in Congress and elsewhere to promote various kinds of restrictions or limitations on our trading partners (particularly Japan), even though such measures might invite retaliation and a wholesale shrinkage of the volume of trade between the U.S. and other countries.

   Without taking sides on this heated issue, we should at least make note of the fact that most economists believe that there are important *general* reasons for leaving international trade as free and open as is feasible. These reasons are usually summed up in what is called the *doctrine of comparative advantage*. Roughly speaking, this doctrine states that whenever any two countries face somewhat different productive conditions so that each country can produce certain products relatively more cheaply than the other country (a condition almost always fulfilled), then trade between the two countries will be *mutually advantageous*, that is, both countries will gain in real terms. In other words, trade isn't a case where if country A wins, country B loses. In the *general* case, both A and B will gain from trade, and both will lose if trade is curtailed or interrupted.[1]

In short, for all the problems trade may cause, the main reason we have had such an expansion of trade in recent decades is that it has been advantageous to the United States—and to other countries—to engage in such transactions.

BALANCE OF PAYMENTS ACCOUNTING

Although trade is usually beneficial in real terms, it is very seldom conducted in real terms, that is, on a barter basis. We use money in our international trade transactions, and, of course, a variety of different national currencies are involved. This brings us to the important subject of *balance of payments accounting*.

A Simplified Balance of Payments Example

Let us begin with the simplest possible case, where we have only two countries trading in merchandise exports and imports and where the outstanding balances between the two countries are settled, as they were in olden times, by shipments of gold. The country whose balance of payments is represented in Table 16-1 is enjoying a surplus of exports over imports, or what is sometimes called a *favorable balance of trade*. Such a favorable balance was much sought after by mercantilist statesmen and writers of the sixteenth and seventeenth centuries since it led, among other things, to an increase in national "treasure." In our particular case, the $200 million export surplus is being paid for by gold imported by this country from its trading partner.

As simplified as it is, this table brings home an important point: namely, that there is a certain accounting sense in which trade must always be in balance. The final sum of all credit and debit items must be zero. The "economic" significance of this point is that it forces us to realize that every transaction in international trade is essentially two-sided. Every good that we import from abroad must be paid for in one way or another. If we import an automobile from a European country, we must pay for it either by exporting goods of equivalent value or by exporting gold or, in more complicated

---

[1] This is necessarily a very abbreviated version of the doctrine of comparative advantage. It is a somewhat complicated doctrine to state since it involves, at a minimum, two different countries and two different goods. It can be illustrated by the use of two production-possibility curves, one for each of the trading countries. For a more careful development of the doctrine, see my microeconomics text that is a companion to this text. (*Economics and the Private Interest*. In press.)

TABLE 16-1 A Simplified Hypothetical Balance of Payments
(Millions of Dollars)

Merchandise	Amount	Balances
Exports (+)*	+500	
Imports (−)	−300	
Merchandise balance (net)		**+200**
Gold imports (−)	−200	
Formal accounting balance		**0**

*Plus signs represent credit items; minus signs, debit items.

cases, by transferring dollars to a foreign account or by sending an IOU to the foreign country (in which case the foreign country is increasing its investment in the United States) and so on. When all the plus items (credits) and all the minus items (debits) are added up, the final result must always be zero. Indeed, as we shall see in a moment, when they don't add up to zero, accountants use the term "statistical discrepancy" to make up the difference.

Classification of Items

If trade must always balance in an accounting sense, why then do we ever worry about our "balance" of payments? Clearly, it makes a great difference what the particular credit and debit items are. For example, in Table 16-1, although our given country might be happy to be receiving a debit item of $200 million in gold imports, its trading partner might be greatly alarmed at having a credit item of that same amount on its balance of payments account. We must come to a clear understanding of exactly what credit and debit items are.

As far as the classification of items is concerned, the fundamental rule is that any transaction that creates a demand for your currency—say dollars—is a credit item. By contrast, any transaction that involves a supply of your currency seeking other currencies—say dollars being offered in exchange for francs or pounds—is a debit item.

Consider the $500 million export item in Table 16-1. Let us suppose that these are exports going from America to Germany. The German importer has marks in his possession, but he wants to buy goods from an American who wants to be paid in dollars. The German goes to his bank and uses his marks to buy dollars at whatever the going "exchange rate" is between these two currencies and then sends the $500 million in dollars to the American firm in exchange for the merchandise. The details are more complex than this, of course, but the central fact is clear: these exports have created a demand for dollars in terms of a foreign currency (marks), and, thus, these exports are considered a credit item for the United States.

The reader can easily apply the same logic in reverse to the case of American imports from Germany. But what about the third item in Table 16-1—gold imports? Why are these considered a debit item? The principle is exactly the same. When a foreign country ships gold to us, it receives dollars in exchange, and, thus, the supply of dollars has been increased. To follow it through: the German exporter of gold receives dollars for the gold, which he then uses to buy marks (or, alternatively, simply to pay for the extra merchandise imports from America). Thus, gold imports are a debit item, and gold exports are a credit item.

An Actual Balance of Payments Account

Once this general principle is clear, it becomes possible to apply it to the many complex items that make up a country's actual balance of payments; for example, tourist expenditures of Americans abroad, our military expenditures abroad, interest and dividend payments to foreign owners of U.S. securities, U.S. private investment abroad, and so on. Take, for example, a long-term investment by an American firm in a factory in France. Does this create a demand for dollars or a supply of dollars? The American puts up the dollars, which are then exchanged for francs to pay workmen in France to build the factory. Hence, the answer is that the supply of dollars seeking to purchase foreign currencies has been increased and that U.S. investment abroad is to be treated as a debit item. Conversely, Japanese investment in the United States creates a supply of a foreign currency (yen) seeking to purchase dollars and is to be treated as a credit item in the U.S. balance of payments.

In Table 16-2, we present the actual (although still very simplified) balance-of-payments account for the United States in 1988. You should be able to explain several of the items already, for example, investment income from abroad. This is a credit item because Americans were receiving net payments of $2.2 billion on their investments abroad, and these payments were generated in foreign currencies (yen, marks, lire, and so on), which then created a demand for dollars to pay off the American investors. We had a very large credit item for private capital inflows. What this meant is that private foreign investors were investing much more (a net of $98.9 billion) in the United States than American investors were investing abroad. Foreign investment in the U.S., as we have already indicated, creates a demand for dollars in terms of foreign currencies.

Of course, over time, foreign investment in the United States creates claims on U.S. investment income by foreign investors. Outflows of investment income are a debit item on the U.S. balance of payments. The same is true of foreign official assets in the United States. When foreign governments buy U.S. government bonds, this is a credit item for the U.S., amounting to

TABLE 16-2 U.S. Balance of Payments, 1988 (Billions of Dollars)

Type of Transaction	Amount	Balances
Merchandise		
Exports (+)	+319.3	
Imports (−)	−446.5	
Merchandise balance (net)		**−127.2**
Investment income (net)	+2.2	
Military transactions (net)	−4.6	
Travel and transportation (net)	−2.6	
Other services	+20.3	
Balance on goods and services		**−111.9**
Unilateral transfers	−14.7	
Balance on current account		**−126.6**
Private capital flow (net) (inflow, +)	+98.9	
U.S. government foreign assets (net) (increase, −)	−0.6	
Foreign official assets in the U.S. (increase, +)	+38.9	
Balance on capital account	**+137.2**	
Statistical discrepancy	−10.6	
Total	+126.6	
Formal accounting balance		**0**

SOURCE: *Economic Report of the President*, 1990, tab. C-102, adapted by the author.

$38.9 billion in 1988. When interest is paid on these bonds, however, it is a debit item. Over the long run, it is of concern to us that these potentially debit-creating foreign investments in the U.S. are growing so rapidly. In 1989, for the first time in the postwar era, our net investment income turned negative.

A Run-through of the Balances

We will discuss the significance of the U.S. balance of payments condition later in this chapter. For the moment, we will simply give a brief run-through of various balances listed. We imported many more goods than we exported in 1988, meaning that our merchandise balance (what we have previously called the *balance of trade*) was negative, or "unfavorable." This negative balance was increased by our military expenditures abroad and by the fact that American shippers and tourists spent somewhat more ($2.6 billion) than foreign shippers and tourists spent here. However, we did have a small positive investment income as already mentioned and considerable services income to offset these negatives. In total, our *balance on goods and services* was still negative (−$111.9 billion), but not by quite as much as our trade balance.

When we add one more item here—unilateral transfers (private remittances abroad and also the U.S. nonmilitary foreign aid program)—we come down to the *balance on current account.* This is the balance that is usually meant when we say that our balance of payments shows a surplus or a deficit. In 1988, this balance was in deficit by the not-unprecedented, but still substantial, sum of $126.6 billion.

We said earlier that every import a country receives has to be paid for in one way or another. Essentially, our excess of imports in 1988 was paid for by capital flowing into this country, both private and government. This is what the next items in the *capital account* tell us. In the simplest terms, in exchange for letting us have more of their goods, foreigners took payment in the form of ownership of stocks, bonds, real estate, and factories in the United States. Needless to say, these were not usually the same individuals or governments on both sides of the transactions; it's just the totals that come out that way.

Finally, since the totals don't *exactly* come out that way, we have our "statistical discrepancy" to remind us that the basic principle can never be violated. Under this heading are all the transactions flowing across our borders that somehow didn't get counted. While we don't know exactly what items are in this total, we do know what the total itself has to be—in this case, −$10.6 billion. For only then can we get to the required final result: a zero formal accounting balance.

DIFFERENT EXCHANGE MECHANISMS—FIXED VERSUS FLEXIBLE

We have been talking about the supply and demand of dollars in relation to foreign currencies. We now ask, How is the exchange rate between the dollar and these other currencies established? Fundamentally, there are two mechanisms (with many variations) that can be used: (1) fixed exchange rates and (2) flexible exchange rates.

Fixed Exchange Rates—The Gold Standard

The simplest way (conceptually) of determining the exchange rates between different currencies is to fix them all at a given level. One dollar is equal to so many marks, so many yen, so many pounds, and so on. This can be accomplished by setting a fixed price on some common means of payment—historically, this was gold—in terms of each of the other currencies. If the price of gold is fixed in terms of dollars, marks, yen, and pounds, then the exchange rates of these currencies are also fixed, or, more accurately, are fixed within the limits set by the cost of transferring gold from one country to another. If currency A becomes more expensive in terms of currency B, people pay in gold rather than in currency A.

Under such a mechanism, the way in which a deficit in a country's balance of payments manifests itself is through exports of gold. If a country is buying more abroad than it is selling and also investing more abroad than it is receiving in foreign investments, then it will tend to lose gold. More generally, a deficit in the balance of payments under a fixed exchange standard will show itself in terms of pressure on the country's supply of reserve assets (gold or other universally acceptable means of payment, such as "hard" foreign currencies).

Completely Flexible Exchange Rates

At the opposite extreme (and, as we have said, there are infinite variations possible) is the case of completely flexible exchanges. Here, the value of a currency in terms of other currencies will be determined by supply and demand. The supply curve of German marks seeking to buy U.S. dollars in Figure 16-2 will reflect the desire of Germans to import goods from the United States and to invest in this country. As the price of the mark in terms of dollars goes up, U.S. goods will be cheaper for Germans in terms of

Figure 16-2 Supply and Demand Determination of Exchange Rates

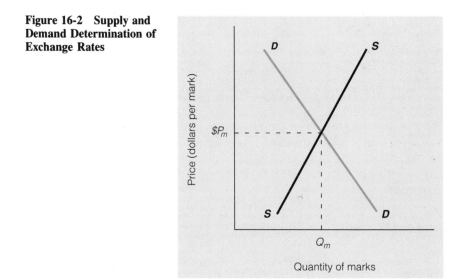

Quantity of marks

marks; therefore, they will presumably want to buy more U.S. goods. For this reason, the supply curve will go upward to the left.

The demand curve for marks reflects the desire of Americans to buy German goods and to invest in Germany. As the price of the mark goes down in terms of dollars, the price of German goods goes down in terms of dollars. Therefore, we will presumably want to buy more German goods, that is, demand more German marks. Thus, the demand curve will slope downward to the right.

The exchange rate is then, of course, determined where supply equals demand. The equilibrium dollar price of marks is represented by P_m in this diagram. Of course, this exchange rate can change weekly, daily, even hourly under completely flexible exchanges. It will depend simply on the forces of supply and demand.

Under the flexible exchange mechanism, the way in which a deficit in a country's balance of payments ordinarily shows itself is through a fall in the value of that currency.[2] If a country is trying to buy more abroad at a given exchange rate than foreigners want to buy there at that same exchange rate, there will be an excess supply of that country's currency trying to buy other currencies, and the result of supply and demand will be a fall in the exchange rate. No shipments of gold are required.

THE CLASSICAL GOLD STANDARD

Historically, the appeal of the gold standard (and there are some who yearn for its return today) proceeded from the fact that it created a great degree of certainty in international trade—you did not have to consult your daily paper to discover whether the price of your currency or of foreign currencies had changed drastically overnight—and also from the fact that it seemed to have its own corrective mechanism in case of difficulties. Could it be shown that if one country had a deficit in its balance of payments and another had a surplus, that these imbalances would lead to forces that would remove these imbalances and restore equilibrium?

The British classical economists, and especially the philosopher and friend of Adam Smith, David Hume (1711–1776), thought that just such a corrective mechanism did exist. Assuming (1) that a gold flow into (or out

---

[2] We say "ordinarily" because it is theoretically possible for a country to have a deficit in its current account balance but to have so great a foreign demand to invest in that country that the value of its currency rises even while the deficit continues. This is not only a theoretical possibility, but an accurate description of what happened to the U.S. dollar in 1988–1989. From the first quarter of 1988 to the third quarter of 1989, the dollar appreciated in value with respect to foreign currencies by over 10 percent, and yet the U.S. had a major deficit on current account during this whole period. The reason: the strong desire of foreign investors to buy U.S. bonds, securities, and property.

of) a country is matched by a roughly proportionate increase (or decrease) in the country's money supply and (2) that the quantity theory of money[3] holds true—that is, that changes in a country's money supply will lead to proportionate changes in its price level—they presented the following argument:

> Two countries, A and B, are trading together. Country A has a surplus with country B, as in Table 16-1. Country B has an equal and opposite deficit with country A. Gold flows will now take place between the two countries, gold going from country B to country A. As a result of the gold flows, the money supply in country A will rise and the money supply in country B will fall. Because of the quantity theory of money, these changes in the money supplies will result in a rise in the price level in country A and a fall in the price level in country B. These changes in the price levels, however, will lead to consequences for the trading positions of the two countries. Country A's exports are now more expensive, while exports from country B are less expensive. Citizens in country A will now want to purchase more goods from country B, while the citizens of country B will curtail their purchases of the now more expensive goods from A. Under ideal circumstances, these changes will lead to a correction of the original trade imbalance and a cessation of the gold flow. The net result will be a redistribution of the world's gold supply between country A and country B.

Indeed, we can put the classical case quite simply by saying that the original problem between country A and country B was a maldistribution of gold stocks. Country A had too little gold (hence, its prices were too low, and, thus, its exports were too high), and country B had too much (with consequent high prices and a poor export performance). At one stroke, the market mechanism—this was usually called the "price-specie-flow" mechanism—corrected the trade imbalance and the gold maldistribution and brought overall equilibrium to both countries.

Any theory, unfortunately, is only as good as its assumptions. In this case, neither of the two basic assumptions have usually been fulfilled. Nations are not willing to allow their money supplies to be determined purely and simply by inflows or outflows of gold from abroad (assumption one). In the United States, for example, the Federal Reserve Board might "neutralize" the gold flows by open-market operations. For example, in 1939–1941, when the U.S. gold stock rose by over $5 billion, most of the increase was neutralized by open-market sales of government securities. The opposite happened in 1961–1963, when a loss of $4.4 billion was completely offset by the Federal Reserve Board's actions. Even if the nation did allow its monetary policy to be determined purely by international considerations, however, the quantity theory of money (assumption two) is unlikely to work in the simple, effortless way suggested by the classical theorists.

In a certain sense, the major flaw in the gold standard was that it in-

---

[3] Recall our discussion of the quantity theory on pp. 211–214.

volved the "tail wagging the dog." Imbalances in international trade required massive readjustments of each country's domestic economy (by the inflation or deflation of its price level, but also, in practice, by changes in its levels of real national income and employment). In the crunch, few deficit countries are likely to take the risk of plunging the nation into recession or depression simply to sustain the value of their currencies abroad.

THE ABANDONMENT OF FIXED EXCHANGE RATES

For all these reasons, it is not surprising that the attempt to maintain fixed exchange rates was largely abandoned by the United States and the rest of the world in the early 1970s. One of the important reasons for the move toward flexible (or "floating," as they are sometimes called) exchange rates was the changed trading position of the United States, which we described earlier in this chapter. As a result of the rapid growth of the Japanese and European economies, the United States began showing persistent deficits in its balance of payments from 1950 on. Since the dollar was pegged to gold at the price of $35 an ounce, we financed this deficit in part by the export of gold. The U.S. gold stock in 1949 was running in the neighborhood of $25 billion; by 1974, it had fallen to less than $12 billion.

Our accumulated deficit was, however, much larger than the decline in our gold stock, and the fact is that by far the greater part of the deficit was financed by the export of dollars. For approximately 20 years after 1950, the dollar served along with gold as a generally acceptable medium of exchange for the purposes of international transactions. In fact, the matter in its most favorable light could be put this way: The United States' balance of payments deficit was a significant means of expanding the total supply of international "liquidity," during the postwar period. In the absence of vast new discoveries of gold, this expansion of dollars held by foreigners facilitated the enormous (and mutually beneficial) expansion of world trade that has been one of the most striking features of the last few decades.

Unfortunately, however, such a system could last only while the dollar was accepted in this unique way, that is, considered "as good as gold." By 1971, after years of deficits, this had become impossible. Our liquid liabilities to foreigners exceeded our gold stock by a factor of five; indeed, the central bank of Germany alone held enough U.S. dollars to exhaust our entire gold stock at $35 an ounce. The dollar was clearly overvalued; its ties with gold had to be severed.

From 1971 to 1973, in a series of stages, the entire system was overhauled. The official price of gold and the private price of gold were separated. The dollar was devalued. Crises still occurred. The dollar was devalued again. The last remaining ties between the dollar and gold were severed. In short, by mid 1973, the attempt to operate with any form of fixed exchange rates was largely abandoned in the United States and abroad. We moved into the world of floating exchange rates, a system that had long been predicted and increasingly urged by a majority of economists.

PROS AND CONS OF FLOATING EXCHANGE RATES

One of the main reasons many economists prefer flexible exchange rates is that they permit, as we have noted, more freedom of maneuver for domestic policies. This same argument, however, can be used *against* flexible exchanges. Lacking the "discipline" of the gold standard, it is claimed, countries can follow highly inflationary domestic policies without having to pay the consequences in terms of their balances of payments. They simply allow their currencies to depreciate. This depreciation, in its turn, may heighten inflationary pressures within the country since it means increases in the domestic prices of foreign imports. One can imagine (and, indeed, this seems to have happened in the case of certain Latin American countries) a vicious circle of inflationary domestic policies, exchange depreciation, higher rates of inflation, more exchange depreciation, and so on. Under fixed exchange rates, this could not happen. The country would either have to reduce its inflation or face the total depletion of its international reserves and cease to be able to trade at all.

An even stronger argument against flexible exchange rates is that they add still one more uncertainty to a world where, because of high and variable inflation, uncertainty is already a major impediment to economic prosperity, growth, investment, and trade. In order to carry out an international transaction, we have to estimate not only the future course of prices here and abroad, but also the future course of exchange rates between the currencies involved. These price movements and exchange rate movements are not, of course, wholly independent of one another. In general, we should expect that the exchange rates between currencies will adjust to price differences between countries in such a way that a dollar, say, will purchase roughly the same quantity of goods in Japan, France, or Pakistan as it does in the United States. Otherwise, international demand would flow to the countries where prices were cheaper. This view is called the *purchasing-power parity theory.*

However, there are many slips 'twixt cup and lip in this long-run adjustment process, meaning that exchange rate variations can themselves be an independent source of uncertainty. Figure 16-3 makes it clear that there has been extraordinary volatility in the value of the dollar in foreign exchange markets during the decade of the 1980s. The dollar went up more than 60 percent against the currencies of its main trading partners in the early 1980s, then down an equal amount, and then began rising again at the close of the decade.

Furthermore, adjustments under flexible changes often disappoint ex-

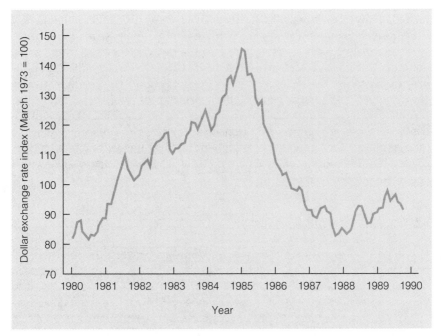

Figure 16-3   U.S. Dollar Exchange Rate, 1980–1989   This chart shows the changing value of the U.S. dollar with respect to other foreign currencies during the decade of the 1980s. The volatility of the U.S. exchange rate is striking.
SOURCE: Board of Governors of the Federal Reserve System.

Note: Data are monthly.

pectations, because they take time to work out. Imagine a country with a deficit in its balance of trade with a result that its currency starts to fall in value. The *first* impact of that decline in the exchange rate is to make foreign goods (imports) more expensive to citizens in the deficit country. In the long run, this should help remove the deficit, but in the short run, it could make it worse. If the deficit country temporarily continues to buy the same, or nearly the same, physical quantities of goods from its trading partner, its deficit will actually *increase for a time.*[4]

Having said all this, however, we should probably give floating exchanges a number of very positive marks for their performance during the past 20 years. One reason for saying this is that this period included a number of serious "shocks" to the international trading system, particularly in the mid- and late 1970s, when OPEC was raising havoc with balances of pay-

---

[4] Economists call this the *J-curve effect.* What it says is that a country's deficit may at first worsen when its currency depreciates and will improve only after long-run adjustments have taken place. In

ments all over the world. To have survived these difficulties without any overall breakdowns in the system is a reasonably impressive achievement.

The main reason for at least mild applause is, however, a very simple one. It is what is suggested in our Figure 16-1, where we show the extraordinary expansion of U.S. exports in recent years, actually tripling in real value since the early 1970s. In general, the expansion of world trade under the floating exchange regime has been extremely impressive. This isn't wholly a tribute to the new regime—government intervention to influence exchange rates has never been completely absent during this time period[5]—but it does suggest that any move back to a more rigid system must be approached with a certain amount of caution.

AMERICA AND THE TWIN DEFICITS

It is time now to indicate the broad relationship between the international position of the United States and some of the domestic issues we have been considering in this text, particularly the levels of savings and investment in the U.S. (a major factor in our future economic growth) and the federal deficit. If we were to sum up the basic relationship in a few words, it would go like this:

> The United States has in recent years been accumulating large deficits in its current account balance and also large deficits in the federal budget. The federal deficit has

---

the accompanying figure, we are dealing with a country with an unfavorable balance of trade, measured on the y-axis. On the x-axis, we measure the length of time since the depreciation. Under average conditions, there might be a lag of a year or two before the country reduces its deficit to zero, at point C.

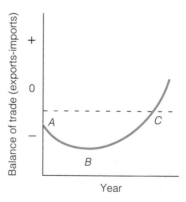

Time since depreciation

---

[5] Frequent interventions by governments and central banks all over the world mean that we do not have a *pure* floating exchange system (any more than we have a *pure* market economy). The present system is sometimes referred to as a "managed float," or, more colorfully, a "dirty float."

effectively reduced our total domestic savings rate, but our investment rate has not gone down equivalently. It has been possible to maintain the level of investment because foreign investors have effectively been doing our saving for us. Net capital inflows have filled the gap caused by the budget deficit and our inadequate total domestic savings. In this fundamental sense, it can be said that we have been living beyond our means and that foreign investors have basically been financing the additions to our national debt.

In the remaining few pages of this chapter, let us briefly examine these propositions.[6]

National Income and International Trade

If we go back to our earlier presentation in chapters 7 and 8, when we were dealing with an economy with constant prices, we can see an important way in which international trade enters into national income analysis. A condition of equilibrium in that analysis was that consumer and investment demand plus government spending must be equal to the national income produced (Y). We did this graphically, but we could also represent it by the following equation:

$$Y = C + I + G$$

Now, when we bring exports and imports into the picture, it is not difficult to understand that we must change the demand side of this equation to reflect two facts: (1) Exports (X) represent demand for our production from foreigners. To the American producer it makes no intrinsic difference whether the demand for his product comes from a domestic or a foreign consumer. Thus, X must be added to the demand side, so that we have $C + I + G + X$. (2) Imports (I_m), by contrast, represent a subtraction from demand for domestic production. Again, to the American producer, if the consumer buys foreign goods, it is just the same to him as if the consumer didn't spend the money at all, that is, saved it. Consequently, I_m must be subtracted from total demand, leaving us with this general condition:

$$Y = C + I + G + (X - I_m)$$

($X - I_m$) represents net exports or, equivalently, our balance of trade.

---

[6] As in our discussion of the federal debt (pp. 250–253), we have to acknowledge that there is a similar disagreement among economists as to how big our international deficit is, a major factor being an undervaluation of U.S. assets abroad. The frequently heard claim that the U.S. is now the "world's greatest debtor nation" should probably be taken with a certain grain of salt. See Robert Eisner, "Divergences of Measurement and Theory and Some Implications for Economic Policy," *American Economic Review*, vol. 75, no. 1 (March 1989): 5–6.

This equation is interesting for a variety of reasons. For one thing, it helps explain why countries suffering from recessions might particularly like to have a favorable balance of trade. When positive, the term $X - I_m$ represents an addition to aggregate demand in the same way that added C or I or G would. Writing in the Depression years, Keynes presented a defense of mercantilism along these lines, arguing that these early writers, in their search for a "favorable balance of trade," were trying to stimulate demand to keep the domestic economy prosperous.

If we go further and add the not-unreasonable notion that countries tend to import more goods as their national income rises, then we can glean some further insights from this equation. If we have two countries and one is growing more rapidly than the other, then there will be a tendency (other things equal, of course) for the more rapidly growing country to increase its imports more and the less rapidly growing country to increase its imports less. If we start from a position in which the balance of trade is zero for both countries, then this growth differential would tend to produce an unfavorable balance in the rapid-growth nation and a favorable balance in the slow-growth nation. On such grounds, some observers in the United States were arguing in recent years that our trading partners, particularly in Europe, should be stimulating their economies more vigorously so that our trade deficit might be reduced.

Another point that becomes clear from this analysis is that we have uncovered still another reason, beside those mentioned in chapter 13 (pp. 246–250), for lowering the value of the national income multiplier. Suppose there is an increase in aggregate demand due to an increase in G (or I or C). Now we have to take into account the fact that some of the increased income that results will go into added imports, and added imports represent a subtraction from aggregate demand. Depending on the size of our increased imports—a function of our *marginal propensity to import* out of increased income—the multiplier will be reduced more or less by this additional factor.

The Relation of the Trade Deficit to the Federal Deficit

Our special interest at the moment is to explain the relationship between our persistent trade deficits in recent years and our persistent federal budget deficits. Recall that we indicated earlier (pp. 258–259) that in our domestic economy, the way we made provision for government spending and private investment was through taxes and saving, or:

$$G + I = T + S$$

When we consider an economy engaged in trade (often referred to technically as an "open economy"), however, we must also consider another source for investment, that is, net capital inflows. In this case, we would have to rewrite the equation:

$$G + I = T + S + \text{capital inflows}$$

Ignoring complications (like services income, the statistical discrepancy, and so on), we know that capital inflows must be equal to the excess of our imports over our exports, or $I_m - X$. Thus, we must add this term to our equation, or, equivalently, subtract net exports $(X - I_m)$:

$$G + I = T + S - (X - I_m)$$

We can now rearrange terms so as to make the budget deficit, $G - T$, appear explicitly:

$$G - T = (S - I) - (X - I_m)$$

And what these equations tell us is that for a given level of S and I, the bigger the budget deficit (that is, the more G exceeds T) the more we will have to rely on capital inflows (that is, the more I_m will have to exceed X).

Of course, the levels of private domestic saving and investment are not simple givens in any realistic economic account. For example, we could have a large budget deficit without a trade deficit if, say, private savings were to go way up or if investment in the American economy were to go way down. Then we would not need foreign savers to come in and finance our budget deficit and investment expenditures. In point of fact, however, neither of these possibilities occurred during the 1980s. Instead, our total private savings (business and personal) remained relatively constant as a percentage of GNP, as did our investment. Under these circumstances, the *only* way our budget deficit could be financed in real terms was by foreign capital inflows—an excess of I_m over X.

Why Foreign Capital Flowed to the United States

The trouble with equations like those above is that they make a rather complex process seem much more mechanical than it is in fact. The truth is that foreign investors, whether private or government, did not *have* to buy our government bonds, our stocks, our real estate. No one was forcing them to do so. To some degree, the inflow of foreign capital during the 1980s is a tribute to the American economy: we were a politically stable, investor-friendly, growing economy—why not put their money here?

But we can also see some interrelationships between the fiscal and trade deficits of an indirect kind. Let us suppose that a country is experiencing a large fiscal deficit but is maintaining a reasonably tight monetary policy. We know from our analyses in chapters 13 and 14 that interest rates will tend to rise under these circumstances. Government borrowing will tend to compete with private borrowing, generally forcing up interest rates. This rise in interest rates, however, may make the country's capital market more attractive to foreign investors. Thus, by this roundabout route, a country's fiscal deficits can lead to an increased capital inflow, thus making possible a persistent current account trade deficit.

Does this mechanism have any bearing on the case of the United States during the 1980s? Some economists believe so. During the early 1980s especially, the combination of large fiscal deficits, a restrictive monetary policy, and high real interest rates made foreigners willing to sustain the necessary U.S. trade deficit, or so it is argued. Had foreign investors not come in, then we would have been unable to continue to "live beyond our means," and either we would have had to pull in our belts and save much more domestically, or investment would have had to fall sharply, with possibly large consequences for our future level of national income.

How Worried Should We Be about the Twin Deficits?

We have to say "some economists" in the preceding paragraph because, as we have already noted, there is some disagreement in the profession about the proper analysis here, and even about the proper interpretation of the statistics. How big *is* our fiscal deficit when properly measured? Or our trade deficit? It is of some interest to note that although we seem, by certain measures, to have been a major debtor nation for some years now, it was only in 1989 that the investment income we had to pay foreigners began to exceed the investment income we received from them. Until 1988, in fact, we had a very substantial investment income balance in our favor.

Also, we should note that fears of foreign citizens taking over our economy are often exaggerated. In 1988, for example, as a percentage of the host country's GNP, the United States had far higher direct investments in most of our trading partners than they had in the United States. Direct investments—as opposed to portfolio investments, which involve purchases of stocks or bonds—involve actually buying tangible assets, like buildings or factories, or buying a 10-percent or greater interest in a domestic company. Interestingly, in terms of such direct investments in the U.S., Japan in 1988 ranked below not only the United Kingdom, but the Netherlands. Finally, one can add that relative to GNP, there was some decline in our current account deficit from 1987 through early 1989.

Still, most economists do feel it highly desirable that both these deficits be reduced. Insofar as our national debt has increasingly become an *external* debt, then we are accumulating increasing burdens for the shoulders of future American generations. Also, it does not escape notice that in our basic failure to save enough domestically to finance our needed investment we are doing very little to prepare for a future day when such investment may prove to have been highly desirable. Here we touch on a subject that we will return to in the next chapter: namely, the policy mix most likely to promote future economic growth.

We conclude for the moment with a general assessment: There is no reason for panic, but we still can undoubtedly do better than we have if we face our problems squarely.

SUMMARY

International trade has become increasingly important to the American economy in recent years, while at the same time the dominating position of the U.S. in world trade has declined. The general expansion of world trade during this period had undoubtedly brought real benefits to all trading nations, as suggested by the doctrine of comparative advantage.

To understand international trade transactions, one must first learn the rudiments of balance-of-payments accounting. Basically, credit items are those that create a demand for a country's currency, while debit items are those that involve a supply of the country's currency seeking to purchase other currencies. The effects of a surplus or deficit in a country's balance of payments depend on the exchange rate mechanism employed. Under a fixed exchange rate system (such as the classical gold standard), deficits will lead to exports of gold or to other forms of pressure on a country's reserve assets. Under flexible exchanges, the exchange rates between currencies will be determined by supply and demand, and deficits in a country's current account will tend, other things equal, to lower the value of a given country's currency in terms of those of other nations.

The classical gold standard had much appeal historically because it meant stable (or nearly stable) exchange rates and also because it seemed to have a built-in corrective mechanism. The classical economists showed how, through the price-specie-flow mechanism, countries on the gold standard would lose gold if their balance of payments were in deficit and gain gold if it were in surplus. These gold flows would, on the quantity theory of money and other assumptions, bring rises in price levels in surplus countries, declines in price levels in deficit countries, and, ultimately, a correction of the balance-of-payments disequilibrium.

Under pressure from structural changes (including the changed position of the dollar) in the postwar period, relatively fixed exchanges gave way to flexible (or floating) exchanges in the early 1970s. Although there are concerns about their effects—particularly the volatility of exchange rates, including the dollar exchange rate—there is no doubt that world trade has expanded rapidly under the floating (or "managed" floating) regime.

In the late 1980s and early 1990s, much concern has been expressed about our trade deficit and its relationship to our federal budget deficit. It is possible to show that the two deficits are, in fact, related, since in the absence of an increase in domestic private savings or a fall in investment, an increase in the budget deficit will require an inflow of capital from abroad (an excess of imports over exports). There is disagreement among economists as to the seriousness of our "twin deficits," although majority opinion is that they represent a fairly serious drag on our future prospects and that steps should be taken to reduce them.

Key Concepts for Review

Benefits of trade (comparative advantage)
Balance of payments
Credit items versus debit items
Different balances
    Merchandise balance (balance of trade)
    Goods and services balance
    Balance on current account
    Balance on capital account
    Formal accounting balance = 0
Statistical discrepancy
Fixed exchange rates (classical gold standard)

Price-specie-flow mechanism
Flexible (floating) exchange rates
Supply and demand for a currency
Volatility of exchange rates
Purchasing-power parity theory
J-curve effect
Twin deficits
Multiplier in an open economy
Marginal propensity to import
$G - T = (S - I) - (X - I_m)$
Capital inflows = current account deficit
Foreign direct investment
Living beyond our means

Questions for Discussion

1. Classify the following items as credits or debits in the United States' balance of payments and explain your reasoning: exports of computer hardware to Italy, German tourist expenditures in the U.S., the United States renting the services of Norwegian ships, a U.S. foreign aid grant to Israel, imports of Japanese automobiles, U.S. investment in a factory in Brazil, income for U.S. investors from a factory in France, income from a U.S. government bond cashed in by a Korean national.

2. Ignoring the "statistical discrepancy," explain why any deficit (or surplus) on the current account must be balanced by an equal surplus (or deficit) on the capital account.

3. Explain how trade deficits or surpluses are corrected on the gold standard by the price-specie-flow mechanism. What flaws do you find in this mechanism from a theoretical point of view? Why is it sometimes said that a regime of fixed exchanges involves the "international tail wagging the domestic dog"?

4. Some economists today are advocating a return to relatively fixed exchanges. What arguments would you offer pro and con with respect to this position?

5. Explain in words why the value of the national income multiplier will be lowered if a country's imports tend to rise with its level of national income. Referring back to Figure 8-6 (p. 000), show how the introduction of this principle might affect the *slope* of the $C + I + G$ curve.

6. If a country's private domestic saving level is constant and equal to its private investment level, explain why its public budget deficit must be matched by an equal trade deficit (ignoring statistical discrepancies). Suppose there were no foreign investors around to finance the excess imports (= the capital inflow), what would have to give if the government persisted in running a large budget deficit?

C H A P T E R   17

GROWTH PROSPECTS FOR DEVELOPED AND LESS DEVELOPED COUNTRIES

In this final chapter, we shall extend our discussion into the future, posing some questions about the growth prospects of the various economies of the world, including our own. When we take this large view of our subject, we immediately have to face an extremely important fact: namely, that the process of modern growth that so revolutionized the economies of Europe, North America, and Japan largely bypassed vast areas of the globe containing half or more of the world's populations, or, at least, did so until very recent decades.

In considering global growth prospects, we have, therefore, divided the question into two main parts—prospects for the less developed world and prospects for the already developed world. The issues can be quite different in these two contexts. In the industrialized countries, many have been asking in recent years whether further economic growth is desirable. In areas where massive poverty is still a predominant fact of life, such a question never arises.

Let us begin with the less developed countries (LDCs) since we have not yet had an opportunity to discuss their problems directly.

THE UNEVEN IMPACT OF ECONOMIC DEVELOPMENT

That serious poverty still exists in the world is attested by national statistics on many different measures—for example, life expectancies, calories in the diet, number of teachers or doctors per capita, steel output or electrical power output per capita, miles of road, sanitation facilities, and so on. Because modern economic growth is defined in terms of a continually rising real GNP per capita, economists usually use this index as a general measure of the degree of poverty or "underdevelopment" in any particular country. In Table 17-1, the nations of the world are ranked into various categories according to their GNPs per capita in 1986.

This table has to be taken with a certain grain of salt. Statistical collections in many poor countries leave much to be desired; also, there are deep philosophical problems involved in trying to compare standards of living in countries where the whole plan and pattern of economic life is radically different. Nevertheless, the gap in levels of GNP per capita between the rich and the poor countries of the world is so great that even the very rough statistics we are able to gather tell a meaningful and dramatic story. The countries in group A in Table 17-1 all have measured outputs per capita (equaling, of course, annual real incomes per capita) of under $450 in terms of 1986 U.S. dollars. The average in group A is about $270 a year. And the countries in group A alone comprise roughly *half the world's population!* Even if we correct these numbers upward, as we probably should (could anyone actually have lived on $270 a year in the United States in 1986?), the fact remains that perhaps a majority of the people of the world survive on a tenth of the income the average citizen of the industrialized world takes for granted.

HISTORICAL VERSUS PRESENT-DAY DEVELOPMENT

In their attempt to close this large gap, the LDCs must, of course, cope with the same basic factors that we encountered in the case of Western development: technological progress, capital accumulation, and population growth. For a number of reasons, however, these basic factors do not present themselves in the same patterns that confronted the nations that industrialized earlier. In some cases, the modern LDC has certain advantages over its predecessors on the path of modern growth; in other cases, it has equal or perhaps even greater disadvantages. Consequently, in judging its growth prospects, we cannot safely perform a simple extrapolation from the past experience of the developed world. We must, indeed, reconsider each of the basic growth factors.

Technological Progress

One respect in which modern LDCs appear to have a clear advantage over their predecessors is in the area of technological progress. They do not have to reinvent the steam engine, the railroad, electricity, the computer, and so on. Unlike the situation facing eighteenth-century England or early-nineteenth-century America, there is an enormous store of new technology

TABLE 17-1 GNP Per Capita, 1986* (in 1986 Dollars)

Group A: Annual Per Capita Output of $0–$449	Group B: Annual Per Capita Output of $450–$899	Group C: Annual Per Capita Output of $900–$1,799
Africa	*Africa*	*Africa*
Benin	Botswana	Cameroon
Burkina Faso	Côte d'Ivoire	Congo, People's Republic
Central African Republic	Egypt	Mauritius
Ethiopia	Lesotho	Tunisia
Ghana	Liberia	
Kenya	Morocco	*Asia and the Middle East* ˜
Madagascar	Nigeria	
Malawi	Zimbabwe	Jordan
Mali		Syrian Arab Republic
Mauritania	*Asia and the Middle East*	Turkey
Mozambique	Indonesia	
Niger	Papua New Guinea	*Latin America*
Rwanda	Philippines	Chile
Senegal	Thailand	Colombia
Sierra Leone	Yemen, Arab Republic	Costa Rica
Somalia	Yemen, People's Demo-	Ecuador
Sudan	cratic Republic	Guatemala
Tanzania		Paraguay
Togo	*Latin America*	Peru
Uganda	Bolivia	
Zaire	Dominican Republic	
Zambia	El Salvador	
	Jamaica	
Asia and the Middle East	Nicaragua	
Afghanistan		
Bangladesh		
Bhutan		
Burma		
China		
India		
Nepal		
Pakistan		
Sri Lanka		
Latin America		
Haiti		

SOURCE: Adapted by the author from the *World Development Report* (International Bank for Reconstruction and Development, 1988), 222–23.

*For reporting nations with populations of 1 million or more.

Group D: Annual Per Capita Output of $1,800–$3,599	Group E: Annual Per Capita Output of $3,600–$9,999	Group F: Annual Per Capita Output of $10,000 and Above	
Africa	*Asia and the Middle East*	*Asia and the Middle East*	
Algeria	Hong Kong	Japan	$12,840
Gabon	Israel	Kuwait	13,890
South Africa	Oman	United Arab	
	Saudi Arabia	Emirates	14,680
Asia and the Middle East	Singapore		
Korea, Republic of	*Europe*	*Europe*	
Malaysia		Denmark	12,600
	Austria	Finland	12,600
Europe	Belgium	France	10,720
Hungary	Greece	Germany,	
Poland	Ireland	Federal Republic	12,080
Portugal	Italy	Netherlands	10,020
Yugoslavia	Spain	Norway	15,400
	United Kingdom	Sweden	13,160
Latin America		Switzerland	17,680
Argentina	*Latin America*		
Brazil	Trinidad and Tobago	*North America*	
Mexico		Canada	14,120
Panama	*Oceania*	United States	17,480
Uruguay	New Zealand		
Venezuela		*Oceania*	
		Australia	11,920

potentially available even to the poorest and most backward countries. Since technological progress is an important (perhaps the most important) factor in modern growth, this advantage constitutes the main reason for being optimistic about the ultimate prospects of the less developed world.

At the same time, it must be said that this advantage is at least partly offset by the fact that the advanced technology of the West is, in most cases, ill suited to the economic conditions prevalent in the LDCs. Many of these countries are characterized by (1) an abundance of unskilled, semiliterate laborers and (2) a shortage of trained workers and managers and of machinery and other capital goods. The advanced technology of the West, however, requires both skilled labor and a great deal of capital. Furthermore, many of the capital goods necessary for the installation of modern technology have to be imported from abroad. This can cause serious balance of payments problems. The mounting external debts of many LDCs in the late 1970s and 1980s have become, in fact, a major source of worldwide alarm.

Capital Accumulation

Because many of the poor countries of the world are seeking what would historically be considered very rapid development and because the technology that would make such rapid development possible uses (as we have just noted) a great deal of capital, the need for very high rates of saving and investment in these countries is apparent. However, many of them are extremely poor, even poorer than England and the United States when they were starting out. Capital accumulation requires saving, but if output per capita is very low, people may wish to consume all or nearly all of their very meager incomes. It used to be said that many of these countries face a "vicious circle of poverty": low incomes → low savings → low investment → low incomes. These vicious circles are obviously not completely closed—the LDCs have, in fact, raised their savings rates substantially in recent decades—but they do emphasize the special strains that the development process can encounter in its modern setting.

Such strains can, of course, be somewhat offset by foreign aid. The existence of substantial official developmental assistance from individual countries and also from multilateral institutions like the World Bank marks another important difference between present-day and historical development. The possibility of such aid clearly must be accounted an advantage of beginning development in a world in which there are already a number of very rich, potential donor countries. Again, however, this advantage is not without its drawbacks. Faced with their own domestic problems (including balance of payments problems), donor countries can lose interest in large foreign aid programs. Aid from developed countries has been falling as a percentage of their GNPs for many years; in the United States, our official development assistance fell from something over a half of 1 percent of GNP in 1960 to around a quarter of 1 percent in 1986. These are very small numbers as compared, say, with our Marshall Plan effort in Europe after World War II.

It is not just the unreliability of aid sources that is the problem, however. For the fact is that aid is, to some degree, a two-edged sword. Take food assistance, for example. When people are starving, or at least near the edge of serious malnutrition, it seems humanitarian to send substantial food aid; also, it can be argued, the food aid permits the poor country to concentrate its labor and capital on development projects—roads, dams, steel plants, whatever. But if such food assistance takes away markets from farmers, processors, and distributors in the domestic agricultural sector, then it may reduce incentives for production and development within that sector. If—as many commentators believe—it is agricultural development that holds the real key to success in many of these very poor countries, then the dumping of cheap or free agricultural products from abroad on fragile local markets may be counterproductive. This problem may be particularly serious in those countries where, for political reasons, governments purposely keep food prices low for the urban populations at the expense of farmers. In these cases, raising domestic agricultural productivity may be initially impossible.[1]

Population Growth

If the picture facing modern LDCs with respect to capital accumulation and technological progress is somewhat mixed, there is little question that when it comes to the third factor—population growth—they are at a marked disadvantage compared to their historical predecessors. In chapter 15, we noted that many of the leading early-nineteenth-century British economists, especially Malthus and Ricardo, took a pessimistic view about the future possibilities of economic progress. The main reason they did so was that they believed in the so-called Malthusian theory of population. This theory, in essence, states the following:

> The consequence of a rising standard of living will be that the birth rate will rise and the death rate will fall and there will be a massive increase in population. Because of the law of diminishing returns (population pressing against the "fixed" natural resources of the society), this rise in population will force the average standard of living back down to the subsistence level. Thus, although societies may progress for a time, the ultimate future is dismal. Population growth will inevitably

---

[1] Unfortunate government agricultural policies are a prominent problem in many African countries: "Of all the steps that governments can take to raise agricultural productivity in Africa, a reorientation of food price policies is the most important." (Lester R. Brown and Edward C. Wolf, "Revising Africa's Decline," in *State of the World, 1986,* eds. Brown et al. [New York: W. W. Norton, 1986], 190.)

expand to the limits of the economy's means of providing for that population, reducing the mass of mankind to the barest of subsistence.[2]

These predictions failed for the countries to which they were meant to
apply (economically advancing countries such as Britain) because technological progress and capital accumulation took place much more rapidly than
had been anticipated, outdistancing the rate of population growth. But, also,
the pattern of population growth was quite different from what Malthus had
predicted.

In Figure 17-1(a), we can see that while the death rate in the developed
countries did fall with economic progress as Malthusian theory dictates, the
birth rate in those countries also fell. Rising living standards produced not
higher but lower birth rates. The role of the family became altered in an increasingly urbanized society. More women wanted careers. Parents began to
want more education and other spiritual and material benefits for their off-
spring. In consequence, families in these advancing economies began to have
not more but fewer children. The rate of population increase in all these
countries fell far below Malthus's biological maximum.

When we look at Figure 17-1(b), however, we face a radically different
situation. Death rates in the LDCs started falling earlier in the development
process and much more sharply than did those of their predecessors. Moreover, birthrates have remained extremely high in these countries, beginning
to fall only in very recent years. The rate of population increase in these
countries, measured by the difference between the birth and death rates, has
thus been extremely high. Moreover, this high rate of population growth has
taken place, in many cases, in areas that already have an extremely heavy
population density. Such population growth may well constitute the main
single obstacle to successful development in many of the LDCs.

The reason for this Malthusian problem has very little to do with Malthusian theory. After all, these high birth rates are occurring in countries that
are poor, not rich. The central fact is that it has been possible to apply even in
very poor countries many of the techniques of modern medicine, disease pre-
vention, malaria control, public health, sanitation, and the like. Almost
ironically, this aspect of Western technology has been quite easily transferred
even to very backward countries. Hence, death rates have been brought down
very drastically and in advance of actual economic development. In the absence of the other accoutrements of development, birth rates have begun to
decline only relatively recently. The result: the population explosion of modern times of which we have all read so much.

---

[2] In his famous *Essay on the Principle of Population* (1798), Malthus put the problem in the dramatic
form of two "ratios." He saw population growth as tending to occur at a "geometric ratio" (that is,
1, 2, 4, 8, 16, 32 . . .), and he believed that food production could increase only at an "arithmetic
ratio" (that is, 1, 2, 3, 4, 5, 6 . . .). Ultimately, food supplies would run out, population growth
would be brought to a halt, and everyone would live in a state of misery.

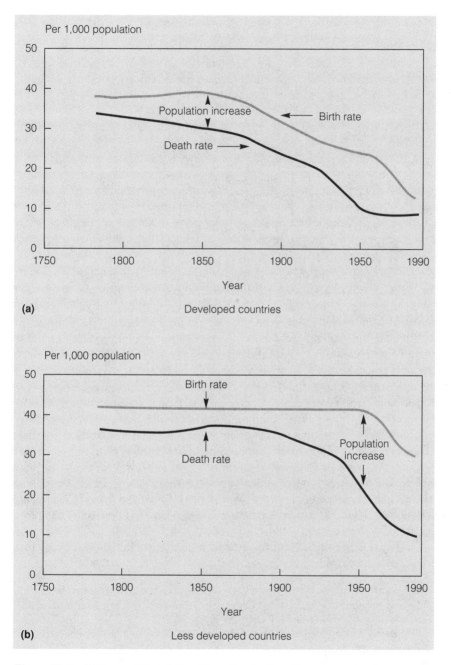

Figure 17-1   Patterns of Population Growth   In these diagrams, to get the percentage rate of population increase per year, subtract the death rate from the birth rate and divide by 1,000.

SOURCE: Adapted by the author from the *World Development Reports*, 1982, 1988.

POSTWAR DEVELOPMENT IN THE LDCs

Given their advantages and also the special obstacles they face, the LDCs could not expect to duplicate the exact features of historic Western development. And, in fact, development results in these countries have been variable, both over time and from region to region.

The Overall Growth Record

In the immediate decades after World War II, there was considerable optimism about the growth prospects of the LDCs, fueled perhaps by the evidence of rapid growth (amounting to "miracles") in war-devastated Europe and Japan. By 1970, a more pessimistic view had taken hold, the pessimism applying to growth in the industrial nations as well as the LDCs (see below, p. 352). During the 1980s, optimism returned again, although it was not universally shared, and it had to be applied rather selectively.

Such evidence as there is suggests quite major economic achievements for the majority of LDCs during the postwar period as a whole. Professor Lloyd Reynolds, founder of Yale's Economic Growth Center, distinguishes between a country's *extensive growth,* where total production just keeps up with population growth, and *intensive growth,* where total production grows faster than population. Only in the latter case do we have an increase in output per capita. Looking at the more populous LDCs—for example, China, India, Pakistan, Indonesia, Egypt—Reynolds found that in each case, the transition to positive per capita income growth took place after World War II. The crucial "turning points" have all occurred in these recent decades.[3]

Similarly, development economist Gerald Meier found that for the LDCs as a whole, GNP growth far outpaced population growth in the period 1955–1980. He found the average rate of growth in GNP per capita during this period to be 3.1 percent per year—"a remarkable rate." The 1988 *World Development Report* of the World Bank found the same 3.1 percent per capita growth for group A countries (see Table 17-1, pp. 338–339) for the period 1965–1986.

This is a very high rate of growth. Meier, for example, sums up his overall assessment thus:

> Compared with their own past records and the record of the presently developed countries in their initial phases of development, many LDCs have exceeded expectations in the growth of GNP and GNP per head. . . . The period since 1950 can certainly be viewed as the best period in history for people in the poor countries of the world.[4]

---

[3] Lloyd G. Reynolds, *Economic Growth in the Third World, 1850–1980* (New Haven: Yale University Press, 1985).

[4] Gerald M. Meier, *Emerging from Poverty* (New York: Oxford University Press, 1984), 55–56.

This same favorable outlook was evident in a 1982 Nobel symposium on development issues. Nobel laureate economist Wassily Leontief used his input-output analysis to forecast the growth of output per capita in the LDCs to the year 2030. He and his colleague Ira Sohn developed both a "pessimistic" and an "optimistic" forecast, but even the former foresaw annual rates of growth of output per capita of between 1.38 and 1.52 percent, rates which are quite comparable to those achieved by the industrial nations in the half-century before World War I. And these were the lowest forecasts.[5]

In short, taking the broadest overall view (and one we shall have to qualify in a moment), the news from the LDCs has basically been good news. After centuries of poverty, improvements are occurring and may very likely continue to occur in the future.

Developments on the Population Front

But what of the major obstacle posed by population growth? Won't this problem eventually catch up with even the most successful LDCs, dooming their best efforts in the long run?

Here again, a certain optimism has crept in in recent years. For one thing, it is difficult to ignore the fact that the greatest progress in terms of *per capita* output growth in the LDCs has occurred during the period when their population explosion was *at its height*—that is, during the post–World War II decades. This conjunction of developments has even suggested to some observers that population growth may be an important factor in stimulating technological improvements in the economy, particularly in the pivotal agricultural sector. Population pressures, while clearly part of the problem, may also be part of the solution to the problem they have created.[6]

Ultimately, of course, the "carrying capacity" of the earth has some finite limit, and, therefore, in the long run, population growth in the LDCs will have to come to a halt. The main source of optimism in this respect is the evidence of substantial declines in fertility in these countries in recent decades. Reynolds found in his study that birth rates fell in 35 of the 37 LDCs studied over the period 1960–1980 (the two exceptions were Uganda and the Sudan). In the *World Development Report,* low-income countries (group A in Table 17-1) showed an average decline in birth rates from 42 per thousand in 1965 to 30 per thousand in 1986.

A more significant measure is the *total fertility rate,* which, ideally,

---

[5] Wassily Leontief and Ira Sohn, "Economic Growth," in *Population and the World Economy in the 21st Century,* ed. Just Faaland, Norwegian Nobel Institute (New York: St. Martin's Press, 1982), 96–127.

[6] For development of this view, see Mitchell Kellman, *World Hunger: A Neo-Malthusian Perspective* (New York: Praeger, 1987). He develops an "induced innovation" model: "An induced innovation process, triggered by demographic or density pressures, may affect the choice of a new technology so as to economize on the scarce factor [land]." (p. 189)

measures the average number of children a woman will have during her entire childbearing years. According to World Bank estimates, this rate also fell for our group A countries, from 6.4 in 1965 to 3.9 in 1986.

Furthermore, many students of the population problem in the LDCs suggest that the present "population explosion" is essentially a transient phenomenon. Richard Easterlin and Eileen Crimmins have developed a supply and demand analysis of fertility change and applied it to both household data and aggregate data in Sri Lanka, Colombia, India, and Taiwan. They believe that the fall in death rates in the LDCs, which has been a main factor in causing the population explosion, will also operate to bring about fertility reduction. As the supply of children increases, they argue, families in the LDCs will have increased motivation to practice birth control;[7] also, they will be pressured to do so by their governments.

China represents a major case in point, where the government has in recent years undertaken serious steps to reduce fertility. It was not always so. Marxism has historically been disinclined to take population problems seriously (Marx himself called Malthusianism a "libel on the human race!"), and Chairman Mao often referred to China's huge population as an asset rather than a liability. Since the late 1970s, however, China has adopted a "one-couple-one-child" principle, this principle being enforced through penalties, rewards, publicity, persuasion, and, according to some Western reports, coercion. This vigorous policy has had at least some success, and China's population growth rate, which was estimated at 2.6 percent per year in the period 1962–1973, had fallen to an estimated 1.1 percent by 1985.

Thus, it would appear that in addition to the natural tendency of birth rates to fall with development, as occurred in the Western world, there may be added governmental and other pressures to reduce fertility in the LDCs. It is quite possible that as they have experienced more rapid falls in their death rates, these countries may also experience more rapid declines in their birth rates.

All this is on the hopeful side of the population question. On the less hopeful side, we must acknowledge that fertility rates are still far higher in the LDCs than in the industrial countries and that the younger age structures of many of these countries guarantee enormous future populations, even when there are marked behavioral changes taking place with respect to family limitation. Table 17-2 presents some Census Bureau estimates of LDC populations in the year 2050. In these 10 countries alone, total population is expected to reach around 5.4 billion in 2050—larger than the estimated population of the *entire world in 1990!*

Furthermore, government policies are by no means always effective in

---

[7] See Richard Easterlin and Eileen Crimmins, *The Fertility Revolution: A Supply and Demand Analysis* (Chicago: Chicago University Press, 1985).

TABLE 17-2 Population Projections for Populous LDCs

Country	Population Projection for the Year 2050 (in Millions)
India	1,591
China	1,555
Nigeria	471
Pakistan	424
Indonesia	360
Bangladesh	266
Ethiopia	243
Vietnam	166
Kenya	166
Zaire	158
Total for these 10 nations	5,400

SOURCE: U.S. Bureau of the Census.

the population area. In China, for example, there was evidence that population growth began to rise again in the mid-1980s, as economic liberalization made families richer. Also, of course, policies may change. China, as we know (pp. 57–59), has been going through a major political upheaval. Whether her family planning policies will be strengthened, weakened, or even abandoned in the uncertain period that lies ahead, no one can possibly know.

Thus, any optimism one feels about the population problem in the LDCs must be cautious at best. And this is particularly true when we turn to areas of the world where the development process seems to be sustaining very serious defeats.

Sub-Saharan Africa—A Tragedy in the Making?

If we went back to Table 17-1 and did some further calculations with respect to the low-income countries in group A, we would soon discover that even the poorest LDCs have some very different characteristics. If, for example, China and India are removed from the group, average per capita income falls from $270 a year to $200 a year. Furthermore, the average rate of per capita income growth falls from 3.1 percent to 0.5 percent, and the average total fertility rate rises from 3.5 live births per woman to 5.1 live births.

If we studied the relevant statistics in even greater detail, we would come up with this alarming fact: Of the world's 36 poorest nations, 22 are in sub-Saharan Africa.[8] The crude death rate in sub-Saharan Africa has been falling, but the birth rate has remained basically constant—and very high. Thus, this region is the only major region of the world that has experienced an *increasing* rate of population growth in recent decades, rising from about 2.5 percent a year in the 1960s to around 3 percent in the 1980s. At this rate of increase, populations double every 23 years.

In this region, moreover, food production has not kept pace with population growth. In many African countries, despite the introduction of some new technologies, grain yields per acre are falling. Indeed, in the effort to expand production, Africa is encountering what many observers feel is a serious deterioration of her agricultural resource base through erosion, soil degradation, deforestation, and desertification. Now, requiring food as well as other crucial imports, many of these countries also face declining prices for some of their commodity exports and potentially crushing external debt problems. It does not help that these burdens are carried by countries with *declining* annual per capita incomes in many cases. Examples for the period 1965–1986: Zaire, −2.2 percent annual per capita GNP growth; Uganda, −2.6 percent; Tanzania, −0.3 percent; Niger, −2.2 percent; Zambia, −1.7 percent; Ghana, −1.7 percent; Senegal, −0.6 percent.

Finally, with respect to the population problem, we have to note that it is only recently that most African governments have awakened to the need for population control policies, and the impact of such policies, as there are, is doubtful. Kenya, for example, has had such a policy for some time, yet in 1988 the World Bank estimated Kenya's annual population growth at around 4 percent, one of the highest in the world. The extent of the problem is indicated by the fact that in 1989, Kenya announced with pride that during the previous five years, her fertility rate had dropped from 7.7 to 6.7. (For comparison, the U.S. fertility rate in 1989 was 1.9; at the *height* of our Baby Boom it was 3.8.)

All these facts must be put into a context that makes them even more alarming: in many African countries, almost half the population is under 15, This virtually guarantees massive population growth in the future—unless, in a tragic working out of the old Malthusian "solution," inadequate food supplies and a return to high death rates bring it to a halt.

In short, development successes are occurring and will undoubtedly continue to occur in many of the world's poorest countries—but not necessarily everywhere. The problems of sub-Saharan Africa, in particular, will challenge mankind's ability to overcome poverty in perhaps the harshest single test of the next century.

---

[8] The following section relies heavily on R. Gill, N. Glazer, and S. Thernstrom, *Our Changing Population.* Forthcoming.

THE DEVELOPED COUNTRIES—IS MODERN GROWTH SUSTAINABLE?

But what of the developed countries of the world? Will they continue to grow economically during the next decade and well into the next century? What are the prospects of the United States in particular?

No Clear Evidence of Declining Growth

If we take a broad look at the history of the United States and other Western nations, we see no clear evidence that our rate of economic growth is in a state of decline. Professor Goldsmith's early survey showed that the rate of growth of U.S. per capita output was the same in the period 1919–1959 as it was for the whole period 1839–1959. Maddison found that the growth of total output for 16 industrial countries was substantially higher in the years 1950–1979 than it was in the years 1870–1950. Even during the slowdown years of 1973–1979, Maddison found growth in these 16 countries to be the same as it was in 1870–1913 (2.5 percent per year) and higher than it was in 1913–1950 (1.9 percent).

As far as productivity increase in the United States is concerned, the declines of the 1970s have been at least partially reversed during the mid- to late 1980s. We must remember that the years immediately after World War II were quite exceptionally vigorous in terms of our total history. Also, we have the view of some commentators (see above, p. 310) that our failure to give adequate weight to productivity increases in the now-dominant service sectors of the economy tends to understate GNP growth, and has perhaps even exaggerated the extent of our productivity slowdown in the late 1970s.

In short, history creates a presumption that economic growth in the developed world will continue on into the future, though, of course, nothing even close to a guarantee.

Labor Force Changes That May Affect Future Growth

Whether growth does or does not continue will depend in part on the quality of the labor force that emerges in the years ahead. In the United States, there are at least two aspects of our future labor force that are relevant here, and they will probably affect our prospects in opposite ways:

1. *The increasing age and experience of our labor force.* One of the reasons given to explain our slower productivity growth in the 1970s was that with the Baby Boom generation reaching working age in large numbers and with the dramatic increase in the number of women in the labor force, the general levels of age and experience in our work force fell considerably. With the Baby Bust generation now entering the labor force in much smaller numbers and with a large part of the increasing percentage of women in the labor

force already having occurred, we will be dealing with a much more experienced labor force, on average, in the years ahead. This should be a plus factor as far as future productivity growth is concerned.

2. *Skill and educational levels.* On the opposite side of the ledger is the possibility that we will be dealing with a labor force that exhibits declining skills, or at least skills declining relative to the demands of the high tech industries of an advancing economy. The educational system of the country is widely believed to be in a crisis condition, with low or falling test scores placing the United States very near the bottom of all industrial societies. This is true of both verbal and mathematical skills. Furthermore, the ethnic composition of our future labor force will be skewed toward groups with lower educational and achievement levels. Black, Hispanic, and other minority groups supplied only 18.4 percent of the net increase in the U.S. labor force between 1970 and 1985, but they will provide an estimated 29 percent of the new addition between 1985 and the year 2000. Tests of achievement have so far shown these groups to be substantially behind the national average.[9] Moreover, this skill deficit will be occurring when, according to the Labor Department, the supply of high-skill jobs will be increasing almost twice as fast as that of low-skill jobs.

Thus, labor force factors can be seen to be cutting both ways as far as future productivity growth is concerned.

Policies to Promote Growth

These labor force factors should not, however, be taken as givens. They can be altered by policies. Our immigration policies will, for example, clearly affect the character of the U.S. labor force of the future. There are already voices urging that instead of family-member preferences, we should increasingly emphasize skills in our immigration mix. Improving education in the U.S. has now become a high priority item, with President Bush expressing the wish that he be known as "the education president." At a minimum, the problem of educational decline is now widely recognized as requiring serious attention.

Moreover, assuming that we *want* continued economic growth (an assumption we will discuss in a moment), we should be able to adopt macroeconomic policies designed to foster the process. How, we might ask, are we doing on this particular score?

---

[9] Thus, the National Assessment of Educational Progress in 1978 determined that while 13 percent of all American 17-year-olds could be judged to be "functionally illiterate," the corresponding figure for that age group among blacks was 56 percent and among Hispanics 44 percent. (John Palmer and Gregory B. Mills, "Budget Policy," in *The Reagan Experiment*, eds. John Palmer and Isabel V. Sawhill [Washington, DC: Urban Institute Press, 1982], 78.) Of course, it is hoped that the recent emphasis on higher standards in U.S. education will alter these discouraging results.

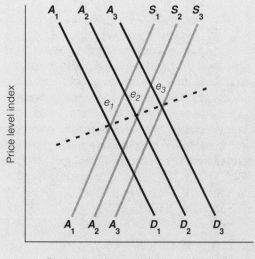

Figure 17-2   Growth with Low Inflation   If supply-side policies successfully move the aggregate supply curve to the right as we go from period 1 to period 2 to period 3, and so on, then we may have continued growth with only mild (or possibly even zero) inflation.

The answer here is decidedly mixed. Insofar as recent years have seen a new emphasis on supply-side economics (an emphasis shared by many who do not qualify as "supply-siders" of the Laffer curve variety [p. 278]), then it may be said that macroeconomic policy in the United States has been attempting to create conditions under which noninflationary growth can take place. The goals of supply-side economics are suggested in Figure 17-2. By policies designed to increase technological progress (such as educational reform), promote capital accumulation, and stimulate and reward ability, effort, and productivity in general, supply-side economics hopes to be able to keep shifting the aggregate supply curve out to the right so that even with substantial shifts in the aggregate demand curve, noninflationary (or, in Figure 17-2, mildly inflationary) growth can take place in real national income. The advantage of supply-side as opposed to demand-side policies is that the former policies—if successful—both stimulate growth and reduce inflationary pressures, while the latter tend to promote growth and inflation simultaneously.

On the negative side is the fact that the general balance of our macroeconomic policies for some years has tended to be antigrowth rather than progrowth. A progrowth policy would be one that encouraged investment, both public and private, as opposed to consumption. This would imply, as far as private investment is concerned, a relatively expansionary monetary policy ("easy" money, low real interest rates) complemented by a relatively contractionary fiscal policy (budget surpluses or at least reduced deficits). It would also require that public expenditures be increasingly devoted to investment purposes (say building up the nation's infrastructure), as opposed to consumption (say paying farmers not to produce crops, or providing income for nonworking retirees). Finally, it would attempt to shift taxes so that they fell more heavily on consumption and less heavily on capital accumulation.

On almost all these scores, the United States has been deficient in recent years—with high real interest rates, substantial (though debatable, as we know) federal budget deficits, neglect of infrastructure investment, and a reluctance to reduce capital gains taxes. By 1990, however, there was evidence of concern on all these issues. This concern was particularly heightened by an awareness that early in the next century, when the Baby Boomers start retiring, there will be tremendous *consumption* demands placed on our GNP. If we do not promote capital accumulation beforehand, serious trouble could await us later on.

Still, as far as the "sustainability" of modern growth is concerned, the main lesson of U.S. experience in recent years is that such growth can continue to take place—and fairly vigorously—even when macroeconomic policies are far from optimal with respect to growth promotion.

Global Concerns

But is such growth really sustainable from a *worldwide* perspective? During the decade of the 1970s, many books and articles proclaimed the approaching collapse of the process of modern economic growth. A well-known report of that period put it this way:

> The principal defect of the industrial way of life with its ethos of expansion is that it is not sustainable. Its termination within the lifetime of someone born today is inevitable—unless it continues to be sustained for a while longer by an entrenched minority at the cost of imposing great suffering on the rest of mankind. We can be certain, however, that sooner or later it will end (only the precise time and circumstances are in doubt).[10]

The basic threats that the writers of this statement (and a number of similar so-called "Doomsday" writers) saw to the continuation of growth were the exhaustion of natural resources, especially energy resources, and pollution. (In the case of the LDCs, they also worried about population and food supplies, in a modernized version of Malthusian doctrine.) They cautioned that the huge, rapidly growing industrial economies were gobbling up the world's nonreplaceable resources at an unsustainable rate and creating levels of pollution that would ultimately cancel out, or reverse, positive GNP growth.

Two decades after the great outburst of Doomsday alarm, concern over

---

[10] From "A Blueprint for Survival," *The Ecologist,* 1972, published by Tom Stacey Ltd. and Penguin Books, p. 2.

resource depletion has somewhat abated. Mainly, this is because the "energy crises" of the 1970s gave way to frequent "energy gluts" in the 1980s, with OPEC struggling to keep production down so that oil prices would not plummet even further in real terms. These "gluts" could conceivably be reversed in the 1990s as turmoil in the Middle East after Iraq's seizure of Kuwait could lead the world back to energy "crises" once again.

Both "gluts" and "crises" are, of course, merely temporary phenomena. When we try to get at the underlying truth about natural resource scarcities, the picture is quite mixed. At about the same time the above quotation was written, highly respected economists William Nordhaus and James Tobin were tentatively concluding that natural resource scarcities had become rather *less* of a limitation on U.S. growth than they were 50 years before.[11] The ability of humanity to accommodate to resource scarcity by the substitution of other factors of production and by the development of resource-saving technology has been dominant in the industrial nations. When we think about it, indeed, this is really the same story as that which occurred at the very beginning of the industrial revolution in Britain. The shortage of timber at that time was an important factor in promoting the use of a coal-based technology. The consequence: not a slowdown, but an enormous acceleration in the rate of industrial growth.

But if concern about resource depletion has somewhat lessened, concern about pollution seems to have increased sharply in the last two decades. Three major perils are seen when a global perspective is taken on the growth-pollution problem: (1) *the greenhouse effect*—fossil fuel combustion is believed to be producing excessive carbon dioxide in the atmosphere, which will cause global warming, coastal flooding, and other disasters; (2) *stratospheric ozone depletion*—the use of chlorofluorocarbons (CFCs) in air conditioners, refrigerators, aerosols, and plastics is thought to be destroying the world's protective ozone layer, exposing us to hazardous ultraviolet rays (and also contributing to the greenhouse effect); and (3) *acid rain*—sulfur and other emissions from coal-fired furnaces are producing acid rain, which is destroying our lakes and forests. To these problems can be added a very generalized concern about using nuclear power to replace fossil fuel sources because of the problems of (1) storing nuclear waste and (2) the possibility of a catastrophic accident. The costs of the Chernobyl accident in the Soviet Union, both in human and economic terms, seem to be mounting higher and higher with every new study of the tragedy.

An economist has no special tools for evaluating these concerns. New

---

[11] See William Nordhaus and James Tobin, "Is Growth Obsolete?" in *Economic Growth: Fiftieth Anniversary Colloquium V*, National Bureau of Economic Research (New York: Columbia University Press, 1972), app. B, pp. 60–70.

scientific knowledge may show that the growth process ultimately is, in fact, "doomed" by these *external diseconomies*.[12] Or, on the contrary, new research may show that these concerns have been vastly exaggerated. All the economist can add to the discussion here is that in trying to reduce pollution, we should take economic considerations into account. By this, we essentially mean that, wherever possible, society should use its tax and subsidy policies so as to *internalize* these various external effects—briefly, the "polluter pays" principle. To institute yes-or-no rules and regulations without taking economic costs and benefits into account is almost never likely to produce the desired social result.[13]

Taking a global perspective, then, and peering into the very distant future, no one can be sure whether or not modern economic growth is sustainable indefinitely. Perhaps the greatest comfort for growth enthusiasts comes from an awareness that many alarms have been sounded historically only to have been proved largely false alarms. Human ingenuity has so far been up to the tasks that have been specifically created by the growth process.

IS GROWTH DESIRABLE?

But why should we have to cope with such tasks? Why should we want growth to continue anyway?

Anyone who has read extensively the Doomsday literature of the 1970s or the environmental literature of the early 1990s will realize that many of these writers don't really *like* economic growth. They seem at times to be afraid that natural resources *won't* run out and that growth actually might continue for another century or two. In this feeling, they are at one with a number of earlier writers. Even during the heady days of the industrial revolution in Britain, the great philosopher-economist John Stuart Mill yearned for the time when mankind would look for "better things" than a constant "struggle for riches." Mill wrote:

> I confess I am not charmed with an ideal of life held out by those who think that the normal state of human beings is that of struggling to get on; that the trampling, crushing, elbowing, and treading on each other's heels, which form the existing type of social life, are the most desirable lot of human kind, or anything but the disagreeable symptoms of one of the phases of industrial progress.

---

[12] Recall our discussion of private and social costs in chapter 4, pp. 69–70. These social costs are sometimes called *external diseconomies,* pollution being a prime example. Firms or individuals pollute the environment but are not *charged* for such pollution in a pure market economy. The costs fall on others ("external" to the firm or individual).

[13] For further discussion of this large subject, see my *Economics and the Private Interest.* In press.

Mill actually looked forward to the coming of a "stationary state," providing, of course, that the Malthusian population problem could be handled and a decent standard of life guaranteed the working classes.

Do the Costs of Growth Exceed Its Benefits?

In the United States, in the last decade of the twentieth century, we have achieved a standard of life for the average person that far exceeds anything Mill could have hoped for. In consequence, there are those who argue that the time has now come to reconsider the pivotal role of economic growth in our social life.

These critics point first to the declining benefits of modern growth in the affluent society. Why do we want more goods? they ask. Certainly not out of economic necessity, not even for added material comfort; historically, people have been content with far less abundance than we now enjoy. Essentially, they answer, we want more goods because a growing society creates the very wants it in turn supplies. These wants may be created by other consumers in the manner of "keeping up with the Joneses": my neighbor has a new and fancy automobile, and, thus, I must have a new and fancy automobile. Or they may be created by the industrial producers through advertising and other means of public persuasion: if you do not buy such-and-such a product, your personal and social life will be jeopardized, if not ruined. In either event, a kind of self-canceling process of want-creation and want-satisfaction is established. If I buy more because my neighbor buys more, and if my neighbor buys more because I buy more, then we can both keep on accumulating purchases indefinitely without either being any better off. Similarly, in the case of producer-induced demand, business firms advertise to convince consumers that they need the goods that they would not have missed had the advertising and additional production never occurred.

Few critics would claim that these are the "only" motives that make consumers wish for additional goods or services—for example, I might wish to undergo expensive medical treatment so as to live longer, not just because my neighbor is also living longer!—but such motives do clearly enter into many of our purchases, and to this degree, the benefits that accrue from still additional economic growth are far less than they appear in the statistics. As the society becomes ever more affluent, these benefits can be expected to decline continually.

While these benefits are declining, the critics go on, the costs of growth are mounting dramatically. Growth has always had associated costs. Indeed, even the measurement of growth is made difficult by the fact that many of the products that we include in our GNP may actually be nothing but the costs of an industrial-urban society. Suppose we lay tracks and set up a commuter train service from the suburbs to the city. Should we consider this act of production an addition to GNP, or should we argue that commuter services are simply a required cost of having an industrial-urban society and would have no value were our society organized differently.

More generally, there are all those external diseconomies of growth that we were just talking about. Quite apart from concerns over the greenhouse effect and other global phenomena, there are the numerous unpleasantnesses of growth: traffic jams, noise, smog, billboards, the constant rush and bustle of a time-pressured, overwrought society. Plus, of course, the threat to various animal species, the violation of wilderness areas, the ugliness of strip mining, oil spills, and the paving over of millions of acres of land to make roads and parking lots. Is it not a paradox, the critics ask, that the richest societies in history should be creating not great works of art and beauty and culture, but the megalopolis, the freeway, and the ghetto?

A World without Growth?

Before we wholeheartedly embrace this litany of criticisms, we must pause a moment to consider what a world without economic growth would mean in actual fact. In terms of the two main economic problems that have concerned us in this book—inflation and unemployment—a growthless world would, at least in the first instance, be a disaster. Continued real growth is at one and the same time a major force reducing inflationary pressures and increasing employment opportunities. No one could claim that it is impossible to have full employment and stable prices in a completely stationary society. In the transition to this society, however, the slowing of economic expansion would pose problems of such difficulty that it is doubtful we possess the political and social means for solving them.

Even if we could solve these great macroeconomic problems, we would still have major problems concerned with the distribution of income. From a *worldwide* perspective, the distribution of income among nations would pose almost unbearable dilemmas. If there were to be no growth throughout the world, then we would either have to freeze the present disparities of income between rich and poor nations or engage in a truly massive transfer of income from rich to poor nations to achieve some rough parity among them. This second path would mean absolute *declines* in living standards in the economically advanced countries. Would this be tolerated? Or would a third alternative—freezing development in the advanced countries while permitting development in the poor, high-population-growth countries—be any more attractive? Can one imagine the rich countries standing idly by while the world's resources were poured into a frantic (and not necessarily even successful) race with the growing billions of poor people around the world?

Even within the developed countries, a freeze on growth would involve serious distributional problems. In the United States (and all industrial nations), we have always had rich and poor within our borders. One factor that has kept these income disparities from leading to Marxian style "class conflict" has been that, on the average, everybody—rich or poor—has been getting better off over time. Without growth to ameliorate these divisions, however, *relative* income distribution would undoubtedly become a much more intense social issue. We could easily become a "society of envy." Would this really be more attractive than a society built on vigorous competition, growth, change?

Indeed, perhaps the most difficult issue of all concerns the psychological impact of a growthless society. Ever since the industrial revolution, the idea of progress—economic, political, social—has been a dominating one in the eyes of Western man. This is a future-oriented idea. We make sacrifices and lead our lives in certain ways today because of the benefits that will thus accrue to our posterity. In other words, it is (or at least has been) extremely important to us *today* to believe that the world will be a better place in which to live *tomorrow*. In a growthless society, such an attitude could not long persist. But then what would our goals be? How would we guide and justify our daily lives?

Faced with such global questions, economics alone can hardly provide decisive answers. Hopefully, however, it will form a useful background for their intelligent discussion.

INDEX

DATE DUE
